Saint of the Wilderness

A Biographical Novel Depicting the Life and Works of Robert Sayers Sheffey

Jess Carr

ISBN 978-1-64140-400-6 (paperback)
ISBN 978-1-64258-377-9 (hardcover)
ISBN 978-1-64140-401-3 (digital)

Christian Faith Publishing, Inc.
832 Park Avenue
Meadville, PA 16335
www.christianfaithpublishing.com

Printed in the United States of America

Dedicated to the memory of my paternal grandparents, George and Sallie Carr, whom I never knew; and to my maternal grandparents, Esca and Minnie Mitchell, who helped inspire this story; and most of all, to my own dear Mother and Father, without whose love and guidance this story would have held no importance at all.

Rev. Robert S. Sheffey

INTRODUCTION

The birth of this book, viewed in retrospect, seems almost a circumstance of fate. The chain of events leading to the final writing, viewed singularly, at first appeared of no particular consequence; but viewed as a subject that seemed always to be unfolding before the author's eyes over a period of forty years an element of continuity is present, which rightfully denies dismissal.

I heard first of Robert Sayers Sheffey at the feet of my maternal grandmother and grandfather. At the same time thousands of other children like myself were hearing the same story, just as our own mothers and fathers and grandmothers and grandfathers had before us. How much this old saint of the wilderness captured my imagination! How I longed even as a child to meet him, rejecting every thought that for nearly half a century he had lain rotting in his grave.

The subsequent years of my growth were spent in part by trying to grasp the person and personality of a man reputedly so kind that tears were known to drip from his cheeks at seeing the broken wing of a bird. And what must someone be like who stayed in the saddle twelve months of the year, in all kinds of weather, doing good at every opportunity? Every child could understand this man's great love of humanity, learning, further, that his favorite sheep of earth's great flock were the poor and downtrodden.

Not even in Sunday school had I been exposed to a lesson that taught a greater message than this true story of a person who not only preached and taught, but who lived the example of what he preached and taught. That he demanded of others to put the teachings they allegedly believed into practice was a thing later to be marveled at.

A man usually becomes a legend in his own time only if he deserves it. Talleyrand's statement that "The reputation of a man is like his shadow—gigantic when it precedes him, and pygmy in its proportions when it follows," is true only if the subject has failed to do a greater good for humanity than was sought for himself.

In spite of having grown up on the stories of this man who became a legend in his own time over an area of four states, or parts thereof, I nevertheless came to a point in life when I viewed all I thought I knew and believed about him with pseudo-intellectual skepticism. Even if most of my schoolmates and fellow citizens of the ensuing years had also heard and believed—so what? What difference did it make, if the world was made up of good and bad people that at least one man who had lived and worked among us stood head and shoulders above the crowd? Perhaps this old Methodist circuit rider was really crazy after all. Plenty of people thought so. It wasn't normal for even a white-bearded old itinerant to stop his horse and get off to help an upturned turtle back on its legs again; or to take his own socks from his feet and present them to another more needy than himself. And it certainly wasn't normal to make the statement when confronted with a problem or decision that: "I must talk to the Lord about it." Or to pray and believe that that which is asked for not only can be forthcoming, but under the right circumstance will be forthcoming, is a dangerous philosophy, one that has put its practitioners behind bars countless times throughout history. Even in a less complex era, when simple faith went largely unchallenged, too much demonstration of such a principle, frightened the wits out of more sinful men, or provided at least a small measure of discomfort. Being a good Methodist was never reputed to keep a man or woman from sin, but it was claimed to keep enjoyment of such wrongdoing to a minimum. This eccentric servant of God who had found his way into the most remote hollows and nearly impenetrable hills insisted that the true way of Christian living was neither to think, practice, nor enjoy sin, for in so doing the real purpose of life was missed altogether.

The day had not yet arrived when conservation, ecology, civil rights, awareness of natural resources, and similar contemporary problems held any major importance. The world of mostly rural America in the period of 1840–1900 was one of survival of and recovery from three wars. To Robert Sayers Sheffey, however, conservation, ecology, civil rights, and a simple awareness of the goodness that surrounded every man was not visionary wisdom or political foresight; it was, to him, the way God intended mankind to live. Every single thing to which man was exposed was a gift of God to be used if needed, and, if not needed, to be preserved with infinite care until somebody did need it. Man ought to love and cling to one another because God intended *that*, and to do otherwise was really the unnatural thing.

The matter of Robert Sayers Sheffey never left my mind during the ensuing years. In reality such was impossible—the very historic presence of this legendary human being seemed a part of the atmosphere to be breathed.

But in spite of this lingering aura of such a dynamic personality, my own increasing worldly wisdom and fast-growing urbanity began to demand of me that I discount the implied importance attached to this man. He was now a relic of the past. How could any importance be attached to him now? And anyway, for all the multitudes of twice-told tales about the eccentric old Methodist renegade, half of them at least had to be pure fabrication, and another quarter had probably grown monstrously in the telling and retelling. So for me, Robert Sayers Sheffey was gradually put in mothballs, if not into oblivion.

After my own slow growth into adulthood and a tour of duty in the United States Marine Corps during the Korean War, I came back to Virginia, married shortly thereafter, and entered civilian employment. That first job after marriage was a sales position requiring constant traveling. Once on a northeasterly journey from my office I chanced to take a short cut through a section I rarely passed through. In the course of the journey I came to one of the most picturesque rural churches I have seen anywhere in this country, and to the south west of the church building was a well-kept hillside cemetery. I noticed only half consciously that a small group of people stood at a grave, but gave no further thought to the matter until I had driven several miles down the road, where I stopped at a country store for a Coke break. I mentioned to the storekeeper (more to make conversation than out of any real interest, I must confess) the funeral I thought I had noticed in progress. He questioned me about which church and reaffirmed its location, finally telling me that there had been no funeral in the neighborhood on that day. I asked the reason for the entourage of visitors to the cemetery and was told that the grave of Robert Sayers Sheffey was there and that individuals and groups both large and small visited his gravesite all the time, year-round.

I did not go back to the cemetery, although I had the strongest inclination to do so. My appointment hour was set and I traveled on company time and expense. Driving away, I was immediately aware that the ghost of childhood legends and bedtime stories had been not so successfully cast into oblivion. What manner of man is this who still commands even small pilgrimages to his grave one hundred and fifty years after he came into the world? Such were my thoughts as I sped away.

A few more years passed and this subject continued to worm its way into my brain by the most ingenious methods. A friend told me of being stationed in Germany after World War II where he was asked by an elderly German civilian if he had ever heard of a godly man whose name was Herr Robert Sheffey and who rode about the countryside of the southern United States, doing good. The German man had all his facts straight except for the belief that Brother Sheffey still lived at the time of World War I! Here it was again: oral history that had spanned the ocean and come to people who spoke a foreign tongue. Is there something so universal about a good man—a man who demonstrates a profound love of humanity—which commands the love and appreciation of men everywhere? I started asking myself.

At the time I had never written anything, nor had I had any such desire. Nevertheless, I made some halfhearted inquiries as to what had been set down about this old circuit rider, finding that almost nothing in the way of definitive material had been written.

Again the matter slipped away without further conscious pursuit. In 1966 I began to do a little creative writing, mainly because a job with a commercial printing-and-book-publishing firm had inspired my interest. I had no qualifications at all as a writer. College was not one of the advantages of life I had received, and it is doubtful that I could have passed a high school grammar test at the time. Nevertheless, I published my first short-story collection in hardcover in 1970. The next published book was a work of non-fiction entitled *The Second Oldest Profession*, a major work on the illicit-liquor (moonshining) industry in America. It was here that I unexpectedly met Robert Sheffey again. No revenue officer in the entire United States, at any period of history, wrecked more whiskey stills than Robert Sheffey did, or even approached him in the unique methods he employed to get the job done. (As a matter of interest to history buffs, Sheffey destroyed distilleries at periods of history when they were not illegal. His destruction was based on moral grounds; the depths of degradation brought on by whiskey making he could see with his own eyes and wished to eliminate.)

But even this new encounter with an old codger who in my mind's eye now carried an ax in one hand and a Bible in the other did not convince me that I should undertake a work about him that I knew would be difficult, if not impossible—a lengthy process involving assembling never-ending bits and pieces of information, or, at the other extreme, finding little information at all.

Again fate dangled a morsel in front of my eyes, showing me the true magnitude of the character no one would allow to die. A young woman mentioned to me one day that one of the highest-ranking officers in the Pentagon, where she worked, had asked her to tell him all she knew about a godly old man who in Civil War times had ridden about the Virginia countryside, devoting his life to doing good. The young woman was a Virginian, a fact which possibly precipitated the question, but the heart is warmed to know that overseers of America's military empire might pause for a few fleeting moments to inquire about a humble itinerrant who had somehow accomplished things greater than the questioner had, in spite of all the money and sophisticated machinery at the latter's disposal.

Finally the day came when I took my aging father to Sheffey's gravesite and was told by a custodian of the church who lived nearby that the streams of visitors seemed never ending—usually small groups or single families. "What manner of man?" The question kept repeating itself. And the words so moving upon the tombstone seemed a magnet, holding one fast and demanding a pause to consider. I was fast becoming hooked, and I began to pick up a fact here, an assortment of facts there, until I found out that my subject had grown up amidst great wealth at the home of an uncle. Again, "What manner of man?" would willingly, gladly, leave the promise of wealth and social position to flush out the most remote frontiersman and remind him that there was no wilderness so deep where man could hide from God.

All that then remained for my interest to be goaded into action was the moving and unique story of Robert Sheffey's own conversion. From that point on, there was, for me, no turning back.

Rediscovered was the man who believed and practiced a total integration with every facet of life—a man who showed a unique appreciation for every gift bestowed by a loving and very personal God. The tiniest bug and the most gigantic tree were friends who breathed a very special breath and paid a very special tribute of living testimony.

This St. Francis of the wilderness carried his message and lived the example of his life for sixty-three years after his own conversion. Although the extent of his own travel throughout his life was confined to parts of four states, his spiritual stepchildren still oversee the missionary posts of the world and sit in the highest councils of government. He was only one of many who helped to shape the real character of the American frontier. No American may with impunity disregard the dynamic influence of the pioneer circuit rider. No American can disregard Robert Sayers Sheffey as one of the great chiefs among them. And now step back into history and ride in the saddle with the man who was called The Saint of the Wilderness.

JC

So when they had dined, Jesus saith to Simon Peter, Simon, son of Jonas, lovest thou me more than these? He saith unto him, Yea, Lord; thou knowest that I love thee. He saith unto him, Feed my lambs.

He saith to him again the second time, Simon, son of Jonas, lovest thou me? He saith unto him, Yea, Lord; thou knowest that I love thee. He saith unto him, Feed my sheep.

He saith unto him the third time, Simon, son of Jonas, lovest thou me? Peter was grieved because he said unto him the third time, Lovest thou me? And he said unto him, Lord, thou knowest all things; thou knowest that I love thee. Jesus saith unto him, Feed my sheep.

—St. John 21:15–17

CHAPTER I

The streets of Abingdon, in Virginia's far southwest, were deserted on a predawn morning in July of 1838, except for the two dozen or more Negro servants who scurried about, doing their assigned tasks. They worked in semi darkness; first, sweeping the walks or stepping stones leading to their masters' houses, then gradually working their way out toward the brick sidewalks. The results of their work would be short-lived. Each servant had done this task before and knew full well that at dawning visitors from every direction would be coming into Abingdon for the two days of celebration, bringing fresh dirt and dust with them. The next task—watering down the macadamized street would be short-lived also. By an early morning hour, or by the time one hundred sets of wagon wheels had passed over the oak-lined street, dust would again be the victor.

No sooner had the final bucket of water been drunk up by the compacted stone-and-red-clay thoroughfare when full daylight and the first wagons arrived together. Sounds of activity about the impressive houses of Court and Main streets could be heard; human voices, too, penetrated the early-morning hour as windows were raised to combat heat already in evidence.

By the time the breakfast hour was nearly over, traffic on Main Street, all the way to the front of Colonel James White's home, was heavy with travelers on foot, on horseback, and in hacks and wagons. Colonel White sat at the north end of the long dining-room table and gazed past the row of younger people on each side of the table, over the head of his wife, Elizabeth, and through the window facing Main Street. He watched the steady stream of travelers for a minute, then commented to his wife, "Elizabeth, Abingdon isn't going to hold them all today. They'll be sleeping on the rooftops and roosting in the trees if they keep coming."

"I don't mind if they use the rooftops," his wife replied, "but our trees and shrubbery have too noble a history to die an unheroic death."

"Big Edmund will keep the people out of our yard," Milton, the youngest child, said.

"All of the slaves get to go to the celebration today, except for the kitchen help," Elizabeth White reminded her family.

Colonel White still looked beyond the window. He liked a celebration. He liked people. He liked seeing people together, laughing and talking and telling stories. He watched the scene for a moment longer, until a wagon stopped in front of the window. It was heavily laden with a large family and all the belongings needed for a one- or two-day sojourn to their county seat. The mother of the group sat rigidly beside her husband, holding an infant in one arm and a small child in the other.

"Poor little fellow is tuckered out already," the colonel said absently.

The others at the table looked again to the window, in an effort to make sense of the older man's statement.

"They've been up since before daylight," Elizabeth White speculated. "Likely as not none of them could sleep last night thinking about today."

"I didn't sleep good last night either." Robert Sheffey spoke almost timidly.

All eyes focused on him immediately, but his aunt and uncle did not need to ask the source of his discomfort.

Elizabeth White saw the flush on her husband's face, but quietly took the prerogative of speaking first. "Robert, I know our discussion of last night upset you, but we believe our counsel to be wise."

His aunt's voice was calm and quiet, as always, and the softness of her dark eyes reassured him of the sincerity of her statement.

Colonel White's approach was not so gentle, and his fingers continued to drum on the table. "Robert, you would not have such an aversion to education if you could visualize the future growth of this infant nation as I envision it. There is a fortune to be made in most any enterprise a man would undertake...but the country needs smart men, not slackers."

"Yes, sir, you told me that," Robert Sheffey said with no intent to mock. He knew better than to try mockery and he also knew that up to a point he was being given a choice.

"Then why not believe me?" The colonel's voice was raised slightly. "I have tried to treat you like my own sons and my counsel is for your benefit and not for mine."

"I just don't have the feeling of needing a lot of learning," Robert Sheffey replied," and I don't care about gettin' rich either."

The colonel did not answer his nephew, for he had heard the same weak defense before. The older man's massive chest heaved slightly in response to his rejection of so stupid a statement. Presently he excused himself and pushed his muscular bulk from the chair. He stood towering over the family table, authority magnified, but his voice was calm. "Robert, Professor Collins and Professor Wiley will be at the celebration today. We will seek our opportunity to talk to them. Perhaps their wisdom will put fresh thoughts into your head."

Robert said, "Yes, sir," and stared at the massive back of his uncle until, with giant strides, Colonel White had cleared the room.

The formal atmosphere at the table lessened somewhat with the exit of the master of the house, and Robert Sheffey felt contemptuous eyes falling upon him from both sides. Seven of the eleven White children still sat at their father's table, and Robert was aware that the older ones, at least, must feel contempt for his apparent ungratefulness. But how could he tell them more plainly than he already had: education was fine for some people, but he did not feel inclined in that direction. In his own heart he waited for something. He knew not what, but he did not feel that it was higher education. His own brother Lawrence, who also sat at the table, understood, or at least Robert felt that he did. For Lawrence, education was a good thing. The right thing. For in Lawrence there was the hunger of the scholar, the fascination in exploring the known and the unknown. Lawrence looked sympathetically across the table at his brother but continued eating in the near silence he had maintained throughout the course of the meal. The two of them understood each other—respected each other.

Robert's face saddened as, finally, the others resumed more light-hearted chatter about the things they would do on this Independence Day and about the horde of guests who would come and go over the threshold of the stately frontier mansion. He excused himself; sure that no one remembered the second reason that this day was important.

"Happy birthday, Robert!" Elizabeth White called behind him. He returned the smile on her olive face and made his way to the front door.

Upon reaching the front steps he stretched his arms and swallowed a deep breath of morning air. All of the other slaves working on the lawns and sidewalks had finished except for Big Edmund, who wielded a grass rake.

"They tromped the grass down a-carrin' water acrost it," Big Edmund said. He labored for a few moments, raking the sickle-cut stubble back to an upright position. Robert watched him closely; he found the servant's approach to the job almost comical. "That looks good, Big Edmund," the boy said.

But the Negro would not concede the accuracy of this observation until he had lain flat on his belly, surveying with one closed eye, across the top of the grass blades to make sure that all of them stood at even height.

"Yas, sir. But de visitors won't take no mind of that stubble now."

Big Edmund stood up, and Robert was conscious, on this day more than any other, of his own physical size in relation to that of other men. Big Edmund stood over six and one-half feet tall, while Robert's own height was almost six inches under six feet. This feeling was the same in the presence of his uncle, for the colonel stood three inches over six feet tall, his abundant gray hair with a tendency to curl, making him look even taller.

But these were not matters to worry about, he told himself deceptively, even on his eighteenth birthday. Sometime after his sixteenth birthday—he didn't remember just when—he had partially reconciled himself to his lack of physical attractiveness.

Big Edmund picked up his tools and started to exit from the yard.

"Are you going to do it again this year?" Robert called to him.

Big Edmund tried to look serious, as if he didn't know what Robert was talking about. But when Robert grinned, the tall slave did too. "If'n theys a new horseshoe 'round here that ain't too thin I might," he said.

"Every homesteader from here to Wytheville will have a horseshoe for you," Robert assured him.

Big Edmund walked away, with Robert's eyes following him. There would be more people on hand than he who could hardly wait to see this Herculean Negro take a newly forged horseshoe and bend it double with his bare hands. That amazing demonstration all by itself would bring two hundred men to Abingdon on the Fourth of July.

Horse and wheel traffic were coming closer together now. Most of the people waved or called to Robert as they passed—people who on other occasions would be more restrained. He looked to the south of town and beheld a dust cloud coming from the direction of Black's Fort and another to the west. It was a sure bet that every mountain road, including the remotest ones, would be filled with the movement of buggies and surreys headed for the town square, where festivities would officially begin at the eleven-o'clock hour.

Now he himself was getting caught up in the festive atmosphere and anxious to see the final trimmings of the public square. He had stepped toward the street when a hand restrained him.

"How does it feel to be eighteen?" his brother Lawrence asked.

Robert stiffened his body and threw back his head of strawberry-blond hair. "I've still got a way to go before I reach you," he said.

"Every litter has a runt," Lawrence said jokingly. Robert didn't smile. He might have any time except today. "I was just joshing," Lawrence assured him. "It doesn't matter what size a man is—it's what's under the top of his skull that makes a man different from a mule."

Robert remained in thought for a moment and said, "What if a man don't have muscles or brains either?"

"You've got brains—as good as any man. You just need more practice and schoolin' to use them. Uncle James and Aunt Elizabeth are both right. There's no reason why you can't go to Emory and Henry with me in the winter, when we've helped Uncle James with the last of the crops."

"Let Uncle James and Aunt Elizabeth stop worrying about the orphans in their house and brag on their own sons. You recollect he didn't say anything about us going to Princeton like his own boy did. He wants us to go to Emory and Henry and do farm work."

"It won't hurt us to work a little for our books, but we can't earn it all and we might as well own up to being beholden to Uncle James and our own brother. Besides, Princeton isn't the only place honors can be won, and Francis isn't the only one who can win them."

"I told you—I'm not going to college. I'll work or do something else," Robert insisted.

"Do what? You didn't get rich working in Greenway's store, and you said you don't like working for Uncle James. Would you rather move to the slave quarters or start boiling salt for somebody?"

"I'd just as soon work with the slaves as anybody. I'm not too awful sure they aren't ahead of the people they work for in some ways."

"Oh, Robert! There's nothing wrong with poor people, but *our* future is bright as the sunrise. Look what Uncle James has amounted to—and we have a lot better chance than he had."

Robert reflected for a moment, and then said, "I don't know what I want to do…I think about it a lot, but…"

"If Father and Mother had lived they would have wanted you to go to college and do the best you could."

"You don't know that," Robert said. "You weren't but four years old when Mama died and I wasn't but two. And Father didn't live but four years longer than Mama. How do you know Mama would think that?

"Mother was Uncle James's sister, and he knew her as well as anybody."

Robert lowered his head for a moment as though he sought the communion of the spirits that the will of his unremembered mother might be made known to him.

Lawrence took advantage of this moment of reflection. "We should be grateful to Uncle James as well as to Aunt Elizabeth. Not every uncle and aunt would take in three orphan boys and give us the chance they have given us."

"I can't deny that Aunt Elizabeth has been like a mother to us, but Uncle James and most of his children don't let us forget for long that we never belonged there."

"That isn't altogether true, Robert. Uncle James has a pretty stiff spine most of the time, but he's a busy man—an important man. Our cousins did remind us a few times we were orphans but that was only to be expected."

Robert said nothing by way of rebuttal and Lawrence hesitated a moment before uttering the statement he felt needed saying. "Robert, you are doing the kind of reflecting today that a young man just turning eighteen shouldn't be doing."

"Then I'll do all my thinking by myself," Robert said and headed out onto the street.

He walked westward from Colonel James White's house and stopped to look at the flags fluttering from the houses on either side of him. The smell of lime and salt from the whitewashed fences still hung in the air. He ran his fingers along a top pole on a fence as he walked and thought how foolish the landowner was to whitewash his fences when they were already covered with dust. He turned the corner at the second block, noticing that already the large crowd had nearly obscured the speaker's platform—and the hour was not yet ten o'clock. Regardless of the time, a festive gaiety was electric in the air.

"Come have a little snort o' brandy with me, Robert!" a heavy-set man called from the open door of a woodshed.

Robert recognized the man as a worker at the tanning yard and said, "My breakfast hasn't settled yet."

The man took a long swig from his demijohn and dried his mouth with one quick swipe of the back of his hand. "You ain't been down at the yard lately. That lye and dead hide smell a-gettin' the best of you?"

"No, I've been gone for a spell, that's all. Went down on the stage to visit my brother James and his wife in Marion."

"He's the one what married Colonel John Preston's daughter, ain't he? Big lawyer now, I understand."

"He's the one. He says he'll help pay my college expenses to Emory and Henry if I'll go."

"Nothin' wrong in book learnin' if you've got a need for it. It wouldn't help me none a-scrapin' hides."

"Between my brother James and my Uncle James, I don't have much say-so but to go—but my mind's not made up yet."

"You listen to Colonel White," the other admonished. "He's nigh the biggest man in Washington County, and there ain't nobody what don't listen to him. Maybe he's fixin' you up to take over one of his farms or salt mines. Got a big interest in the lead mines down in Wythe County too, I understand."

"He's got plenty of his own sons to look after his money. I don't think that's going to be any worry of mine."

Again the demijohn was held out to Robert and again he declined. "I'll have a dram with you later," he said. "I've got to get on to the speaker's platform and see somebody. Won't have a chance to after all that oratory gets started."

"And bless Providence if it ain't hot enough already," the other said, mopping his brow with his shirt sleeve.

Robert pushed his way toward the large, stage like speaker's stand. It was built the same way every year and had stood in the same place for as long as he could remember. It looked like the front porch of a house, complete with railings at the front and sides, and was entered by steps coming from the rear. It had no roof, but the ladies who sat by their important husbands always brought their parasols anyway, so what was the need? Red, white, and blue banners were intertwined in the platform railing, and where the hewn pine framing of the porch wasn't covered, resin dripped from the cooking of the hot sun.

Robert had not worked on the platform, as some of his friends had, but he thought it looked just right. Good enough, in fact, for the President of the United States to stand on. But President Van Buren would be speaking from a much bigger platform at the Capitol or somewhere else, he imagined. The turnout in Abingdon was bigger than usual, not because President Van Buren was expected, but because citizens from Washington and surrounding counties felt that Governor David Campbell would be the next-best speaker they could expect to hear, and he was a native son, to boot.

Robert ascended the platform, where chairs were being readied. More elbow room was being given the center chair, and Robert supposed that the governor would be seated there. He would speak before the noon hour, and other dignitaries in the afternoon.

Under a shade tree on the ground to the rear of the platform stood Robert's uncle, who, upon meeting Robert' s eyes, motioned the younger man to join him. "Robert, I want you to meet Reverend Ephraim Wiley. Reverend Wiley is professor of ancient languages and literature at Emory and Henry College."

Robert shook hands after being himself introduced.

"I have already spoken to Reverend Wiley about you," Colonel White said, "and I want you to speak with him frankly. I will leave the two of you now and help with some of the program arrangements."

Reverend Wiley leveled at Robert the most piercing gray eyes he had ever seen and lost no time in pursuing the subject obviously under discussion before Robert had arrived. "So you place no value on learning?" the older man began, accusingly.

"I just don't feel the need…"

"Pray tell me why not?"

"I reckon it just goes against my grain, sir." Robert tried to face his elder unflinchingly.

"What do you hope to become someday?"

"I don't know, sir."

"Surely you must have some inkling? A lawyer? An engineer or surveyor, perhaps?"

"I like to walk in the woods and talk to people," Robert said. "Maybe fish a little, too."

"Those might be all right as pastimes, but your uncle tells me you would hang around the tanning yard or dangle your feet in the Holston most of the time if you were free to do so. The type of men who hang around the tanning yard and grogshop are not the best kind of men to cultivate."

"I don't stay with them in the tavern very much—Aunt Elizabeth never would hear of it—but I'm eighteen now."

"That's the perfect year to stop wandering about the meadow and to start thinking about your future," Reverend Wiley bore on. "Robert, your uncle is a very wealthy man, probably the wealthiest man in the county. Someday, if you prepare for it, there will most likely be a place of great responsibility for you. Few young men are so lucky as to have family-owned lead mines, salt mines, vast farmlands and extensive mercantile interests to lure them with a promising future."

"Uncle James's sons and daughters will be looking after all that, I 'magine."

"There can still be a responsible place for you if you prepare for it. And even if you don't want to be employed by your uncle, you'll be better enabled to work for yourself or somebody else."

Robert was listening in earnest, and the professor continued. "We feel that we have a good plan at Emory and Henry. We're only a few miles away and our young men work part of the time and study part of the time. You will be given credit for your work. The rate of pay is five cents per hour. All the young men study from five o'clock in the morning until one o'clock in the afternoon. After the noon meal, field or barn work is assigned until five o'clock. Each person then has two hours to rest, change his clothing, and prepare for the supper hour. From seven o'clock to nine o'clock is the final study period of the day."

"That doesn't leave much time for walking in the fields and fishing," Robert observed, unsmiling.

"Our young men see all of the fields they care to. Their fishing is for knowledge, in preference to the scaled variety."

"My brother Lawrence is going to sign up for the winter term. I just might come with him," Robert said.

"Let me hear when you and your uncle have decided. We like to know our expected enrollment in advance. I will also be talking with one of your former teachers. I want to learn what I may expect from you. McViccar taught you at Abingdon Academy, didn't he?"

"Yes, sir. And if you've a mind to, you can talk with Mr. Gillenwaters. He taught me drawing and penmanship. Said I was right good at it, too."

"I want you to do some serious thinking about this, Robert. I must go now and join Colonel White on the platform. We want everything to be in order." Robert said a "thank you" and wandered off into the crowd.

By the hour of half after ten the entire White family (excepting the colonel and his wife, who would be among the honored guests on the platform) were taking their places on the reserved benches to the front. Robert watched his brother Lawrence join them, but he himself elected to mill about in the crowd until the presence of the governor would bring the people to silence.

He was not aware of the approaching entourage of dignitaries until all the onlookers had risen to their feet, clapping wildly. A long line of finely dressed men and women made their way from Findley House, across the street, to the platform.

Finally, with the invocation and a series of introductions out of the way, Governor Campbell was on his feet. Robert marveled at how much more austere-looking the gentlemen had become since he had left Abingdon as clerk of the county court to occupy the governor's mansion.

The governor looked long upon the crowd and kept silent until they themselves did likewise. The stiff collar of his shirt rose high against his cheeks and seemed to hold not only his velvet bow tie in place but his head as well.

He was a good speaker, Robert thought, but he was going on too long. Sure now that he had been wise to hang back to the rear of the crowd, Robert crept from the view of the speaker's platform and hoped his retreat was not witnessed by the colonel. He could still understand the governor's words but somehow, being now more distantly removed, and sprawling under the shade of a large elm, the whole affair seemed more tolerable. He got out his knife and began a lone game of mumblety-peg, safely distant from the family who shared the shade of the same tree. Presently a slender young woman with long black hair, and dressed in dotted linsey, obscured his view of the speaker's platform.

She hesitated with her question until their eyes met. "Could you tell me where the town spring is? We need to fill up our demijohn," she said.

He started to point, but there was something about her dark brown eyes that compelled him to maintain the close distance now between them. "I'll take you there," he said, rising more rapidly than he had reclined.

She was taller than himself—not much, but enough so that it mattered—and he attempted to walk on the balls of his feet, until he thought how peculiar it must look. He glanced at her sideways from the corners of his eyes, and when she shifted the demijohn from one hand to the other, he offered to carry it. Before she removed her finger from the jug, he held it so that their hands touched. Her forearms were firm and red, like a man's, and sunburned. There was no hardness in her pretty face, however, and as they walked, the sun danced in her hair until they passed under a shady area again.

"What did the governor mean when he was talking about the schools?" she asked.

"I think he wants all the counties to have schools for everyone. The state would help pay the tuition, I believe." Now he wished he had listened more closely so he could impress her with his knowledge of state affairs.

"There wouldn't be no more private teachers or church schools, then?" She pressed him further.

"I think that's right," he said as positively as possible. "Uncle James's brother said it wouldn't work, though. He said not everybody could be educated."

"Is your uncle James's brother one of the talkers?" she asked.

"No. Uncle James is on the speaker's platform. Colonel James White. You don't know him?"

"No. My family lives in Wythe County. I'm just visiting my kin during the celebration."

"I didn't even ask your name," Robert remembered.

"It's Elizabeth Swecker. What's yours?"

"Robert Sheffey."

They both seemed to run out of words at the same moment, and he removed the corncob stopper and filled the demijohn to the top. He purposely did not offer her a drink.

"Would you go to the cider wagon with me?" he asked.

The faintest smile crossed her lips. "If we're not gone too long a spell," she said.

The constable set a limit as to how close the cider wagon could be positioned to the speaker's stand, and he kept it at a considerable distance so the activity and noise would not displease the notables who occupied the places of honor. In spite of the distance from the stand, the cider seller was not short of business. He looked at Robert and, when Robert failed to produce cups of his own, as was the custom, hesitated to take his order. Finally, the cider seller reached down into the wagon and produced two pewter beer steins that he filled and admonished the users to wash out for him after use.

Robert allowed the girl to drink first and when she didn't slurp, he tried not to also. He was not successful, and he wished silently that he had listened to Aunt Elizabeth as to how it was properly done.

"It's good and cool," the girl said.

"He likely as not soaked the rocks all night," Robert said.

"He done what?" she asked.

"The way he keeps the cider cool in the barrels is to soak large limestone rocks in a cold spring all night. When he takes them out and puts them in the cider barrels they keep the cider cool for several hours."

When her cup was empty she remembered her errand. "We'd best get this water back to my kin." Robert agreed but reminded her that they would need to go back to the town spring and wash out their cups. Neither reminded the other that the washing could be done with water from the demijohn.

They walked by way of Valley Street this time and turned the corner at Court Street until once again they were back on Main and near the front of Colonel James White's house.

"That's where I live," Robert said with a mixture of pride and humility.

"I've never seen such a big house," Elizabeth Swecker said as she surveyed the three stories of brick. "Is it a new house?—it looks well-nigh new."

"It was built the year I was born—1820. You want to hear some tales about it?"

She nodded.

"Daniel Boone was one of the first people to see all this land around the forks of the Holston River. One night he fought off a pack of wolves on this very spot. In fact the wolves came out of a cave to the back of the house. Abingdon was first known as Wolf Hills—did you know that?"

"No, I never heard it before," the girl said.

"The very street we're standing on was first known as Boone's Trace."

Robert proceeded to tell Elizabeth the story of James White: how he had been a young clerk in a mercantile firm in Baltimore and had come to southwest Virginia and found success beyond his wildest dreams; how in the War of 1812 he had been commissioned a colonel, and how before that, in 1799, a captain, in the state militia. Before Robert had finished telling of the family holdings, which reached into four states, he was ashamed of himself. It was wrong of him to try to impress this girl, who might well be poor, with another's splendor. It was the first time he had spoken to anyone with such a sense of pride about his uncle. He didn't understand it himself. He suddenly felt very foolish and embarrassed.

Fortunately he could not continue, even if he had wanted to. The hour for dinner had arrived, and great throngs made their way toward the fashionable houses along Main and Valley streets. The speaking and festivities would resume after bellies were full, and that was the prime consideration of the moment. "I can't ask you to break bread with us," Robert said. "Aunt Elizabeth is entertaining more people now than we've got plates."

"It's all right," Elizabeth Swecker said, lowering her head. "We brought a spread to have in the shade."

She wanted to walk back by herself but he refused to let her go unescorted. Aunt Elizabeth had taught him that much.

When they reached the town square again, a large throng was still gathered near the speaker's stand, and Robert could not understand this, since the dinnertime recess had been called. He was confused only until he could see the head of Big Edmund nearly a foot above anybody else, could see the slave's gritted teeth and the neck muscles standing out like individual spider webs with sweat running down the gullies, indicating correctly that between the Negro's vise-like hands a horseshoe crumbled under superior strength.

When he returned to his own house one half of the aristocracy he had seen in the public square seemed to be there. In the rear yard, under the trees, sweating kitchen slaves hustled back and forth until the tables labored so heavily under their burden that Robert doubted their ability to sustain another loaf of bread.

He headed for somewhere near the front of the line. The glance Elizabeth White gave him would have frozen a ghost in its tracks. She brushed close and whispered, "Wait for our guests to be served first!"

He moved away and joined the circle of men who had the governor captive among them.

"Why is the Lynchburg and Tennessee Railroad running behind schedule?" someone asked. "What's taking the improvement of the turnpike road to the Kentucky line so long?" another wanted to know.

Robert slipped away from the men and into the kitchen. He stuffed a pants pocket full of trimmed onions and with both hands helped himself to biscuits and fried chicken. Then he made his way through the house and out the front door.

He decided not to go back to the public square lest he need to explain his presence to Elizabeth Swecker after he told her of all their guests. She would want to know why he hadn't stayed to entertain them, and he wasn't sure he could define it. There was something false about important people. They just didn't ring true. They were not like the men down at the tanning yard or those at the wagon shop. Those men somehow had open hearts, and he relished their friendship and confidence. He liked looking into their souls and he liked sharing the view into his own.

Yes, he would go to the tanning yard. The men would not be working but they would congregate there for their dinner. That would give Elizabeth Swecker and her kin time to eat at leisure, and then he would find an excuse to see her again.

Wild clapping in the distance signaled the renewal of activities at the public square. He had stayed longer at the tanning yard than he realized, but it was so easy and pleasant to fight the Battle of King's Mountain all over again. And listening to the old veterans tell about it, it was precisely like firing the long-barreled rifles himself, and bleeding and crying a little with the men too.

Robert walked toward the square with two of the veterans, both over eighty years old. They carried their rifles, shot pouches, and powder horns for later use—traditional on this day. He parted company with the elderly men after giving each of them a pat on the back. After orienting himself, he hurried to the proper tree. New faces smiled up at him and offered a seat in the shade. No, Elizabeth Swecker was unknown to them—they had just arrived. Elizabeth Swecker was gone.

Robert searched the grounds and went again to the town spring the two of them had visited. There was no sign of her. Perhaps tomorrow—the final day of celebration—she would be there, smiling up at him from the shade of the tree.

By ten o'clock on the following day torrential rains brought to a conclusion what remained of the holiday celebration. Dust was turned to mud. Families ripped down makeshift tents and improvised wagon coverings before they headed for home, wet but happy. Before many of them had left, Robert circulated among them. He had one more idea. He remembered a few families that he knew who quilts had spread on the ground next to Elizabeth Swecker and her kin. If one of these was acquainted with the girl's kin and could tell where they lived, his luck would not have run out.

"By grannies, o' course I know them people," a bewhiskered old homesteader Robert knew from Greenway's store said to him. "That family lives up purty nigh the north fork of the Holston."

Robert paused just long enough to get the exact location and name of the family, then ran to the stable in back of his uncle's house. "Saddle Ginger, and hurry!" he called to Big Edmund.

The big slave headed for the stable and Robert raced for the kitchen. While Ann, the oldest Negro cook, had her back conveniently turned, Robert stuffed his mouth with all the honeycomb it would hold. He accidentally dropped what was left in the dish, and the crash brought Ann's silver-white head into motion.

"I tol' you I'd box yo jaws fer stealin' the table honey," she said on the run.

Robert dodged the flying broomstraw about his head and leaped into the saddle. He tried to call out a frantic "hurry up" to Big Edmund, but the chunk of honey in his mouth seemed to swell rather than diminish. "Mmmmm...mmmmm...un...," was the best he could manage.

"I'se moseying fast," Big Edmund assured him, "but I ain't sho' what's gwine to happen to me. Colonel White done tol' me not to let you go flyin' to the fields and mountains all night."

Robert grunted and dug his heels into the horse's flanks.

The house Elizabeth Swecker's kin lived in lay more than a mile south of the Holston's north fork. Even as he first sighted it, Robert envisioned what it would be like to walk with the girl along the banks of the river. He would find deep-blue mussel shells for her and she would look at him with those eyes again—eyes that mirrored a soul of honesty and simplicity and beauty.

Robert introduced himself to a man working diligently to the west of his log house with a bared back and swinging scythe. "Might I see Miss Elizabeth for a little spell?" Robert asked.

"We put her on the eastbound stage this morning."

"I wanted to see her again," Robert said unashamedly.

"I noticed you was lookin' at her right smartly yesterday."

"She lives in Wythe County, doesn't she?"

"That's right. She's been visiting us a few days. I'm her uncle."

"You reckon she'll be back any time soon?" Robert asked.

"We're not alookin' for her any time soon. Far as I know, this visit to us was the first time she's ever been out of her home county—first time she's ever been on a stage—I know that for a fact."

"I reckon I'll be goin' then."

Robert started for his horse, but the man called him back. "I might oughta' tell you…if you're thinking of sparkin' Elizabeth, she's purty nigh twenty-two years old. If I'm any judge of a feller I'd say you're not more'n fifteen or sixteen at most."

Robert started to answer him. Yesterday had been his eighteenth birthday! Then, instinctively, he ran his thumb and forefinger around his chin and silently cursed the apple skin smoothness of hide that hadn't yet grown one visible whisker.

The colonel could bring out the whole town and most of the state militia, Robert decided in his disappointment and humiliation. He would spend the night on the bank of the Holston and listen to the melody of the ripples. Maybe he would spend two or three nights, if he could find a bee tree filled with wild honey.

Chapter II

As August came and went, the issue of Robert's attendance at college during the second session was not so much in the forefront of things. It was understood that both he and Lawrence would help with the work of summer and fall. The holdings of his uncle were growing by leaps and bounds and ever farther apart they were spreading. So productive were the colonel's salt mines that in order to market the output of the hundreds of boiling cauldrons, he was seeking the opportunity to barter salt for land. To this end he was successful with the help of agents and the small band of emissaries that included his older sons and the husbands of his older daughters. Before long, salt by the barge load floated down the Tennessee River as far as Alabama, and deed recordations were showing such things as land transferred with the "consideration being thirty thousand bushels of salt."

Robert's problems were not so complex. The corn grew healthily and the wheat grew large-headed and developed a golden hue. But the nourishing sun did not do as well on Robert's fertile chin. He thought, however, he had found the answer to that problem.

Down near Black's Fort there lived an old Indian who supported himself by digging and selling herbs. According to a story Robert had heard at the tanning yard, the oldest man who worked there had a healthy crop of black hair at the age of seventy-three and all because the Indian herb doctor had applied the blood of the wild grapevine to the patient's once bald head. That revelation didn't leave much to ponder about. If the blood of the wild grapevine could grow thick black hair, surely it could grow stiff red whiskers.

From midsummer until early fall, Big Edmund didn't have to ask Robert where he was going each time the horse was saddled for him, but, out of habit, he did so anyhow.

"What yo' goin' up to the mountains agin fer? Everybody done think yo is out of yo haid now."

Today Robert felt like agreeing with the slave. The horseback trips that once were just for the benefit of solitude and meditation now had a dual purpose: he could meditate while his chin rested in a bowl of wild grapevine blood. As he sat hunch-shouldered, his chin growing cold and numb, he wondered whether Elizabeth Swecker could possibly appreciate the effort he was going through on her behalf. At times the awful thought seized him: she must be twenty-two by now, going on twenty-three, and he hadn't grown the first whisker!

Robert had nearly run out of new excuses for not wanting an education. He had finally narrowed his reasons down to the axiom that wisdom and education was not necessarily the same thing. The former he wanted; the latter was, he felt, unnecessary. The deadlock was broken by Colonel White one day in early September.

"Robert," the colonel said, "I understand you have not yet made up your mind about college in spite of our many talks. I have work lined up for you at the Goose Creek saltworks just in case. You will load salt on the mule wagons ten hours a day. I am told each box to be emptied weighs approximately one hundred and twenty-eight pounds. If my figuring is correct, you will handle over seven tons of salt daily. Let us know when you have made your decision."

By the middle of October both he and Lawrence looked forward to beginning their studies at Emory and Henry. Most of the money they had earned by working for their uncle was spent for clothes they would need. Their brother James was financially able to provide one half of the tuition and board money—their uncle James would make up the balance—so that all of their plans were in order. Robert mentioned his thoughts to nobody, but he wished his brother James could afford all the expenses. He did not feel right about taking money from his uncle, in spite of his wealth. He thought he felt resentment in his uncle when expenditures were made on his and Lawrence's behalf. Still, he couldn't justify the feeling with evidence. His uncle had, after all, encouraged his enrollment at college. With all Robert's rationalization, the feeling just wouldn't go away—it was a feeling that, Robert realized, had been with him since his earliest years. But he would keep his thoughts to himself. If brother James was still in the notion to help, he would consider himself lucky.

Robert and Lawrence boarded the eastbound stage on the morning of October 21, 1838, and headed for Marion, some twenty-five miles away. The stagecoach rumbled along, its wheels occasionally striking an upturned rock, making the sound of grating metal against stone. The sound and the boat like roll of the moving coach provided a hypnotic repetition of sounds and motion that caused Lawrence's head to nod sleepily.

Robert nudged his brother in the ribs with an elbow. "I don't see how you can sleep on this kind of a ride," he said.

"I can't. Something keeps poking me in the ribs," Lawrence said without looking up.

The passenger to the other side of Lawrence kept his silence and moved away, slightly.

"We just took on a passenger at Sulphur Springs," Robert murmured. Lawrence's head still bobbled. Robert leaned over close to his brother's ear. "She's pretty," he stated.

Lawrence looked up suddenly to confront at close range the bewhiskered face of an old woman, horribly witchlike in appearance. While Lawrence's mouth yet hung open, the old woman attempted to add life to the captive condition they all shared.

"Understand we're goin' to cross a new county line on this trip," she volunteered.

"Yes, ma'm," the passenger next to Lawrence said, "but it's not so new now. Smyth County was formed five or six years ago."

"I didn't know that," she said. "I don't git out aright smart."

"Where do you live?" Robert asked.

"Just south of Fort Chiswell—in Wythe County."

"Do you know a family of Sweckers ?"

The woman fingered her stubbled chin and thought. "Only family I heard of by that name live over on Cripple Creek. What's the name of the Sweckers you're lookin' fer?"

"I don't know—I can't remember," Robert said. He started to give the woman Elizabeth's name, then thought better of it since he did not know the name of Elizabeth's father.

"I don't know them Sweckers personal-like myself, but they got the name of being God-fearin' folks. I'll mosey around and find out for you," the old woman said.

Robert smiled, knowing he would probably never see her again. "Thank you just the same. We're stopping in Marion to see my brother. He's a lawyer there and he probably knows of the family."

James Sheffey was working laboriously at a roll top desk when his brothers entered his office. He paid them little mind while attempting to finish the line he was writing. Robert started out the door before the young lawyer could finish, and "put on" his most annoyed air: "Well, Sir Lawrence, shall we take our affairs elsewhere?"

At the mere hint of a loss of business, James Sheffey rested his quill against the inkwell and turned to face the gentry to his rear.

"Robert! Lawrence! It's good to see you both." He clasped each of their hands. "Come, sit down and tell me all about yourselves."

"Sit where?" Lawrence said, noticing only one extra chair, which Robert took.

James pushed his own desk chair to Lawrence and he himself sat upon a pine storage box. "One of these days maybe I'll have cane bottom chairs lining my share of the walls—but maybe by then the fees will be a little higher and coming in a little faster."

"I think we chose a bad week to come, Robert," Lawrence said.

"I believe I know your reason for coming," James smiled, "and never fear, I intend to make good on my offer. I didn't say our business was bad, just that it could improve."

"Land transfers should be good," Lawrence said. "Uncle James said that when the railroad actually got under way, we'd really see a landslide of activity."

"I agree with Uncle James, except for one thing," James said. "I'm not sure we're going to see the coming of the railroad for twenty-five years. For the Virginia general assembly to incorporate the Lynchburg and Tennessee and authorize subscriptions is one thing; getting the tracks laid over some of this country and hearing a puffing locomotive coming down the tracks is another. Uncle James was in here yesterday and we talked about this very thing. And Uncle James can see starlight through the storm clouds, as you know."

"What was Uncle James doing down here? He didn't say anything about coming to Marion," Robert said.

"I don't think you have any idea of the extent of your uncle's holdings," James said. "His interest in the Buddle Furnace alone will make him a quarter million dollars and even more if he can get full control of it. That's what you saw me working on. We're trying to deal with the Jackson heirs and get a controlling interest. That area of Wythe County is like a goldmine. In case you've forgotten," James reminded them, "those mines furnished bullets for the patriots of seventy-six, and you can bet your boots the redcoats at King's Mountain won't forget the lead in their rumps that was mined right here in this area."

"Do you get a great deal of business from Uncle James?" Lawrence asked.

"I'm much beholden to him," James confessed. "You asked what he was doing here. I don't think he would mind my telling you, as long as the news doesn't pass beyond the family. He is in Wytheville on official court business, but he has some other things in mind also: namely, negotiations to acquire Graham's Forge. I don't have to tell you what that means."

"Looks like we ought not to be looking to you for any help toward our tuition and board—looks like Uncle James wouldn't miss what little it took."

"No," James interrupted Lawrence. "I want to help, and it is my duty. When we are able to earn our own way it is not up to our uncle to help us, no matter what his wealth."

"I'll repay you someday," Robert volunteered.

"No, that is not at issue," James said. "I wish I could pay it all for both of you, but it'll take me a few years yet to really get going."

"I have a feeling you'll succeed in a big way, James," Lawrence said.

"These are wonderful times for all of us to get started. There's a fortune to be made everywhere a man looks. Do you know that zinc is being found around Ivanhoe, testing ninety-six per cent grade? Iron ore lies around here on the ground like culled potatoes. Why, good farms abound by the dozen, to be had for the asking—some of them can be bought only for the taxes due. There's no real way to ship produce and livestock right now except by wagon—but you wait until the railroad does finally come and every farm within fifty miles of the track will multiply its worth ten times."

"I get excited just hearing you talk about it," Lawrence said.

Robert was silent, and James eyed him suspiciously. "What's the matter, Robert, you having trouble figuring out how to make your first million dollars?" he asked.

"It's not worrying me none," Robert said.

"Well, you'll probably end up being worth more than anyone in the family—maybe even worth more than all of us put together." James and Lawrence both laughed.

"You mentioned the good grade of zinc at Ivanhoe. I suppose they haven't found any on our old homestead?" Lawrence asked.

"No. All we're getting is the rent—that accounts for little more than paying the taxes and keeping the place in repair. I'm afraid our father didn't pick one of the lucky spots. The best ore and zinc deposits seem to be in pocket areas. It's something we want to be thinking about. Robert will be twenty-one in three more years. We can sell the farm then, or hold on and hope that in years to come when mining techniques become a little more advanced, they will be able to dig deeper and find something on our place. I don't see anything to do but go on renting it for farmland—unless you both disagree with me."

"You go on handling it, for my say-so," Lawrence said.

"What about you, Robert? I want your opinion."

"You do what's best. I just don't want to sell it, that's all," Robert said. "I'm the only one that can't even remember Mama or Papa. One day I want to go back to Wythe County and walk over every inch of it. Maybe I'll feel something I've never felt before."

"I'll check with the other brothers too, but anyway beginning next fall you will be in charge of collecting the rent," James said. "Then you can walk over it all you want. It's been paid this year, but next year you start for sure. It'll be a good time for you to begin learning a little about business, and a college man ought to be up on how to figure with a right fine pencil point...Now—that's talk enough about business. You all come along with me and Ellen can put two more plates on the table."

They left the frame offices and crossed the street to the brick sidewalk that ran beside the courthouse. Lawrence paused. "Still shows its birthday suit pretty well, doesn't it?" he said, viewing the new-looking courthouse.

"A lot of history has passed through it already, and long may it stand," James said, laying a hand upon the shoulder of each brother as they walked.

Ellen Preston Sheffey would hear of no talk about business at her dinner table. As soon as the meal was properly served, she dismissed the kitchen servant and sat down to absorb every word of what she expected to be a stimulating conversation. "You promised that business would not be discussed," she would remind gently when the conversation seemed pointed that way. "You've told me how all the family are, but surely something else that's interesting has happened in Abingdon since we were last there."

Lawrence didn't offer anything, but Robert grinned as he remembered a tale from his tanning-yard visits.

"We had a man with a powwow put on him," he began, "a man outside of Abingdon by the name of Marsh who came down with a bad case of scrofula. He dreamed his disease was brought on by a conjure man by the name of Yates. This wizard could remove his curse if he wanted to, Marsh believed, but Marsh was pretty scared of him—..."

"Now, wait a spell. Why did he do it in the first place?" Ellen asked.

"I think Marsh just imagined his neck swelling was a curse put on him, but he really believed it, the men told me."

"Well, did the king's evil go away?" James asked impatiently.

"No, and by and by Marsh sent for Yates, the conjure man—who turned out to be an Indian, by the way—and Yates administered his nostrums for the cure."

"Then Marsh turned into a frog," Ellen anticipated the ending.

"You're getting ahead of me," Robert said with a scowl, "and this is a true story."

"Pay no attention to my wife," James said, "she's not only pretty but she has an imagination that is far too healthy."

"Anyway," Robert continued, "Marsh got worse instead of better and decided by some twist of the mind that if he got rid of Yates by a powwow method of his own his troubles would be over. Well, Marsh drew a likeness of Yates on a tree and shot at it several times with bullets containing portions of silver. It was clear to Marsh that his powwow hadn't worked when, in a few days, Yates passed by, perfectly normal. Before Yates was out of sight Marsh loaded an old musket with two balls and shot the wizard in the back of the neck. But Yates didn't die and Uncle James's court sent Marsh to the penitentiary."

Ellen Sheffey's blue eyes gleamed like those of a child hearing nursery rhymes. "Does Robert dream up these fairy tales while he's off alone in the woods somewhere or do those smelly old hide-scrapers down in the bottom really tell him these things?" Ellen asked Lawrence.

"I can't tell you that," Lawrence confessed. "Maybe he got that story from some of those frontier travelers heading for the gap of the Cumberlands."

"You still keep an eye on Black's Fort and the Great Road?" James inquired.

"Uncle James accuses me of being Washington County's ambassador to the settlers going west. I guess I do like to sit around and talk a little and watch those in a hurry go on by," Robert said.

"Do you want to go with them?" Ellen asked.

"I don't rightly know. I don't know whether I'm supposed to go with them or not. I get a funny feeling about it."

"You just like to watch them pass?"

"Yes," he said.

James looked at his youngest brother with a searching eye but made no comment until Ellen reminded him of the time.

"I do have to get back to my desk and take care of a few matters. Lawrence, you and Robert wander about our little village or stay here with Ellen as you like. You will of course spend the night?"

"If your good wife won't be obliged to go to a lot of trouble," Lawrence said.

"Nonsense," Ellen scoffed, "you'll be no bother, and Robert can study the humanity in Smyth County. Perhaps he will find them even more virtuous than those of Washington County.

Robert was caught off guard by the perception of his brother's wife, and he looked upon her with new affection. She was more than pretty and more than the essence of grace. She brushed the lint from the lapel of her well-dressed husband and sent him back to his work. As she began to clear the table, Robert watched her birdlike movements. Occasionally she smiled at him, and he found it hard, surrounded by this aura of feminine sweetness, not to think of Elizabeth Swecker.

Elizabeth Swecker's name was not mentioned, however, until the following morning at breakfast.

"I know of no family by that name, personally," James said. "Perhaps I can inquire the next time I attend court in Wytheville. What part of the county are they from and what is the householder's full name?"

It was like the old woman in the stagecoach all over again, Robert thought.

"I don't know that, but I think they may live near Cripple Creek. All I'm sure of is the girl's name." Robert blurted it out as quickly as he could.

James, by six years his younger brother's senior, approached the matter cautiously. "Elizabeth, you say. Well, all we need to do is find Elizabeth's father. Might this be serious enough to put several people on the trail?"

"No," she's a whole lot older than me," Robert said shyly. "I was just wondering—that's all."

"It's just as well," Ellen Sheffey said. "You're going to be in college and there won't be much time for sparking anyway. Girl's faces have a way of getting in front of text books."

That sounded too motherly for Ellen, Robert thought, and he ate the rest of his breakfast resenting her advice. Nevertheless, their parting for the return trip to Abingdon was congenial.

"Tell Mother Elizabeth it is her turn next to visit us!" Ellen called as they departed the house.

Before the west bound stage was due, James showed his brothers around the new court house and they watched with interest a session going full blast and a red-faced lawyer, well lathered with sweat, arguing on behalf of his client.

Back in James's office, Robert was the first recipient of his brother's outstretched hand. "I'll send some more as soon as I can," he promised, and handed Robert two five-dollar gold pieces. Lawrence received the same. "I'll try to keep ahead of the treasurer at the college, but if you need more help, let me know."

They thanked him, but he brushed the words aside quickly. "I'll walk with you to the stage stop. And remember, not a word about Uncle James's private affairs.

Within the quarter-hour winded horses brought the stage coach to a dusty stop in front of Hinkman's Hotel. The sky was overcast and the air was chill for October, enough so that streams of vapor rose from the flared nostrils of the panting animals. Livery workmen unhitched the team with a minimal loss of time and the stage driver lowered the baggage of passengers whose destination had been reached.

"Spread the word!" the driver called to the ever-present body of onlookers. "Colonel James White dropped dead in Wytheville this morning!"

James stepped nearer to the driver. "What did you say?"

"I said Colonel White died this morning in Wytheville.

Colonel James White of Abingdon—he died during the opening of the court session."

"Do you know who was dispatched to bring word to his widow?" James asked.

"No, sir. I know some men left Wytheville going to Abingdon by hack—Jabe Cochran at the livery stable told me—but I don't know who they were."

Robert saw the face of his older brother suddenly drained of blood, and he himself started to tremble.

"What ought we to do?" Lawrence murmured.

James paused unduly long, and then said, "I will tell Ellen and then I'll go to Wytheville and accompany the body back to Abingdon. I think both of you had best go ahead on the stage. Somebody will have gotten the word to Aunt Elizabeth before you get there—but I'm sure you can be a great comfort to her."

Fresh horses, with the vigor of their thrust, snapped back Robert's head unexpectedly and slammed it against the corner brace of the coach. Indeed, he was not dreaming. It started to rain, and through the steamed up window of the stagecoach, he could still see James walking stoop-shouldered against the rain.

When Robert and Lawrence arrived back in Abingdon and hastily made their way home, two strangers and Reuben Bradley, who had accompanied the two men from Wytheville, still sat in the parlor. Only five of the White children, including James Lowry, the oldest son, sat in a circle about their mother. Six of the children had yet to learn of their father's death.

Presently Reuben Bradley got up from his chair and whispered suggestions of things he could do.

"We have taken advantage of your kindness already, Reuben," Elizabeth White said. "Please have the gentlemen return home. The days are short and I fear they will be getting home after dark. Is it still raining?"

"No, Elizabeth, it has stopped."

Robert had never seen tears in his aunt's eyes, nor did he see them now. Still, he was aware of her suffering. Her movements were restrained to the point where her motionlessness seemed an unuttered scream. He walked among the others and kissed his aunt upon the cheek. Her face was cold. This woman who had taught him his prayers, who had been the only real mother in the world he had ever known, was cold. Why did not one of her own place his arms about her? For he hadn't the right. He tiptoed to one of the cooks and asked for his aunt's shawl. Having received it from the wet-eyed servant, he placed it around her shoulders.

By the supper hour word had spread and friends and neighbors filled the spacious rooms whose congenial warmth had long been known to most of them.

More than once during the evening Robert saw acquaintances and business associates of his uncle circulate through the house and finally find themselves standing before the colonel's favorite rocking chair. The misty-eyed onlooker would invariably give the chair the slightest push, and then watch it, until the lack of motion seemed to the onlooker some sort of private benediction.

By morning the parlor was rearranged to accommodate the casket of the master of the house. Robert stayed in his room until his uncle's wife and children had stood at the side of their legendary husband and father, admitting in silence and for the first time, he thought, that every man is mortal. When the room was silent and empty again, Robert made his own casket-side visit, to view the profile that looked as commanding in death as in life. He, too, as the others had done, stood gazing upon the face of this man who was both friend and foe, servant and lord, companion and antagonist.

Robert touched his uncle's hand. For a fleeting moment he wanted to shake it in some form of abstract reconciliation, some final pronouncement of acquiescence to the superior man.

Throughout the day this feeling did not leave him, nor had it gone when the final hour arrived and he sat as a family member on the front bench of his uncle's church. There was a sense of peace in the minister's voice; he spoke with great compassion about his deceased friend. His gaze was fixed steadfastly on the eyes of Elizabeth White, as though to convince her that his words were not only well chosen but instinctively true.

Robert was not any more sure of how his uncle really felt about the church than he was about how he himself felt. The quiet Presbyterianism the White family practiced seemed a simple part of weekly routine rather than any predominating force in their lives. He did remember hearing the colonel say on one occasion that being a Presbyterian allowed one the privilege of practicing worship without getting excited about it. Robert had felt that, like so many of his uncle's observations, this one might not convey the real depth of the colonel's feeling on the matter. Although in Robert's memory Colonel White had not given any special emphasis to religious matters, Robert suspected that he had a deep and abiding respect for things spiritual.

About his Aunt Elizabeth, though, he was certain. He could not recall a time when she had not encouraged him to read his Bible, to keep his person clean, and to attend church. Equally forceful were his aunt's lectures about keeping good company and developing high ideals. All of these things were to be attained with and practiced with a special sort of dignity that Elizabeth White felt was becoming to every man.

Robert shivered a little in the presence of the church surrounding him. This was not a good place to lie even to oneself. It was odd that he chose this time and this place for his soul-searching, but he had not very often taken to heart the teachings and ideals of his aunt.

Colonel James White had not lain in his grave for more than a month when Robert approached his brother one day with a proposal he felt now needed to be made.

"Lawrence, Aunt Elizabeth hasn't mentioned anything about either one of us going to college. I don't think she wants us to spend the money."

"I know only what little I've overheard," Lawrence said, "but I think it's more complicated than that."

"She can't spend it, you mean?"

"I know this much—an accounting has to be made of Uncle James's estate and his heirs ruled on by the court. Alexander Findlay, one of the appraisers, told me it would be several years before all of our uncle's estate would be settled."

"Sounds to me like there won't be any money for college or anything else," Robert said.

"There won't be any shortage of money after everything is resolved, but that may take a long time. All the debtors and creditors Uncle James had will have to settle with the administrator of the estate. Aunt Elizabeth may have to live the best she can until everything is finalized, and my guess is that it will be a year's time at least."

"That kind of arrangement doesn't seem fair to me," Robert argued.

"Fair or not, the law says a man's affairs have to be put in order before anybody can get his money or property."

"Aunt Elizabeth could get a loan of some kind so that Uncle James's wishes for us could be carried out," Robert suggested.

"I suppose she could, but under the circumstances she will probably be given a maintenance fee by the administrator until matters are settled. Aunt Elizabeth doesn't have a head for business, and you know as well as I that she will be dependent on the court-appointed trustees and her own children."

"Do you think we can expect anything from Uncle James's estate?" Robert asked.

"Don't hope for it," Lawrence said. "There are eleven children, you know, and some of them are minors. They may have court-appointed guardians. I think we can expect our lives to take a much different turn now."

Robert already had surmised this himself, and now he blurted out the plan he had previously formulated. "I'm the youngest and I'll find some work while you go to college. Our brother can't send us both and pay all the expenses."

"Don't be saying that until we can talk to him."

"It doesn't matter now," Robert said. "For a long time I didn't really want to go to college—and in some ways I still don't—but I can almost hear Uncle James admonishing me from his grave. I guess I owe it to him to go."

"Let's not anticipate any move whatsoever until we have talked to James."

"If he wants you to have the money he gave me, he's not in for much luck," Robert said.

"You lost it?" Lawrence gasped.

"No. I gave five dollars of it to a family going to Kentucky."

"What in the world for? James will be mad enough to hang you!"

"They needed it worse than I did. They were going home steadin' on nothing but a team of horses and a couple of axes and maybe a hoe and mattock. They didn't have enough kitchenware in that wagon to cook for two people—and hardly any bed clothing that I could see."

"You can observe that kind of sight nearly every day you sit around Black's Fort. I don't understand why one family is any more deserving than another or why you think they need your brother's money more than you do!"

"I just knew it—that's all. I had the money in my pocket that day and I knew when that family came along I was supposed to give it to them."

"I hope our brother believes that story."

"If I can explain to him what that woman's face looked like, he won't need to know anything else. She had a baby in each arm and her tears pretty near washed them all off the wagon seat."

James confirmed what Robert and Lawrence had already discussed. Legal entanglement over their uncle's estate was a matter that pressed heavily upon the mind of their aunt. To add to her lack of knowledge, and consequent anguish, in such things, family problems over matters of the estate had begun to surface. Now a new kind of turmoil was added to the burden of a terrible loneliness that was getting worse rather than better. James Sheffey insisted that his brothers not mention the subject of finance to their aunt and thereby remove at least some slight burden of worry from her shoulders.

Robert's plan was finally the one found acceptable. He would not enter college, thus allowing Lawrence the privilege of going first, supported in full by their brother James.

Robert, for the first time in his life, now sought the prospects of a regular job. James promised to help his brother in the search for employment, but the fall of 1838 was not a year of promise for a young man of eighteen whose qualifications for work consisted of good penmanship, some artistic talent, and no history at all of a real need to labor with hands or head.

Robert was not asked to return the remaining gold piece his brother had given him. Perhaps James believed the story Robert told him of sharing his money with someone else. James had merely smiled and refrained from the expected chastisement, Robert recalled later, but he did remember James saying something to himself about "A fool and his money ..."

CHAPTER III

By the first of December, Robert obtained a position to which his meager talents seemed adaptable. His brother James did some fast talking toward convincing Andrew Russell, clerk of Washington County, that Robert had a genuine gift as a scribe. Robert learned later that Andrew Russell was not an easy man to persuade, in spite of family friendships. Nevertheless, upon seeing a facsimile deed that Robert had copied in his best penmanship, the aging old public servant was convinced that never in his more than forty years of service had he seen any better scribe.

During Robert's first day on the job it pleased him that Mr. Russell looked over his shoulder as he worked and occasionally brought one of the deputy clerks, who would smile his pleasure at the deft strokes of Robert's tortoiseshell nibs.

Although his superiors were pleased with his work, by the arrival of the first Saturday he had begun to tire of the job. The lump of three dollars and fifty cents in wages was welcome, but he did not look forward with any particular joy to the coming of Monday. His buttocks were sore from the precarious perch on the high stool for a week's duration, and he realized, too, that each succeeding day would be exactly like the previous one.

After work Robert made his way to Shoate's tavern, where he spoke to some of the wagoners who frequented the establishment and joined them in a mug of rum. Some of them looked at his clean clothes suspiciously, for they themselves smelled of their own sweat and that of the animals with which they came in contact. But those men who knew him seemed undistracted by the cleanliness of his person, and their tone of voice was one of brotherhood.

The young man who dominated the conversation was not a mule skinner or wagon master, as most of the men were, but a blacksmith whose jovial good humor made a tavern visit a daily tonic.

"Well, what about it, Robert? The county court has obliged us with gettin' a gun house put up on the public lot, and Captain Stevens is securing all the artillery we need. Are you goin' to join us?"

"Uncle James said before he died that the Texas agitation wouldn't spread *this* far," Robert argued.

"Well, now, I ain't doubtin' Colonel White was a smart man, but there's others who are athinkin' trouble with them Mexicans will be bustin' out all over the place."

"I might just join up," Robert said with a grin.

It was no trouble at all for him to imagine himself a part of the elite company of volunteers who would be forming Captain John W. Stevens' artillery company. It was just possible that the patriotic youth of Abingdon might one day march to the Mexican border.

Robert looked at the arm of his blacksmith friend and saw there a physical power second only to that of Big Edmund. He could visualize with ease this master of the hammer and anvil tamping the hungry mouths of the cannon. When this bright-eyed, big-jawed smithy grinned at him, he knew that the grin asked the question of whether or not he himself really desired to be a man—a real man.

"I might just join up," Robert said again, as if there had been no pause since he had made the same statement.

Another round of rum passed the lips of would-be cannoneers, and still another, until the entire strategy necessary for the defeat of Mexico had been planned and discussed in such detail that victory would be a certainty.

Robert left the tavern in a state of alcoholic euphoria, aware of two things: Aunt Elizabeth would not like his being late for supper, and his brother James would growl a firm "no" at the mention of his possible participation in the volunteer artillery company. As he walked home his mind was occupied with how best to approach his brother on this issue. Patriotism? Yes, James was not only an up-and-coming lawyer but a patriot if ever there was one. But perhaps he would join with or without James's consent. Another thought lurked in the back of his mind: a colorful uniform representing the Abingdon artillery volunteers might be enough to fool Elizabeth Swecker even if the wearer still had no whiskers. And that was another round he was going to have with his brother. James hadn't written one word about whether he had located Elizabeth Swecker's family. Robert could go back to the home of her kin near the Holston, but he had been disappointed there once. He would not risk a second chance. Ellen Sheffey's words came back to him then. Maybe Ellen had discouraged James from passing along any information he had learned about Elizabeth Swecker. If that were true then Ellen was being too motherly and protective again. But then maybe his pining for a girl he had been with for less than two hours was a little silly. And to make matters worse, he had told James that finding Elizabeth wasn't important. Elizabeth might even be married by now, but the thought of it brought a terrible ache to his heart.

The chill nights of December forced a clear headedness as he walked across Main Street to his aunt's house. He could see the White family and Lawrence seated at the table as he ascended the front steps. He washed and took his place at the table, apologizing for his lateness. Elizabeth White eyed him suspiciously, but instructed the kitchen servant to bring his plate.

The meal hour concluded with the same dismal silence that had become normal since the death of his uncle James, in spite of Elizabeth White's valiant fight to bring back to her table some semblance of the carefree chatter so much a part of former mealtimes. The family drifted from the table one by one, but Lawrence remained to eye Robert disapprovingly, as did his Aunt Elizabeth.

"You do not honor your uncle's home by coming to his table smelling of rum and animal sweat," Elizabeth White said.

"Is rum any less honorable than Madeira? Or sherry? Uncle James did not object to the smell of those in his house," Robert said.

"There is a difference—and there is a time and place."

"A drink is a drink whether it's in a tavern or in a ballroom," Robert argued, "and some of your own sons might agree with me."

"Your tongue seems whetted with unusual wisdom and vehemence tonight, Robert. You will excuse me if I remove myself."

No sooner had the sad eyes of Elizabeth White ceased to search his face than those of Lawrence continued the surveillance.

"You disapprove of me too, Lawrence?"

"We should not add to Aunt Elizabeth's burden in any way," Lawrence said. "You are wrong to distress her when her grief still hangs heavy on her shoulders. Neither has she gotten any additional word from Alabama in the last two days. James Lowry could well be dead by now, -and she knows it."

The implications of Lawrence's words were sobering, and Robert suddenly felt a fraternal closeness to his cousin. Of all the children of his aunt and uncle, he was more drawn to James Lowry, for they had been more nearly like older and younger brother than sometimes-hostile cousins.

"No word from him could mean he's getting better, couldn't it?" Robert asked.

"I hope so, but there's no way of knowing. Word travels so slowly."

"If anything happens to him Aunt Elizabeth would just go crawl in a cave," Robert said abstractly.

"We should know something by tomorrow," Lawrence said. "Word will be coming up the river."

Robert lay in his bed until the effects of the rum had left nothing but dull head pains and a stinging remorse. If anything happened to James Lowry it would be like losing his uncle James all over again. James Lowry had been the one salvation of the whole family; he had stepped into his father's shoes, admittedly lacking the skill of a business administrator but not the courage and benevolence of his father. Nor was energy any less evident in the younger man, and it was this, perhaps, that lay at the seat of his feverish collapse in the pursuit of his father's business.

Well past the midnight hour Robert's sobriety continued to condemn him to wakefulness. He slipped from his room, feeling his way with familiarity down the hall to the stairway. A beam of lamplight escaped from beneath the door of Elizabeth White's room. He paused there a moment, wondering if he should knock and try to comfort her. No sound came from the room, but there would be none. His aunt would not be crying, but her dark eyes would be luminous with passionate pleading to heaven that her oldest and most-needed be delivered from harm. Robert turned from her door and made his way down the stairs and to the parlor and the dying embers of the hearthside.

By dawn he, awakened, chilled, in spite of the quilt about him and a few coals still glowing red. Frost covered the windows, obscuring the daylight beyond.

Presently one of the younger servants made her way from the kitchen, carrying a basket of kindling and pine knots. For a moment she was startled at Robert's presence in a place he ought not to be so early in the morning. She stirred the ashes with the poker and added chips of wood until, a blaze leaped for the throat of the fireplace. Having gotten a good blaze going, she added several pine knots and turned her back to the warmth, in a manner that was just like the one she had observed in the refined ladies who visited the White household—when no gentlemen were present! Robert observed her imitative antics without comment.

"Never nobody sits by the hearthside all night lessen they is havin' love troubles er painin' in the soul. Ain't that right, Mr. Robert?"

"That's what they say," Robert answered with a yawn.

"Is you havin' love troubles?"

He grinned now at her young brashness; he treasured the lack of formality he enjoyed with all the servants. "No, I'm not having any love troubles," he said. "Everybody tells me you can't even think about loving anybody until you've taken a straight razor to yourself a few times."

She looked closely at his chin. "Well, lawsy me, ain't it a shame? Sure as you're born though, you'll be sproutin' the same time as the spring corn and onions." She started to run her finger over his chin, but he backed away in shame. "If'n you ain't got love troubles, what you painin' in the soul about?" she persisted.

He didn't want to answer, but she still stood there, sincere and expectant.

"Have you ever been lost?" he asked.

"Lawsy me, yes, but I'm on my way to glory now, hallelujah!"

"I don't mean that kind of lost exactly ...but that might be part of it... I mean lost at a crossroads or in the mountains and not know which way to go."

"Gracious no, Mr. Robert. I ain't hardy been out of this house since I been born—lest it be to fetch sumpin' out of the fields or from a neighbor."

"You wouldn't understand then," he found himself saying.

He turned his face then to the fire, and it felt good. "You'd better get some chunk wood to put on the fire," he said finally.

She nodded, and he called behind her, "I'll get the heavy logs. It's going to be cold today—may even be snowing by midday!"

He returned with a second log of yellow locust; the first one he had placed on the and irons was popping noisily and sending tiny sparks hopping in all directions. Elizabeth White moved aside to allow the second log to be placed.

"You didn't rest well either, did you, Robert? I heard you come downstairs last night."

"No, I was restless."

"It helps us to be alone sometimes. I remember sitting alone at this very same fireplace many nights and for many reasons."

"Waiting for Uncle James to come back from some of his trips, I 'magine."

"Yes, sometimes. Sometimes it was one of the babies with colic so bad I knew he might not last the night. We lost two babies. Such precious little things they were. Our second child was taken from us four years after I married your uncle. He was a little boy, hardly over a year old. And we lost Mary Young—she was next to Milton and lived not quite a year."

"Life doesn't seem worth living sometimes—least to me it doesn't, and I reckon with all the trouble you've had you've been thinkin' the same thing."

"A part of life is trouble and hardship, Robert. Be forewarned. Maybe time will make it easier for those of you who are younger. Abingdon is not the wilderness it was when we moved here before the turn of the century. The War of '76 was still fresh on everybody's mind when I settled this wilderness as a young bride of sixteen. There was stillness at eventide far more frightening than the marauding Indians who stirred up trouble on occasion."

"Did you ever feel like running away?"

"Yes, many times. I sat by the hearthside often, both crying and praying to see Pittsylvania County again, and be under the roof of my mother and father."

"But you toughed it out?" Robert said.

"Yes. It wasn't easy, but we planted our seed—worked it through sunshine and shadow, and now we see it growing and bearing fruit. There is one lesson you must learn from your uncle's life if you learn no other, Robert. Your uncle believed in everything he did. He made some serious mistakes but he did not fret over them. No mistake he made was great enough to make him even pause before he plunged wholeheartedly into some new enterprise. Believe in what you do, Robert, with your whole heart and mind and spirit. If it is a worthy task and your dedication to it is complete and unyielding, you will wear a crown that neither God nor man will ever forget."

"I can't ever amount to what Uncle James was. I know that. I don't even want to try. All my brothers do, and they goad me. They've called me everything but the black sheep in the family, and when I make them mad enough they'll be hankering to call me that."

"You are young yet, Robert. Your greatest task now is to see that you do not take the wrong road until you have a chance to come to the right one. Your uncle's death has upset some of our plans, but we will make arrangements somehow to help with your college expenses."

"Our brother has taken care of helping Lawrence, and I am going to wait for another year—if I don't change my mind. Besides, you have your own children to think about."

"I have talked to Lawrence and James both. Your brother has acted most nobly during this period when my affairs have been so unsettled, but he may be undertaking more than he realizes. We will simply do the best we can, and I hope you will use this year of waiting most wisely. Do your work honestly so that your employer will speak well of you, and pay much heed to the company you keep."

Robert wondered if now was the proper time to tell his aunt that he was tiring of his position after only a week, but others were congregating in the room now, making frequent inspections of the dining-room table, so he hadn't the privacy required for such a declaration. The timing would be bad and would certainly insure a rebuttal in forceful tones from his aunt.

They were all seated shortly. Robert noticed that his aunt was hardly aware that complete silence prevailed—that all eyes watched her and awaited the customary blessing over the food. Finally her tired gaze turned to them all, and Robert was sure he alone knew of her sleepless, prayerful night. The conclusion of the grace she uttered over their food left no doubt where her thoughts were: "… and if it be thy will, dear Lord, deliver our son and brother from the pain of his illness and see him safely from that distant land so far from home and those who love him . Amen."

The younger White children were prompted by their mother's prayer to ask questions as to why no one knew whether their oldest brother was better or sicker now that the third day had come with no further word. The older children knew without asking.

"We will not learn anything new unless a courier is sent or until the canal boats come up the Tennessee River with the mail," Elizabeth White explained.

"Don't they have doctors in Alabama?" Milton asked.

"Yes, child." Elizabeth White smiled lovingly at her eight-year-old. "I just hope he got to one in time."

"I didn't understand the contradiction in the first message," Lawrence Sheffey said. "I thought that James Lowry was at the Jackson County farm, but the courier indicated that he was considerably upriver."

"The courier who reached us was the fifth or sixth in the relay, and after word has been passed on several times it always gets mixed up."

All speculation as to the fate of James Lowry White ceased by midmorning of the same day, when Robert heard the pounding of swift hooves against the stone surface of Main Street. A breathless courier on a breathless animal brought a message that seemed clear and complete. James Lowry White was dead and had been since the previous day. He had indeed been stricken ill with high fever on his way home from far upriver, from Jackson County, Alabama. For over two weeks he had fought the fever that ultimately consumed him. Elizabeth White had spent the night praying for a son who was already dead.

Robert did not let the solemnity of his cousin's memorial service deter him from seeking his brother James's approval of his joining the volunteer artillery company, but James thought the occasion not the time or place to discuss the subject in detail and told Robert he would think on the matter and write his reply. The tone of his brother's voice took on a surprising likeness to that of his uncle.

Robert trudged back to his stool and desk on Tuesday, weary from the sight of new bereavement in a household that had not rid itself of an earlier one and was ill prepared for a second. Now his aunt had not only the memory of a lost oldest son to sadden her but a feeling of responsibility for a daughter-in-law and her fatherless children. By the day's end Robert realized that Andrew Russell's probing side glances were not purposeless and that he had copied little on his journal paper. He felt a deep loneliness when he thought of James Lowry dead. The kind and amiable character of one who had tried so hard to span the chasm left by his uncle haunted him in the very midst of activity. He dreaded going home and seeing his aunt try so hard to hold back her tears and trying to give a certain dignity to her fate.

Every day for the rest of the week he hurried back to the house, only to conclude that he wasn't needed. His aunt seemed not even aware when he was in the house and when he was not. Sometimes those of her own family circle would surround her, but as often as not she sat rocking with misty eyes that were oblivious to all movement.

Almost a week before Christmas a letter came from James, in Marion. Robert had already washed his hands for supper before tearing the envelope open. He frowned as he read the first few lines, and by the time he shoved the letter into his coat pocket and stalked from the house his face had flushed crimson.

Minutes later he burst through the heavy oak door of Shoate's tavern. While the door yet oscillated back and forth from the impact, the muscled arm of the blacksmith steadied Robert's shoulder.

"Cool down a little," Muley Grant said with a twinkle of mirth in his voice. "Ain't nothing in all thunderation that bad."

"My brother doesn't want me to join!" Robert blurted out, and held the letter at the nose of his friend.

"What did he say?" Muley asked.

"He said I would have his permission to join only when the Mexicans were sailing up the south fork of the Holston."

"The dern fool!" shouted Muley. "Don't he know we're goin' to have to catch them brown-skinned bandits before too many of 'em get over the border?"

"He knows all right. He's just clownin' me by sayin' we are makin' up a war that isn't goin' to happen."

"Well, I don't know about that." Muley scratched his head doubtfully.

"I'll join up without his permission," Robert said, only partially calmed.

"That might not go—"

"I'm man enough to do my own thinkin," Robert interrupted. "I've been babied too long, that's the whole trouble in a nutshell. Let's have a mug of rum and then go lookin' for Captain Stevens—I want to join up tonight."

"I don't know that there's any hurry," Muley said, "and besides, you don't have to go lookin' nowhere for Captain Stevens. He's sittin' over in the corner there."

Hastily Robert finished his rum, and, backed up by Muley, made his way to the table of Captain Stevens.

Robert's first desire, to join the artillery volunteers, the captain already understood, but Robert's temperament at the moment caused a furrow in the officer's brow. After some minutes of questioning, Robert told all.

"I could not encourage you to join if permission of your brother and other family members here in Abingdon is not forthcoming. This is not conscription and it isn't wartime—"

"But boys fourteen and sixteen years old fought in the Revolution," Robert argued.

"That they did," Captain Stevens admitted. "This is nothing like that, or circumstances would be different. You are old enough, Robert, but the volunteer militia would just as soon not get on the wrong side of the family. If war was at our back door there would be no question."

"Them brown-skinned devils might come a-sailin' up the Holston one of these days," Muley said comfortingly. "Then you'd be in it for sure."

The captain said he didn't understand Muley, nor Robert's antagonistic attitude. He pressed Robert about it until Robert shoved the letter in his face.

Captain Stevens read it and handed it back. "Tell your brother you'll make a bargain with him. Tell him you will agree to wait only until the Mexicans cross the Mississippi."

The captain's attempted humor infuriated Robert all the more. "All of you think I've got to be forty years old before there's any man in me! I'll show you! I'll figger a way to show you!" he vowed and went to fill his mug again.

After Robert's temper showed signs of cooling, Muley soon joined him. Within another few minutes Captain Stevens stood on the other side of him.

"I know you're disappointed, Robert," the captain began, "but I couldn't help noticing the postscript at the bottom of the letter. I wonder if that might not be the cocklebur under the saddle blanket!"

Robert sipped at his rum and stared straight ahead. "Don't make any difference," he said after an uncomfortable silence. "I haven't seen her for a long time anyway."

He looked down into the half-empty mug and could almost see the last three lines his brother had written floating mirrorlike on the surface of the liquid. As if it were an unimportant afterthought, James had scribbled in crooked lines at the edge of the sheet: "Elizabeth

Swecker is the daughter of Wendell Swecker and they live on Cripple Creek in Wythe County. I understand from reliable sources that the girl is betrothed to a young man by the name of Greever who works at the Chatwell forge."

Lord Almighty! How shameless he was in hoping—maybe even praying a little bit—that this enemy he had never met would rob his employer and be sent away to the penitentiary for a hundred years! Even fifty years would do it… not even fifty, just five or ten—he would settle for that. And that wouldn't be unfair punishment for a thief who would steal the woman whose eyes were implanted on his soul as surely as he breathed the breath of life.

"Why don't you go on home now and get some sleep?" the captain suggested. "You've had a lot of bereavement at your house, and it looks like I didn't make it any easier on you tonight."

"I'm not sleepy, thank you," Robert said stiffly. "Besides, Muley and me might just do a little hell-raising tonight."

Muley looked bewildered. "There ain't no place to raise hell tonight unless you're hankering to go down to the tanyard and tear the hides off the drying frames," he said.

"No, I guess there's not," Robert said.

He paused no longer then, and setting his mug upon the polished chestnut counter top, he walked out of the tavern.

Snow fluttered lightly from the heavens, but he did not hurry his steps. It was late and the streets were deserted, but several lamps glowed from windows along Main and Court streets. He went out of his way until he came to the court—house building where he worked. Insufficient snow had fallen to make snowballs, and he soon gave up the effort, but as a last resort, he gave the corner of the building nearest to his own office a vigorous kick, then trod wearily down the street to his own door.

He made no effort to enter the house quietly, for through the parlor window he could see Elizabeth White rocking back and forth, watching the snow through the street window. He stepped through the door to the parlor, but his aunt did not change her position nor acknowledge his presence. He said a "good night" anyway and went to his room.

He could not remember saying his prayers for many years, years that dated back to when he knelt beside his bed with Elizabeth White's warm hand upon his neck. But on this night he uttered a stumbling, tearful prayer to a God he was not sure existed, and asked, childlike, that Elizabeth Swecker be preserved in all her sweetness for him and him alone.

Every child and grandchild of Elizabeth White congregated at her side on Christmas day. A special effort toward family harmony for this one occasion was the unspoken creed that prevailed—but with fragile success. The absence of two family members seemed obscured by sheer force of numbers, but it was still with misty eyes through which Elizabeth White appeared to view them all. Robert remained all day with the family group and assisted in their little game. Each took turns asking questions of his mother, grandmother, or aunt; or tried other tactics to keep her mind engaged in happenings of the present.

It was New Year's Day before Robert found out about more drastic changes the White household would be undergoing. He would not have known of them even then, he supposed, had not he come upon Big Edmund in the stable with tears streaming down his face.

"Come plantin' time, I is goin' to be hired out," Big Edmund whimpered.

"It won't be for long," Robert speculated.

"Miz White say she don't know how long."

"I'll talk to her about it," Robert promised. "You try not to worry about it."

"It ain't only me what's leavin'. Ann 'n' George 'n' Moses is agoin' too. We is all bein' hired out."

Robert confirmed this with his aunt, and she told him it was true. They were all four her best slaves, but they would also bring the highest rental. He tried not to think ill of his aunt, for he was aware that the empire his uncle had built was no longer so widespread. In fact, things were going downhill now, and his aunt and her sons and daughters could consider themselves lucky if they could build on the portions each would eventually hold title to. This opinion was widely held; in fact, Robert had heard the subject discussed around the courthouse, as the complex legal procedures regarding the estate wore on.

Still, he could not condone his aunt completely in her action with regard to the slaves. The renting out of human beings was sinister and wrong. It was especially wrong to pick those who had served most faithfully. None of them would leave the household before March, but he had seen each one of them crying every day.

None of the slaves was more upset than Ann, the oldest and best of the kitchen servants. He watched her both crying and praying aloud as she went about her tasks until his own heart seemed about to be torn from his breast.

Two days after New Year's he could stand it no longer. He and Muley Grant got drunk enough to throw a rock through the window of the female academy, hoping to cause havoc to reign supreme. When no screams erupted through the broken glass, Robert remembered that the academy was not in session. He avoided Muley's company the rest of the week, for he was deeply ashamed of their antics. Every solitary thing in his life seemed to be crumbling like the walls of Jericho. He did things he himself didn't understand, and winter, with snow on the ground, was no time to ride off to the north fork of the Holston and meditate on his life and destiny. It saddened him to realize that Big Edmund might never saddle his horse again when the buds of spring and the whispering trees called him.

The court-appointed appraisers of his uncle's estate had set the worth of Big Edmund at nine hundred dollars. Ann and Moses and George, all together, were appraised at one thousand, nine hundred dollars. For the first time in his life Robert wanted to be rich—to be able to reach into his gold pouch and bring out twenty-eight hundred dollars and free the souls of friends who showed him unmercifully, their bondage.

On the night of January ninth he could stand his own haunting loneliness no longer. The sight of Ann darting about her kitchen, wringing her hands, plagued him at home, and the ever more critical eyes of Andrew Russell plagued him at work, urging him almost daily to better his copying speed of the previous day.

As he walked toward Shoate's tavern, he half hoped that Muley would not be there. His aunt Elizabeth did not approve of the blacksmith, and Robert had begun to see the wisdom of her objections, although he would never admit it. He liked Muley, but at the same time he felt inner evil, of which previously he had thought himself incapable, being generated. It was only part of the time that he felt this with Muley. On other occasions their spirits seemed to be soaring with the highest harmony, their banter drawing a larger following of men who desired to join in and share the fun.

Muley himself was not the only one present, at Shoate's tavern as Robert entered; the smithy had two mule skinners in tow and the three of them were merry with rum. Robert thought he would back out the door as if he had forgotten something, but Muley called to him from across the smokefilled room: "C'mere, Robert. I want you to hear the tales these fellers from Baltimore is tellin'."

Robert crossed the room to the hewn log table and bench occupied by his friend and received an introduction to the two mule skinners. Muley was already on a first-name basis with them, and he gave Robert a quick report.

"Clefus and Shem come down the valley from Baltimore," he said, "and they done unloaded their goods at the mercantile houses. Reckon we can show 'em a good night's fun, Robert?"

"Perhaps so. What are you taking back on your wagons?" he asked, to make conversation.

"Loadin' up at daylight in the mornin'. Both of us is takin' all the saddles and horse harness we can haul. Abingdon is purty well thought of for the leather the tanyards are aputtin' out," Clefus said.

"There's a dern good thing about haulin' leather," Shem grinned. "If a feller wears out his whips acrost the hide of them mules goin' up the valley of Virginia, he can just make some strops outta the harness."

"These fellers think we're still in Indian country," Muley said to Robert. "What we goin' to do to show 'em we're plumb civilized?"

"Maybe they'd just as soon stay in here by the fire. Must be gettin' cold enough out there to freeze over the Holston," Robert said.

One of the mule skinners looked about the walls of the crowded tavern. He shivered a little and pulled the collar of his sheepskin coat more tightly around his neck.

"Wanna' move a little nearer piece to the fireplace?" Muley asked.

"Naw, I'll go get us all a mugful of hot coals we can drown in our stomachs." He got up, crossed the room to the open fireplace, and paused to warm himself in front and behind. The fireplace, big enough for a man to stand in, roared with a furious fire, but for those who sat or stood near the outer walls it was sheer accident if the heat ever reached them when the wind whistled icy cold through the hewn logs and woodshingled roof of the tavern.

Robert also pulled his greatcoat tighter around his neck and thought he would have one mug of rum or a dram of brandy to be sociable and then go home. It was too cold to wander about the streets, and the two mule skinners might decide that they did not want to head north, facing a chill wind, without a good night's sleep.

Clefus returned to the table with four mugs of rum and a grin on his face. "Well, I've heard a lot of mule stories in my time but I ain't never heard that one before."

"Who told you one?" Muley asked.

Clefus pointed. "That feller talkin' to the tavern keeper."

"Why, that's old Rufe Ewing. He's been driving mules down the valley since 'fore you was born," Muley said. "I've probably heard the story, but you tell it."

Clefus repeated the story and got a spontaneous round of belly-laughter.

"Clefus, you can take that'n with you clean back to Baltimore," Muley said, still laughing. "I reckon it's my turn to buy a round, unless you want to volunteer first, Robert?"

The word "volunteer" struck a sensitive nerve somewhere in Robert and suddenly he came to life.

"Set 'em up all around," he said. "I'd just as soon spend my week's wages for that as anything I know. Old Man Russell would pop a gut for sure if he knew I was doing that with my money."

"I 'spect he might already," Muley said, and headed for the tavern keeper with Robert's money.

Robert shivered as he acknowledged the prospect of Muley's suspicions being well-founded, and his tablemates noticed his lack of ease.

"You work for this Russell feller?" Clefus asked. "I work for the county, and he's over me."

"How you goin' to keep him from a-knowin'?"

"I'm not trying to, I reckon," Robert confessed, "but I'd just as soon he didn't find out."

Muley plopped the mugs on the rough table and Shem made a grab for one of them, spilled most of it, and let out an oath.

"Well, at least you're sayin' *somethin'*," Clefus said. "Thought you was a-dying layin' against that wall—er froze to death."

Shem cursed his partner and sat looking at the nearly empty mug.

"I'll take *that* one," Robert said and gave Shem his own in exchange. "I don't want any more anyway."

Shem let out another oath to the effect that Abingdon was dull and full of dull people who went to bed with the chickens—and he wished he was back in Baltimore where he had plenty of women and chances for real hell-raising.

"He gets plumb ornery when he's had a few," Clefus explained.

"Next time I get a round I'll get the tavern keeper to lace his rum with some egg whites. I understand them spirits hide in little balls of egg whites and won't bust till daylight," Muley said.

Clefus disagreed. "That won't do. There won't be any road between here and Lexington wide enough to keep the wagon in. He sure don't need no bubbles full of rum abustin' in his stumach."

Robert watched Shem sip his rum faster than he should, and instinctively he pushed his own mug away.

"Say, what's all the people leaving fer?" Clefus asked.

"I ain't sure," Muley said, looking toward the door. "Most times they stay till the doors is locked, and the night ain't hardly started. I'll find out for you. Something is goin' on." He came back on the run.

"They's a revival happenin' up over Greenway's store! Some of the fellers is goin' and make it hot for the old sin-socker."

Clefus shook the arm of Shem and brought his sleepy head from his forearms.

"Wrap yourself tight. We're goin' to sober you up in that January weather out there or we're goin' to let that-there evangelist do it fer us. You may be just about right to get saved! How'd you like to wake up in the mornin' and know you was plumb, teetotally saved!"

Muley laughed as heartily as Clefus, and between them Shem staggered first against one and then the other. The three of them reached the door before Muley relinquished his hold on Shem so that he could pass through the entrance. Robert had not moved.

Muley looked back at their table. "Come on, Robert!

Ain't you comin'?"

"You-all go on. I think I'll head home and hit the bed."

"We can't go out ahell-raisin' without you. You want them fellers to think you are a man, or some kid what sneaked away from the academy?"

"You go ahead and tell them I hope they don't get snowed in before they get back to Baltimore."

"I ain't goin' to do it. Nearly everybody's left here now. See—there ain't a dozen people. You know they all saw you here and they'll be awonderin' why you didn't have nerve enough to come and pelt that old sin-socker with corncobs."

"He hasn't done me any harm," Robert said.

"I been thinkin' lately—you gettin' too good for us fellers what sweats a little for our livin'?"

"No, that isn't it."

Clefus called impatiently from the doorway. He was minus his partner, Shem. "I knowed you wasn't man enough to be in the volunteers! If we was in battle we couldn't count on you to reach us the gunpowder. You'd be as scared as a sucklin' kid. You're scared of a big-mouthed old preacher!" Muley said.

"I am scared of nothing!"

"Then don't stand here talkin' about it. We ain't goin' to get seats, and all the corncobs will be gone. Let's get goin'!"

Muley pulled the bench out of Robert's path and the way was clear to the door. Robert looked at Muley and the blacksmith grinned wide, until his yellow teeth showed. Robert crossed the distance hurriedly and they were out in the street. Muley called to Clefus, "Let's get goin'! Make Shem take a deep breath of this cold air. If that don't sober him up it'll give him a coughin' fit and shake loose his liver and he can let it all out."

When the four of them reached the top of the stairs over Greenway's store, the third-floor room still had vacant seats. Robert could tell the serious worshipers from most of the faces he had seen in the tavern. There was little need to draw a line of division, for many of the tavern patrons sat en masse to the rear of the large room. There could not have been more than twenty-five or thirty people in attendance before the men from the tavern arrived. Now the congregation numbered sixty or seventy. Having come last, Robert could not be certain, but the old man who stood before them, thin but tall, with his bony knees and elbows outlined against his worn clothes, had an inquiring look on his face. It was not hard to see the brightness in the aged man's eyes when he first began to notice the empty benches starting to fill. Although the revival must have been half finished, the countenance of this old evangelist strongly suggested to Robert his willingness to start the meeting all over again if there were those who would benefit and if their attendance was sincere.

Bony hands caressed each other as the old man tried to smile and welcome the newcomers. The skin of his face was wrinkled and loose, and he stooped slightly, though he tried to stand erect. He walked across the front of the room to pick up something, and the arch of his back became much more apparent. It seemed to start at the base of the spine and continue to the base of the neck—the type of arch a man would develop when he had ridden a horse for many more years than his strength had been sufficient to hold him erect.

The object the old man fetched was a pitch pipe.

"The Lord has blessed us with many who have come late. Since they have not joined us in fellowship by the singing of a hymn, we will sing together that old hymn you all know, 'Blessed Be the Name of the Lord.' Sister Louise will pass out the songbooks, but we don't have many. Please share them with a Christian brother by your side."

The preacher blew the "C" note on the pitch pipe, and led the singing. Those near the front sang vigorously, but only a few in the back joined in, and then only until they were stared down by their fellow tavern patrons.

By the middle of the second verse the copper kettle sitting to the side of the single Ben Franklin stove began to yield what few corn cobs yet remained of the kindling. In the absence of more corncobs, someone reached for wood chips, but an older man nearby squeezed the taker's wrist until the chips were dropped. "Don't use chips on him," the older man whispered. "We don't want to kill him—or blind him—we just want to slow him down."

A corncob was passed to Robert. He held it in his hands for a moment, and passed it on. Not a corncob was in sight when the hymn was concluded; each man concealed his weapon with the same skill with which he concealed his intentions.

Robert knew about when to expect the onslaught. He had heard the men at the tavern talk about how they had carried out this devilment before. They would let the visiting itinerant work himself into a sweat, and when the invitation to penitence was issued the corncobs would begin to fly through the air until the helpless preacher looked like an awkward schoolboy fighting off a swarm of bees.

The crowd all listened, and Robert sensed that this man who stood before them was not of the common variety of itinerants Greenway's meeting room was rented to. Not only did he sense it, but some of the men sitting close to him were looking on with a degree of concentration that was not just good acting.

The white-thatched preacher pushed a strand of hair from his forehead after his opening remarks were made and announced his text.

"Our Scripture tonight will be taken from Second Kings, Chapter Two. To those of you who do not have your Bibles, our Scripture deals with the last days of Elijah and his companion, Elisha. In this chapter we see by the hand of God, Elijah taken in to heaven in a fiery chariot, drawn by fiery horses. Elijah, as he rises toward heaven in a whirlwind, drops his mantle, or cloak, and Elisha catches it and receives the divine powers God had given Elijah."

A grunt and then a snicker originated from someone near the stove. Robert saw Shem sit up straight and slap his knee. "You reckon my mules will catch fire on the way back to Baltimore, Preacher?"

Although Shem laughed heartily and Muley and Clefus chuckled, few others made any sound.

The old preacher ignored the outburst and continued.

"When Elisha received the powers originally bestowed on Elijah, he went and stood by the river Jordan and smote it with the cloak of Elijah, and it parted so that he walked across the river on dry land. Elisha tarried in Jericho and used his God-given power to purify the water and enrich the land so the people might prosper. But, my friends, I must tell you tonight that everyone did not receive God's servant Elisha without mockery. Be not deceived, God will not be mocked… But let us not leave Elisha. We must examine what happened to God's servant Elisha in the closing verses of the chapter. Follow me in the Scriptures if you will:

'And he went up from thence unto Bethel: and as he was going by the way, there came forth little children out of the city, and mocked him, and said unto him, Go up, thou baldhead; go up, thou baldhead.

'And he turned back, and looked on them, and cursed them in the name of the Lord. And there came forth two she bears out of the woods, and tare forty and two children of them.

'And he went from thence to Mount Carmel, and from thence he returned to Samaria'."

Suddenly Shem stood in front of his bench and hurled a cob, which missed its mark.

"My brothers and sisters, it is not God's will that any should perish but that all should have everlasting life. Are there those among us tonight who search for something without knowing for what they search? Or those who forsake God to seek their own selfish desires? What would *you* give in exchange for *your* soul? Is God your loving father, who walks with you each day, holding your hand as a little child? Your enemy to be feared? Does He give you the wind and the sun and the rain and the flowers and the trees and smile down at you with His blessing to enjoy them and use them?"

Shem and Muley were both on their feet now, letting a barrage of corncobs fly with all their might. Clefus kept the two others supplied, and occasional cobs flew from further behind him. At the beginning the preacher tried to dodge the raspy and cutting objects, but as they kept coming he stood immobile. His strategy stopped the cob throwers only for a moment; then they were incited to throw harder and faster.

Muley connected with a hit directly on the nose and Clefus, after two tries, knocked the preacher's glasses to the floor.

When Robert saw blood dripping from the face of the old man, he could stand it no longer. Leaping over three other men, he picked up the copper kettle by the stove and brought it down hard on the heads of Shem and Clefus. When they appeared dazed, he turned it over, brought it down on the head of Muley and left it there.

The preacher wiped the blood from his face and proceeded to speak. His sermon consumed the better part of an hour but even before he had ended his pleas, a line had formed. His invitation to more penitents was all that remained.

Robert sat on his bench with head bowed and his eyes wet with tears. He did not enter the line of converts; in fact, he was ready to leave the building. He resisted raising his head for fear the pleading eyes of the older man would be there searching out his own.

Presently an unsteady arm rested on his shoulder.

"Let's get out of here, Robert. I didn't know we was makin' you mad. We just wanted to do a little hell-raisin'. You plumb near knocked me senseless. Clefus and Shem still can't hardly get on their feet."

"Go away," Robert whispered.

"I ain't goin' to leave you."

Women and children near the front of the room started to sing as he pushed Muley away from him.

"Come on, Robert."

"I've got to go down there."

"You outa' your head? Why that old sin-socker is just runnin' this business for the money," Muley argued.

"Not this one. He didn't even take up a collection, and it wouldn't matter anyway. I've got to go down there. Get out of my way."

Muley stood aside until Robert made his way down the aisle and fell upon the wrinkled neck of his deliverer.

When the building was cleared of all the other people, Robert faced the elderly preacher, who now stood shivering from the cold. Suddenly the boy felt drained of words, and he too was shivering. He picked up two of the corncobs at the preacher's feet and gripped his fist tightly around each until he could feel the sharp edges of the outer cob collapse.

"Maybe if I put a few of these in the stove we could get some heat back in this place," Robert said.

The older man stopped blotting the shallow cuts on his face and put his red bandanna handkerchief in his hip pocket. "I can't think of any better use for them." He chuckled and assisted Robert.

"I want to apologize for the way the men from the tavern acted," Robert began. "They're not such bad people—not so bad at all."

"Most of the smoke and anguish of hell will surely come from people who don't think themselves bad."

Robert swallowed hard and made his confession complete. "I was with them. I came from the tavern. So were three other men who were in the line and made their professions of faith in Christ."

"God bless each of you"—the older man smiled again—"and we'll keep working on all the rest of them. They will probably look upon you and the three others with contempt. The four of you will be a reminder to them—a painful reminder they would just as soon forget but cannot."

"I will certainly do my best to see that no rowdy crowd comes up here again and bothers you—even if I have to knock them down the stairs with this poker."

"That is not the way of the Savior, my young brother. You do want to be more like Him?"

"Yes."

"Then he who would be more like the Christ must study the Bible and learn of His life and works. Imitate Him in all your thoughts and deeds. You are not so foolish as to think that that will come easy?"

"No," Robert said.

The short life of the burning corncobs left the room chilled again, and the older man stood with great effort. "My aging joints do not work well in the cold," he said apologetically. "One day you will be old, and understand."

"Will I see you again?" Robert asked.

"Oh yes. Our business is not complete. We cannot baptize in the cold months of winter, but I shall be back in the spring—about May—with a host of others, God willing, and we shall cause the waters of the Holston to froth as they carry away the sins of His new sheep."

He told no one in his household about his conversion, but within a month his Aunt Elizabeth had heard of it. Robert learned later that she had found about it from Muley while patronizing his blacksmith shop.

One day in early February his aunt confronted him with her knowledge of his attendance at the revival meeting. "Robert, your friend Muley tells me you two attended the revival together. Does our family church not suit your liking?"

"We didn't go there to 'go to church,' exactly," Robert confessed humbly.

"Then it was all the more wrong."

"Yes, I know it was."

"What denomination was the minister who held the meeting?" his aunt asked.

"I don't know."

"But I thought Muley said you had been converted."

"Yes, I was."

"You made a profession in a ramshackle store building and didn't even find out the denomination of the minister?"

"It didn't seem to matter."

"Robert, I have tried to give you, as well as all my children, the foundation of a faith to be built on. In the case of you and your brothers, I have not tried to dictate your religious life, knowing that someday you would prefer to make these decisions yourselves. It is hard to believe that you have chosen conversion at the hands of an itinerant whose denomination you do not know and who chooses to hold his 'meetings' on the second floor of a rundown store. Do you even know his name?"

"No, I didn't ask him and I didn't hear—but I liked him."

"It doesn't matter now. I can find out later if it becomes of any importance."

Somehow she was shaming him, and he hadn't expected that, nor the need to explain his actions. But he re-examined his thoughts on both points and knew that he had lied to himself. Why hadn't he told her if he didn't feel subconsciously that the act had been clandestine?

"Robert, the religious affiliation of one's life is very personal, and I will not intrude on the meaning this has for you. I am disappointed that you have not chosen to make this commitment in a different way. By your failure to give allegiance to your family church and the dignity befitting it you lay further grief on my shoulders."

"I don't feel good about hurting you, Aunt Elizabeth, but I'm not sorry for what I did. It was the right thing, and I hope you will share my new joy."

"If there is any joy for me, it will not be in this world. All that I have known of earthly happiness seems to have ebbed away. The foundations of the floor on which I kneel to pray seem to be cracking and falling."

"I wish I could share more of your grief—now more than ever, I wish I could," Robert said.

"You would not want any of the load I carry, you can be sure of that. Death and more death and the sicknesses of greed, avarice, and family dishonor do not make joyful music in my daily life."

"Have I, too, brought family dishonor?"

She looked at him searchingly for a moment, and her eyes were harder than he ever remembered seeing them. He knew her answer would not be one issued in anger but only after due deliberation.

"Yes, Robert. Not one of us has the right to tear down the name and dignity of your uncle and all that he's built and stood for. We are not the sheep of itinerants. The acts of each one of us adds to or takes from the whole of his name and honor. The hope for each one of us must lie in the heritage of our forebears added to our own, that multiplied esteem and integrity may be ours."

Robert raised his head finally and saw his aunt trembling with the intensity of her troubled emotions. "I am neither sorry," he said, "for my act of faith nor for discovering, after all these years, the misplaced values of the White household."

That night he packed a carpetbag with all the winter clothes it would hold. On retiring he wrote a letter to Lawrence at Emory and Henry College and left it on his dresser. The next morning, before any of the household had stirred, he picked up the carpetbag and all the gold coins he had saved and wrapped himself warmly in his greatcoat. At dawn he stood by the Great Road at Black's Fort.

CHAPTER IV

Had the month been April rather than February, the Great Road (or, as it was now being called by the younger citizens and westward travelers, the Wilderness Road) would have been laden with travelers of all varieties. Part of Robert's fascination with Black's Fort during the many hours he had spent there was the observance of diverse humanity on the move; that, and the aura of history surrounding the once-active pioneer outpost.

On this bitter cold morning there was no one to observe. No one. He stood by the road, feeling that not even the breathing pores of his body could dispel the faintest whisper of his loneliness. The smallest sound would have been welcome as he stood there, but there was none. Winter dawn ushered in the day with a deathlike stillness. The very atmosphere of it caused Robert to pull his greatcoat tighter and twist his heel in the roadside stone for the creation of a sound—any kind of sound.

He looked to the east for the first flicker of the sun, but it had not yet appeared. He then looked north. The servants would be up now at Elizabeth White's house, scurrying about and fixing the fires. Ann would be putting wood chips, corncobs, and pine knots in the fire under the big iron skillets where the side meat would be sizzling as soon as the flames rose. She would be crying too, for her days in the White household would come to an end within another six weeks.

There was still time to change his mind. Wasn't even a house growing slowly ill with depression and betrayal, and living on memories and creeds of earlier and happier days, preferable to the ugly, freezing gray dawn that surrounded him? But there was the matter of dishonor. He blew on his hands and held them to his ears. The warmth felt good, but it was short-lived.

Now, the first hint of sunlight appeared to the east, but on the farthermost horizons, there was no sign of travel from either direction. He would go the way a ride was offered. It didn't matter. If no traveler appeared on the road within the hour, he could always take the eastbound stage. But that would tempt him to stop in Marion, and right now he did not relish the house or company of his brother. Nor did he want to spend his gold for the stagecoach fare. Westward it would be, if he had to stand in the cold until his boots froze solid to the soil.

When a larger crescent of sun appeared over the mountains to the east one lone wagon could be seen in the distance. It made a solitary picture emerging through the haze, with the entire world seemingly behind it. Two horses snorted and sent chilled vapors of hot breath skyward as they labored under their burden. The wagon seemed born from the womb of the sun as it approached, and so welcome was the sight that Robert kept his eyes affixed to it until a solemn-faced man pulled abreast of him and stopped.

"You look like you're waitin' for a hitch, but you can see I ain't got much room."

Robert looked around the bed of the wagon and saw that every square foot appeared to have people, from infancy to dotage, wrapped in heavy clothing or quilts. "I'll get a ride before long," he said.

"I knowed I couldn't haul you," the man said, "but I didn't want to be unneighborly and pass on by."

"I'm much obliged," Robert said. "Somebody else will be along shortly."

The wagon driver snapped the whip over the back of the lead horse and Robert watched the grating wagon wheels chew into the stone again. The family wagon moved farther away, and so did the eyes peering at him from over the tailgate. All soon passed into the distance.

The sun was half high when two buggies approached from the east. The first stopped; the second kept going.

"I never offer transportation until I determine the character of the man," the stranger said. He got out and walked around Robert, standing above him only slightly in height but well making two of him in girth, and looked him over as if contemplating the purchase of a first class racehorse. When he had made the full circle around Robert, he faced him squarely.

"You are either running away from home or you are an adventurous position seeker. I won't ask you which you are just yet. In either case, you are welcome to the space beside me. I might add, that seat has held the buttocks of both the finest of ladies and the most notorious of rascals."

Robert cast a startled glance at the man and said, "Hope they left the seat warm."

The older man's grin, abundant with perfect teeth, spread to the top of his forehead and into the same shade of strawberry-blond hair Robert possessed. Before Robert could say, "Thank you," or, "No, thank you," a large but uncalloused hand jutted in his direction.

"Name's Yancy Womack. I'm headed through the gap of the Cumberlands and maybe points beyond. You're welcome to go as far as you want."

Robert introduced himself and climbed into the buggy. While depositing his carpetbag behind the seat he noticed a satchel not unlike those the doctors of Abingdon carried.

"You sized me up pretty well back there," Robert said. "I had you sized up as a gambler or a drummer. Now I see I was wrong. You're a doctor."

"You're right; I am a doctor—among other things. My hands always give me away. In fact, you're right on all three counts. A doctor does have to gamble and be a good salesman on occasion. What do *you* do, Robert?"

"I was supposed to go to college this year but things didn't work out and I took a job as a scribe at the county courthouse."

"Do you draw or paint?"

"Yes. My teacher said I was pretty good at it." Robert beamed.

"Ah. I knew you had it, standing there in the morning sunlight—the soul of an artist ... that kind of man for whom fate has reserved a special kind of spite. You plan to follow the trade of a scribe wherever you go?"

"I don't know."

"You did bring a letter of recommendation? It will be impossible for you without it—there are so many fugitives who *seem* on the square."

Robert didn't answer, and the doctor faced him inquiringly.

"No, there was not time to get one. Perhaps I should seek another trade anyway." He shivered, partially from the cold, but more so for the tardy realization of what he was doing and what might face him.

The doctor reached for his inside coat pocket and withdrew a flask. "Here, have a drink of brandy. That'll send the blood down to your toes."

Robert paused, and then declined, and the older man took a long drink. "Don't do any imbibing, huh? Well, every man must steer his own course. If you're not having any liquid heat you can use that horse blanket under my satchel. Put it across your legs and you'll ride comfortably."

By the time they arrived at the intersection of the stage road and the public road due east of Walnut Grove, Robert's traveling companion had requested that he be called "Yancy-doc." Robert felt that either name would have sufficed by itself, but he did not challenge the usage.

The doctor looked at both roads and questioned Robert. "The stage road goes through Blountsville, Tennessee, doesn't it?"

"Yes. The public road goes through Estellsville—that's the Virginia route, pretty near due west. We can get to Cumberland Gap by either route."

"Well, now. Point of decision. Do we go south or west? It should not really be hard to decide. Where is the nearest tavern with ale spilling over the fingers of fair lasses before it is drunk?"

"I haven't been any farther west than Wallen's Ridge, but I know there is one tavern called the Old Block House twenty or thirty miles from here."

"Let us hope your estimate of distance is on the short side, for if it isn't, you will have a very late dinner indeed.

When the fireside of Old Block Tavern had been reached, Yancy-doc delayed no longer in getting to know Robert more intimately. Although the older man sat almost wordless, eating his salty meat, baked potatoes, and muffins, Robert found it easy to talk about even the more private things in his life. Yancy-doc commented sparingly about things Robert said and the conversation was punctuated by an occasional grunt, or a belch from an oversized gulp of ale. Between bites, he encouraged Robert to keep on talking even though Robert's platter was noticeably untouched. Only when Yancy-doc had run out of ale, and while he squeezed the hand of the tavern maid and ordered another, did Robert begin the consumption of his own food.

He ate while Yancy-doc wandered about the tavern, speaking here and there to an interesting-looking stranger and always to a tavern maid if she gave him half a chance.

When Robert had finished he found that Yancy-doc had already paid for both of them. He was bothered by this gesture. "I'm obliged for the ride, but I don't expect to have my vittles paid for," he said.

"Never frown on good fortune," Yancy-doc admonished, "and we are headed for more good fortune. The one-legged man by the window says that much good plantation land is to be had in the north-central interior of Kentucky. We shall go through the gap of the Cumberlands with all due haste and see for ourselves."

"Is that your hope—to own much land?"

"Only part of it," Yancy-doc said. "The other requirements must include a populated and well-to-do community where I can practice my profession, and last, but most important of all, an abundance of beautiful women."

Yancy-doc paid the liveryman for the horse feed and Robert again wrapped the blanket about his knees. His companion seemed as comfortable in the chill air of the buggy as he had by the fireside of the tavern. Robert could not help wondering about him: for a man who appeared to be in his late forties, he possessed an enviable amount of stamina.

Yancy-doc lit his pipe and gave his horse a flick of the whip.

"I told you pretty near everything about me in there," Robert said. "And I don't know anything about you."

"Well, it's a long story," the physician said, and stopped. He remained silent and Robert commented, "We ought to have plenty of time if we're going all the way to Kentucky." Yancy-doc grinned at Robert's persistence and beat out the ashes of his pipe on the side of the buggy. Robert could sense that information would be given with reluctance, but he was entitled to a fair exchange.

"Not much to tell until I got to be a man. I studied medicine in Baltimore and finished up in eighteen-eleven. My father was a physician in Norfolk, Virginia, and the original plan was for me to join him in a family practice."

"Sounds like a good future to me," Robert said.

"Maybe, but I liked Baltimore so much I wasn't in any hurry to get home or to begin practice either. My father was at Norfolk stewing because I wasn't putting my training into practice. I was in Baltimore stewing from a seven -day-a-week dose of alcohol and too many parties. I went for a week sometimes without three hours' sleep. I spent over a year on that treadmill."

"Don't see how you stood it, but it doesn't seem to have hurt you any," Robert said.

"Don't make that judgment until you hear the full story. I was on one of those week-long alcohol dreams when I woke up in Norfolk at a medical station near the coast. I never did know how I got there but my father had enlisted me in the army as a doctor. I hadn't really been sober for three months, but I knew pretty quickly we were engaged in war with the British. Wasn't that a hell of a way to find out about the War of 1812?"

"My uncle James served at Norfolk during the war. Did your father ever speak of Colonel James White?"

"He spoke of nothing. I didn't see him for over two years after that."

"You didn't stay in Norfolk?"

"No. There were attempted invasions of Norfolk a couple of times—once while I was there—but I was sent to New Orleans, where the real trouble was expected. Father finally did write me, but he didn't apologize. I deserved what I got. I knew it and he knew it and I have to admit the experience made a man out of me. Of course,

I would have benefited little with my head blown off from the naval bombardment that was soon in coming."

"We talked about the war at Abingdon Academy, but it's hard for me to remember about New Orleans..."

"Well, I can tell you from memory," Yancy-doc began. "'The British thought they had us at New Orleans, but we stomped the hell out of them. They had Sir Edward Pakenham pouring everything they had at us. All of we doctors worked from sunup until sunup for days on end, and the casualties kept coming."

"Are you a surgeon?" Robert asked.

"No, I'm not a surgeon but I did surgery—we all did everything there was to do. The most tragic damn thing about the war was that a settlement had been negotiated long before anybody at New Orleans knew anything about it. Some of the worst battles we had were going on until the middle of January of 1815—long after the war was officially over."

"You really mean it about not being angry with your father?" Robert asked.

"I really mean it. To some extent my experience accomplished what my father hoped it would. I was jarred out of my childish vision of life. And I was forced to practice my profession."

"Did you go back to Norfolk after the war?"

"Yes, and we had a family practice until Father died about five years later. My father lived for his work. He believed a man should aim himself like a rifle at a worthy target and never take his eye from that target. He practiced what he preached, I'll give him that."

"My uncle I told you about was a lot like that—except he wasn't quite so– well, cold."

"Father's manner might seem cold in description or observation too, for that matter—but he was anything but cold. I know he cared deeply for me and my brothers, though I believe he always knew I'd never make the grade as the kind of doctor he wanted me to become. He went at his profession with the zeal of a martyred Christian. He believed as a servant of mankind that to do the job right he had to be totally immersed in humanity."

"I think I can get a picture of him," Robert said.

"No, I doubt that you can. I'm not sure even I ever fully grasped the depth of my father's character. I heard him say once that if he'd had his life to live over again he'd be four people for a while before settling down to being one. He said he would have been a teacher, a farmer, a preacher, and a doctor, in that order."

"I don't understand his reasons," Robert said.

"They were fundamental. First, he would teach humanity to discover how weighted down in ignorance they were. He would have been a farmer, he said, to learn that all men live best and find their greatest humility from the soil. He would have preached, he said, to convey the message of hope and love that ought to bind men together and help them endure. But as wise and compassionate as my father was, he wanted most to be a doctor, for he knew that however worthy the other three occupations, the bulk of humanity would need a doctor as they succumbed to sickness of mind or body or spirit. It was among these he wanted to walk."

"You make me feel that I would have liked to know him," Robert said.

"Father escaped one thing, and that was the practice of military medicine. I wished more than once that he had been with us at New Orleans. I wonder how much better he could have stood the screaming and the dying—how much easier he might have sawed a leg or an arm off when there was neither enough medicine nor time."

"He'd have done it the same as you."

"No, Robert. Somehow he'd have done it better. Really, he would have. I remember a Creole boy who called me to him one night and said, 'Tell me, Yancy-doc, why I must give my legs? If you cannot tell me that, I will shoot in my mouth with a pistol.' I couldn't give him even one reason why he had to lose his legs. He did as he said he would do. My father could have given him some profound answer that he could live with and think upon, and be the richer for having heard it."

"All that was a long time ago," Robert said.

"You're right. I've drowned those cries in hundreds of self-prescribed drunks and overnight stays in houses of pleasure. I suppose you're wondering if I'm ashamed of the life I've led?"

"No, I wasn't going to ask you that."

"Well, the answer is I'm not ashamed of it. I lost the respect of my father and the love of my wife but I'm not ashamed of it. There are people who just weren't made to fit in a certain mold and stay there. I want to soar free like a silver hawk. I have served my time and earned my freedom. If a man immerses himself in humanity like my father did, he can bet on one thing: he'll drown himself just as certain as that buggy wheel is turning."

"Did your father drown like that?"

"He drown right in the middle of his office floor. He never had two days' pleasure in his whole life. I buried him, stored my belongings, and here I am. I will find some good land and raise fine horses and work when I feel like it and loaf when I feel like it. If the patients don't want to pay my fees they can go to the nearest Indian herb doctor or the devil. Let it be their choice. At least I won't be seeing the wharf women and seafaring scum who used to crowd my father's office."

As they crossed through and entered Kentucky, the gap of the Cumberlands was a sight to behold. Yancy-doc drove only a mile into the new state before he stopped the buggy and looked back. Along the crests and down into the gap, ice covered every foot of the high ground, or so it seemed. It was morning, and the sun danced rays of rainbow colors from the gap, in a prism effect, making the gap look like a giant door decorated for a holiday welcome, and a most merry one at that.

"I'll drink to that," Yancy-doc said, and pulled out his flask again. When he had viewed the sight as long as he wanted, he turned to Robert with a grin. "You think you could draw a picture of that, Robert?"

"Yes. If I had anything to draw with, I could."

"You really did leave in a hurry, didn't you? When you get settled are you going to send for your things?"

"I have all of my things with me," Robert said.

"I kind of got the idea from your clothes and bearing that you might have a good deal to send for. In fact, from some of the things you've said along the way, if your material and family financial position is as strong as your pride, we might have to send a wagon train back to Abingdon."

The ice they encountered in the gap of the Cumberlands was mild compared to that which they began to battle as they drove northwesterly onto steep wagon roads near the village of Heidrick. Almost a half day of travel from the gap had taken them only twelve or fifteen miles—and precarious miles, at that. More than once the buggy seemed about to slide from the road entirely and land in some awesome gully below. Several times the horse fell to her knees, and Robert looked toward Yancy-doc with a glance of uneasiness.

"It's getting too bad out there to travel much farther," the doctor agreed. "We're going to need a blacksmith soon or we'll have a horse with a broken leg."

"Ice nails in her shoes may help for a while," Robert said. "But look at that sky. If we don't soon get to shelter it may not matter a bit about ice nails."

Snow was coming in blinding waves by the time they reached Heidrick. The wayfarer, who, during a water-stop, had told them about the village, had described it accurately. There was a very large blacksmith shop operated in conjunction with a wheelwright's shop and a large adjoining building for wagon-making. A boot shop and a mercantile establishment were on the same side of the road. On the other side stood an inn, a carpenter shop, and, almost out of sight and farther on down by a stream, a water-driven gristmill. Although snow covered the ground heavily and made the small village appear dwarfed in the hewn-out wilderness, every building seemed to fit in its place with no room left over.

The innkeeper was unusually congenial, for the winter season evidently allowed him to slacken his pace and possibly, even enjoy his guests. The stable boy took the horse and buggy after first being told to see that the animal was taken to the blacksmith shop in the morning for re-shoeing with ice nails.

After thawing themselves loose from snow-swept clothing by the heat of the fireplace, Robert and Yancy-doc hung their wet outer clothing on wall pegs near the fire and made their way to a table. The inn was nearly empty, except for six men, and themselves. The six would probably be drummers or couriers, or perhaps a businessman or two whose affairs were sufficiently pressing to necessitate travel in any weather. The tavern maids seemed to like the drummers best, and if that belief held true in Kentucky as well as Virginia, Robert picked three of the men to be drummers. He relayed his guesses to Yancy-doc and waited for one of the girls to come to their table and confirm it.

Yancy-doc took the girl's hand when she waited on their table. She blushed the color of her red hair, but it made her slightly freckled face even prettier.

"My friend here says that three of the men there are drummers. Is he right?"

"Yes," she said in astonishment. How did you know?"

"I just watched the men you and the other tavern maids paid the most attention to," Robert said.

"I'm going to have to do something about this, Robert," Yancy-doc said and ordered himself a rye whiskey while his food was being served.

When they had finished their supper Yancy-doc said that he did not want to go to his room just yet, but he asked Robert to retire and offered him money for another room.

"I'm likely to be up half of the night. Sometimes I get a little noisy when I'm drinking. You go on to bed in your own room and I won't bother you when I come in."

Robert paused before agreeing, but he declined the money altogether. He would like to sit by the hearth and do some thinking. There seemed to be fire in Yancy-doc's eyes, and he knew that his friend had made not a request but a demand. He went to his room and sank between the quilts and feather tick. Thoughts of Abingdon and home began to invade his mind, and the snow and sleet pecked at the window unmercifully. Soon he was warm but not sleepy. Where would he go in Kentucky? Who would vouch for his character if he was lucky enough to find a job? These and other problems plagued him, and he wondered if perhaps he would not be happier if he were more like Yancy-doc, and able to take everything so masterfully in stride.

A troubled sleep gave him refuge until some predawn hour. Human voices penetrated the walls on both sides of him. For a moment he could not decide whether everyone had risen for the day or if they simply had not gone to bed. He lay very still and concentrated on the sounds he could hear. High-pitched female laughter carried through the walls on both sides of him.

When morning was a certainty, in spite of overcast darkness and heavy falling snow, he washed his face from the pitcher of water on the dresser and descended the stairs. Only one of the men he had noticed the previous night was being served his breakfast. He wanted to eat with the man, for the loneliness he had felt in his bed during the night still occupied his mind.

"Looks like you and I are the only ones with any get-up and-go this morning," Robert said.

The man returned a friendly smile and said, "Sit down, sit down. We may have the 'get up' but there won't be any 'go' today. Look out the window."

"That's pretty near as deep as a wagon wheel," Robert agreed.

"Where are you headed for?"

"We're driving farther on into Kentucky to look at some land," Robert said, aware of the deceptive "we" he had used.

"I'm going on to Lexington. You ought to look around that part of the country. Some of the prettiest land God ever made. Going to start tobacco raising or stock grazing?"

"We don't know what we're going to do yet," Robert said. "We're just going to do some looking around."

Robert had finished his breakfast and a long conversation with his new-found friend before Yancy-doc descended the stairs. He took one look out the window and dropped into the nearest chair. Robert got up and joined him, though Yancy-doc's behavior was less than hospitable. His eyes were red and swollen and he smelled of the sourness of fermented fruit.

"Didn't count on gettin' snowed down in a one-horse village," Yancy-doc growled.

"It won't last but a day or two."

Yancy-doc ignored him and growled at the innkeeper, "Where's my breakfast?"

Presently the same freckled tavern maid who had served them the previous night hurried to their table with fried potatoes and eggs. Yancy-doc cast an evil grin at her, but she would not look at him. This seemed to annoy Yancy-doc, and he whacked her on the buttocks.

"What's a matter?" he said. "You liked me well enough last night."

The girl hurried from the table, and Robert reported all he had learned from his early morning breakfast companion.

"Hell, I knew about the place a long time ago. I patched up the back of a boy from Lexington at New Orleans—or what there was left of his back, that is. A volley of grapeshot took the fat off his back down to the spine. That boy used to lay and moan and talk about Lexington like it was the Garden of Eden, if there ever was such a damn place. If it's half as good as he said it was I want to own at least half of it."

Yancy-doc seemed to eat more hurriedly, the more they talked about the land, and his disposition got better as he filled his stomach. His mood changed again for the worse, however, when he stepped outside and saw again the impossibility of travel for that day—and several more if a rapid thaw did not quickly take place.

Throughout the day Robert expected the various tradesmen to break through the snow and open their shops. Most of them lived only a mile or two away, he was told by the inn keeper. Yancy-doc paced the floor in obvious foul humor. He guessed aloud that the blacksmith wasn't going to try to open his shop and that consequently his horse would not be shod with new shoes and ice nails. He expressed his certainty to Robert that on the following day most of the two-foot snow would .be melted and they could be on their way.

That night a howling wind beat upon the inn and Robert didn't need to guess what sight would be visible when he came down to breakfast. Snowdrifts held fast the front door to the latch. It was the same at the doors and windows of all the buildings he could see. The road was scarcely visible except where some wind-swept spots revealed mud and stone, and farther along, as the road turned north, shoulder-high drifts could be observed.

Yancy-doc took one look at what Robert had seen and let go with a thunderous oath.

"Might as well calm down," the innkeeper suggested. "Last year we stayed landlocked like this for nearly two weeks. What happens is the wind piles it up in one direction one night and piles it in another place the next night and—"

"Damn the wind—we want to get out of here and be on our way to Lexington!" Yancy-doc snorted.

"So do we, mister," one of the other men declared.

"We've got plenty of grub," the innkeeper said. "We get caught like this every winter—ain't nothin' to worry about."

"Well, if you've got plenty to drink, the situation might be a little more tolerable," Yancy-doc said.

None of the shops were opened during that day either, Robert observed. As the innkeeper had said, what was the use? Almost all the village trade depended upon the travelers going north or west, and if there was no travel, it was easier just to stay home with one's family.

Yancy-doc drank heavily all day, but he was sober enough to patch the shoulder of the stable boy who had been forced against a broken door hinge by an unruly horse. The boy took his treatment with a few shrieks of pain and trudged home through the snow. All the captive guests and tavern maids started calling the physician "Doc" then, with increased respect that he did not return. By nightfall Yancy-doc was drunk, and Robert led him to his bed. Each morning he came downstairs, looked out, and carried a bottle back to bed.

It was on a Sunday, five days later when the first break in the weather came. By midmorning a warming sun sent slides of snow tumbling from the roofs, and cedar shingles popped and crackled in the drying sun. By Tuesday all snow had disappeared except for the massive drifts, shoulder-high and abundant in number.

One or two shops in the village were opened again and only because their owners were not prevented from so doing by drifts between their places of business and their cabins, Robert surmised. What had once been snow now flowed down the mountainside and flooded the creeks and branches. Shop owners and workers who had no drifts to cross now found themselves captives of high-water conditions.

Of the village people, there were two distinct groups, the innkeeper told Robert. North, along the same creek that fed the waterwheel of the gristmill, lived nearly all of the craft-shop owners and additional workers. A short distance to the west were the homesteaders and trappers.

"Them creek people are law-abidin', do their day's work, and go home without botherin' anybody," the innkeeper said.

"And what about the others?" Robert inquired.

"They're a little like your friend upstairs. They can be jolly or downright hostile. Some of 'em are the scrapin's of the earth and some of 'em are as humble and God-fearin' folks as you'll find. That first bunch I was tellin' you about by the creek, they got hooked up with those Moravian missionaries that come through here from North Carolina. Whatever their religion is, they practice it downright honest, you can count on that."

Snowdrifts remaining in the road could be crossed with a horse and buggy when the following Sunday arrived. Robert looked forward to leaving the village and heading for Lexington. The same cabin fever from which the others suffered was beginning to affect him too. Yancy-doc did not come down to breakfast, but Robert ate with the other six guests in what he knew would be a farewell breakfast. He chose to sit with the first of the men he had met and the one who had told him about the good land around Lexington. They had become almost friends during their captive days together and Robert had learned Peter Reed's name as well as his occupation.

"A stonemason can't do much work until the weather warms up, can he?" Robert asked.

"Not much. The days have got to be warm enough so's the mortar will dry and not freeze…You never did tell me *your* present occupation," Peter Reed said.

"I don't have a *present* one," Robert said, lowering his eyes. "I used to be a scribe. If we go on to Lexington I guess I'll be looking for something."

"You're not traveling permanent-like with the other fellow? I thought you two was going to buy up a big parcel of land."

"I guess I gave you cause to think that—but I'm just riding with Doc until I want to get off," Robert said.

"I hope he turns out to be a good farmer or stock raiser...I'd think twice afore I'd let him doctor me for anything more than sour stomach."

"He's a nice enough fellow when he's not drinking," Robert said.

"I got my doubts about that. Drinkin' don't change a feller—it just brings out what's already in him."

"Maybe so," Robert said. "I won't be with him much longer anyway."

"My guess is that that'll be your good fortune. The two of you don't fit together somehow. You got a good look in the eyes, young feller. I'm ahopin' you do well." Peter Reed got up and shook Robert's hand.

Within the hour all of the guests had mounted their horses or climbed into their buggies to continue toward their destinations. If they didn't come back in an hour or so it would mean that all the drifts were passable and the swollen streams could be forded. Maybe half sober; Yancy-doc was playing it smart after all. If the others didn't get through, he wouldn't have wasted his time. Robert grinned at the thought.

About midafternoon Yancy-doc staggered down the stairs, his blue eyes bloodshot and hazy.

"Where's my damn breakfast?" he bellowed.

The innkeeper told him that both breakfast and dinner had come and gone.

"Well, fix me some breakfast anyway. We're leaving this God-forsaken wilderness today if we have to swim."

Fried meat and herb tea put a congeniality back into Yancydoc that Robert had despaired of seeing ever again. They gathered their things from their rooms and faced a smiling innkeeper who, Robert was sure, appreciated their leaving as much as the extra coin Yancy-doc placed in his hand.

In the absence of a stable boy, the innkeeper went to get the horse and buggy for his remaining guests. When he delivered them, Robert and Yancy-doc stood talking to the youth, who had returned to the inn, but not alone. A team of horses pulled the family wagon, and the boy sat astride the lead animal. He pointed to the wagon, which looked empty.

"They're alayin' in there," he said.

Yancy-doc did not move toward the wagon, and the boy's eyes remained upon him.

"I was ahopin' you'd still be here to doctor 'em," the boy said.

Yancy-doc lowered his head for a moment, appearing reluctant to step forward. He finally looked up at Robert, and Robert knew what he was thinking.

"Please, Doc. They're awful sick," the boy pleaded.

Robert and Yancy-doc took quick strides to the wagon and looked in. Yancy-doc pulled back the quilts in which a middle aged man was wrapped. A sickening stench reached their nostrils as soon as the man was fully uncovered. The purging of his bowels penetrated his clothing and his face lay bathed in his own vomit. He was conscious but unmoving. Robert moved automatically to the other side of the wagon and helped Yancy-doc pull the quilt from the other person.

"That's my brother," the stable boy said as Yancy-doc and Robert observed the same sickness in the boy as in his father.

"How long has your pa been sick?" Yancy-doc asked.

"The next day after you patched up my shoulder he got to feelin' poorly. In two days more he was bad sick and then Brother got bad sick."

"Are any of the other people who live near you sick with the same thing?" Yancy-doc asked.

"I don't know. Ain't no way we could get around and get help with the snowdrifts and floodin' and all. The road in both directions from our place has been under water. Today was the first day we could get out."

"Are any other members of your family sick?" Yancy-doc inquired.

"No. Least they wasn't a few minutes ago."

Yancy-doc turned to Robert and said: "Well? You want to try your hand at doctoring or go to Lexington?"

Robert didn't hesitate a second. "What can I do?"

"I don't know, but let's get them back to their house first. We can't do anything but wash them off in that wagon bed. If you've got the stomach for it you can help me do that."

Robert nodded his willingness and Yancy-doc instructed the stable boy to drive the wagon home as fast as he could.

CHAPTER V

In spots the trio still had to dodge floodwaters as they wound their way along the creek for about three-quarters of a mile, to where the well-built log house sat among large hemlocks and laurel thickets. Yancy-doc did not allow time for introductions when a middle-aged, plumpish woman stepped out on the porch.

"Get us a kettle of hot water now and put another one on the fire," he ordered. "Bring us scrap cloth and two more quilts. We're going to clean them up out here."

Robert worked faithfully with Yancy-doc and between his frequent gagging he questioned the physician. "What's the matter with them? They look near dead to me."

"They're pretty much gone, and my guess is that they won't make it. As to what the matter is, I'm not altogether sure, but I'll bet it's cholera."

"Anything you can do for it? You got any medicine with you?"

"We'll have to do some studying first. I've never treated this disease before, and hadn't heard a lot about it until a few years ago. There was a big outbreak of it in India and China not long after we left New Orleans. And I learned while I was still at Norfolk that it was spreading over Great Britain."

"How you suppose it got across the ocean?"

"I'm not sure I'm right, but if I am, disease travels where people travel."

Yancy-doc worked on until the boy and his father were clean and wrapped in dry quilts. Robert watched his friend with a new admiration. He was not the same man who a few hours earlier in the day staggered drunk and abusive down the stairway of the inn. He might not have wanted to come and clean up the vomit of a sick man but once started he did the job quickly and in good spirits.

Both of the sick were placed on the same feather tick and Yancy-doc asked again if any of the others of the house hold felt feverish or had signs of purging or vomiting. The woman, who introduced herself as Millie Caudle, assured them that she and her three daughters had no symptoms of the illness. All the children looked old enough to report their physical condition with accuracy and Yancy-Doc accepted the woman's assurances without question. The sick boy appeared the oldest of the children—about seventeen or eighteen—and the stable boy next, with all the girls being younger and about a year between them.

Yancy-doc explained to the sick man's wife what he thought the sickness was, but said that he wanted to consult his medical books. He excused himself to get them from the buggy.

The woman attended her husband, then her son. They moved about but little and their heaving stomachs generated only watery fluid. She bathed their foreheads with cool cloths and motioned the oldest girl to take over the chore.

There were no tears from the woman, but her face was grave and her lips were pale. She searched Robert's eyes unduly long and stepped near to him with a whispered request.

"The countenance of God is in your face. Will you pray for my man and my boy?"

The question stunned him. He had never before uttered a prayer in the presence of a stranger. He wanted to, and he wanted the inner power to, he knew that. What strength he lacked he soon found in her pleading gaze. He started a simple prayer, and sought the woman's eyes, that she might know that his words were sincere as far as they went.

It was dark now, and Yancy-doc studied the books by the lamp-light. Within the hour he stood up, convinced. "It's bound to be cholera," he said. "All the symptoms are there. And now for the hard part—the remedy. For the recommended treatment we have poor substitutes." The doctor scratched his head a moment in contemplation and spoke sharply to Robert. "Go out in the buggy and get my satchel. There's an extra flask of brandy in it. We'll need that."

Robert was back quickly. Yancy-doc stood over his patients. "We're going to need more brandy. Do you have any?" he asked Millie Caudle.

"We've got all you'll be aneedin'," she said.

"What about flaxseed for tea, and dried mustard?"

"We got a little of both in the garret, but it won't be much."

"It won't take much," Yancy-doc said. "Robert, I want you to warm this bottle of paregoric in your hands for a few minutes and shake it up good."

Robert helped administer the first dosage of medicine to each patient before he and Yancy-doc were offered supper. He had not the slightest appetite under the conditions at hand, but Yancy-doc ate heartily.

When they all had eaten, Millie Caudle had her girls get out of the garret two small straw ticks, which she placed on the floor.

"You and the doctor can sleep on these," she said to Robert. "They ain't much but they're better than a pallet."

Robert went to bed when Yancy-doc assured him that he could be of no further help. The sick man groaned mournfully, preventing his sleep, and he wondered if by morning they would be dead. Calvin Caudle was the chief miller at the gristmill, Robert had learned, but one thing he knew—Calvin Caudle wouldn't be sacking any cornmeal any time soon.

Before daylight Calvin Caudle was dead. Before lunch time, the boy was dead. Worse yet, by the end of the day the youngest girl started vomiting copiously.

At Yancy-doc's insistence the dead were to be buried the next morning and not later. The necessity of immediate burial, while reflecting the medical wisdom of Yancy-doc, nevertheless had an adverse effect on neighboring families, Robert learned. This information came that evening from one Matthew Cullegin, who, according to Millie Caudle, was the self-ordained preacher who was their spiritual leader.

"We will do as you say, Doctor. Brother Caudle and his son will be buried in the morning, before the sun is half high. This urgency has frightened our people, and our midwife will not prepare the body after her usual custom. I will lay them out myself," Matthew Cullegin said, "but I will need some assistance to move them."

"We'll help you." Yancy-doc volunteered himself and Robert. "I can't be with you long, but Robert will aid you as long as you need him."

Robert felt his stomach turn against his will, but he said nothing and followed Matthew Cullegin.

They used Calvin Caudle's own wagon and moved the bodies to Matthew Cullegin's barn. Robert was sure that he would be allowed to walk back as soon as the bodies were unloaded. The wagon would have to be left to take the bodies to the cemetery the next morning, but he would gladly walk any distance.

Matthew Cullegin soon revealed himself as a man who could do any job well and without being selective about it. But Robert wasn't allowed to leave. Every half-minute Robert would say he'd be going and Matthew Cullegin would intone, "Just a minute now, son, I want you to do this or get that for me." Robert tried to ask all sorts of questions to consume the waiting. In only two or three minutes he learned that Matthew Cullegin had lived in Heidrick for twenty years and that he had a wife and two daughters. He had been converted by Moravian missionaries and later ordained himself as a preacher of the free-will church he himself had raised "from the foundation to the rafters."

The more Robert talked to Matthew Cullegin, the more he liked him. He was a rather serious man, and yet there was mirth in his voice at times. His responses were quick, and he reminded Robert of paintings he had seen of the Catholic friars of Italy. He was bald in a saucer-shape on top of his head, but the side hair was thick, curly, and sand-colored. He was both older and heavier than Yancy-doc.

After what seemed an eternity of time, Robert heard the resonant voice of Matthew Cullegin call out that the laying-out was done. The corpses looked as natural as possible under the circumstances and their meeting clothes had never fit them better. The pride of an unusual job well done was still one of humility, Robert felt.

He had only to look upon Matthew Cullegin's face to believe he had served his God by this work just as much as he might have in the pulpit with the split-log benches crowded with people.

When the older man had washed his hands with salt and rinsed them in the watering trough he fixed his deep blue eyes upon Robert. "There are many ways to serve the Lord, Brother Robert. Long before I read it for myself our Moravian friends used to teach: 'Inasmuch as ye have done it unto the least of these my brethren ye have done it unto me.' Do you believe that, Robert?"

"Yes, sir," he answered obediently, without quite knowing why.

"Come eat with my family and me and then we will load the bodies back on the wagon so they will be ready for their last earthly journey when daylight comes."

Robert took a deep breath and followed the plump frame of the older man to his cabin.

By mid-morning of the next day the burial was over. It had been attended by few. The reason was not the time of day nor a lack of knowledge of the death. Fear had kept some of the people away, but Matthew Cullegin had learned something else at the time of burial: Two other families had illness in their households—illness with all the symptoms too well known, now, by every householder of Heidrick.

After the news of Yancy-doc's presence in the community became known there was no time for sleep and little for taking food. Yancy-doc left the young Caudle child reluctantly, but others were worse off.

Two days after the Caudle funerals, households with the illness numbered eight. In two homes all family members were ill.

Robert made the rounds with Yancy-doc and became an expert in mixing dosages and ingredients needed for various patients. He sensed what Yancy-doc might be thinking but had not said: they were fighting a losing battle, and what medicines they had were running in short supply. Yancy-doc had no more paregoric and he needed more flaxseed and dried mustard. Brandy was the only thing in abundance.

At the invitation of Matthew Cullegin, Robert and Yancydoc made their headquarters at his house after the Caudle funerals. Even on the subject of medicine Matthew Cullegin had some suggestions.

"The people along the creek here don't raise much flax," he said. "Most of them make their living at the craft shops. You will need to go to the homesteaders for more flaxseed and dried mustard."

"Go there immediately, Robert." Yancy-doc acted on the suggestion. "Take the stable boy—the Caudle son—with you to show you the way."

"Most of them are centered west of the village," Matthew Cullegin directed. "In a way I ought to go with you, but I'm needed here. If it's the Lord's will, I'll prepare their bodies and preach their funerals … and dig their graves too, if need be."

"At least you won't be alone." Yancy-doc managed a tired grin. "I notice your midwife has got her courage back."

"Yes, she's bad scared, but she wants to follow this part of her calling. I have a hunch that that barn is going to see a lot of bodies being fixed before going to rest. I'm not doubting your doctoring now, don't get me wrong—I've just seen a lot of this kind of thing—"

"I'm afraid you might be right," Yancy-doc interrupted, then to Robert: "Be gone with you now and get at least three pecks of flaxseed and half as much dried mustard. Tell Mrs. Caudle I'll check on her girl sometime today. Get back as soon as you can. I need you."

Robert picked up his passenger and delivered Yancy-doc's message. Millie Caudle had tears in her eyes this time, and before he knew it Robert had some in his own.

They drove to the inn, where the Caudle boy wanted to stop to assure his employer that he would return to work as soon as he could leave his mother—and to please wait on him, for he needed the work now more than ever.

The innkeeper seemed agreeable but on learning their destination gave a word of warning: "They may not welcome your comin'. They don't have no sickness over there, and some of them was in the village yesterday and learned about it. They got outta here like a scared hant when they heard the news."

"They'll be obliged to help," Robert said confidently.

Later that day Robert returned with only a small portion of the items he had been sent for. The innkeeper was right; they had not been welcome among the homesteaders and trappers and had in fact been chased from the settlement. All the flaxseed and dried mustard Robert had was gleaned on the way back from one elderly couple living in isolation nearer to the village.

Returning up the creek, he met Yancy-doc on one of Matthew Cullegin's horses and told him of the misfortune.

"They'll be more helpful when the scourge starts taking its toll among them," Yancy-doc said.

"You're sure it'll spread over there?"

"I'll bet on it."

"They don't think it will if we stay away from them. They said so and let us know that if we came back they'd bury us alive."

"They'll learn," Yancy-doc said. "Now you go on back to the cabin and start compounding what medicine we've got. I'll finish my rounds and be home long enough to eat and lie down for a few minutes. Help Cullegin all you can. He's got his hands full now. There are four bodies in the barn since you left."

Robert didn't ask who. He didn't want to know.

That night after supper Robert sat at his stool, compounding more medicine, while Yancy-doc slept. Matthew Cullegin's oldest daughter had made a homemade pestle that she used to powder the dried mustard in a small dough tray. She worked tirelessly, brushing the raven-black locks from her sweating face only rarely. Then, abruptly, the color of her pretty face changed and she became pallid. Suddenly she ran from Robert's presence to the out-of-doors, where even the log walls could not suppress the sounds of her violent retching.

Presently she re-entered the cabin, supported by her father.

"It's struck home now," Matthew Cullegin said, and the girl's mother was only then aware that even her own house was not immune.

"I'll wake Yancy-doc," Robert offered.

"I guess you'll have to," Matthew Cullegin said. "I want to talk something else over with him. Me and the midwife decided—you may as well know too—we can't keep laying out these corpses. It's too much for both of us. Two more bodies were brought to us a little while ago."

"What are you going to do then?" Robert asked.

"We're going to be obliged to bury them as soon as they die. It's not the right way, but it's the only way."

In a few minutes Yancy-doc lumbered down the steps and to the bed of the sick girl. He wiped the sweat from her forehead and gave her a dosage of paregoric. He had told Robert that he had no more of this, the most vital of his medicines.

"There is nothing more we can do here," Matthew Cullegin said after his daughter rested, "but we are needed at the barn. Robert, would you come and help us load the bodies back on the wagon? We're going to have to stack them crossways on slats to get them all on."

Robert agreed and followed the older man to the barn. The midwife stood preparing the body of a child. The child was the little daughter of Millie Caudle.

Before all the prepared bodies were loaded, Robert saw Yancy-doc ride off into the night with another man who had come for him. Presently Matthew Cullegin's wife came to the barn and called her husband aside. They conferred in whispers until finally he sent her back to the cabin. As he stepped back toward the lamplight Robert could see that his face was both flushed and troubled.

By dawn of the next day two horsemen stopped at Matthew Cullegin's cabin. Yancy-doc had not finished his breakfast but he rose from the table without question. Matthew Cullegin did not know the men, he said, but he guessed that the visitors meant one thing: the scourge had finally found its way to the settlement west of the inn. After talking to the strangers his guess was confirmed.

"How does it spread?" had been a question often asked, and Robert had seen Yancy-doc shake his head and say, "In the floodwater or maybe bad drinking water, or poison milk or bad air…" The guesses were endless and unsatisfying.

Yancy-Doc was certain to be gone all day and, as instructed, Robert delivered doses of medicine to all the known sick along the creek. Matthew Cullegin had before him the task of burying seven people, one of whom had not been laid out. Robert promised to meet the older man back at the cemetery and help when his own errands had been done.

When he did finish and return, the meetinghouse was full of those members of the seven families not too sick to travel or too scared of exposure to attend. He finally worked his way down the dirt aisle and took a crowded space beside Millie Caudle and her three remaining children. Matthew Cullegin preached a long and weary sermon and remained afterward until the last shovelful of dirt covered the dead. Robert stayed with him, and at the preacher's request, he tied his own horse to the tailgate and rode in the wagon.

"Let us hope we do not go home to find new guests in our barn," Matthew Cullegin said. As an afterthought he added, "And it is getting cold again."

Robert knew what he meant. Since the illness had engulfed them a warming of the weather had prevailed. Now winter appeared to be upon them again.

Matthew Cullegin pulled his frock coat tighter about him and eyed Robert gravely. "Robert, how long have you been acquainted with the doctor?"

Robert told him and asked in return if he was thinking about asking Yancy-doc to stay in the community permanently.

"I had no such thing in mind," Matthew Cullegin replied.

"Just the opposite, in a manner of speaking."

"I don't understand," Robert said, surprised.

"Oh, I know he's doctored us all, day and night, and that's being the good shepherd, but there's a lot of the wolf in him too."

Robert knew better than anybody the two men who lived in the skin of Yancy-doc, but he defended him anyway.

"Yes, and there's a lot of evil in him too," Cullegin argued. "I felt it the first night he stayed in our home. The way he looks at our girls don't ease my doubts none."

"But he's taken care of everybody like they were his own kin," Robert said.

"That's what makes it so hard," Cullegin agreed. "But some strange whisperings have been reaching my ears from others, and I didn't have any more doubts after last night. You saw my wife come to the barn. She told me that your doctor friend was lookin' over our sick girl in a way he shouldn't've been. She saw part of it for herself, and the girl told her mother more about it."

Robert didn't know what to say. For one thing, this information helped to explain things about Yancy-doc that were otherwise unexplainable, and, second, he wondered how they would all live together now if the sickness continued, and made it necessary.

By dinnertime of the next day Yancy-doc had returned. He asked if any more deaths had occurred. Informed there had been none, he told Robert that he would take the medicine and make the rounds himself this time. He gave Robert an extra set of saddlebags full of flaxseed and dried mustard. He also had new medicines he had thought of and found in some of the garrets of the homesteaders: dried peppermint and fermented rhubarb. In the first new remedy he placed great hope, for if the near-dead survived they would need to take nourishment after the flux or purging subsided, and peppermint tea would help condition their stomachs for food. In the fermented rhubarb he had good medicinal syrup. He set Robert and the youngest Cullegin girl to pulverizing the flaxseed. The milky white tea, as sticky as egg whites, could be a lifesaver for those with bloody flux. The medicine would help to heal the lesions deep in their intestines, Yancy-doc explained.

That night standing water froze solid and for the second day in a row no one died. Matthew Cullegin's girl was able to get out of bed although she was still far from well. Yancy-doc had an equally good report after returning from his rounds. There were no new deaths and no new cases of the sickness. Some of the patients were still in the life-and-death struggle, but the peppermint tea was helping. Some were keeping down nourishment after drinking the tea.

Yancy-doc ate with the rest of the family and told them that he would ride to the settlement west of the inn. More new cases might develop there, he said, since the disease had spread. He said he would spend the night and told where he could be reached if needed. Robert asked to go along but was told to stay where he was and rest up. If things got bad among the homesteaders and trappers he would be sent for.

For the first night in a long while Robert slept well. The garret of Matthew Cullegin's cabin had begun to seem like home. In the morning after breakfast he and his host made the calls to all of the sick, taking to each a fresh batch of powdered peppermint. Robert enjoyed the outing with Matthew Cullegin and felt in his presence fatherly wisdom and new insight into compassion and humble servitude. He told him so.

"I don't hanker to see you leave either, Robert. I'm sorry I can't say the same for your traveling companion. Where will the two of you go?"

Robert told him of their original plans.

"Sounds to me like you're running away *from* something—not to something," the older man said.

Robert felt chastened by his opinion, but there was something about the force and conviction with which he had spoken that stuck in Robert's consciousness.

That night by the fireside Matthew Cullegin's words still had not left him. Just where was he going and why? What was better about Lexington or any part of Kentucky than his own native Virginia? The longer he thought about it, the more it disturbed him. Finally he asked for a pen and parchment and wrote to Lawrence at Emory and Henry College, telling him only of where he was and what had happened. He was tempted to say in the letter that he wanted to come home, but he didn't.

When Robert had finished the letter Matthew Cullegin gathered his family about the fireside and asked Robert if he would join them in thanking God for delivering them all through the trials of the scourge and for a blessing on those who had lost loved ones or were yet sick. Robert bowed his head submissively and felt that if ever a man talked directly to God, Matthew Cullegin was doing so. But the preacher did not stop in his prayers with requests for comfort of the ill and courage for the bereaved. He prayed for Robert by name, that he might be used as a special servant of his Creator.

Robert was more than touched by the prayer. He trembled from the deep conviction of the preacher's words and the thought suddenly occurred to him that an attentive God might be answering the petition as it was being uttered. Robert was quiet after the devotions as they all sat about the fire. It was good to hear the banter of a family again.

After a while his host said to him, "I am, going to bed, but you may stay up if you like. Would you like something to read? The Bible or another book perhaps?"

Robert said he would like to read, and his host brought the Bible in one hand and Bunyan's *Pilgrim's Progress* in the other. Robert chose the latter.

"My father brought that book from England. It won't stand much more wear, but you can touch it and almost feel the sweat and holiness of its author. You will not be the same man when you finish this allegory, Robert. Know that in advance."

Yancy-doc did not come back the next day or the next. Maybe all the sickness that was disappearing along the creek was finding its way to the west of the village. Still, Yancy-doc had not sent for Robert or for any more of the medicine he and the Cullegin girls had compounded.

Robert finished his book and waited two more days. He told the Cullegins during the noon meal that he was going after Yancy-doc the following morning if he did not show up by nightfall. Matthew Cullegin reacted without comment to Robert's suggestion except to assure Robert that he was welcome to stay where he was as long as he wanted.

By midafternoon, the sound of horses' hooves were thought to be the return of Yancy-doc. A frantic pounding on the door indicated otherwise.

Matthew Cullegin reached the door first. "Yes, what is it?"

"Is this where the doctor was stayin'?"

"Yes."

"You better come and get him. He's been shot."

"Where is he?" Robert gasped.

"I'll take you to him," the messenger said.

They saddled two horses quickly and followed the informant at a gallop. Westward, past the inn, they traveled the same road that Robert had taken to get the extra medicine, but turned off short of the main settlement onto a steep mountain road. When the leader came to a halt they were facing a small but new-looking cabin. On the eastern side the outside wall was nearly covered with stretched and drying hides.

The man led the way to the small barn. A single milk cow occupied the stall, and they passed through the stall door into the feedroom. On the hay-covered floor lay Yancy-doc. Robert and Cullegin knelt beside him and saw no blood. His eyes were open and he breathed laboriously.

"But you said he was shot!" Robert said.

"Try turning his worthless hide over," the man said.

"He's been shot in the back!" Matthew Cullegin exclaimed.

"Ain't that the only target a man would have if he was layin' on a woman?"

"Your wife?" Cullegin asked.

"No. The woman is my sister. Her husband is in the cabin, sick."

"Did you shoot him?" Robert asked.

"No, he did. Her husband."

They turned their attention to Yancy-doc, whose mouth opened, emitting blood rather than sound. Robert wiped the blood with the tail of his shirt. They propped him up on the hay so that his oral bleeding would not choke him. He seemed to gather a little strength, and Robert steadied his shoulders.

"Preacher... Robert," he said in a whisper. They held him on each side.

"Press no charges... I take the blame... Robert, you... should have been... surgeon...you could take pistol ball out of... my back."

"Be easy, brother, we'll do all we can for you," Matthew Cullegin whispered.

"Nothing you... can do... Robert, we won't... get to... Kentucky... wonder if—if it was like Eden... Write my wife... tell her I loved... her much..."

They sat with the dying man until Robert felt as if he was growing numb all over. He wiped blood from his friend's mouth until there was no dry spot left on his shirt. Matthew Cullegin removed his own without being asked.

Once they thought the doctor was gone, but he rallied and opened his eyes. He tried to speak and could not until they swabbed his mouth dry. "Bury... me... by the creek... with my patients... I did my best ... I tried to save... them."

He tried then to cough and could not. Bubbles of blood formed on his mouth, and he was gone.

"Where are his horse and buggy? We will take him away," Robert said.

The man led them to the rear of the cabin, and Robert brought the buggy around to the front. A heavily bearded man supported himself against a porch post and talked to Matthew Cullegin. He looked almost too sick to stand, but he did, and spoke his piece to the preacher.

"I don't hold with killin'," he was saying, "but what you goin' to do with a snake what pretends to doctor you and all the time he's atryin' to get your wife down in the hay?"

The man awaited their response, but there was none they could make. "It ain't right," he continued. "I was plumb near death—and that doctor thought I was too—but he learned one thing. I weren't so near dead I didn't know what was goin' on. I woulda' paid him for doctorin' me, but I'd kill another'un just as quick for takin' what ain't his'n. The poor thing is simpleminded anyhow—reckons you know she'd have to be to live with me in this trappin' country."

Robert turned the buggy toward the barn and prepared to load the body of his friend. He pushed the door open and saw kneeling on the hay beside the dead man the smallest wisp of a woman—not even a woman, perhaps, for she appeared in her teens. Tears streaked her face as she continued to run her slender fingers through the hair of the dead man. The girl's brother took her away and Yancy-doc rode his buggy to the inn for the last time.

He was buried where he wished, among many fresh graves.

Early the next day Robert prepared to go. His heart was heavy.

"I will mail all his personal effects to his wife and tell her of his death and burial place. Neither will I forget to include your letter," Matthew Cullegin said.

"Will you tell her how he died?"

"If I said he died at the end of a cholera epidemic it would not be an untruth, would it?"

"No sir"—Robert grinned—"and tell her how well he cared for the people when they were sick—I did."

"I will, Robert, but we must not dismiss the main message we have learned here. Do not ever forget that truth cannot travel in the cloak of a lie nor can an angel's mercy be gilded in the black death of the devil's deception."

"I will not forget, but I will always have love in my heart for Yancy-doc."

"Bless you. That is God's mercy shining through you. But do not be deceived by evil, and that evil which is half-truth and half lie is the worst kind of all—a despicable mockery to a just God. May hell consume you if you ever use a gift of Providence, as your friend did, for the destruction of your neighbor."

Robert could talk no more; his heavy heart was getting heavier.

"Where will you go, Robert? You have not told me."

"I don't know. Perhaps farther on into Kentucky, but maybe back to Virginia. Tell Yancy-doc's wife I will send her a draft for the amount the horse and buggy are sold for when I reach my destination."

"I think you should keep them. You've earned them, and she would likely agree."

Robert leaned from the seat and extended his hand. To those on the porch he waved.

"I have prayed the same prayer more than once, Robert. The countenance of God is in your face. Serve Him well."

The inn was filled with travelers, and spring would soon be coming. Most of the people were going west, and Robert had over half the gold with which he had left Abingdon. Still, Matthew Cullegin's words asked of him again whether he ran *to* something or *away* from something. He cracked the buggy whip and turned east toward the gap of the Cumberlands.

There was no snow or ice on the return journey, and he did not tarry until he reached the beautiful mountain range and the picturesque gap, cut as perfectly from the stone as a bite from a biscuit. He stopped the buggy and withdrew the quill and ink and parchment Matthew Cullegin had given him. Patiently he formed the lines and shadows that seemed to move the mountain gap from its place of repose onto the fine texture of his parchment. Yancy-doc would have liked that. Perhaps he would mail the drawing to Yancy-doc's wife in Norfolk or, if not, perhaps to James's law office in Marion.

CHAPTER VI

Robert told his story to his brother, and at James's and Ellen's invitation took up residence with them in Marion. He would not have accepted his brother's hospitality a month previously. It was different now. It was different for more reasons than Robert could fathom, but he *felt* them all whether he could explain them or not.

For one thing, the month was April—a little over six weeks since he had stepped into Yancy-doc's buggy for the first time. It seemed to him more like six years. April was a good time to think things out and a good time simply to be alive. Soon the dogwoods and the Judas trees would be in bloom and all would seem fresh and new. Abingdon would be most beautiful of all, for even in this year of 1839, Washington County and the town itself were old—over sixty years old—and forsythia, apple japonica, spirea, and other flowering shrubbery from the mother county (many times divided and replanted) added magnificently to those native colors that of themselves painted a canvas of breathtaking beauty. He did not think it strange that Abingdon seemed so exquisite in the eyes of his mind, for he felt now that it would be the only way he would see it ever again.

Both James and Ellen were sympathetic to his feelings of hurt at the hands of his aunt Elizabeth. He thought, however, that they didn't fully understand, *couldn't* fully understand; James had made some passing remark about pride and mentioned the matter no more. James informed him soon afterward that he himself was more interested in the years ahead rather than the past. In that connection he advised Robert to be thinking about his plans for the future. Robert did so, first keeping his appointment on the banks of the Holston, where he was baptized.

With James's help he had gotten a summer job clerking in Tate's store, a dry-goods establishment located near the hotel and stage stop.

The next suggestion James made took him by surprise. "Robert, college is not going to be easy for you. You will be the first to admit your lack of zeal for learning. After closing hours at your store job I have arranged to have you tutored by a very scholarly gentleman here in Marion. His name is George Washington Buchanan, and you will like him. He takes to scholarship with the same dedication as that of a beautiful woman to her mirror."

"But I'll be going to college in June," Robert protested.

"That's the idea. I want you to be adequately prepared for college. You will be working on the college farm part of the time, and when you get to the classroom you must be ready. If you are not a serious student they will tell you quickly to go home and stay."

Robert consented and went to his tutor faithfully every Tuesday and Thursday evenings, and a half-day on Saturday. It was not long before the names of Plato, Alexander the Great, Ramses II, Pliny the Elder and Younger, not to mention the great composers and poets of the world, became well known to him. There were some his tutor mentioned of necessity but with a shudder. Voltaire was foremost among these, with Calas and La Barre not far behind.

It was bad enough to be anti-Christian, Mr. Buchanan explained, but in the case of Voltaire, to be a writer of naughty plays and a mocker of public figures was just too much. To have been so loved for his devilment that admiring lady friends would, at his death, have his heart cut out and preserved in a silver box was downright ludicrous, Mr. Buchanan said. Still, the man was too historically important to ignore.

Robert's tutor not only breathed the breath of life into the great and near-great of the world, but he was equally fascinated by algebra and logic, and he admitted to lying awake nights, packing his brain with the latest developments in chemistry as well.

George Washington Buchanan frequently reminded his student of the short amount of time they had to work together. If it was possible to cram a man's head with knowledge, like the barrel of a muzzle-loading rifle is tamped with powder and shot, Robert was quite sure that his tutor was so doing.

The first of June came none too soon. Classes at Emory and Henry did not commence until the latter part of July, but Robert did as most of his classmates were doing, working a month ahead to build up work credits.

The work to be done on the college farm during midsummer consisted mostly of raising and processing food for either the students and faculty or the farm animals. One rarely had the choice of working in the gardens or the hay field. Work was by assignment. It was in the hay field where he met Zeno Sprinkle, Raleigh Stinson, and Hiram Strong, students like himself.

During the first part of July the four of them worked steadily. Zeno, the chunky one of the four, maintained his vigil around the hay pole, seeing more and more of the pole disappears as the hay rose higher and higher. He walked around and around the pole, packing the hay with his feet, and as the stack rose higher his perch became more precarious. His wiry red hair seemed to stand out in all directions when the haystack reached a needle point and the walking surface narrowed to nothing. Robert and Hiram Strong tilted the ladder upright against the haystack and Raleigh Stinson started up the ladder with the "weights," two fence rails tied together that would be looped around the hay pole and allowed to hang down the stack to keep the wind from blowing any of the hay away.

Their field master, who during the academic sessions would probably be just as precise in the classroom as he was in the field, explained to them the desirability of getting the weights on properly. "If the wind does not take any of the hay from the stack, then the stack remains peaked at the top and turns the rain well," he said.

Zeno said that he was not impressed with such a detailed explanation of fundamental logic and he asked Robert and the others why the field-master-teacher didn't realize that every boy in the field was experienced in this task long before he came to college. Zeno then said, "Maybe I'd better change my mind about becoming a teacher if they all get feebleminded."

They laughed, because Zeno was always making observations like that. And the truth was that none of them could quite envision Zeno as a teacher. They had discussed it as the time for classes to begin came nearer.

Each boy except Robert seemed pretty positive about his life's work. Raleigh Stinson, like Zeno, wanted to be a teacher. Raleigh, however, seemed the epitome of what a teacher should be: articulate, commanding, and with a personal vibrancy that would be a great asset in the classroom. He even looked like the stereotype of the schoolmaster, with bushy hair, a gaunt frame, and the pointed intellectual nose.

Hiram Strong resembled Raleigh Stinson in physical appearance but he was much more prone to weigh his words before speaking, and when he did speak his words seemed to carry such conviction that they were most times incontestable. But, strangely, this evidence of powerful intellect did not seem to detract from a capacity for compassion. They were not bad attributes for a minister, Robert thought, if Hiram continued his plans in that direction.

Such were Robert's closest friends as they began the more serious part of the school term.

Lawrence Sheffey had his own friends at the college but he did help his brother to adjust in every way possible. Although the college proper sat in the midst of six hundred acres, five hundred and ninety of those acres could still be considered farmland. The main college building was a large brick one, four stories high in the center with a wing on each side of the main building rising three stories high. The building had a deep basement and a steep-pitched garret, neither of which was wasted room.

Squire Henry, the Negro janitor, lived in the basement, but if anybody thought his duties consisted only of keeping the living quarters and classrooms clean they simply did not know the college tradition. Squire Henry was friend and confidant to every boy in the school and a self-taught authority on the Revolutionary War. He could also quote the works of Chaucer from memory.

By July twentieth the boys had their class assignments and their work accounts reconciled. Robert, Zeno, Hiram, and Raleigh had each accumulated about one hundred and sixty hours' work credit, and figured at the set rate of five cents per hour, they had about eight dollars to apply toward tuition, board, books, and the fee for the use of the library.

"It sure isn't any way to get rich," Zeno expressed what seemed to be a universal opinion. All of them, including Lawrence and his friends and still others, were not discouraged, however, from the hard schedule. Study started at five o'clock in the morning and lasted until one pm After lunch they all did farm work from two o'clock until five o'clock pm, and from seven pm until nine pm studying was again the order of the day. But it wasn't too much for any boy, or, if it was, not one would admit it.

Robert worked hard as one week passed into another. Often at his side, sharing both knowledge and encouragement, was Lawrence. Much of what was to be learned seemed to Robert a useless waste of time. Zeno agreed with him, but Raleigh and Hiram would make no complaint.

"It will all come in handy," Hiram would say authoritatively, meaning that all learning would find application somewhere. Robert and Zeno would grudgingly concede the momentary wisdom of the statement and buckle down to Hedge's *Logic*, Wayland's *Political Economy*, Turner's *Chemistry* or Kingsley's *Tacitus*, and others.

There were reviews with each professor at the end of every month of the session.

"Robert, your Uncle James would be proud of you, were he still living," Ephraim Wiley said at the end of the first review month.

Robert thanked the professor and remembered how much more hostile his elder had seemed when they first talked at the Fourth-of-July celebration in Abingdon.

"I want you to do as well the rest of the session. I suspect you will like some of the literature we will be studying, as well as your chance at oratory," Professor Wiley said.

Robert said he probably would and chuckled to himself, remembering Zeno practicing his elocution in advance while rounding up the milk cows in the late afternoon. His resonant voice sounding the sharp A's and round O's, was enough to sour the cow's milk, Hiram

Strong would say without the hint of a smile. Robert too would work on his elocution in the fields, among the animals and everywhere else.

"Your voice is too soft," Raleigh opined, "and you're not getting any roll in your O's—"

"Nor any force and depth in your voice," Hiram added.

Zeno practiced gestures while Robert tried again and again.

When the time came to put all his rehearsals into application, Robert was a miserable failure at oratory. His high voice went even higher, he forgot how to use his hands, and his short arms hung limply at his sides. As if all that wasn't bad enough, his speech displayed no continuity of thought and his delivery ended up in a jumbled outpouring of unrelated half-thoughts. He was embarrassed, as were his classmates, who couldn't help showing it. His embarrassment turned to despondency when there was no noticeable improvement in succeeding days. Nothing Lawrence or his friends said to him seemed to compensate for this failure.

Professor Wiley approached him one day after the class had adjourned. "Robert, not all men are born to speak well, nor can some of them be taught. It is no disgrace. Many of our students go on to become farmers or merchants. If one does not intend to become a teacher or minister or lawyer, proficiency in oratory is not mandatory."

"I know that. Thank you, sir," Robert said formally, and left the room. He wanted to say more to his professor, but the time had not seemed right. He had told no one what he wanted to be although he had felt the birth pangs of it months ago. If this ambition ever really came to fruition he would need the ability that seemed to flee from him.

That night during the study period he closed his books and left the building. To the northwest of the structure a steep hill overlooked the college grounds. He climbed to the crest, knowing well that his act was contrary to college rules: he ought to be studying, and by nine-thirty he was supposed to be in bed.

The thought of it bothered him little—but the moon was bright and the night only slightly chill. It was the first week of September, and he knew that winter would soon be upon the campus. Thinking about that, he became still more chilled, and put his hands under his armpits for warmth. In the distance he could see the lamplight in the dormitory windows, looking like another world to him, with an ocean separating the orange glow of the windows from his solitary perch. Suddenly he jumped from his seated position and ran a ways down the opposite side of the hill.

The night air invigorated him, and he wished he could keep on running or, better still, that he could be upon the saddled back of Ginger, headed by harvest moonlight to the banks of the Holston. He thought about Big Edmund and Ann and how they were getting along. He thought also of Yancy-doc, and wondered if the flesh had rotted from his bones, and which place in the unseen eternity the soul of his friend had found refuge. The thought that Yancy-doc might be roasting in a never-ending hell caused Robert to grit his teeth in a kind of inner pain. He could not put the doctor out of his mind. No matter how much he tried, it could not be done. At the strangest times the face of Yancy-doc appeared to him. Sometimes in the visions his friend would be doing a great kindness, and at other times he would be submerged in the blackest of evil. Robert felt that if he could justify the doctor's life and philosophy in some way the visions would disappear and no longer bother him. At times he felt as if Yancy-doc called to him from the farthest reaches of eternity. But the call had no message. What could possibly explain a man like Yancy-doc? Had there been both a devil and an angel beneath his skin, and while one worked the other slept? Robert thought of his own conversion and how quietly and serenely his own being was being changed. He had as yet talked deeply to no one about it, in the sense of what it meant to him. He had hoped to do so with his aunt Elizabeth, and casually he had mentioned it to Yancy-doc, but his friend had cut him off with a definite signal of disinterest. Once when he and Yancy-doc were working among the sick he started to open his heart to Matthew Cullegin, but something always seemed to interrupt.

All in all his life up to now didn't add up to much. He felt the peace of God in his heart, but he hadn't done much about it. Indeed it was not at all clear what God expected him to do, if anything. Lately he had experienced a sense of mission but maybe "the sense" was too weak to be real and he was not sure whether his thoughts were more those of fantasy than of guidance. One thing was certain: whatever things he felt in his heart would have to stay there. Throughout the week he had proved to himself, his classmates, and his professor that he had no ability to speak convincingly about them in any well-prepared and professional manner.

Now his head started to spin and his heart was heavy. He descended the hill wearily, feeling the dew soak into his brogans and making his feet as wet as his eyes. He tiptoed through the dark halls and fell onto his bed.

The next afternoon he and Zeno were assigned to clean out some of the stalls, but they had worked only a few minutes when Lawrence stuck his head through the door. "I'm afraid I have some bad news, Robert. Aunt Elizabeth has sent a courier to tell us that Francis has died."

"Was he at home?" Robert asked.

"No, in Florence, Alabama. He had been ill with fever, Aunt Elizabeth said—almost a duplication of the tragedy James Lowry suffered."

Robert began to wonder if family investments in the state of Alabama had not turned into a sinister omen.

"Will you go to Aunt Elizabeth?" Robert asked.

"Yes. Will you accompany me?"

"I don't feel I could give her any comfort."

"Very well then. I will be back tomorrow."

Zeno looked at him strangely, with questioning eyes.

Finally he said, "Your cousin? Did I understand right?"

"Yes, my aunt's third son. He was just admitted to the bar a few months ago. He was only twenty-four and was graduated from Princeton with honors," Robert added as a sort of final tribute.

Toward the end of September, Robert's monthly conference was scheduled not with Professor Wiley but with Reverend Charles Collins, president of the college. Lawrence, aware of his brother's nightly wanderings, had told Robert that the conference would cover the subject of rule breaking. Lawrence's warning did not frighten him; and he was prepared to tell Reverend Collins or anybody else that he could search for life's answers at the top of the hill in the moonlight just as well or better than in the classroom.

"You know you have broken the rules of the college," Reverend Collins began firmly but calmly.

"Yes, sir," Robert confessed.

"The evening hours before bedtime are set aside for study."

"Begging your pardon, sir, but I *have* been studying," Robert said.

"I mean the conventional kind, Robert: with your books open by lamplight. Your college work has been going downhill lately. You are aware of that, aren't you?"

"I can't understand some of the chemical formulations, and logic sometimes gets hard for me."

"It's more than that. Your whole attitude has changed. Professor Wiley thinks part of your trouble has to do with your failure at oratory. Why is this so important to you? Do you hope to go into law? Teaching?"

"I wanted to be able to speak. I don't know altogether why—and I don't know what I want to be for sure yet."

"Robert, you must learn to conform to the college rules, and if you expect to stay here you will find us harsher than before. I suggest you put your failure at oratory out of your mind and settle down to work. I admire your desire to grasp something you obviously cannot, but Professor Wiley assures me that this is not one of your talents. You might as well accept the fact that, whatever life holds for you, public speaking will not be a part of it."

"I'll sure miss walking up the hill. I'm getting a lot straight up there. It's the most peaceable place in the world to get your thoughts in order."

"Do your walking after supper or Sundays after church," Reverend Collins said and dismissed him.

Robert tried to keep the rules for a while, but when the first snow came in November he was not deterred from climbing to the peak. Sometimes he would ask Zeno or Raleigh and Hiram to accompany him, but most times he preferred to go by himself. Once he sketched a landscape scene from the top of the hill for Lawrence to hang in his room.

During church one day at the end of the month a second and very heavy snow fell. He could not wait to trudge his way to the peak, for his soul felt full and the morning sermon had opened his eyes to something. The minister had preached long and eloquently. His theme was that most of mankind did not respond to the call of God because they did not feel His lovingkindness.

After his dinner Robert walked up the hill alone, thinking of the responsive chord that this message had struck in his heart. In truth, he knew not why the thought moved him so, but immediately his thoughts turned to Yancy-doc. His friend had surely been exposed to the teachings of the Bible and must have bypassed the call to conversion dozens of times; he had implied as much. Then why had no one been able to reach him?

No matter how Robert approached the question—from Yancy-doc's point of view or his own—the answer came out the same: the doctor had not found the peace of God simply because he had never felt nor been shown God's lovingkindness and grace . Nobody had stood halfway between God and Yancy-doc to be the convincing messenger, to point the way. Yancy-doc had either missed the entire mission of Christ or ignored it altogether, and no minister or friend was ever able to bridge the gap as intermediary.

The first session of college ended just before Christmas, and Robert came back to James's and Ellen's house, more learned but more confused. He was even thinking about dropping out of college before the February term began. James's reaction to the pronouncement was a quick re-establishment of tutorial services from George Washington Buchanan. Robert was told that if he kept up his studies during the interim of six weeks between sessions he would not lose interest in going back in February. It was a poor kind of logic, Robert thought, but neither James nor his tutor agreed.

Robert made his appearance at the home of Mr. Buchanan the day after Christmas. He was minus a greatcoat even though the day was bitterly cold and the wind howled with ferocity.

"Do you wish to destroy yourself by coming out in this weather without a greatcoat?" George Washington Buchanan asked.

"I don't have one, and James said he would not buy another until I learned my lesson. I must say it occurred to me what he had in mind just walking over here. I am chilled to the marrow of my bones."

"In the name of Jehoshaphat, what happened to your greatcoat? Did you get careless and lose it?"

"In a way, I suppose. I went down to the dry-goods store where I worked last summer to pay my respects and then stopped by the hotel for a few minutes. A man got off the westbound stage without a coat, and his body shook so bad from the cold that he could hardly stand up."

"And you gave him your coat?"

"Yes," Robert confessed. "James said if I went without one for a while and checked the price of a new one I might appreciate ownership a little more."

"You cannot be charitable to every rum-guzzler you meet. Your brother works hard at his practice, and keeping you in school adds to his burden. Purchases of extra greatcoats do not ease his situation."

One day shortly after New Year's, Robert made clear to his tutor his reluctance to study. He did want to talk of other things, however.

"Have you ever thought that too much learning might be the work of the devil?" Robert asked.

"What!" Mr. Buchanan's glasses nearly fell from their place far down on his bulbous nose as he jerked to attention.

"I mean, couldn't a man get so smart that he thought he knew everything and had no humbleness at all?"

"I should think it would be very hard to get *that* smart. Very hard indeed!"

"But it could happen, couldn't it?" Robert pressed the question.

"I suppose it could—maybe." The other retreated a little.

"Even if it just happened a little, wouldn't it be wrong?"

"Well—humility is not always virtuous," Mr. Buchanan hedged a little.

"I have lately come to think otherwise. I don't have enough, and I have been awakened to it. I am sinful with pride—"

"Now wait, Robert. I do not hear confessions. I enlighten minds when given half a chance." And he peered mockingly at Robert over the top of his glasses.

Robert ceased his probing that day and studied half-heartedly thereafter until it was time to re-enter Emory and Henry in February.

There was more time for reflection and study in the second session than in the first. The weather was too bad to do anything out-of-doors except clean the barns and see that the animals were fed. If one did not relish books there was an abundance of time on hand. Robert made an honest effort at study and spent longer periods in conversation with Zeno and Raleigh, and Hiram too, when he could command the latter's time and attention. Lawrence tried to get him interested in drama, for during the winter months thespian endeavors especially seemed to flourish. Robert paid scant attention to the art of the theatre, saying that all men were acting all the time and that no need existed to pay attention to their acting at a given time or place.

He started the long outside walks again whenever he felt the need. At first no one said anything, for the winter was unusually severe and many of the students felt an unsuppressible cabin fever. The professors recognized this and relaxed the regulations a little. Robert's interest in his studies began to decline again in March, and once more he sat before Reverend Collins.

Robert extended to Reverend Collins the courtesy of speaking first but made his own point quickly. "I wish to leave college," he said.

"All of your actions indicate that you do, but why?" Reverend Collins asked.

"The learning is wrong for me. Too much of it would make me more haughty and proud."

"There is no reason that you should not be proud of learning," Reverend Collins said, "and whatever you do, you will need this and more."

"I have been thinking for many weeks about knowledge. Isn't it true that all knowledge comes from God? That everything you and the other professors know comes from Him? Even that all things to be known will come from God?"

Robert could see that the magnitude of the question stunned Reverend Collins somewhat, but his elder answered quickly.

"Yes, Robert, in a manner of speaking, but this does not remove from us the obligation to do our part in gaining such knowledge."

"I do not agree, sir. If I give my life to God He will give me all the wisdom I need to be His advocate."

"Robert, I had not thought of you in the ministry. I mean no offense, but you are in no way qualified, and I must discourage you. Now promise me once more you will pay serious mind to your studies. Have you ever given thought to becoming a teacher?"

Robert said he had but didn't believe that he could address a room full of older children.

"Give some thought to tutoring smaller children then," Reverend Collins said. "And you will need more than divine help for that task also," he added with a smile.

Robert made no promises, and within a week he was gone. He came back to Marion and tried to explain to his brother and sister-in-law why he had left college. He asked to stay in their house, promising to get his job back at Tate's and pay his own room and board.

The arrangement worked well, and James soon appeared to accept the fact that Robert would never return to college. Robert kept to his own room or otherwise took pains not to interfere in the social or business life of his brother.

By midsummer he started attending all the revivals within a day's riding distance of Marion. When there were no revivals, he would simply drop in to a church at random, paying little attention to the denomination or the appearance of the church building. Neither did he observe the color of the congregation, and one Sunday, in the community of Adkins, he unintentionally interrupted a Negro church service. He walked into the building in the middle of a rousing spiritual and recognized Ann, whom he immediately sought out and hugged vigorously. He must have given the impression that a white man was attempting to drag the woman from the building when her shouts went up. Moments later the verses of the hymn resounded from the log rafters again.

In August he attended a revival in the village of Saltville, where the sweating Baptist minister in his closing pleas was getting few converts. Robert noticed a man a little older than himself who appeared to be in deep travail. Several times the man would seem in an anguish of indecision and yet unable to move from his bench. Robert got up from his seat and went to him, kneeling at his side and offering words of comfort and encouragement. The minister observed Robert's efforts and prolonged the service with more pleas and singing. Soon Robert came walking down the aisle with the young man and sat with him on the penitents' seat.

When the service was over, the exhausted preacher came to Robert with outstretched hand. "Do I have a visiting brother of the cloth in my midst?" he asked.

"No, I am not a preacher, I just saw a brother who lacked only the lovingkindness of God to make his journey to the front."

"Bless you for your exhortation, my brother. Without you our convert might be sitting at the point of indecision until this time next year."

Robert disclaimed the credit; and yet his success was more than a little startling.

"The hand of God is upon the exhorter as well as the preacher. Do you consider this work a calling?"

"I don't know," Robert said earnestly.

He thought about it, riding back to Marion. The word "exhorter" was almost as new to him as was what was expected of such a person. More thought and study on the matter revealed that such a calling was indeed a divine one. In Philippians he read of Euodias and Syntyche, and he learned of those non-clergical men throughout history who had been intermediaries between a loving God and a reluctantly yielding Mankind.

The revivals around Marion did not end until the passing of the New Year. By then the weather prevented attendance, or no warm place could be found to conduct them. But as long as they lasted Robert made the rounds—sometimes to more than one on the same day.

An exhorter did not get paid, but Robert was saving a little money from the meager pay at his store job. Soon he would own his horse and James would not frown at him each time he saddled up and rode off.

By the spring of 1841 Robert was again in the saddle, covering even greater distances than he had the previous year.

Before daylight on Sundays he would ready his own horse and quietly leave Marion. As often as not he would return by the light of the moon.

This rigorous schedule extracted a toll from him and he found it hard to keep his mind on his work at the dry-goods store. His employer spoke to him, but not as severely as he might have, for he had heard of Robert's good work.

Nevertheless, the conflict grew greater for him. He wanted to do an honest day's work in the store during the week, but half-days on Saturday and one full day on Sunday limited the range of his travels and the amount of time he could spend in his exhortations. He knew he had no ability to address a group, but his exhortations directed to one man or one woman at a church or in a home or, more and more frequently, along the roadways, were abundantly fruitful. Increasingly he found the opportunity to stop at homes along the byways and the less-traveled roads and pathways of the mountains.

During the months of summer he started traveling short distances during the week after his regular working hours had ended. But he couldn't go far in the three or four hours of daylight left after work. If one man or woman, however, felt after hearing his exhortations that God's grace and loving kindness were things of reality to be drunk into one's soul, he considered the time well spent.

During one week in late July he returned home unusually late to find that James had left a lamp burning in his room with a note propped against the base. The words written in James's hurried scroll, said:

"Tragedy has again struck and we have lost another cousin. Lawrence Alexander died today from the accidental discharge of his gun. We got the message after supper. Will you accompany us to Abingdon?"

Robert put the note back on his dresser. Now the fifth son of Elizabeth White was gone. It was easy to remember his cousin's age, for Robert exceeded him there by only four months.

He had never felt a close kinship to Lawrence Alexander, in spite of the proximity of their ages. He remembered with pain coming to the White household in Abingdon after his father had died and his stepmother made plans to marry again.

Lawrence Alexander had been the first to torment him and call him a dirty orphan. His cousin's hostility had seemed to grow with the passing of the years until it manifested itself by Lawrence Alexander's simply ignoring him altogether in favor of more exciting and socially acceptable friends. But that was all over now. Death was the greater equalizer.

He would not go to Elizabeth White. God forgive him, but he could not go just yet. Perhaps he would even embarrass her if he went. He agonized over the hypocrisy of what he wanted to be and what he was. But then and there by the lamplight he vowed to bury his pride and hurt sometime in the future and be reconciled to his aunt again. It could not be now; it would take more time than that. Much more time.

After telling Ellen that he would not be going to Abingdon he left the house before breakfast the next morning. All day, during work, he saw the grieving face of Elizabeth White. The loss of a husband and three sons would, he feared, leave her a withered, lethargic shell. Gone would be the bright sparkle in her nearly black eyes, and that perfectly blended mixture of frontier woman and genteel lady would have faded, remembered only by those of an earlier day when Elizabeth White's patrician nose and taut olive skin showed not a care nor wrinkle. For those who had seen her cut down bit by bit the former days would not be so easily remembered, Robert suspected. But he remembered, and his heart grew sadder as the day progressed.

The winter of 1841–42 was not as severe as it had been the previous year, and Robert kept up his travels with some regularity. Often his trips would amount to nothing more than a Sunday church service and then a visit with two winter bound old people or an arthritic ex-slave holed up in a mountain cabin.

As he rode the winter trails he often thought of how badly he wanted to stand before large groups and be able to speak with force and eloquence. The scenes he remembered of trying to learn oratory at college still left him red-faced. He practiced speaking some days as he rode along, but his high-pitched monotone and the jumbled expression of his thoughts caused his horse to prick up her ears and then gyrate them wildly in what could be interpreted as a gross offense even to an animal!

In January at Blue Springs, southeast of Marion and near the Wythe County line, Robert was invited to a golden-wedding anniversary celebration of a man he had led to conversion only the previous year. After numerous guests had consumed a savory dinner of roast turkey a mild-mannered man of about thirty-five whom Robert had been introduced to upon his arrival sought him out.

"I have been hearing of you and your good works, but I wonder if your talents do not extend beyond your reputation."

Robert did not know what he meant, and said so.

"I mean, I would guess you have talent as a teacher. I am connected with the Raven Cliff iron furnace on Cripple Creek. I will be a partner with Mr. Gleaves, the present owner, and we are interested in hiring a teacher for our own children and those of our workmen. There are other children nearby, and added to our own they all could make up a class of nine or ten—maybe even a dozen children."

Robert's face brightened instantly. "I've been thinking about this very thing lately. My present job doesn't suit me too well, and teaching would give me a little speaking experience and six months of the year free."

"If you're interested and consider yourself qualified, with some good references to back you up, the job is yours. The pay will be adequate, and we'll provide the supplies, building, and heat."

Robert shook the hand of Cass Wilkerson and sealed the gentleman's agreement. He was riding back to Marion before the thought struck him: had he not been so quick to agree, the salary offered might have been higher. But he never had possessed a head for business. Maybe he possessed no ability as a teacher either, but with great enthusiasm he looked forward to trying.

CHAPTER VII

Robert kept his job at Tate's dry-goods store until the last of July, nearly a month after he had received a handwritten contract from Cass Wilkerson confirming his employment as a teacher. "For teaching during the period of October 1, 1842, until March 31, 1843, we the undersigned promise to pay Robert Sayers Sheffey at the rate of $30.00 per month, payable on the last Saturday of each month," the contract said in part. The new position would pay him almost double what he had received at Tate's. But had the pay been half as much it would have mattered little.

His resignation from Tate's two months before his new job began was not without purpose. During August and September he wished to carry his exhortations to some of the areas having revivals, and, more particularly, to extend his range of work to other counties—if time and opportunity allowed, into the fringes of Tennessee and Kentucky.

As he traveled from county to county and village to village, he wrote Lawrence of the joy of human fellowship among strangers. But they weren't really strangers he said in the letters, for the moment they all prayed or broke bread together, some impenetrable bond seemed to hold them fast. He spoke also of the mounting interest in the establishment of camp meeting grounds throughout the areas he traveled. The Methodists in particular were pushing this movement, and Robert told Lawrence how much the Methodists impressed him with their energy, piety, and zeal. They would be a good group to join, Robert opined, and what did Lawrence think of that?

By the middle of September, Robert returned to Marion. He looked as though he had been on the trail for months; his clothes were dirty and worn, and his horse seemed to rattle from three broken shoes that slapped annoyingly against her hooves.

James and Ellen showed only remote interest in his work and travels, he sensed, but he gave them a full accounting anyway. He told them of warmhearted, hospitable people whom he had met and with whom he had often stayed overnight, or, in some cases, several days. Sometimes they were people of wealth with plantation homes and acreage, but as often as not his host might be the owner of a one-room log cabin. In either case the household would hear his prayers and exhortations and sometimes be moved to join him at a nearby revival. There he would continue his work inside, outside, before and after services, or take his usual place on the back pew to watch for those who wavered back and forth in their decisions.

He had also slept out under the stars when the distance between villages was great and the landscape sparsely settled. His eyes shone when he told them that, for the experience was just like riding to the banks of the Holston again and drinking of the purity of nature. Now it was even better than that, for the scope of his purpose was enlarged and, it seemed at times, divinely defined.

He had little to pack as he prepared to leave Marion the third week of September. He had his clothes (which had been added to by Ellen when she contributed some oversized castoffs of her husband) and a few books. That was the sum total of his worth except for the forty dollars he had saved from his earnings at Tate's. All combined, they did not provide an excessive burden on the back of his animal as he headed for Cripple Creek in Wythe County, some thirty-five miles' distant.

He had no definite place to stay upon reaching Cripple Creek, and, since the creek ran the entire length of the county, he would need to orient himself.

He had little trouble locating Messrs. Gleaves and Wilkerson, since their Raven Cliff iron furnace was a hub of activity and of great local interest. The enterprise was only one of several like it along the sparkling waters of Cripple Creek, but, Robert learned, this firm boasted better than thirty years of successful existence.

Cass Wilkerson took charge of him once a tour of the iron furnace was concluded. "Your schoolroom isn't much," he said as they reined their horses to a stop in front of a combination stone-and-log building about twenty feet square.

"Looks like somebody started to build it out of creek rock and got tired or ran out of rock," Robert said.

"It was built by a German mining assayer. He used it for his tools and ore samples and once in a while for his company's workers to guzzle a little Saturday-night brandy."

"Looks substantial enough for a classroom," Robert said.

"Substantial it is, but it'll take work to put it in shape. They say that assayer never did trust the waters of Cripple Creek. That's the reason he built it half high out of rock."

"Can you offer any suggestions as to where I might find room and board?"

"I figured you'd ask that, and I found a couple of places. Neither one of them is very close to the building here, but I guess it won't hurt you to ride a ways. Most of the children have a good distance to come too."

Wilkerson then handed Robert a sheet of torn ledger with the names of two people on it and gave him instructions on how to find them. "Either place ought to be comfortable enough for you. The first one belongs to an old widow lady. She could use the money if you like the accommodations. Let me know when you get settled and we'll move all your supplies into the building. Might as well go ahead and put up the stove too."

They shook hands and Robert started to ride off. He wheeled his horse around, however, before Cass Wilkerson had moved.

"I used to know of a family of Sweckers—Wendell Swecker—living somewhere along Cripple Creek. Ever hear of them?"

"Can't say that I have. Of course they could live at either end of the creek. That's a long way."

Robert thanked him and said he'd find out about the family and it wasn't really important anyway.

Cass Wilkerson had described Bertha Kincannon as an "old widow lady," but when Robert found her, farther west along the creek, if she was a day over sixty, she carried her years well. When he walked into the yard of her well-kept brick house she was spreading black walnuts upon the ground for drying. Her movements were sprightly, but she tilted her spine excessively backward as if to unlatch a crick when she saw him approach her. He introduced himself and commented on the large size of the walnuts and her foresight in preserving some for cracking during the winter months.

"They *are* big ones. It's been a good growing year." She dislodged the hull from two or three of the walnuts with her foot. "The hull maggots don't seem to be doing such a good job of loosening up the hulls. Wonder why that is?"

He had no informed answer to this, but said, "Since they're so big and the hulls so thick, maybe the maggots need a little longer to cut through." She chuckled at the simplicity of his answer and her stout body shook. He liked the woman almost instantly. She was homely, with round pink cheeks and disheveled gray hair, but possessed warmth he could feel immediately.

"You would be the young man coming to teach?" Her blue eyes focused questioningly upon him. "Cass asked me if I'd be willing to board you."

"Yes. We will use the old stone building three or four miles down the creek. Looks like I might have two dozen students, according to Mr. Wilkerson."

"I know most of the families," she said. "One or two of those young'uns you could just as well do without."

"Well, I suppose there's no job without its own problems," he said.

"A lot of the foreigners that have come in here to work these ore mines are funny people. They don't think like you and me. Well, now, I guess you'd like to look at the room?"

"I'm sure it's nice," he said and followed her.

She turned around and faced him. "Don't be sure about nothin' until you've seen it for yourself," she said brusquely and wrinkled her gray, bushy eyebrows into a scowl.

She took him to an upstairs room that was spacious and had a large poster bed, a dresser, and a highboy. She stepped on the first step of the little ladder needed to climb onto the bed and brought her hand down with force on the feather tick. "Look at the size of that hole! Is that soft enough for you?"

He looked at the indentation and at the artistic patchwork quilt.

"Do you have a white counter pane for the bed?" he said. "I like a white counter pane."

She was stunned for a moment and, he feared, offended.

"You're the first man I ever saw that could even say the word, much less know what one was. You a nephew of the Marquis de Lafayette? Where'd you ever get used to a white counterpane on a bed?"

"My aunt Elizabeth, who raised me, she always kept my bed covered with a white counterpane and clean bed linen. She used to say you could tell what people were like just by looking at their beds."

She stared at him severely for a minute while fingering a wisp of her hair. "I don't suppose I'll ever meet your aunt Elizabeth, but I can tell you right now she's already made a peck of trouble for some woman if and when you ever get married. Why, a women would have her fingers rubbed raw on a scrub board keeping a white counterpane clean on a bed all the time."

He said nothing, now certain he had offended.

Finally, when her second oration had run down, she said, "Yes, I've got a white counterpane I'll put on the bed. Far be it from me to discourage our new schoolmaster from his rest if it takes a white counterpane to make content his slumber. I won't even raise the room-and-board price for doing it. Is ten dollars a month all right?"

He said it was and that he'd pay extra to have his washing done.

By the first school day in October he had scrubbed the cobwebs and dirt from the class room walls. Cass Wilkerson had more supplies than Robert had anticipated; a wagon load of handmade stools with short legs (milking stools, the children laughingly called them) arrived along with a hand-planed desk of thick walnut for himself. Next to be unloaded were the more commonplace items: slates and chalk and a few books.

About one thing Robert was ecstatic from the beginning: addressing his class of seven- to twelve-years-olds seemed so natural he could hardly believe the steadiness of his own voice.

Bertha Kincannon helped him to understand the phenomenon even better during the evening meals of those first few days. "When the nut sets in its own pod it fits well," she said philosophically. "You're doing what comes easy to you if you can just keep the false fears away of believing you can't do it."

Robert became accustomed to Bertha Kincannon quickly. She was like some lost member of the family whom he had overlooked all these years. Perhaps she was. Certainly she had every characteristic of those German and Dutch ancestors of his own, whose lives, fortunes, and temperament were well known to him.

By the middle of October he commented to Mrs. Kincannon that he felt now that he had the class under control and every student save one in the jug with the stopper plugged tight. The exception was a twelve-year-old girl who was a mystery to him—"To put it mildly," he said.

"And you don't have to tell me which one," Mrs. Kincannon said. "It has to be Wanda Lewinski. She's the daughter of one of those Polish families who came here to work in the furnaces and ore trenches. The child is either crazy or just plain mean– or maybe got a little witchery in her."

"If they haven't been in this country long, maybe she's just frightened."

"No, I don't think it's that. As I understand it the Lewinski's lived up north for fifteen years before they came here, and they speak English good. Some of these furnaces and ore fields are owned by northern capitalists, you know. Wythe County people weren't good enough for them. They wanted to send some of their own workers down. They say that Europeans who have worked in trench mines know more about them than anybody else, and claim they have a special knack for smelting and forging ore."

"If the child's mind is affected we can't keep her in the class. God bless her, but it would disrupt the other children. If it's meanness, maybe we can cure that."

They spoke no more of the child, but Bertha Kincannon promised to aid him by finding out all she could about the family. He forgot the matter for the time being, both because it was Saturday, and the days were still almost as hot as summer, and because he had other things on his mind. He first oriented himself a little better by determining the exact location of his place of lodging. Mrs. Kincannon told him they lived east of the community of Simmerman, near the junction of Thorn Creek and Cripple Creek.

"If you rode along Cripple Creek all day you wouldn't need a jug of brandy, you'd be drunk just following the twists and turns," she said.

"Somewhere along this creek there's a man called Wendell Swecker. He has a daughter named Elizabeth… I heard a long time ago she was getting married to a young man who works at one of the forges. Do you know of them?"

"Law, yes. I remember Wendell Swecker. He helped us haul ore back when my family had the old Bell-Kincannon ironworks. He was a young man then, but he was one of the quietest, most honest men I ever knew. He wasn't an educated man, but nobody was any harder a worker than he was."

"Which direction do they live along the creek?"

Bertha Kincannon eyed him suspiciously and grinned. "Are you hoping she is married or not married?"

"Oh, it's a sure thing she's married by now, but I just knew her and wondered where she lived."

Mrs. Kincannon changed her tone to one of seriousness because his own demeanor was one of stiff propriety now. "I don't know his family at all, but they moved on after working for us. The last I heard they lived near the community of Huddle way on down the creek. I don't know distances, but it's a half day's ride or better."

"I guess it's just curiosity. Of course I'll have to ride in that direction anyway someday soon. I told my brother James I'd ride down to Ivanhoe and give him a report on how our renter is taking care of our home place."

"You never mentioned you came from this section."

He told her his history and that he had been too young to remember when they had lived at Ivanhoe. She still eyed him suspiciously as if she thought he was concocting the trip to Ivanhoe.

Suddenly he wished he had found out about Elizabeth Swecker's father from somebody else.

The following Saturday the rising sun had barely winked a greeting across the mountain range before he was on his way eastward along the creek. A slight fog rose from the chill water of Cripple Creek, and in the stillness of early morning the lilting lap of the water rushing over rocks seemed magnified and especially melodious. It was the kind of quietness that should not be broken except by some sound more melodious still, he thought, but then he shattered the silence he himself had declared sacred. "Thank you, Lord, for water so pure and sunlight so bright and breaths of fog that fall at night." He had not meant to make a rhyme and he smiled in wonder at the way his praise came from his lips. He had not lowered his voice when speaking the first time, but he repeated the phrase louder a second time so that his voice would travel afar.

Men were already at work as he passed the Raven Cliff ironworks. The lot behind the furnace seemed covered with huge bowl-like objects, the identity and purpose of which he did not know. The power-furnishing waterwheel turned with a labored groan that he could hear long after the building had disappeared from sight. Soon he passed wagons coming and going, heavily laden with either bar iron or fresh ore.

Bertha Kincannon couldn't be disputed on one point. Cripple Creek was like a dying snake at sundown. It twisted in every direction, and the narrow dirt road followed the serpentine meanderings almost perfectly. When he approached what seemed to match Bertha Kincannon's description of Huddle he stopped his horse. While he waited for someone to come along and confirm his assumptions, he pulled cheesecloth from his saddlebag, unwrapped it, and began eating a meat biscuit. He consumed the rest of his meal and, still seeing no one, proceeded to crack some of the black walnuts lying in the road and dehulled by churning wagon wheels or plodding hooves.

By the time a rider came by, the road lay littered with cracked nuts and Robert's hands were colored the rusty stain of the walnut hulls. He had gone too far east, he was told by the rider, if it was

Wendell Swecker's house he wanted. He could not understand the hare lipped man well and he listened carefully to the man's complicated directions on how to leave the main road and find the right hollow.

"Do you know his daughter, Elizabeth? Do she and her husband live nearby?" Robert asked.

"I don't know no women. I ain't hardly the kind of feller they'd be a-botherin'."

When he found Wendell Swecker's house he rode on by it. Near to the house two men and three women worked in a corn field, loading pumpkins onto a one-horse sled. Robert craned his neck as the landscape passed all too quickly. The younger of the two men must be Elizabeth's husband, he thought. They hadn't even looked toward him, none of them. Any other time his horse would have whinnied at the sight of strangers and the proximity to other animals. He should have pitched a small stone at the house or barn roof, he thought. The noise would only have sounded like a falling walnut or broken tree limb, but they would have looked up and faced the direction of the sound.

He had hardly gotten out of sight of the house when he turned around to make another pass He could just stop at the house and inquire of the best route to Ivanhoe... make the occasion so natural it would look accidental—but then an explanation would be needed as to why he was off the main road, and he could not lie. All the people came into view again and he thought that he recognized Elizabeth, for one of the women had long black hair falling nearly to the waist. Then and there he knew once and for all that he had to see Elizabeth Swecker one more time.

He dismounted in front of the log house and hitched his horse to a small ash tree. Chickens and geese scattered to the right and left of him, noisily announcing his presence. Presently a lanky, slightly stooped man came toward him from out of the field. Robert extended his hand and had it grasped by a large calloused hand on which prominent blood vessels seemed to stand up in little ridges.

Equally prominent were blood vessels running up the neck, and the man's brown eyes were bulging but congenial.

"I'm Robert Sheffey and I was just passing through—" He stopped, unable to tell it all.

"Obliged to meetcha."

"Would you be Elizabeth Swecker's father? I was just passing by and I knew her… and I wanted to pass the time of day… "

"Elizabeth's my girl. She and her sisters and brother is workin' in the pumpkin patch. You want me to get her, er' you comin' on to the patch?"

"I'd be obliged if you'd ask her if I might speak to her a moment."

He waited, shifting his weight first from one foot, then to the other, and hoping his shaking knees did not show. Did he dare assume she had not married? He watched each end of the long house; it looked as if each room had been laid end to end rather than placed one behind the other, foursquare. She appeared around the right end of the house, and her approach slowed when she saw him. Then she stopped altogether.

"It's me, Elizabeth. Robert Sheffey."

She continued toward him then until they were face to face. Her hair, almost as blue-black as a crow's wing and shining in like manner, hung down to the small of her back. She had not changed, except that the indelible caress of her eyes penetrated him even more deeply than before, if that was possible. Still, there was a distinct sadness about them.

"Elizabeth, I told your father I was just passing through, and part of that is true, but I remembered you and wanted to see you again." He thought he might as well get it all out at one time and added, "I understand you got married to one of the furnace workers. Are you living here at your father's place?"

She covered her hand and ring finger quickly, instinctively.

But then she uncovered it, for the question had already been answered.

"We—we didn't get married," she said, voice cracking.

"I understood you *were*," he said stupidly, instead of, "I'm sorry," or, "I'm glad," or, "There's plenty of time for a thing like that…"

"No, we didn't. I thought we were but we didn't—he's gone away from here now."

Now his heart jumped with glee, but he dare not show it overtly. "Elizabeth, I thought about you a whole lot after that first day we walked to the town spring. I wondered what happened to you. I didn't forget you."

"For a while I recollected being with you too."

"Did your kin from Washington County tell you I came out to see you?"

"No, they never wrote nothing about it. It pleasures me that you thought about doing it ."

"I would have ridden down here except"—he fingered his chin, rough now with red-blond stubble—"except I ran away from home and afterward went to college and…heard you were marrying."

"Won't you come in and sit a spell?" she asked when he allowed the silence to persist.

"Won't your father be expecting you back in the pumpkin patch?"

"He won't growl none if we just sit and talk a short while. Papa don't think much of a feller trying to make a mash on the weekdays, though."

They talked in the parlor for the better part of an hour and it was agreed that he would stop on the following day on his way back from Ivanhoe and have Sunday dinner. He left Wendell Swecker's house and unhitched his horse. Twice his foot missed its aim into the stirrup, but finally he was mounted and on his way to Ivanhoe. The rhythm of the horse's trotting hooves and the palpitation of his own heart were beating in near perfect time.

When he sat at Wendell Swecker's table on the following day his skittishness had subsided to a feeling of well-being. Wendell Swecker said a long thanksgiving, and his soft-spoken wife, Rebecca, served their guest with grace, as was the household custom.

"Did you find everything at your farm in good shape? I didn't make no connection with who you was till Elizabeth straightened me out," Wendell Swecker said.

"Everything looks well-kept to me, and I enjoyed staying the night. My brother just wanted me to take a look around. That was our home place. My father was Henry Sheffey. Ever hear of him around here?"

"I never knowed him, personal-like. I knowed *of* him, and your uncle Daniel too. They used to tell that your uncle Daniel walked down the valley of Virginia from Baltimore with a cobbler's kit on his back. They tell me he was one of the smartest fellers ever hit this country and that what he didn't know he learnt in a hurry."

"That story has been passed down in the family," Robert said.

"He cobbled shoes and studied for a while and then apprenticed hisself to a lawyer, didn't he?"

"Yes, sir. Alexander Smyth—the one Smyth County was named for. He left this section after a few years of law practice and went to Augusta County, Virginia. That's where two of my brothers went to live—with him. The other three of us went to live in Abingdon with our mother's brother. Uncle Daniel served in the House of Representatives, but I can hardly remember it. He died when I was ten years old."

"Your pa married again, didn't he—after your mother died?" Rebecca Swecker asked.

"Yes, he married Sena Nuckolls, and then he died after his son by her—Ezra—was born. That's when we were all split up. My stepmother married again to a man both of you might know, by the name of Joshua Jackson. Ever hear of him?"

"I know of him, but seems to me they left this section of the county," Wendell Swecker said. "Well, you're gettin' pretty close to home agin after all. Goin' to farmin' agin?"

"Robert is teaching school down a ways from Simmerman," Elizabeth said.

"Well, it's gettin' thick-settled up there now. You ought to have a big school," Wendell Swecker said.

"No, it isn't large. They have a school at Speedwell and they've got one at Fogle furnace. Mine is sort of in between, and it's too far for the children to go either way to the other schools. Why, some of my students walk or ride six or eight miles."

Elizabeth's sister Leah had been quiet, listening, but she smiled at him then and said, "Are you ready to hire an old maid for a helper? I can't get no teaching job around here, or nothing else."

Robert was almost embarrassed to say he needed no help. Because of the distance he didn't think she was serious, unless she anticipated boarding away from home.

Elizabeth's other sister, Sarah, and brother, Ben, laughingly told Leah that they had her employment problems all taken care of if she'd just marry a certain neighborhood farmer of the area who was quite wealthy.

"Maybe bein' a rich man's darling wouldn't be so bad if the man was under seventy," Leah said. But this one wasn't, Robert found out, and he joined in the family joke.

After they had eaten he walked with Elizabeth to the spring at the side of the house. It was an abundant and unusual spring for he could see hundreds of rising bubbles seemingly popping from the sandy bottom, then rising upward to the surface and bursting.

"It's the strangest thing I ever saw!" Robert exclaimed.

"Nobody knows what causes it," Elizabeth said. "There's been dozens of people come to look at it. That German assayer who used to run all up and down Cripple Creek said it was some kind of strong air down under the ground trying to get out."

Robert looked up at the sun and knew that it would be after dark before he got back to Bertha Kincannon's, but he couldn't tear himself away.

"You'd better be gettin' along," Elizabeth said. "You don't know this section yet, and you could get lost after night."

"It's pretty country, and I'd like to see more of it. What I'm really saying is that I want to see *you* some more."

"I thank you, Robert, but I don't expect that will do."

"Don't your folks approve of somebody who doesn't live in the neighborhood?"

"I'm over the age of needin' to ask Mamma or Papa about things like that."

Suddenly he felt foolish for saying what he had. "I just meant I didn't understand why I can't call anymore."

"It just won't do. Not for now, anyway," she repeated.

Riding off with a heavy heart, Robert tried to recall if he had said or done anything that could possibly have angered Elizabeth Swecker. He could think of nothing—except that it was easy enough to tell that Elizabeth's brother Ben did not show a genuine friendliness toward him. Maybe he, Robert, had pressed her too much about having heard that she was married. No, it wasn't that, for then she wouldn't have asked him to Sunday dinner. Maybe the age difference worried her. Maybe seeing him reminded her of the other man who wouldn't go through with their marriage. But that would be foolish. She wouldn't judge him by another man. No answer made any sense to him, and he was still thinking about it when he unsaddled his horse in the moonlight outside Bertha Kincannon's barn.

The following week, and still another, Robert knew that if he had done any teaching at all he had done it subconsciously, instinctively. He saw visions of Elizabeth Swecker dancing angel-like on his desk during the day, and she was the unseen table guest when he dined with Bertha Kincannon at night.

He suspected that Mrs. Kincannon recognized the signs of his melancholy, although he hadn't told her all the complications. Nevertheless, when he felt his spirit ebb, she would make little attempts to cheer him up or change the pattern of his thinking.

"Robert, some of the older folks I've talked to sure are pleased with the good work you're doing with the young'uns. If it's not just bragging parents you must have some real little scholars in your school."

"All of them are smart enough except for two or three. Cass Wilkerson's oldest boy will make a fine lawyer one of these days—you wait and see."

"Has there been any change in the Lewinski girl?"

"No. She's getting worse, if anything. She's always disrupting the class, looking for things. Her little brother shows the same signs, but not as bad. The girl just won't mind, and she's jerky and nervous and does the craziest things for no good reason. And you never know when she's going to do them."

"I promised you I'd find out more about the family and I haven't done it. Give me a week. I'll get out while the weather is still pretty," Bertha Kincannon said.

In the middle of the week, when he had dismissed the students for the day, Robert sat down and wrote a letter to Elizabeth. He didn't ask to see her—he'd go slow on that—but he felt that if he wrote occasionally and told her of his work and problems he might get a reply and some feeling of unity between them. He wrote of Bertha Kincannon's fine home and how her ancestors had hand-molded and fire-kilned the red clay bricks used for the building. He wrote of Cass Wilkerson and what a fine businessman he was and how much he was helping the Cripple Creek valley to grow, with new jobs and new products for shipment elsewhere. He wrote of Wanda Lewinski—at the very moment when the child burst back into the classroom, weeping and knocking over the stools.

"What is it?" Robert rose quickly from behind his desk.

The child ran from one side of the room to the other, upturning books on the tables and shattering slates in her frantic search.

"What is it, child?" Robert demanded.

"I've got to find my caul! I can't find it nowhere! I'll die if I don't find it!"

"I don't understand, child," Robert said. "Is it something you lost during class today?"

"It's my caul. Don't you understand? Mamma said I would die if I didn't find it!"

He began to help her look, not knowing at all what they were searching for. While he helped her she calmed down, and her frantic babbling subsided to a barely audible whimper. He placed his arm around her shoulder. "Wanda, child, what is it? I want to help you, but I don't understand."

"It don't matter none. I'll find it one of these days. I'm agoin' home now," she said with a slightly Slavic accent mixed with the mountain dialect.

That night he told Bertha Kincannon what had happened. "It's the worst she's ever acted," Robert said. "And what is a caul, anyway?"

"I can see you've never met any midwives. A caul is a baby's skullcap or head covering at birth. In some places when a baby is born the midwife, or sometimes even the mother, will sell this caul. It is supposed to bring luck and protection. Many sailors buy them in the seaport cities of the world as protection against drowning."

Robert was a little embarrassed, but he was too deep into the subject to drop it now. "You mean it's a part of the afterbirth?"

"Yes, but all is cut away except that portion which covered the infant's head. It dries out like the shed skin of a snake and I suppose the owner carries it around his neck or attaches it to his body in some way."

"Well, they didn't teach us that at Emory and Henry."

"You have learned something today." Bertha Kincannon smiled. "I have heard that the caul of a princess or the offspring of a very important person brings an exceedingly high price. And it's passed down from one generation to another. It is one possession that traditionally is never taken from the owner by murder or theft. To do so destroys its good-luck powers for an unworthy owner."

"Now I know what a caul is, but why would a twelve-year old child search for her own?"

"Maybe I can cast some light on that. I told you I would do some checking around. I did. I talked to a woman who lived near the Lewinski family when they first came here and lived on Gleaves Knob. Mrs. Lewinski was crazy then, and I guess she's still crazy."

"You think she puts all these ideas in her children's heads and they don't know she's not right?"

"I'm thinking they know that *something* is not right, but they don't know her good times from her bad ones. They've lived with it too long."

"Yes, that *would* explain it," Robert said.

"If we ever find out the truth, I'll wager Mrs. Lewinski sold her child's caul and now in her twisted mind she has convinced the girl that if she doesn't find it she will die."

Robert pondered her statement without saying anything.

"It wouldn't be hard to believe if we remember that the child has probably heard her mother's ravings since she was very small."

"Yes, I guess it would work that way, "he said. "Now, what to do about it is the next question."

"My guess is you'll have to take her out of school. I know you'll want to talk to Cass about it first. There's not much else to do if the child keeps the others from learning and upsets them."

When he mentioned the incident and Bertha Kincannon's findings about the Lewinski family to Cass Wilkerson, the latter said, "Our sons have been telling us about the Lewinski children. Stanislaw Lewinski doesn't work for us, but I know him. I've heard talk that there was some family trouble there, but since they moved farther up on the mountain I haven't heard any more about it. I suppose as long as Mrs. Lewinski stays away from people they make out all right."

"Yes, I suppose so," Robert said. "Except for the children, that is."

"Do you think we ought to take the Lewinskis out of school?"

"I've had it on my mind a lot, and I wish we didn't have to. I've got an idea, but I want to reread some of the notes I took at college. A visiting professor from London talked to us once about a case like this. I'll tell you more when I study a little."

"I hope you can handle it. I must say you've been doing a fine job here, Robert. The children think you're somewhat peculiar in your ways, but they're learning, and that's the important thing."

"Thank you."

"I regret I haven't been able to help you more, but as you can tell, I've had my hands full. See? We've got the lot full of salt kettles and now we're spilling over into the meadow."

"So they're cauldrons. I wondered what they were."

"Yep, most of these go to Saltville. There's an awful lot of people using an awful lot of salt, that's all I've got to say."

"The country is growing," Robert agreed, "and if we ever get the railroad we'll really see something."

"The railroad won't get here until we break the backs of those capitalists promoting the canals. Canals may be fine for Lynchburg and Richmond, but I'd like to see a canal boat coming down New River, and it fast flowing north!"

Robert agreed with him, for Lawrence had mailed an Abingdon paper and it had said the very same thing.

"Well, at any rate, when the railroad does come we'll be selling more plow points, nails, and bridge spikes...Let me know what you decide about the other."

The notes Robert searched for were those taken during a lecture given early in the first college term. Recorded were certain theories of British philosophers pertaining to the human mind. The visiting professor had expounded on this, saying how easily a child could be either properly guided or corrupted by philosophies or specific suggestions repeated over and over again. This influence in the home, most times innocent and natural, was what made people as they were. The danger, according to the professor, lay in the fact that a wrongful suggestion could be as impressive if repeated continuously as a right one. The cure for such a misguided person was either to drive the false learning from his mind completely or to cause him to question the truth of his learning each time the occasion arose to use it or think about it. In serious cases, just telling a person that his learning was based on a lie and potentially harmful would not have much effect, the professor had explained. The will had to be broken and the mind subjected to self-examination.

Now Robert had the idea for dealing with his classroom problem with Wanda Lewinski, but a practical means of execution was another matter. He outlined his plans to Bertha Kincannon at supper one night and solicited her aid.

"Of course I'll help, but I want to know if it's all right with the child's father. Have you talked it over with Cass, and does *he* approve?"

"I discussed it with Cass first. He spoke to Mr. Lewinski and Mr. Lewinski told him that the business about the caul was only one of the crazy notions the girl's mother was putting into the child's head."

"Cass said to go ahead then?"

"Yes, he said that as long as we didn't hurt the child, he and the child's father were willing to try anything. Cass doesn't have much faith in the method, but he knows we've got to do *something*—or make her leave school."

"People will think we're plumb crazy when they hear about it."

Robert couldn't sleep during the early hours of the night, and he lit the lamp by his bed and wrote a long letter to Elizabeth. Again he did not ask to see her but tried hard in his writing to achieve a sense of needing and longing for her. As a final touch he pen-sketched at the bottom of the paper a drawing of the rising sun coming anew upon the Cripple Creek valley. In the foreground a young man and woman walked across Cripple Creek on a foot log and the man held the woman's hand so she would not fall. The young woman had hair falling to her waist. He drew his pen back and forth across her hair until the blackness penetrated the paper.

During the week that followed, Wanda Lewinski seemed to suffer from melancholy but there were no outbreaks of temper or destructiveness. When the school day was over on Friday, Robert pulled the girl into the saddle behind him and took her toward the home of Bertha Kincannon, as they had previously planned. The child had been told earlier in the week that she would be staying with Bertha Kincannon, so it was not lack of preparedness which caused her to tremble in the saddle behind him. Comfortingly he spoke to her as they rode along.

"You'll like staying with Mrs. Kincannon. She is nice and has pretty things. On Monday after school I'll take you home and tell your papa what a good time you had."

That night Bertha Kincannon fixed a meal with all the trimmings. The child gnawed hungrily at the leg of the rooster and handled the English silver of her hostess with both visible wonder and care.

Later in the evening, when all of them sat in the parlor, Robert began the approach he had both agonized and prayed over.

"Wanda, Mrs. Kincannon and I asked you to stay here this weekend so we could help you. Do you believe that?" he asked.

The child rubbed her hands together in her lap and nodded slightly.

"I believe in some ways you have adult understanding, Wanda. In other ways you are still a very small child. Do you really believe you must find your caul?" Robert asked.

"Mamma says I gotta find it or I'll die," Wanda said, trembling.

"Your mamma loves you, child, but she is sick," Bertha Kincannon said.

"She's good as anybody!" the child blurted angrily.

"Of course she is," Robert agreed. "She's just sick, and she can't help that. She's sick like other people when they run a fever or get sick to their stomachs."

"We have no way to help her, but maybe we can help *you*," Bertha Kincannon said.

"What you goin' do to me? You ain't goin' to hurt me!"

"No, child. We wouldn't hurt you for anything. You must believe that," Bertha Kincannon said and rose from her chair to put her arm around Wanda's shoulders.

"The only thing we want to do is help you forget about the caul. If you can't forget it you must learn that it isn't important any longer and that some of the things your mother says, you needn't listen to," Robert said.

"Papa's been telling that to us lately, but we ain't sure about believin' him. Mamma says she can see things other people can't see. She tells me and my brother's scary stories all the time and they's so real the hair on my neck stands up."

"But you must learn the true stories from the made-up ones," Robert admonished. "You must forget about finding the caul. You simply must. If you don't you will get sick like your mother, and you might cause your brothers to become sick also. You will need to help them after we help you."

"I believe Mamma. She ain't never done nothin' bad to me. Papa screams at her and says things about Mamma that I don't think are right."

"It's not good for your papa to scream at your mamma, but he doesn't know how to help her and maybe he's scared you will become like her," Bertha Kincannon said.

"He shouldn't ought to scream at her," Wanda said.

"No, he shouldn't," Robert agreed, "but that's why you must understand that your mamma is sick and help her and your little brothers."

"Mamma ain't sick. If anybody is sick it's Papa what's sick."

"No, child," Bertha Kincannon said.

"Wanda, you are going to stay here with Mrs. Kincannon and me tonight, and tomorrow, and Sunday. When I take you back to school on Monday I want you to be changed in two ways. I want you to believe that your mother is sick and that you will not die if you don't ever find your caul. In fact let's get that straight right now. You will never find it. It can't be found," Robert said.

Wanda started to whimper, and then tears rolled down her cheeks until soft sobs echoed throughout the room. Both Robert and Bertha Kincannon pulled their chairs closer to Wanda, that she might feel their nearness.

"I love Mamma. I love Mamma so!" the girl cried.

"We know you do," Robert said, "and that is a good thing. She is lucky to have a fine daughter like you, and she needs a strong healthy girl to help her."

"But Mamma ain't sick or she couldn't love us," Wanda argued.

"She is both well and sick at the same time." Bertha Kincannon tried a new approach. "She can be well in part of her mind and sick in the other parts. Can you understand that, child?"

"I don't believe you. You-all don't like my mamma, and Mr. Sheffey fussed at me when I was lookin' under things for my caul."

"I didn't want you to be looking for something that wasn't there, Wanda. It upsets you, and your behavior upsets the class. We must find a way to help you or you will need to be dismissed from the school."

"No! I don't want to leave!" Wanda rose from the chair in protest. "I like it better than anything a-tall."

Bertha Kincannon seated the child gently and cast a look of desperation toward Robert.

Robert heaved a sigh and began again. "Wanda, for whatever length of time it takes, you are going to change your mind. Mrs. Kincannon and I will stay by your side all night and all of tomorrow, and all of tomorrow night if it takes that long, to make you understand what we are trying to reveal to you."

The child stiffened then. Her posture was not one of fear but of defiance. Robert looked deep into her eyes and saw there a determination to hold her ground and, if necessary, to fight for it.

Alternately he and Bertha Kincannon repeated the same statements to the child: *Your mother is sick. You need not look for your caul. You will never find it and you will not die.*

Even well into the night Wanda showed no signs of fatigue, but Robert's bones seemed to ache from the mental and physical effort he was putting forth. Bertha Kincannon yawned but kept up her efforts to bombard the child verbally.

A rooster crowed in the barnyard before Wanda showed signs of tiring. Then she yawned and her eyelids drooped like weighted objects. Bertha Kincannon walked tiredly to the kitchen and brought back a dish of cold water and a rag with which she bathed the child's face. Then it was like starting all over again.

"Mamma ain't sick. She's weller than you and me. If I don't find my caul I'm a-gonna die."

"No, child. You must believe your mamma is sick. You can never find your caul," Robert pleaded softly but wearily.

Full daylight came and Robert's stomach was stinging from hunger and thirst. He could see the fatigue in Bertha Kincannon's face. Only the child seemed vigilant, as if sustained by some hidden power.

They would not give up, and they would not eat. They must win this battle, Robert thought. They must win, for if they lost now there would not be another chance and there was too much at stake to call retreat.

In an hour he felt the strength of a second wind. Bertha Kincannon had bathed her own face with the wet cloth and looked alert. Bertha Kincannon took her turn and repeated the same statements Robert had made in exactly the same way and in the same strength of voice.

Finally the child showed signs of tiring again. Strangely her fatigue had overtones of victory and not defeat. Robert motioned

Bertha to hand him the wet cloth and the dish it was kept in. He squeezed the cold water out of the rag until the bowl was nearly half full. Without warning he splashed the entire contents of the bowl onto the child's face. Even Bertha Kincannon jumped. Wanda sputtered but didn't cry. She had shown no signs of crying for several hours. Bertha handed Robert a towel, but he waved her away. All of them sat in silence; the child's face still dripping with water and her dress getting wetter and colder. Wanda looked at her clothes and then at Robert and back to Bertha and back to Robert again. As the child's glance moved from one of them to the other Robert could see cold fury in her face. Neither he nor Bertha uttered a sound as they watched the child. Like the moon moving from behind a cloud, they watched Wanda' s face change; the taut, angry lips and gritting teeth of fury became transformed into an expression of almost angelic sadness. Then the welled-up tears burst loose and she sprang from her chair and clung to Bertha Kincannon.

"Mamma is so sick—she's so sick!" the child wailed, and Bertha held her tighter. Robert found himself awkwardly patting the child's back and wiping his own tears.

They all had breakfast then, and mentioned no more the subject that had held them captive for over eight hours. Wanda ate heartily; then Bertha Kincannon put her to bed.

The child slept for the rest of the day and throughout the night. When Sunday came the three of them rode in Bertha's buggy to church at Simmerman. All day Robert and Bertha exchanged glances and smiles of elation at what was obvious to both of them: the heaviest part of a great burden had been lifted and with any luck at all the flower growing under the rock could now be drawn straight and upright toward the sun.

Throughout the school day on Monday, Wanda Lewinski sat in a daze, and Robert made no special demands of her. There were times during the day when he wanted to take the child in his arms and comfort her, but he knew he couldn't. He dismissed the students early and loaded the Lewinski children into Bertha's buggy, which he had borrowed for the day.

He had expected Stanislaw Lewinski's wife to be a wild, raving woman, big in body and excessively animated in movement. Instead he met a mousy woman, short in height and not quite plump. She was also younger than he expected her to be. Only greenish eyes that were not fully conscious of the present gave away her state of mind before her conversation confirmed with certainty an aloofness from reality.

Robert waited until Stanislaw Lewinski came home from work and gave him a detailed report on what he had done.

"I'm glad for you to tell her. Wanda my child, she wouldn't believe me," Mr. Lewinski said.

"Whether Wanda faces the truth or not is up to her—but she does *know* the truth now," Robert said.

"You must stay and eat at my table, Mr. Sheffey. We would have honor to have the teacher of our children. Mamma," he yelled across the yard, "set another plate for Mr. Sheffey!"

Robert sat on the porch of the cabin with Mr. Lewinski until Wanda came to fetch them both to the table. Stanislaw Lewinski looked upon his daughter with a new pride, Robert thought.

The child's father put his arm around her waist before they were seated at the table. "My Wanda is a good girl," he said. "She's a good girl, wouldn't you say, Mamma?"

Mrs. Lewinski looked toward her husband, but Robert could tell she made no sense of what her husband was trying to say.

"It no matter, Mamma, it is so good to have Wanda home again."

Finally the dull eyes of Wanda's mother focused half knowing upon them all and she said, "Lewinski, what you mean you want Wanda home? She's not been nowhere and she ain't goin' nowhere."

Wanda rose from the table and held her mother's face in her hands. "Oh, Mamma," she said, "you need me so much to look after you. I'm never goin' to leave you."

Robert had not come very far down the mountain before he climbed from the buggy and knelt upon the thick moss beneath the trees. He thanked God for the Lewinski family, asking in particular that little Wanda might be a further blessing to her parents, and expressing gratitude that he and Bertha Kincannon had been instruments of healing.

CHAPTER VIII

Every day thereafter Robert had to give Bertha Kincannon a full report on Wanda Lewinski. One day in mid-December he went through the usual routine.

"Well, she started to look under a pile of songbooks today but she stopped and didn't actually pick up one and turn it over. We grinned at each other, and that helped, I think. It's going to take some time yet. Something so well impressed upon the mind is not easily forgotten."

For once Bertha Kincannon made no comment and stood smiling at him. Suddenly she thrust an envelope in his hands. "I thought you might not go up to your room right away so I didn't put it on your dresser," she said.

He had never seen Elizabeth Swecker's handwriting before and could not have identified it except for the return address on the envelope.

"I think I'll go up to my room now," he said.

"I figured you would," she said. "Just don't forget your supper."

"It doesn't feel like there's *that* many pages in the letter."

Night came swiftly in December, and before long his room became too dark to read the letter over again for perhaps the fifth or sixth time. The lamp was lit, and he waited for the flame to brighten. He was disappointed that no word or phrase hinted of feelings of endearment toward him. And it was such a long letter with so many chances for undertones of affection. But what was lacking in warmth was more than compensated for by curiosity. Elizabeth wanted to know all about what had happened to Wanda Lewinski and more about Bertha Kincannon's house and what new things were being made at the Raven Cliff furnace.

Suddenly he looked on the bright side. It *was* a letter. It was communication. The skeleton of an idea formed in his mind then. He would give her the news in such slight doses and so unclearly that she would write often just to find out the missing details. And last he would add, "There is so much to tell you, but it's too long to write. I'll tell you when I see you." The thought of the teaser line so inspired him, and so sure was he that it would work, that he pulled a sheet of paper from his dresser and penned a reply to her letter immediately.

"I thought you weren't going to forget supper!" Bertha called from below.

Before he descended the stairs he reviewed his letter to Elizabeth one more time. Yes. It said what he wanted to say the way he wanted to say it. Before long she would want to see him. It would only be a matter of time.

Within the week he had not only a reply to his letter but an invitation to partake of roast goose and boiled chestnuts at the Swecker home on Christmas Day. Some mention was made of pumpkin pie (and did he remember she was loading pumpkins in the field the last time he saw her?) and games the Swecker family traditionally played at Christmas.

The letter was warm beyond his wildest dreams. He had planned to get Elizabeth a present for Christmas anyway, but now he would buy an even nicer one. Thinking upon the matter of finding just the right gift, he announced his decision to Bertha Kincannon at breakfast.

"I am going into Wytheville on Saturday. Cass has given me money to buy presents for the children. I think I'll buy Elizabeth a high-waisted pelisse dress. You think she would like that for a Christmas present?"

Bertha looked at him quizzically and, without smiling, said, "Robert, it might not be wise for you to give your Elizabeth clothing for Christmas."

"Why not? I'm very knowledgeable along the lines of dry goods. I've had employment in more than one dry-goods establishment."

"It has nothing to do with being able to pick good merchandise. It's just not proper for a young man to give clothing to a young lady."

Robert reddened and coughed a little and said in a low voice, "What shall I give her then?"

"I think some gloves or a chain necklace or some of the playing games she could enjoy during the winter months would please her."

He took her advice with some reluctance and bought all three of the items that she had suggested. On the return trip from Wytheville snow peppered the ground, but it did not stick to the unfrozen soil. Riding along, Robert tried to think of the Christmas program he had planned for the children but thoughts of Elizabeth occupied his mind. How pretty she would have looked in the high-waisted pelisse, with her black hair falling down the garment! In spite of what Bertha had said, he was sorry he hadn't bought the dress. He had even decided on the color of mouse-gray, and now his grandest plans would be unfulfilled and Elizabeth would not stand before the smoldering yule log and look beautiful for him in the dress he himself had selected. Perhaps she had no pretty clothes, and the thought of that saddened him all the more.

On Christmas morning he crawled from bed as silently as possible. Bertha Kincannon and all of the valley people still slept, he supposed, but he wanted to be on his way. There was only faint visibility and that would continue to be so for another two or three hours; but once his horse was on the road and headed in the right direction the animal would instinctively find her way.

He placed his gift for Bertha on the kitchen table and took in exchange several cold biscuits and a baked potato left from supper. Bertha would like the carving knife he had bought for her and would most probably reward him with a roasted goose or gobbler on which to demonstrate the new tool.

He saddled his horse by lantern light and led the animal through the barnyard gate and into the snow-covered main road. The snow was two days old, and a fine sleet that had covered it made an eerie crunching sound under the weight of animal hooves in the chill stillness of morning.

At the full rising of the sun his faithful horse had delivered him a third of the distance to Huddle and, more specifically, Elizabeth Swecker's house. The vision he saw while riding east was that same diamond-like glow of reflected sunlight on ice that he had seen at the gap of the Cumberlands. There the similarity ended, for the mountains now on each side of him were closer, seeming almost to crush him in their grip; Cripple Creek, shallow and narrow, had a unique melody on this morning as clear cold water flowed under ice until, crossing the rock ledges, it rippled merrily downstream. Snow-covered fields sloping down from the mountains looked mirror-like, except for the crisscross of animal tracks coming to water.

Robert sang a song as he rode, knowing there were no ears to offend—unless the horse should throw him from the saddle! He loved to sing, and after a while he sang the little ditty the children had taught him the first week of school:

"Going to Cripple Creek, going on the run,

Going to Cripple Creek to have some fun."

When he turned into the lane of Elizabeth's house there was a look only of silent desolation, but before he dismounted she came through the front door to meet him.

For lack of something better to say he cautioned her about getting her feet wet. They shook hands and Elizabeth smiled at him faintly. He did not let her hand go while his eyes searched her own. They were still sad eyes—movingly sad eyes—and she focused them on the icy ground.

"You must have started before sunrise."

"Yes, I did," Robert said. "I wanted to get here as quickly as I could."

"We would have saved some of the goose for you," she jested.

"I did not come to see the goose."

He joined the Swecker family at their sumptuously laden table soon after midday, but his appetite seemed to have deserted him.

"You're not doing much damage to the goose," Elizabeth's mother said.

"I guess that cold baked potato and biscuits I had for breakfast reduced my appetite," Robert said.

He dug into his sweet potato more vigorously then, but invariably his eyes would lift from his plate and level on those of Elizabeth's, directly across the table. It suddenly occurred to him how much he liked the way she chewed her food and held her fork in such a dainty, ladylike manner. How much Aunt Elizabeth would be impressed with Elizabeth's table manners, and the rigid sitting posture she maintained while eating. Half consciously he mimicked her posture and mannerisms, not mockingly but with a feeling of endearment. He steadied his gaze toward her down-tilted face until her gaze returned his own. The question had occurred to him many times before, but now it pressed down on him with a relentless demand: How could any man repudiate one so lovely, so bathed in sweetness that to behold her was like departing the world and abiding among the angels?

The Sweckers had not the gift of table conversation he was accustomed to, but he did not mind that. He had not come to see Wendell and Rebecca Swecker nor any of their offspring except Elizabeth. A stillness permeated most of the meal, and he missed the mirth and banter of previous Christmas dinners he had enjoyed. There were politely asked and answered questions, and an occasional jest from one of the girls, but not the merriment of volume and numbers he remembered from his holiday dinners at Colonel James White's house.

Presently the bent frame of Wendell Swecker rose from his chair. His son Ben, somewhat dwarfed by his father's height, did likewise.

"The livestock don't know nothing about Christmas," Wendell Swecker said. "I don't feed but once a day when the days get this short, but they're lookin' for it about now."

"I wonder if I might take my horse out to the barn and give him three or four ears of corn and some water?" Robert said.

"I think we can spare that much and not cheat the mice," Wendell Swecker said—more jokingly now that his stomach was full.

He followed Elizabeth's father and brother to the barn and fed his own animal while they trudged through the snow to break open a haystack in the distance and feed the livestock.

As he started back to the house he saw Elizabeth's face at the window. Breaking the crust of sleet, he balled up a fistful of the soft snow and threw it in her direction. He missed the window considerably, which was just as well, although he *thought* the snow too soft to break the glass.

Elizabeth, unsmiling, watched him until he rounded the corner of the house. He took a deep whiff of the smoke swirling upward from the house chimney and, reaching the porch, brushed the snow from his shoes. He took the Christmas gifts from his saddlebags lying on the porch and re-entered the house.

Elizabeth waited for him in the parlor, and from the kitchen he could hear a high-pitched voice as one of the sisters accompanied herself on the dulcimer. He listened to the slap of the goose quill on the strings for a moment, then said to Elizabeth, "Is it Leah or Sarah?"

"Leah does the playin'. Sarah is helping Mama with straight'nin' up the kitchen."

"You suppose we ought to help them?"

"No. Leah, she sits there on the hearth and plays for hours, and Mamma and Sarah gets the work done before they hardly know it."

Robert pulled the homemade chair closer to the parlor fireplace and warmed his hands before handing Elizabeth his gifts. She opened the smallest one first.

"What's this? I don't know what it is!"

"It's a game called dominoes. I'll show you how to play it after a while."

Then her face really came aglow when the small rectangular wooden box revealed a gold-colored chain necklace. "Oh, Robert, it's so pretty! But I don't have many places to wear it."

"Wait a minute. Here's something else that goes with it," he said and handed her the ivory-colored kidskin gloves. She hooked the necklace around her slender neck and he held the gloves so her hands could be inserted. She slid them in gracefully, but not before he could see the wear of summer sweat and winter's chapping cold. She wriggled her fingers in the gloves and looked first at them and then back to him. Her pretty face, devoid now of summer sunburn and looking scrubbed white, came aglow with surprise and pleasure. He felt his own heart would melt at seeing her enjoyment.

"Robert, you oughten to spend your wages on me like this. I'm much pleasured—I know you can tell—but I never gave you any reason to treat me so good."

"I just wanted to, Elizabeth. You're in my thoughts; I might as well tell you that."

"You ought not be lookin' at me, Robert. You're forgettin' I saw the house you lived in in Abingdon, and you've been to college. You ought to be sparkin' some of those high fashion Abingdon girls. I saw them in their straw bonnets and bombazine dresses, paradin' around, and the men couldn't keep their eyes away."

"I'd rather have you in a pair of dirty beaver cloth breeches than every girl in Washington County in the finest Italian silk."

"I can tell by lookin' at you that your talk is straight, and I'm obliged, but there's other considerations."

"What considerations?"

"A man wouldn't want a women another man spurned."

"That's not so, and what happened with you and he is past and done."

"It may be past but it's not done. The cut's too deep to stop bleedin' altogether."

He rested his hand on her own with some trepidation. "I'm sorry you've been brought to distress, but I hoped my caring for you might be a balm toward forgetting."

Her eyes welled up then, but she gave no sound of unhappiness. He kept his hand on her own until it appeared that she was lost in the depths of her own anguish. He gave her hand an affectionate squeeze and she looked back at him anew.

"If it hurts so bad, do you want to talk about it?" he asked.

"There's nothin' much to talk about. We were to be married last summer and before I knew it he was on his way out west."

"He just ran away without telling you goodbye or writing anything?"

"No, he did write me from Tennessee ... but he was gone by then. I wouldn't have stopped him if I could. He sounded as excited as a banty rooster."

"If he was more interested in adventure out west than getting married you're better off where you are."

"I'm tryin' to believe that, Robert. I'm tryin' so hard my teeth ache and my hands sweat—that's how hard I'm tryin'."

She told him that she did not want to talk of it further. He unpacked the dominoes then, and proceeded to show her how to play. She was caught up in the spirit of the game before long, and Sarah and Leah soon joined them. Leah continued her dulcimer playing from the parlor hearth and, at Robert's request, sang a holiday ballad he had loved since childhood. Sarah learned the intricacies of the game more quickly than Elizabeth, but by the time Wendell and Ben Swecker returned to the house all of them had the game of "block-and-draw" mastered.

When the evening meal was over and a once-fat goose lay devoured except for the carcass, Robert pulled the last remaining present from his saddlebag. Although it was intended for family use (and as a gift of appreciation to his host, in conformity with his aunt Elizabeth's training), he handed it to Wendell Swecker first.

"I don't know whether I know what it is or not," Wendell Swecker said.

"It's a checkerboard," Ben Swecker said.

"Now you can put away your old fox-and-goose game," Elizabeth's mother said.

The two men took to the game like excited children. They played by the firelight, aided by one additional lamp on the edge of their playing table. Robert and Elizabeth returned to their game of dominoes at the foot of a small cedar Christmas tree, decorated with homemade candles, strings of popcorn, and colorful Indian corn strung vertically from the top.

Leah stopped playing her dulcimer and asked to take on the winner at the checkerboard. Finally she had her chance and beat her brother three games in a row.

It was beginning to feel like a genuine Christmas now, Robert thought. Elizabeth's mother supplied them all with popcorn, and Wendell Swecker got down his fiddle and tuned up. His large hands dwarfed the neck of the instrument as he crouched over it, locking it firmly in his fist and forearm. He performed no Christmas music, but Robert liked his playing and liked seeing the man so absorbed that his soul seemed to be lifted and so oblivious to others in the room.

As the evening grew late the other members of the family deserted the parlor.

"I don't know when I've ever had a nicer Christmas, Elizabeth."

"Wouldn't you rather be back in Abingdon?"

"No, or I'd have been there."

"At least somebody might've had a Christmas present for you."

"That doesn't matter. You've made my Christmas all by yourself."

"Robert, I can't tell you what I'll be thinkin' about a month or two from now, but when a warm Sunday comes if you want to ride down you can go to church with me."

"I'd like to do that. I'd like to very much."

She told him it was bedtime and that they were keeping the household up. Sarah, who had been stationed out of hearing range but still in sight, was summoned, and she and Elizabeth showed Robert his sleeping place.

He ate sparsely at breakfast the next morning, for Elizabeth again sat directly across from him and she wore the necklace that he had given her. She had on a plaid linsey dress, and he thought surely that God had not made any woman more beautiful in the world. Her eyes sparkled a little through her natural demureness and once she fingered the necklace with one hand as she ate with the other.

Wendell Swecker left the table first and, without being asked, saddled Robert's horse and led her to the front gate. Robert puzzled a moment, not knowing whether the man was just being helpful or if he was telling him that his welcome for the time being was over and that it was departing time. When he stood with Elizabeth unduly long in the parlor, and noticing Ben through the window, holding the horse's bridle in his hands, he knew it was time to go. He shook hands with Elizabeth on the front steps and headed west, for Bertha Kincannon's house. He did not mind the chilling wind. The love in his heart seemed to surge violently throughout his being, and there was a very new form of warmth that he could feel, pounding, pounding away.

School did not get back to normal the first week in January. Absenteeism from sickness was widespread, and it was not until the first of February that each stool was occupied again. As the bitter cold and deepening snows of February descended upon them Robert sometimes felt at the point of tears for the smaller children. It was not rare to see youngsters so cold that they could neither cry nor unclench their hands when they came to him in the mornings. Whether they walked or came in a wagon it was the same. The older children sometimes rode a horse by themselves with a smaller brother or sister behind them, almost too cold to hold on. But they all wanted desperately to learn, and none of them made any harder effort now than Wanda Lewinski.

During the last week of February snow drifted so high that Robert had no alternative but to suspend school until a thaw came. He resented the inconvenience of nature as much as the children did, but for a different reason: he had been to see Elizabeth only once since Christmas, and on that occasion her little Methodist church had been so packed that Absalom Fisher took advantage of the opportunity and preached for nearly two hours. By the time the late dinner was over, he had to rush away to get home by nightfall.

He had wanted to tell her so many things that time, and now his feelings filled him to overflowing. They corresponded in the meanwhile, but the things he wished to say were deep things, and he did not want to write about them if he could explain them to her instead. He wanted to talk to her of his exhortation experiences and of his belief that he was gifted for work in this special way. He wanted to tell her of the places he had been and those places he still wanted to go, on behalf of Christian work, both after schools was over and in his future.

When March came he made up for the prohibitions of February. By the second week of March he had seen Elizabeth twice more. Bertha Kincannon accused him of having marriage plans before school was let out, but he sorrowfully told her that his progress with Elizabeth was slow and subject to changes of her mood.

After he had turned the children out to the call of spring and the many chores that awaited them during the planting season he collected his last wages and headed for Elizabeth's house. He was more than halfway there, having passed Gleaves Knob, when he saw a sight he had not seen in five years. Before he could recognize the man riding, or the man leading his horse, the tinkling of a sheep bell held in the hand of the Negro slave told Robert that his blind brother Daniel was making one of his occasional treks down the valley of Virginia from Staunton to visit his brothers.

Coming abreast of them, he and Randall, the slave, began having a backslapping contest until Daniel made an emphatic inquiry as to what was going on. Robert placed his hand on that of his brother.

"It's me, Daniel, Robert. Where did you come from? I didn't expect to see you this early in the spring—or this year, for that matter."

"Robert! By Jove, I thought I recognized your voice. It's good to see you—there I go saying that again. You know what I mean."

"It's good to see you too, Daniel. It still gets cold nights and some days yet. Why didn't you wait until a little later in the spring?"

"'Cause after I get all my visiting done I want Randall to lead my horse very slowly up the valley of Virginia and I want to smell every blooming thing from Abingdon to Staunton and stop at every wayside and make new friends."

"I'll do it too," Randall said obediently.

"But how did you find me?" Robert wondered.

"I wanted Randall to lead me by Ivanhoe, around the home place, before we went on to Abingdon. I was anxious to see if I could get a feel for our old home... maybe run my hands over the logs and stand in the kitchen where Mamma used to stand. Our renter told me you were at Simmerman. I hate to tell James when we get to Marion, but we're going to lose our renter. He's been thinking about it during the winter and he tells me he's not putting out any spring crops. He wants to be gone by the middle of April. He let us stay the night and said to tell you-all that there were no hard feelings and he'd try to help us find another renter."

"If we can't find one, I could put up there for the summer and maybe get out a corn crop. At least I could watch over the place and see that nothing happens," Robert said.

"I'll talk it over with James and see what he thinks. He might have somebody in mind already. Would you like to ride on to Marion with me?"

"No," Robert said. "I've got some last-minute chores to do, and some of the things in my classroom need storing until the fall session."

"Lawrence wrote me about your teaching. You planning to teach again at the same place?"

"I don't know. I've been offered teaching jobs several places. They want me back, but it depends on a lot of things."

The conversation lagged momentarily; indecision registered on Robert's face. "You can't make it to Marion today anyway, so why not spend the night with me? Mrs. Kincannon—she's my landlady—won't mind, and we can put Randall in the barn."

"Well, I thought you'd never mention it. No reason why we can't visit a while longer. Are we close to home? Where are you heading now?"

Robert told his brother and said that he would like to introduce Elizabeth to him. Daniel agreed, and since they were so close to her house: "It'd be a pity not to," he added.

Such a strange-looking entourage of visitors and the tinkling of the sheep bell Randall carried in his hand aroused the whole Swecker household. The four women stood out in the yard when the trio reined to a stop. Robert introduced them, and one by one, Leah, Sarah, and their mother drifted away. Elizabeth invited them in and took Daniel's other arm as they climbed the front steps. After reaching the porch, Daniel, free of their over-solicitous grasp, turned and called in the direction of Randall. "Water the horse good!"

"Yassir!" Randall shouted back.

"Do you want me to get some corn from the barn?" Elizabeth asked.

"No, I'll feed him when we get back to Robert's place. You are kind, and I thank you," Daniel said warmly.

Elizabeth kept her eyes on Daniel; she looked deep in thought. Suddenly, with no further discretion or hesitation, she said, "How long have you been blind?"

"I started going blind in my teens and everything went black by the time I was twenty-one."

She had a more deeply worried look then. "The doctors—they couldn't help you none?"

"They said I did most of it to myself."

"Daniel has always been the scholar in the family," Robert explained. "He studied himself blind."

"I guess I do have to take the blame," Daniel said. "I remember many a night I'd sneak out of bed and read or study by the firelight. Uncle Daniel never knew I was doing it until my eyesight started to fade."

"What a pity," Elizabeth said, with a tenderness Robert had never before heard her show.

"We reap what we sow." Daniel sighed resignedly.

"It's a shame you can't go on studying. I never had the chance myself, but I like people who learn a lot of things," Elizabeth said.

"But I *can* go on studying, and I *do*," Daniel said. "My brother Hugh—I guess Robert's told you about him—still helps me and reads to me sometimes. He's a Yale man and interested in politics. Oh, I get a lot of information from him and lots of others. There's still plenty to learn. Fact is, I learn something from everybody I meet, and that takes in a lot of people, when you consider the hotels, taverns, and stage stops."

"Tell me, what does it feel like to be blind?" Elizabeth inquired, child-like.

"Well, if you had never had vision I guess it would be different, but in my case it's an easy question to answer. Just close your eyes right now and pretend that they will never open again."

Elizabeth did so and held them closed until Robert felt that she would never relax her eyelids again. When she did, and raised her head, silent tears rolled down her cheeks. "I understand," she said in muted voice.

"It is well that you do." Daniel smiled. "Not for the sake of pity, but for the sake of learning. You see, you will never be the same again, for you have stepped outside of your skin and into that of another. You *cannot* ever be the same again. You cannot be the same again because you have seen further than you've ever seen before. Now you understand my adventures in learning as well."

Daniel and Elizabeth kept up a stream of steady conversation, and Robert sat back, feeling almost like an unwanted third party. Watching the two, he soon realized that what he saw was two people probing the souls of each other. And—he hadn't realized it until then—they were like two wounded souls seeking strength from one of like kind.

"Even in disappointment we should become wiser," Daniel was saying when Leah came into the room and reminded her sister that perhaps the guests would like to join them at dinner.

They all sat down to biscuits of crisp-fried side meat and buttermilk.

"You play *that thing* out there? I wasn't nosin' around or nothin', but I saw it when I took your darky his bread and milk," Wendell Swecker said to Daniel.

"The fiddle, you mean? Yes, I play it riding or walking, or on my lap and behind my neck. Everywhere I stop they ask me to play it."

Everybody but Daniel knows that Wendell Swecker was really saying that he wanted to show his own skill and play a duet with Daniel, Robert thought to himself.

"Would you play some for us?" Leah asked.

"Pass me another biscuit, please, and I'll be ready for a concert," Daniel said.

Daniel played and played until so many feet were keeping time that Robert felt that the porch roof might collapse. Finally Daniel asked Wendell Swecker to get his fiddle and join in.

They tuned up and, faintly, from another room, a dulcimer was tuning in with them. Never had such beautiful music come from the hollow. The whine of the crying strings seemed to glide to the very top of every hickory in the mountains and drift right back down again, only sweeter, traveling on with soothing sorrow or delicious joy, depending on which selections were played.

The spring days were longer now, but they still did not get back to Bertha Kincannon's house until after dark. They walked right in to find Bertha cleaning off the supper table, except for Robert's unused dish and silverware.

"Think you could fill three plates?" Robert said before he introduced his brother.

Bertha Kincannon looked at the eyes shielded by closed lids and then at Robert's hand still upon his brother's more muscular arm. "Sure I can," she said and helped to seat Daniel. Daniel's head of wavy chestnut hair seemed to tower a foot above Robert, even after they both were seated.

"It'd be no wonder if they called you the runt in the family if all your brothers are like this one," Bertha said jovially as she filled their plates as well as one for Randall in the kitchen.

"They do already—but none of them is any taller than Daniel. Nor any smarter, either," Robert added.

"Would I be guessing right that you two ran into each other down the road apiece?" Bertha asked while serving their dinner.

"Yes, Randall and I caught Robert on a romantic journey," Daniel said. "We went with him to do his courting, but I don't think we helped his cause any."

"You helped me too much," Robert said. "Elizabeth paid more attention to you than she did to me."

"What do you think of Robert's Elizabeth?" Bertha asked of Daniel.

"I sense she is very beautiful and full of grace. She has a fertile and inquiring mind too, I think. She's so extra sensitive, though, that Robert will need to be on guard for it."

"I haven't met the girl you know," Bertha said. "I keep hearing more and more about her, but Robert always stops a little short when he speaks of Elizabeth."

"She has the quietest way of picking your mind," Daniel said as an afterthought.

The more they talked about Elizabeth, the more Robert shuffled uncomfortably, and Bertha said, "I think we are making Robert uneasy. Perhaps we had better talk of other things. Tell us the news of the outside world."

"Where shall I begin? Would you like the unusual or the mundane first? I heard that the center chandelier in the hall of the House of Representatives fell to the floor. Somebody else told me that the Federal Party in central Ohio ended up with two-thousand-one-hundred-sixty-eight more votes than they had party members. A couple of days ago when we came by Fort Vause I heard the news about Benjamin Sharp's being thrown from his horse. His head went through the ice of the creek, and he drowned."

"We want to hear important news closer to home," Robert said, "not those tales traveling agents and tavern keepers are always telling you."

"Well, now, there's some hot action in the state legislature. Seems like a group of lawyers down there have sponsored a bill to take the important cases out of county courts and have them tried in superior courts. Uncle James would come out of his grave and fight that one if he could."

They all talked until a late hour, but by hazy daylight the household stirred, breakfast was eaten, and the tinkling of a sheep bell was heard through the mist as Randall and Daniel headed for Marion.

Within a week a letter arrived from James in Marion; he seemed upset about the family farm at Ivanhoe that was lying unrented. He had no tenant in mind and suggested to Robert that since he, Robert, was free during the summer he try to put out a corn crop and generally watch over the place. Tools, seed, supplies, and bedding would be coming down by freight wagon, James said.

By the last of April, Robert had survived his own cooking, nursed his blistered hands, and smiled with pride upon his tilled acreage now pregnant with seed. On top of it all he had a bonus to report to James. The man who had furnished the team and plowed the rich ground wanted to rent the farm. If James approved, the new man would take over the place in the summer when his own hay crop was harvested.

James quickly wrote back his approval of the plan provided that the prospective renter had a good reputation in the community and kept his own place well in order.

Robert tended the corn as it began to come through the ground, but this duty did not prevent him from resuming his travels and exhortations wherever he could find a listener. At first he worked the Cripple Creek valley. He did so for a variety of reasons. First, he felt that since there was a considerable influx of new people coming in to work in the various mines and iron furnaces his work would be especially fruitful. Second, he got to see Elizabeth more often in his comings and goings. He also wanted her to be aware of his Christian work. And third, the area was close enough to Ivanhoe that he could keep an eye on the farm and his corn crop and still have time to do the work he had long planned to accomplish.

Everything seemed to be going well, with one exception. At times he felt that Elizabeth and he were of one accord; at other times she indicated otherwise quite strongly. The fluctuation of her love gnawed at his peace savagely.

He was working in the corn field one day in the latter part of June when this problem began to plague him beyond endurance. He dropped his hoe on the ground, washed himself, changed clothes, and saddled his horse. He ate no dinner and did no worrying about the miles ahead, for the time could be used to devise the most important speech he had ever made in his life.

When his well-rehearsed proposal had been delivered in trembling tones, Elizabeth took her eyes from the floor, and he knew before a word was spoken that he had not won her.

"I don't wish to get married right now, Robert. You do me honor with your askin' but I'm not ready."

He traveled the miles back home, feeling hot and dazed from his effort and disappointment. He had not eaten all day and he was sick to his stomach. He had need of food, but on finally reaching the kitchen, before the first skillet was placed on the fire the events of the day overwhelmed him and he wept.

He did not go back to Elizabeth's house again, though many weeks ago (and before his proposal) she had asked him specifically to come on the Fourth of July, his birthday. The second week in July he received an unexpected and total surprise: a letter from Elizabeth saying, "I might be in the same notion you are. Come and see."

In his instantaneous joy he did not run to the distant pasture field for a horse but glided, half dazed, from the house onto the roadway and, half running, half walking, traversed the miles up Cripple Creek.

"Yes, I'll marry you, Robert. I changed my mind. If you'll look after me I'll be your wife," she said moments after he stood before her in the parlor.

He took both of her hands in his; then suddenly, as if the subject had never occurred to him before, he said, "I want to look after you better than anybody's ever done, but I don't have anything but what I've saved from last winter."

"It won't matter. We'll add onto that when we can and build our own place. I've already talked it over with Papa and we can live here for a while."

"We're not going to fudge on him for our room and board. I'll talk to James and maybe we can use the home place at Ivanhoe."

"I've been thinking about that, but I've got an even better idea. Why don't you and your brothers deed your shares of the home place to Daniel. Somebody's got to look after a blind man. Let him get the benefit of the rent money."

Robert considered a moment and said, "That'd be all right, but I always thought Uncle Daniel's estate would keep him comfortably."

"Even a blind man likes to think he's earning his own keep," Elizabeth offered. "Go ahead and rent it like you planned and give the money to Daniel. I'd be happy over that, and you and me could live with Papa a while yet."

"You're a good woman, Elizabeth. I'll agree for my portion and I think the others will too."

He headed home on a borrowed horse that night, but he could just as well have flown like a chicken hawk, so lofty were his senses. The woman he loved more dearly than he could tell anybody had not only agreed to be his wife but she had given up unselfishly what might have been her first home. No day could crown this day. Never again would all things be so much in harmony that the night bird sounded sweeter than ever under the moonlit sky and the bullfrogs had a lilt to their voices and the waters of Cripple Creek sang and sang to him as he rode along.

On July twenty-second Robert rode with his future father-in-law to Wytheville and executed the marriage bond.

Four days later Absalom Fisher stood in the parlor of Wendell Swecker's house and joined Robert and Elizabeth in holy matrimony.

At the wedding feast thereafter, Bertha Kincannon did not comment when Robert added vinegar to his watercress or when he scooped teaspoonful of sugar over his honey. Neither did she comment when he had his fourth helping of turkey breast, although he saw her eye him suspiciously.

Presently she came to him and said, "Robert, how could a man be thinking about his stomach when he has just got himself such a lovely bride?"

"Have you ever heard of anybody being happy on an empty stomach?"

She said no and asked him one final question. "You're not going to insist on a white counterpane for the bed?"

He nodded "yes" and they both laughed.

"Don't be too demanding and learn patience, Robert. And remember, 'A deaf husband and a blind wife are always a happy couple'."

Chapter IX

Shortly before Thanksgiving in 1844 Wendell Swecker's house resounded with the cries of Elizabeth Swecker Sheffey's first child. Robert had not been there for the birthing. It all happened so suddenly that by the time he was fetched from his new school, east of Huddle, Elizabeth lay smiling in her bed, her labor ended and the proud mother of a son.

After Robert looked at the infant he went out under the pear tree in the side yard and knelt and thanked God for his newborn boy. He stayed there until the cool fall ground had chilled his knees. When he returned to the house, the midwife was preparing to leave, but she asked to be informed of the child's name.

"I'd like to name him James Wesley," Robert said. "I want to honor my brother and Uncle James… and I'd like to think that God would let the little fellow be like John Wesley one of these days."

He looked at Elizabeth for approval. She agreed, and so it was.

Elizabeth was again heavy with child in the late spring of 1846.

"Robert, we've got to have room of our own after this one comes," she said one day early in June.

It was not a point he could argue with. Wendell Swecker had already added more space to his house, but it was still too small, especially since James Wesley had begun to walk.

That weekend Robert took Daniel with him to a revival in Grayson County, near the North Carolina state line. As they rode along, Daniel was playing his violin, and Robert held fast the lead line from his blind brother's horse. He asked his brother to stop playing for a minute.

"Daniel, Elizabeth and I have got to get a place of our own. There's going to be two babies soon and double the amount of chatter isn't going to sit well with the older folks... it unnerves them... and we *are* crowding them."

Daniel said that that sounded logical.

"What I'm thinking is this: Would you be willing to sell me a good lot of the acreage we all deeded to you? Would you just as soon have some money and land both as have nothing but land?"

Daniel fiddled a note or two playfully and said, "Sure, I'll do it. I always did think all of you were too good to me. You should have had a fifth of the farm anyway. The truth is I'd like to have a little money. You know I don't enjoy staying in one place very long, and I'm hankering to take another trip back up the Valley of Virginia. Randall would like that too—he's not so happy being hired out to my renter."

"What part would you be willing to sell?"

Daniel played a few more notes, and then said, "I'll sell you a hundred acres on the south west side. You always did like the creek, and you can build yourself a cabin there."

The bargain was made without stopping a horse. Robert went silent for a while, figuring how much of his savings from teaching would be left to start the cabin after paying Daniel the agreed price of seven hundred dollars for the land.

They rode on to Greenville to spend the night, and there ate the vittles and sweet honey of strangers. The next day, before the service started, Daniel played hymns on his violin while Robert wandered about the churchyard, talking to individuals and small groups of early arrivals about the lovingkindness of a great and good God. Perhaps the preacher would not thank him or even know about his work in advance of the service. One thing was certain, however—and it was the only reward needed—potential converts would fill the church pews a great deal warmer in spirit and more receptive in heart than if he, Robert Sheffey, had not walked among them.

He would sit in a back pew behind his adopted flock, and they would know that he observed their every mood. If someone looked in agony of mind he would kneel by his pew, or, if he had been ineffective, search that person out on the church lawn after the service. If his help was spurned, and if he knew that the pain of the would-be penitent was genuine, he was not adverse to following the man, whether he was on foot or horseback, from the church grounds, calling out his love and concern, praying aloud that the sinner act now, with courage, free of pride or fear of embarrassment.

During the remainder of the summer he continued his travels, but without Daniel, who had told his brother that he believed in the work but found it repetitious and tiring. Robert learned that Daniel enjoyed the variety of friendships and found the diversity he sought in the tavern as well as the church.

The first week in September he returned from a trip to Christiansburg in Montgomery County and found that Elizabeth had given birth to their second child, now nearly a week old. Again a brother was honored, and the boy child was named Hugh Trigg.

When she was up and well again, Elizabeth pleaded with him to forgo his travels and exhortations and stay at home for a while. "Papa has been more than good to us...but Robert...it's not up to him to feed your babies and provide our beds," she said.

Her remarks were not unexpected, for Robert too had noticed Wendell Swecker's manner lately. During the spring his father-in-law had cast hostile glances from the garden where he sweated alone; at other times his words were short, if not downright curt. But surely Elizabeth's father could see the importance of his, Robert's, Christian work.

"I guess I'll have to stay home and see if I can get some men lined up who're good with an adz. Maybe we can have a cabin ready by cold weather," he said, but reluctance showed in his manner as well as his voice.

"Robert, there's nothing wrong with lovin' all of God's children, but your own come first. Can't any man deny that," Elizabeth said.

When the school session started in October the new cabin, placed on a rolling bare spot of ground and in sight of Cripple Creek, was well under way. After school Robert customarily rode back to the home site and pitched in, doing whatever he could to help with the labor. So pleased was he with the rising cabin, and the setting of trees and jutting rocks surrounding it, that he would sometimes draw the scene in chalk for the schoolchildren to see. At other times he would pray about his new home in their morning devotionals. His prayers were long, and he could feel the children's uneasiness. But he knew that they got restless not so much from the length of the prayers as from the fact that he talked simply to God, as if He were perched upon the desk in the very room where all of them sat. He never smiled about it, but it was a little amusing to see the children lift their heads after his prayers and look around, frightened or suspiciously, as if they expected actually to see this Divine Being to whom Robert spoke so lovingly and with such familiarity.

"God is our friend to love and talk to as we talk to our mothers and fathers," he would say. "In fact He is our father – our loving father. Does anybody here not love his father?" he would ask. No child would raise his hand, and he would go on: "You see? You go to your own father and sit upon his knee because you love each other. God is like that, so there's no reason we shouldn't talk to Him as if he were our father—and right here in this room!"

Eight days before Christmas the Robert Sheffeys moved into the nearly completed cabin. Although Robert himself had worked after school hours to stuff the chink and daub between the logs, two rooms were still unfinished. The cabin had four rooms, a limestone fireplace, and a steeply arched roof that allowed for a very roomy garret.

Whatever joy of ownership had been lacking in the beginning quickly disappeared. Robert could see the fruit of his own labors, could remember the sweat he shed in notching the adz-hewn logs with concave and convex Vs so they would dovetail at the corners. He had helped make the shingles also, from short chunks of chestnut that were split into thin boards with a froe. His hands were still callused from gripping and driving the small wooden maul against the blade of the froe, time and time again, until he felt that the mound of thin boards was high enough to cover every house or cabin roof in Huddle.

Yet all the work he had done still comprised the smaller share. Felling the trees, snaking them out of the mountains with horses and log chains, and adz-hewing the logs until they were smooth and straight on two sides had been the biggest jobs of all.

When all the wages and material he had had to buy were added up, he was a hundred dollars in debt. Elizabeth was worried by the indebtedness. "There won't be much Christmas celebrated in this house," she said. "If it's not the wind blowing across our bed that keeps me awake, it's wonderin' how we'll make out if you go to debtors' prison."

"I'll talk to the Lord about it," Robert said. "I've got a hundred and eighty dollars coming for the final school term. That'll pay the debt and keep us this summer, the Lord willing."

By working diligently during the few warm days of late December and early January he was able to finish the chinking and daubing. On the final day it was so cold that the daub was like stale bread in his hands. His work would probably need to be repeated, for he had run out of horsehair, and the daub would probably crumble and fall out without the binding substance. If necessary he'd redo the work in the spring, but if it would keep the chill wind and drifting snow from their sleeping faces now, he wouldn't worry about it.

Cripple Creek flooded her banks when March came, but water three times as high would not endanger the cabin so securely perched on the knoll. During that period when Robert rode home from his school he would find Elizabeth standing in the front door, watching the swirling water wind past their house, rushing frantically for an outlet into New River.

"It is a cleansing of nature," he would say as he paused to watch a few moments with her. "The floods clean and nourish, and spring is not far behind. Praise God for all His blessings!"

During the last week of school Robert took all seventeen of his students for a Creekside walk so they might observe and appreciate the wonders of nature as he did. He found that many of them did so already, while still others seemed hardly aware of the beauties around them. The latter group complained of the foolishness of wandering about the meadows and stream—complained with more vigor than they would have dared use had not it been the last day of school.

Robert realized, too, that some of the malcontents would be backed up by their parents, who would be just as happy having the children at home, preparing the gardens for planting. Nevertheless, he tried to make the nature study interesting. During his walking lectures he told of the parts that melting snow and sunshine played in the growth of budding plants and leafing trees.

Once, as he stopped to make a point, he noticed that half his class was missing. Looking down Cripple Creek, he could observe several of the boys trying to make a dam by breaking off tree limbs and stacking them in the path of a tributary branch emptying into Cripple Creek.

"You musn't break the tree's limbs unless you intend to put them to good use!" Robert called sternly. "They are living things just like you and me. How would you like somebody to twist your arms off?"

Some of the children bowed their heads in shame, and others snickered. Robert did not chastise them further, but walked to the nearest tree and placed his arms about it. "I love the trees," he said. "God made them and breathed a special kind of life into them. If we tear away their limbs and strip them of their bark they will surely die and lose their very special voice of praise."

At last the children were gone until the following October and all Robert's supplies were packed away. First he would help Elizabeth prepare their garden and then he would be on his way to continue his exhortations. During the winter he had been told of the isolation of Burke's Garden, a growing frontier settlement far to the northwest, and of what a beautiful spot it was. He could think of no better place to proclaim God's loving kindness and perhaps to explore that vast domain even farther and follow the meanderings of Wolf Creek and then cross East River Mountain into territories he had never before seen.

As the day drew nearer for the planned departure Elizabeth seemed to grow sad. Part of the reason, he knew, was her knowledge that each year his trips were taking him farther and farther into the wilderness and longer and longer for him to return.

"When will you be back this time?" she asked when the first phase of the planting was done.

"Whenever the Lord's will might be. Don't you worry any, for our needs will be provided."

"Should I ask Papa to help me do the May planting in the garden?"

"No. I will be home by then, the Lord willing." He disappeared into another room and came back with their money box. He handed it to Elizabeth for counting.

"Our debts are paid, and there is seventy-six dollars left, if I counted it right. That ought to keep us until school starts again."

"I won't spend none of it if I don't have to," she assured him.

"I know you won't. You're a good wife, Elizabeth. Keep the money box well hidden, for there are all kinds of new people settling along the creek."

She cooked him a fine dinner that night, of salt-cured hog meat, fried potatoes, and hominy with corn bread and honey. He drank a second glass of buttermilk while she put the boys to an early bed. James Wesley, now three years old, protested with strong lungs, and Robert moved out of hearing range to the front steps. The night was warm for mid-April. Such a sense of peace prevailed that he found himself thinking sorrowfully of leaving this place where the wind whispered through the trees and God's creatures scampered playfully.

He was chastising himself for these selfish thoughts when Elizabeth came to him dressed in a clean flannel nightgown so long that her feet had become entangled in the hem as she walked. She sat beside him, tilting her head backward and giving it a quick shake to distribute the long hair falling down her back.

"Do you ever do any thinkin' about me when you're on your trips?" she asked.

"Yes," he said, and he stroked her silky hair from the crown to the end of the strands. There, the flannel felt good as a resting place for his hand. "Yes. Riding along I'm always thinking of you and the babies. I'm a little lonesome, but doing God's will is a lonesome task sometimes."

"Are you right sure you don't wish you' d never married me and was free to go and come when you please?"

"I haven't changed my first notion, Elizabeth."

She rested the weight of her body against him then and neither of them spoke as they listened to the sounds of spring nighttime. The stars were bright, a warm breeze whispered about them, and Cripple Creek tinkled a louder-than-usual melody.

At daylight she kissed him on the cheek before he climbed onto the saddle.

"But you're not takin' any of the money!" she called.

"The sweet Lord will provide for my every need," he said as his image faded into the hazy dawn.

His exhortations in Burke's Garden were not well received. He himself innocently jeopardized their effectiveness.

When he had topped Walker's Mountain and ridden farther north, until the vast flat, garden-like expanse of land could be entered from the most accessible side, on the east, he had not been prepared for the beauty he was to come upon: as he crested the mountain there lay before him a picturesque valley of fertile land framed by mountains thick with the largest trees he had ever seen. The grass was greener and the air seemingly more pure than in any place he had ever been. Flocks of birds both melodious and colorful flew playfully from ridge to ridge, their voices haunting in the stillness. He could not truly imagine what the Garden of Eden must have looked like, but here, he thought, was the nearest thing to it. He was so taken with this gem of nature set apart in the wilderness that he hitched his horse to a sourwood sapling and knelt upon a moss-covered flat rock to say a prayer. A man came up out of the valley on horseback and passed by him. So peaceful was his communion with the Creator of this beautiful garden of fertile earth that he prayed to keep on praying so that it would not be broken.

He had not finished when the solitary rider returned back down the mountain.

Finally, when he had straightened his stiff knees, mounted his horse, and reached the valley below, he found that he was being looked upon with suspicion. It had already been reported that a certain crazy man had been seen kneeling on the mountain, and it had been observed that his praying had lasted for over four hours.

"Are you a preacher?" Some of the more sympathetic extended the benefit of a doubt.

"No, not exactly," he had to reply.

He left Burke's Garden and an uneasy host before the week was out and followed Wolf Creek along the south side of East River Mountain for a full day's distance. The territory he reached was sparsely settled, and he anticipated the possibility of sleeping under the stars as the distance between houses and cabins grew farther and farther apart.

Wolf Creek began to grow wider and deeper, and he suspected that before he went many more miles the stream which he followed would empty into New River. He was debating whether to keep on his present course or cross East River Mountain to the more populated settlements he had heard about, when his horse gave a warning whinny. Out of the brush ahead of him an elderly man staggered into the road and fell. Robert dismounted and started to wipe the blood from the nose and mouth of the fallen man, who now wept quite openly. While he was yet kneeling over the wounded man a second man, young but husky, sprung out of the brush as if to attack his prey again.

"I whupped hell outta him. He thought he could cuff me around and I whupped hell outta him."

"Who is this man?" Robert asked.

"He's my pa. Look at him laying there, crying like a sucklin' kid. I reckon he won't be bossin' me around no more."

"How old are you, son?"

"What business is it of your'n? Who are you, anyhow?"

Robert told his name and repeated the question.

"I'm pretty nigh sixteen—big enough not to be bossed around! And it ain't your concern."

"Have you ever heard that daughters and sons should honor their fathers and mothers?" Robert asked.

The wounded man started to get up, but fell back, exhausted and bleeding. He was not too weak to talk, however, and his voice trembled with anger, but even more with shame.

"If I was ten years younger I'd wear a razor strop plumb out on your backsides!" he said.

The younger man kicked dirt into his father's face.

Robert restrained him.

"You wanta lose a little blood too—like the old man? You just give me half a reason and I'll whup hell outta both of you—"

The older man wept again and started to pull himself from the road by crawling and pulling at the brush.

"I'm going to help him home," Robert said, and started in the wounded man's direction.

"Leave him be," the younger man growled and jump in front of Robert.

"Then go get your mother—or your brothers and sisters."

"I ain't gettin' nobody! Look at him laying there, blubberin' like an ol' woman."

"He's not crying for himself. He's crying for you. Does it make you feel better to shame your own father? Can you go brag about beating up a man who must be sixty-five or seventy years old? You're a lot more pitiful sight than he is. I said I'm going to get him home. You do what you please."

The young man stood in his way, but Robert calmly stepped around him and helped the older man to his feet.

When they got to the cabin, a quarter-mile or more back in the woods, the occupation of the family became evident. In sight of the house a bold spring gushed out of the rocks, and wooden tubs encircled the spring. Robert guessed that they were not full and fermenting—corn harvest would not be until fall—but the smell of ripe mash and corn whiskey seemed to be coming from every tree.

He sat the man on the front porch of his house, and a scrawny woman half his age came and stood in the doorway.

"He's hurt. I brought him home," Robert said.

"Yeh, I know about it," she said, but made no effort to help her father-in-law.

Robert started to turn away, sure that he could not help further. Why couldn't he help further? The thought suddenly reversed itself. If *this* wasn't the time and place to offer his prayers and exhortations, then there was no right place. He didn't have his Bible—it was in his saddlebag down by the road—but he asked the man if he might pray with him.

"No, that wouldn't do," the man said. "You might get a knife stuck in your back if you was on your knees for a long minute."

Robert gave a quick but passionate prayer for the man and his family just the same. He did not close his eyes while doing it, however.

As he turned away, the wounded man called, "Much obliged," and added, "There's cabins, plenty of 'em, between here and New River. You'll be wantin' to spend the night someplace. It ain't fittin' here or I'd axe you."

When Robert went back down the footpath to the road his horse was gone. For a moment he was frightened, then angered. Either the youth had stolen the horse or he had struck the animal and she had galloped down the road.

With a prayer on his lips, Robert followed the horse's tracks as they wound down the valley, in and out, paralleling the meanderings of the creek. Finally, rounding a turn, he saw the animal, and she looked up, whinnied, and trotted to him.

It was now that time between sundown and darkness—and he had eaten no dinner. His eyes searched both right and left for a house. Daylight had almost given way completely when farther along Wolf Creek he came to a large cabin built partly of creek rock and finished with hewn cedar logs. It reminded him of his first school house, except that the workmanship here was better. He did not pause to consider whether or not he would be welcome. The mountain custom was that no traveler would be turned away if he appeared as an honorable man, especially if he was also hungry and tired.

Hound dogs started a mournful baying when Robert reined in at the front gate. A man of powerful build and flush of face, with a mop of white hair, greeted him with what Robert felt was an equal measure of gladness and suspicion.

Robert got to the point quickly. "Would there be room in your house for a servant of the Lord?"

"Indeed there would, laddie." He was answered in a Scot's brogue. "And have you traveled far?"

Robert told him of the distance but not of the happenings along the way.

"Tie your horse, laddie. We'll oat 'er later, but it's about you I'm thinkin'—you look as lean as my hounds."

Presently Robert stood in the kitchen, where he met his host's wife, sweating at the crane of the fireplace and poking a two-pronged fork periodically into a stewing hen. "You'll be eatin' a tough old hen. We're stewin' her the best we can, laddie, but she's puttin' up a fight," she said good-naturedly.

Before supper was ready Robert had learned Ellie McComb's name and that of her husband, Shed. He marveled at how much this man and his wife looked like brother and sister, for they had the same ruddy complexions and searching blue eyes, not to mention similar white hair and large-boned bodies.

He was about to pluck the stewing hen from the kettle when at last Ellie McCombs invited him to the table.

"Would the advocate of Providence care to thank his Master for this, I suspect, very tough stewing hen?" Shed asked.

Robert paused for a moment, and then said a very long prayer in spite of his hunger. He would not have stopped even then, for there was so much to be thankful for; his host, however, made uneasy sounds, sounds that ceased only when Robert's prayers ended.

When supper was over and his horse fed and turned out into the grazing lot Robert read a chapter from his Bible to his host and hostess.

"You read with the piety of a devout Presbyterian," Shed said.

'"Then I must have read much too slowly," Robert replied, and smiled a little.

"You would be Baptist, then?" Ellie McCombs said, in answer to his jest.

"No, I'm not a preacher exactly, and I'm not lined up with any denomination except by my own conscience. If I were to give you my likes, it'd be Methodist."

"It's a trifle of a shame, laddie," Shed McCombs said. "We're lookin' for a sermoner—within the faith o' course—and we haven't had one for eight months. Pity—raised a new meetin'-house and got nobody to christen it."

"And you helped build it too," Robert said.

"How'd you know that, laddie?"

"Your hands. The joints of your hands are big and your knuckles and skin are shiny. You have been gripping the plane and saw for a long time, and the resin of the pine and the oil of the walnut have polished your skin."

"You are right, laddie, and I made this house and the very bed you will sleep in too."

The talk continued even more congenially then, and Robert told the couple of his travels and exhortations and the experience he had had that very afternoon with the wounded man and his son.

"The old man is the only decent one o' the bunch. But he's out numbered ten to one a-countin' all the in-laws who hang around. His own laddies and lassies—children and stepchildren—mate each other; there's inbreeding on both sides o' the house. You and him both might as well give up on that clan. If they're not likkered up they're pickin' a fight with somebody."

"We can't forget the lost sheep, Brother McCombs," Robert said with a feeling of brotherhood he genuinely felt.

The conversation turned to other subjects the traveler might have heard and could pass on. Where were there new roads? Were there any new cabins along the byways, any new trading posts and crossroad stores? What was the political news in areas he had visited?

Soon what small amount of energy Robert's body held in reserve was completely exhausted. He asked to be shown to his bed, with or without white counterpane. Ellie McCombs started up the stairs, and he followed.

Shed called to him, a tone of mirthful kindness in his voice. "Laddie, sleep well and think on your best sermon. An empty church house is the delight o' the devil. Suppose we disappoint him—very mildly o' course—with a Methodist sermon, come Sunday."

Sunday was two days off, but Robert tossed and turned all night.

Shed McCombs had spread the word himself, Robert learned. The church house was new and the spirit of the occasion would be the same, the older man advised him in advance.

"It's like a hungry laddie a-takin' to food. When the doors have been shut there's more hunger for the Word."

When Sunday came Robert knew he had the confidence of Shed and Ellie Mccombs, but it was small consolation when his own confidence—and, he was sure, that of some sixteen or eighteen other families—was lacking. He had been honest with Shed, and told him time and again that he had never preached from the pulpit before. Yet there was an understanding that had passed between them that buoyed Robert's spirits upward.

Horses and buggies surrounded the church, and every pew was full or near full. Robert's legs trembled violently and his lips stuck together, for there was no moisture in his throat. He dreaded the ending of the first hymn, and hoped that the worshipers would be lenient with him.

At last every voice was silent. Not even a cough interrupted the stillness of the small building, even now smelling of the hewn locust logs Shed McCombs had selected to ensure the longevity of this house of God.

Robert raised his eyes to the rafters as he had seen numerous other preachers do in what he supposed was one last pleading for strength. His Bible was already open to Genesis, his scriptural reference, for the story of Noah and the ark. He had selected *that,* for as Noah had come to rest in a new and uninhibited wilderness, so had the people along Wolf Creek.

As he read the Scriptures his knees banged uncontrollably against each other and the sweat of his hands left moist imprints upon the pages of the Bible. After he closed the Book he paused unduly long, forgetting how he had planned to start his oration. He made a first attempt and his voice went high, like the changing voice of a young boy. Finally he uttered several halting sentences, but none had any relation to the other nor to the passages he had selected. It was no use, and he knew it. He could utter not one single word.

He ran from the pulpit in his humiliation and shame, but Shed caught him at the door.

"I will not let you fail, Brother Sheffey. You are God's man—I am sure of that now, laddie. I will go back with you and you will give any o' your exhortations you can remember. Then you will pray for us."

Suddenly the exhortations he had used in so many different places and so often came from his lips with force and reverence. He prayed, asking God to bless the new church and the wilderness people, and soon he had stopped formal praying and was talking to God as he had done in the schoolroom, oblivious to time and his surroundings.

When he lifted his eyes every pew was empty and every knee clung to the dirt floor. As he finished, seemingly immobile bodies came to life, and countenances were radiant.

"Aye, me thinks the devil is more than a little unhappy today," Shed said to him as they all three rode home in the buggy.

Robert smiled only halfheartedly, for he still felt that he had failed.

"Be patient, laddie. You will be an awesome adversary of the devil in time—I'm sure o' that—but neither did I learn the mastery o' the wood until I had first rendered a mountain of logs into firewood."

The hands of Shed and Ellie McCombs given in parting held his a long time until, with all eyes moist, Robert departed. He followed Wolf Creek westward for a distance, then crossed East River Mountain. In that far-ranging and thinly populated territory to the west he stayed a week, moving from one home to another, one village to the next, always inquiring of the spiritual lives of the inhabitants. His exhortations there had the impact of a single footprint in a field of untouched snow. Someday soon he would return. Of that he was certain.

By the second week of May he had recrossed the mountain, traveling east, until the bed of New River was reached. From there, and often paralleling the wide, northward-rushing stream, he proceeded southwestward, until the waters of Cripple Creek welcomed him home.

He helped Elizabeth with the May garden planting, but his mind was elsewhere. He was re-living his experiences on Wolf Creek a hundred times, and his failure—he still thought of it as that, in spite of the fact that Shed McCombs had written to say how moved some of the people still were at the power of his prayers—in his first pulpit experience a thousand times. Nevertheless, a new world had opened up. He practiced almost daily the sermon he had originally tried to deliver and couldn't, plus a dozen more. Some days he would work in the garden, digging the weeds from a row of beans and, on coming to the end of the row, drop his hoe and preach to the fence rails surrounding the garden. So passionate would his voice become that it seemed to ride the very ripples of Cripple Creek.

"Can't you practice your sermons with the hoe in your hands?" Elizabeth would say time and again when he got carried away and she toiled alone.

His travels and exhortations continued, but it was not until the very early fall of 1849 that his chance to stand in the pulpit alone came again. During this year he had not strayed very far from Elizabeth. She had given birth the previous year to another son—whom Robert decided should be named Daniel Winton, in honor of his brother—and now, only three weeks ago, Elizabeth had been delivered of their first daughter. Robert deferred to his wife's judgment on this occasion, and the child was named Sarah Louise, in honor of the infant's aunt. Elizabeth's recovery after the birth of the baby girl was slow and troublesome. She had pleaded with Robert before and after the infant was born not to leave her for very long, and he honored her wishes.

For that entire summer he did not journey beyond the distance of one full day's ride, coming and going. What he felt at first to be a confinement proved itself a blessing. The temporary shortening of his range had found him discovering small out-of-the-way churches and people in every direction that he might otherwise have missed. Such was the case one day when he found himself only twenty-odd miles from home in the village of Hillsville. He had been there several times—though only once had he given his exhortations—and he was remembered warmly. The congregation was waiting impatiently for its preacher and his guest, a minister from North Carolina, who was to speak as the revival got underway.

An hour later, when the men had not appeared: "Let Brother Sheffey say a few words to us," somebody said, and the message had started from there. Although he received thanks for his sermon, there were no compliments. His prayers however, were highly praised. "I could nigh feel the Lord God a-sittin' on my lap when you prayed!" an old woman said, and the remarks of others were similar. Joy did indeed come by strange routes and small doses and his heart overflowed.

By Christmas, Elizabeth appeared to have made a complete recovery from the problems brought on by childbirth. At least Robert thought she had, until one day when he was approached by Leah.

"Robert, you can't say any of us ever nosed into your and Elizabeth's affairs, but my sister is suffering more than you know."

"Suffering? How?"

"Childbirth is harder for some women than others. With Elizabeth, her first one come easy—but something must've happened, for every one since has been more agony than the one before. Her spirits aren't like they ought to be—you ought to know that."

"I know she gets disheartened when I'm gone from her, but she knows I'm doing the Lord's work. And I have stayed close home this summer."

"I don't want to meddle, but if you want to bring a smile back to your wife's face I'd stay near her until her spirit and her body heals. She's had a broken heart once—I know you know about that—and if you desert her like he did, only this time with a bunch of young'uns I don't know what'll happen to her."

"I must live with a dual longing in my heart: to serve my Lord and to love my family. That is true, whether I have Elizabeth's whole heart or not. Sometimes I don't honestly know what goes on behind those sad eyes that I love as God gives man the right and inclination to love. I just don't know."

"Elizabeth has been a good wife to you."

"She surely has, I'll vouch for that. She keeps many a thing in her soul that never comes out. I can't say I'm not ashamed sometimes when I know she has need of me and I'm not there, but I've never left her for my own self. It has been in the cause of service to the Lord. You know that, and she knows that. And if she's the woman I think she is, and after she ponders on it a while, I won't have to tell her which is the more important."

Robert took the gentle chastisement of his sister-in-law in good grace and acted upon it. After school was let out in the spring of 1850 he kept close to his wife's side, with only occasional exceptions. He did make one long and several short trips, but only because he had actually been sent for. The summer, however, did not pass idly by. He used the time to study his Methodist *Discipline* and in so doing to become convinced that it spoke to and of his own heart. On a sweltering night in August he made up his mind that if the Methodists would have him, he would have them. The inclination might even go farther, if he could learn to preach well. But he wouldn't push in that direction. He would learn as fast as he could, and God would move in His own good time.

He called Elizabeth to him and told her of the decision he had made.

"This has been the best summer we've ever had, Robert, but I guess it's foolishness for me to think you won't strike out again before long," she said.

"Do you realize that it's not for me I'm doing it? There are so many who know nothing of God's lovingkindness."

"I guess I do understand. I couldn't put up with it a-tall if that wasn't the reason."

"You're a good help mate, Elizabeth. I know it's been hard on you, and I won't leave anymore until you feel like you're well and everything is all right again."

"I'll make do. You strike out to where you think you can do the most good."

"Not until I'm sure you're really ready for it," he said, "ready for it in body, mind, and spirit."

Throughout the fall and winter to follow, his school teaching progressed in a routine manner. He gave his best efforts to the classroom work, but during this year a great deal of this had been forced and he knew it. In the back of his mind was the overwhelming desire for spring to come.

Elizabeth had made it through the winter well. Her spirits were high and she looked forward to planting her garden and getting the children outside in the sunshine.

Their firstborn was now seven years old, and he was a constant companion to his mother in the garden while Leah or Sarah took turns visiting and looking after the younger children.

On the fifth day of April, 1851, Robert was preparing for his first missionary journey of the year. After family prayer service that night, and when the children were tucked snugly in their beds, he told Elizabeth of his plans.

"The planting can wait until I make this one trip," he began. "I must ride on to Jeffersonville with all due haste. They need me there."

When he had finished talking, she told him that she was expecting their fifth child, that it was indeed already well on the way.

By daylight of the next morning Robert was riding northwest. Jeffersonville was a village west of Burke's Garden, and although he had never been there he did know the man who had written asking him to come. The man, Shales Thompson, had lived on Morris Knob during the time Robert had been staying with his brother James in Marion. He had met Shales Thompson, a bachelor trapper who lived alone, he recalled, during the early summer of 1840, when he had been giving his exhortations to one mountain family at a time along the ridges of Morris Knob. Robert had stayed with Shales one night—not with particular comfort, he recalled, for the smell of curing hides had saturated the cabin in spite of the fact that it had been summer and no hides had been in evidence.

The letter from Shales Thompson that Robert now carried in his pocket revealed that the man was still a bachelor, still a trapper, though he had moved closer to Jeffersonville. Thompson's request of Robert was a plea to come to the trapping camp Thompson now resided in to help break up a feud among the trappers that had already taken five lives. Robert remembered with joy his being instrumental in the conversion of Shales Thompson, but being a mediator in a feud was a new and unwanted task. Still, he had felt it upon his heart to come, and Shale's pleas were as one Christian brother to another, with the admonition: "You have the power to help us." If that were possible, Robert had no choice but to go.

He found Shales without difficulty. Every resident of the nearby village trembled a little each time a gun went off in the trapper's camp, apparently, and did a daily head count of each other, according to rumor.

After learning that the trouble was caused by disagreement among the trappers as to who had what right to what territory, Robert felt his task of mediation even more impossible. Large landholders would give trapping permission to one trapper and then another trapper would infringe—innocently, Robert was convinced—on this territory, claiming all the while that the land boundary was unknown. As Robert saw it, the only answer to the dilemma was to persuade friendly groups of trappers to stay between streams of water where the boundaries would be easily identifiable and beyond questioning.

With Shales at his side, this proposal was presented at each small cabin along the ridge. Robert closed every visit with a prayer that God would help in the trouble and that the men and their families would forgive one another for past ill will.

Only one family and Shales were willing to abide by the plan. The others disapproved of it totally, claiming that the trapping was better along some streams than others.

When daylight of the next day came Robert left Shales's house without breakfast and took a kneeling position upon a large flat rock in sight of a few of the trappers' cabins along the ridge. Some gathered around him after the breakfast fires had gone out.

"Lord, forgive them for shooting and hating one another," he pleaded so softly as they listened. "And, Lord, I'm going to stay here until they do Your will. I am not going to eat, Lord—although I love the sweet sourwood honey and griddle cakes as much as any man—

and I'm not going to sleep until I fall dead on this rock, unless the good brothers and sisters promise to try and do better."

He repeated his prayer over and over again, sometimes for a new group and then for those who had watched his tired face before. Soon all who had stood before his kneeling body had come, gone, and returned.

Shales Thompson stayed with him, wiping his sweating brow, until the sun mercifully passed behind the mountains.

"You got to get some grub in your stomach," Shales pleaded. "You ain't had nothin' but water, and you can't live on that."

"Lord, forgive them ..." He prayed on.

The moon became visible through the trees before a small group of men stomped through the brush to the rock on which Robert kneeled, feeling almost paralyzed.

"We'll try what you say," one of them offered in a condescending growl. "Ain't no use in you stayin' out here all night on that rock like a hoot owl. Some of the women thinks you're a-doin' it for us."

They had to carry him to Shales's cabin. He had no feeling in his legs. He was seated and given food, but before he began to eat he searched all of their eyes.

"This is not all there is to it," he said. "I want you to hear what the Lord has to say. Let me rest tonight and then I want you all to gather in front of this cabin in the morning before you go about your own business."

Robert had finished his breakfast when he heard them gathering, but he had difficulty standing. His legs were sore, and his knees refused to function in the normal manner. Shales helped him to the cabin door and pushed it open. Robert rested against the doorjamb and begged the group's pardon that his legs would not support him.

"Now, I promised you what our Lord says about the trouble that has come upon us." He then opened his Bible to the marker he had placed there. "Our blessed Jesus said, 'but if ye forgive not men their trespasses, neither will your father forgive your trespasses.' Now, trespasses mean the wrong you have done to a neighbor or the wrong you think he has done to you."

He kept them only a short time with his sermon. Seeing them standing before him, eyes repentant, he felt that a new start had been made, but he couldn't help wondering how long the truce would last. His quick dismissal was really one of personal necessity. The tears forming in his own blue eyes were not so much for them as for him. Before he had gotten half way through his short sermon his own hypocrisy had condemned him. How could any man stand and preach forgiveness when he hadn't extended it himself? His heart was still not forgiving toward his aunt Elizabeth. In spite of time and separation there was still a chasm.

As the moistness in Robert's eyes welled over, Shales Thompson left him alone in the cabin, where the very silence seemed a mocking condemnation. The years had gone by and he had never gone to his aunt Elizabeth for the reconciliation he had promised himself and his God time and time again. Suddenly, sitting there in the cabin with his head resting in his hands, this matter seemed the only thing standing between him and his complete submission to his God.

Vainly he tried to get to the horse he insisted be saddled, but still his legs would not hold him up.

"Brother Sheffey, you'd best stay one more day and rest up," Shales Thompson pleaded.

Robert finally agreed, but no one could know how much he wanted to get to Abingdon and hold his aunt Elizabeth's face in his hands and tell her that all was forgiven, and to hear her make the same declaration if she was so inclined. Now, but not before, he did not need the latter condition, but if it came, there would be even more joy.

It was nearly one and one-half days' ride to Abingdon. Robert's heart swelled with memories and expectation as he crossed the north fork of the Holston, near to where he had fled so many times as a youth. To the east of him, not more than ten or twelve miles, was Emory and Henry College, and he would go there after he made his peace with his aunt Elizabeth. It would be fitting that he return to the college and sit upon the crest of the hill where so many things had been revealed to him. May be he would pay a call upon the president of the college, from whom he had received a complimentary letter pertaining to the humane work and exhortations that "are now well known."

When the north boundary of the town was reached, Robert planned his strategy. He would ride to the back of the house and tie his horse to the stable fence where Big Edmund used to prop his massive foot when nobody hurried him on one chore or another. Then, quietly, he would slip into the back of the house and tiptoe down the hallway into the parlor, where his aunt would be sitting in her rocking chair, looking onto the street. He would kiss her on the cheek before she knew who had invaded the room, and she would turn and recognizes him and cry out for happiness.

His plan worked until he had passed the kitchen door and a servant he didn't know saw him and called out. He put his finger to his lips to silence her and continued forward.

He sprung through the parlor door. The room was empty and the rocking chair deserted. He went back into the hallway to observe the same servant, wide-eyed, her mouth hanging open.

"Where is Aunt Elizabeth?" he asked with a note of foreboding in his voice.

"You ain't heerd?"

"Heard what?"

"Miz White—she done passed on to glory. She been dead and buried fer three days."

He looked at the servant incredulously and dismissed her without telling her who he was.

He still sat in his aunt's chair when a male voice called out before coming into the room, "It must be Cousin Robert! Where are you, Robert?"

A young man who Robert at first did not recognize entered the room. The boy extended his hand. "You would be Cousin Robert. I knew it from the description the kitchen girl gave."

"And you—you would be Milton?" Robert said.

"Yes. The house gets emptier by degrees. You had not heard about Mother until today, I take it?"

"No, I didn't know until I got here. I've been on one of my rounds."

"Your brother James tried to get word to you when she died, but, as I understand it, your wife said you would be gone perhaps for a week or two."

"Yes. There was no way you could have reached me," Robert said.

By lunchtime, which Milton had asked him to share; they were joined by Eleanor White, who now had the distinction of being the second-oldest surviving child of Elizabeth White.

"Mother longed to see you," she said with a sense of his reason for coming that had escaped Milton.

"And I longed to see her. May God forgive me that I waited till too late," he said with tears spilling onto his plate.

The palatial dining room seemed to him then as a tomb. He wished for the time when the table was lined on both sides with young people and family banter echoed about the walls; a time when Colonel White sat at the head and his aunt at the foot and the whole world had had an unshakable stability. Now they all, including Lawrence, his brother, had spread out to other places, with wives and families of their own. All that remained was a memory, and he could see it on the face of Eleanor White as plainly as she must be able to see it on his.

Before preparing to leave, he thanked his cousins for their hospitality.

"Can't you spend the night, Robert?" Eleanor asked.

"No, thank you. I'll drop in on James in Marion. Then I'll have to get home and plant my garden. I've got four hungry little mouths to feed and a fifth one on the way."

He had mounted his horse when Eleanor came running from the back of the house. "Oh, I thought you had gone!" she cried breathlessly. "I just remembered. Wait a minute." It was a dozen minutes before she returned and handed him a flat package wrapped in cheesecloth. "I don't know what it is, but Mother said if you ever came back and she couldn't give you the package herself, I was to do it."

He accepted the flimsy parcel with thanks, made up his mind it was a suit of clothes formerly belonging to one of his dead cousins; and rolled it up for insertion into his saddlebags.

As he rode east toward Marion he passed the college without stopping. Closer looks into the past would not be welcome on this day.

Ellen Sheffey would expect him to be clean, he realized as Marion came nearer. He was no less concerned about it than she, but the practicalities of keeping immaculate while riding the dusty trails was another matter. Nevertheless, a cove formed by offshoots of the middle fork of the Holston provided a private place to wash him.

It was a chill April day, and the water was too cold for an all-over bath, but he scrubbed all the skin he could get to without actually removing his underwear. He cleaned his coat by means of a quick whiplash that sent miniature dust clouds skyward. His breeches were as thin as the cutting edge of his straight razor, and his extra pair in the saddlebags was probably beyond even Elizabeth's skilled needlecraft.

There seemed no better time to open his aunt's package in the hope that the clothing of a smaller cousin had been saved for him. Perhaps he would walk into Ellen Sheffey's house looking like a gentleman of the court.

When the cheesecloth had been removed, he was staring at the wooled hide of a sheep—the sole item within the package. He rubbed his hand over the wool and noted the professional manner with which the sheepskin had been cleaned, trimmed, and prepared for use. He still did not understand until he turned it over and saw the pinned note written in his aunt's hand:

> The sheep is the meekest and most vulnerable of God's creatures. But perhaps its very humility and helplessness is why it is honored of God and man. The lost sheep needs not only rescue, but to remember it is still a sheep.
>
> Ride upon this sheepskin, Robert; pray upon it; sleep upon it; and remember the humbleness of the animal from whose back it came.
>
> I too will do penitence. I have left in my burial instructions that the oldest dress I have (and the

one surviving garment I possess from my first days in Abingdon) now moth-eaten and bare, be used on my body as I am laid to rest. I cannot go out of the world naked as I came into it, but for *my* part I will do the next best thing.

—Elizabeth Wilson White

Chapter X

On August eighteenth the wailing voice of a fifth child broke the stillness of a sweltering and breezeless afternoon.

"We can honor you, Aunt Elizabeth, and my own mother, if you'll agree to Margaret Elizabeth for the name," Robert said when the infant was only hours old. His wife made no protest and sank into a deep sleep.

The room still smelled of the lingering odor of human sweat, for Elizabeth had been in labor since early morning.

"You let Elizabeth's sisters wait on her for a long spell," the midwife admonished as she left. "She's not going to be hopping around so quick after this one."

Robert said that if Elizabeth wanted him to, he would ride to Austinville and fetch the nearest doctor.

Presently Sarah came from out of the kitchen and announced that their evening meal was ready. As he passed Elizabeth's bed he saw large beads of sweat on her forehead and in the hollows of her cheeks. He stooped to dry her face and felt her hot, still-panting breath in his. face. He kissed her dry forehead and stood over her until Sarah called him a second time.

Elizabeth sat with them at the table the next week, but her flesh showed a deathly yellow-white pallor and blue-black circles underscored her listless eyes. She could hardly hold the infant to her breast, and the child always seemed hungry and restless.

The following day Robert brought the doctor from Austinville. His diagnosis was rendered quickly.

"Your wife has lost too much blood. She will need to rest as much as possible and eat well. Her breasts will not produce the amount of milk the baby needs. She can nurse at night and in the early mornings, perhaps. Get a wet nurse and use her throughout the day."

Robert promptly found a slave woman at the crossroads leading to Austinville whose mammoth breasts would by no means be emptied by her own newborn child. Arrangements were made with the woman's owner, who, in a neighborly gesture, gave his permission and a mule for the woman to travel upon.

Elizabeth's slow recovery again prevented extensive travel throughout the rest of August and September. In the interim Robert read his Bible avidly, searched again the pages of his *Discipline* for anything he might have missed, and read thrice over the Abingdon paper to which he now subscribed. The latter would be of benefit in the classroom when October came. He could now tell the children more about Henry Clay and Daniel Webster and a new man they had not heard of, one Abraham Lincoln. The most recent issue of the paper had carried a story about Lincoln's effort while serving in Congress to propose a bill for the gradual and compensated emancipation of slaves in the District of Columbia. Such was to take place with the approval of the free white citizens. According to the paper, however, the bill displeased Abolitionists as well as slaveholders and never was seriously considered.

School hours were over, and Robert stood in his garden, digging the October crop of turnips, when a galloping horse and rider pulled to a halt at the back door of the cabin. Instinctively he dropped his hoe, for across the years he could seem to sense when the unusual or urgent was at hand, and a horse in lather never left any doubt.

He recognized the rider's face but could not recall his name.

"Yes—what is it?" Robert said as the man dismounted.

"Cass Wilkerson sent me to fetch you—there's been a terrible accident!"

"Well, what is it, man?" Robert urged as the messenger paused, wetting his lips with his tongue.

"It's Bertha Kincannon—she's been burned up."

"What do you mean, burned up?"

"That crazy woman of Stanislaw Lewinski's burned the house down in the middle of the night and Bertha alayin' fast asleep."

"Nobody was able to get her out?"

"None of the neighbors seen the fire or smelled the smoke till the roof was fallin' in."

'"Do they have the Lewinski woman in custody?"

"She's in custody, all right. In custody in a pine box. The neighbors said that when they got to the fire last night that lunatic had climbed plumb to the top of that red oak tree between the house and the barn—you remember it?"

Robert said he did and asked the man to continue.

"Well, she was sittin' on a top limb—you could see her plumb ghostlike by the light of the flames—leanin' over farther and farther, tryin' to catch stuff flyin' through the air and goin' up the chimney."

Robert shuddered. "The poor woman was sick."

"Well, she was in good spirits last night, aclimbin' a sixty foot tree and screamin' at the top of her lungs. She kept a-yellin', "Here comes my baby's caul—here it comes!' She would be a-screamin' and lean out of the tree limb and try to catch a piece of trash floatin' in the heat and smoke. She leaned over too far and came tumblin' out of that tree like a shot squirrel."

Robert then asked what Cass Wilkerson would have him do.

"Mr. Wilkerson said the girl—Wanda, I believe her name was—wants you to conduct her mother's funeral."

Robert promised to be there on time the next day. He asked Sarah to stay with Elizabeth and the children, and of Leah he requested that she take her dulcimer to his school and entertain the pupils in his absence.

When he reached the Lewinski cabin Wanda flew into his outstretched arms, inconsolable in her grief. "Oh, Mr. Sheffey!" she cried. "If I hadn't told Mamma you and Mrs. Kincannon helped me she wouldn't a done this terrible thing. It's all my fault!"

"No, no, child. It wouldn't have made any difference—and she'd have heard about it sooner or later anyway. But who'd have thought, even imagined, after all these years … "His words died.

"It went over and over again in her mind. Things like that did sometimes. Mamma would go wild thinkin' about things like that, and she probably believed in her poor sick soul that Mrs. Kincannon had my caul."

"I'm sure that tells the story," Robert said, aware for the first time of the magnitude of the cure he and Bertha Kincannon had affected.

"Come and look at Mamma. We've got her fixed up so purty. I did it myself."

He looked upon the singed face of the woman in the open pine box and was repulsed at the green flies circling about her mouth. Yet, in spite of all the offensive things that he saw, the look of peace that had at last come to the face of Helga Lewinski made all other things negligible.

He stayed with the family then (one of the boys had married, and his wife was there) as they all awaited the funeral hour. No neighbors were present, and no friends, if they had any. He stood at Wanda's side as she prepared a humble meal of fried mush and boiled turnips. She was a grown woman now, a kind of wild, raw beauty that no man had discovered, he was thinking—until she told him otherwise.

"I'm gettin' married at Thanksgiving. My man runs a delivery wagon between here and Wytheville. He thinks an awful lot of me."

"Lord bless you. You've been a good girl, and I hope some of the things I've taught you will help as you pass through this life."

"Most everything I know started when I began school under you."

She told him then that only her youngest brother remained at home and that she and her new husband would live with her father until they had the means to build their own cabin.

By two o'clock Cass Wilkerson, his wife, and several of the men Stanislaw Lewinski worked with made their way up the mountain. Some had brought their wives, and there were also girls that Wanda had gone to school with. He was glad to see them, and since they had held Bertha Kincannon in high esteem he suggested that after the funeral was over they all go to the ashen remains of Bertha's house and hold a memorial service. Stanislaw Lewinski, even in his grief, wanted to be with them. Not even a wall of Bertha's house remained.

A part of the chimney up to about the second floor stood as a grotesque monument of what once had been.

Robert rode around the red oak from which the Lewinski woman had fallen. In the charred branches of the tree, just above the level of his eyes, his outstretched hand grasped a partially blackened piece of the white counterpane Bertha Kincannon had first reluctantly, then lovingly, kept stretched upon his bed. Perhaps Helga Lewinski did see a caul floating upward through the smoke after all… perhaps the blackened cloth he now held in his hands was the thing she reached for. He looked toward the top of the tree, folded the small square of cloth, and put it in his pocket.

Elizabeth had gained some of her strength back by Thanksgiving, and Robert took her for a short ride in the family buggy to the house in which he was born. The trip was not altogether a pleasure trip, for Daniel had written asking Robert to collect his rent. Daniel now wandered from place to place, and it was not unusual for Robert to get a letter from any of a half-dozen counties in western Virginia or any numbers of post offices northward up the Valley of Virginia. Wherever he happened to be Daniel would be happy playing his fiddle, telling stories, talking politics, or generally drinking of the warmth of human fellowship. The relationship he shared with all his brothers was a precious thing to him, even if it depended upon correspondence alone to keep it alive. Lawrence wrote the most often, and indicated that Alabama might become his permanent address. Hugh wrote more rarely than the others, but he always had something important to say, reporting in his last letter the part he had played in the convention of 1850–51 that passed the Manhood Suffrage law, opening the way for non-landowners to be able to vote.

Robert never came back to his birthplace without the same feeling of confused nostalgia. Time and again he had tried to picture what his mother had looked like, what her mannerisms and habits had been, the smallest details that would let him see the woman from whose womb he had sprung. As a small child he could recall being scolded by his uncle James and his other uncles for asking them over and over again to tell him of his mother when she was a young girl.

Now he wanted to call out to the log walls that had witnessed the shadow of his mother's movements and tell her that her womb had borne fruit of which she could be proud.

He did not think that Elizabeth had been particularly cheered by their outing. As they rode home she sat quietly on the buggy seat, her black nun's bonnet pulled low against the chill of November.

"Does this remind you of our courting days?" he asked cheerfully.

She smiled a little then, and straightened. "You never courted me in a buggy. You always rode horseback."

It was true—although they had used her father's buggy a time or two.

"Do you still feel bad, hon?"

"Like every ounce of sap has left me," she tried to say in an undejected tone of voice.

He patted her knee affectionately. "You'll be well by Christmas. You must be. I want you and the children, even the baby, to come to our Christmas program at the school."

"I don't think I'll ever be well, Robert. I can't even feed my own baby without the milk of a slave."

"That's no disgrace. Plenty of women do it. You'd still be my sweetheart if you went as dry as an old jersey cow."

She smiled, but her face took on a suspicious look. "You sure you're not just butterin' me up before you light out again in the spring?"

"No. If I was doing that I'd wait until about the last of February or the first of March."

She looked at him intently then. "Please don't leave me this spring. It's not that I don't want you to do what you're doin', but I've been seein' bad signs about myself."

"You'll get all right, but we'll wait and see," he promised.

Elizabeth was not well by Christmas or by spring either. In anticipation of spending most of the summer at home, Robert put out a corn crop and from the lonely hours spent there a grand idea was born. If Elizabeth's health continued to plague her throughout the summer into the winter and he could not leave her in clear conscience when the following spring came, there was an alternate solution: he would get a preaching license and try to find a small church to serve somewhere within riding distance of home.

His crop did well, and by the time school had opened and the first big frost hit, the corn was in the shock and the pumpkins, for hog feed and home use, in the barn. Elizabeth began to feel like helping him in the husking of the corn, and on many days when he returned from school he would hitch up the one-horse sled and take her output for the day to the corncrib, sorting out first the mound of children that covered his load. By late fall Robert insisted that Elizabeth stop this work. There was a good reason to avoid over strenuous activity: Robert learned that she was pregnant with their sixth child.

John Robert was born July 6, 1853, just two days past the anniversary of his father's birth. When the child was a month old Elizabeth could not stand up for more than an hour. Her breasts had little milk, and she depended entirely upon still another wet nurse that Robert had been able to find.

"Don't go from me anymore this summer, Robert," she pleaded, and he promised he wouldn't.

But he did find himself breaking the promise. First there was a summons from Big Edmund, who was now the property of a plantation owner at Glade Spring, a growing village almost halfway between Abingdon and Marion.

When Robert got there Big Edmund lay dying in the slave quarters, from massive ruptures on both sides of the abdomen. He gave a hug to the suffering man, who burst into tears at this display of kindness and the nostalgia of reunion.

"Your owner told me you just about killed yourself trying to lift a wagon," Robert said.

Big Edmund was whimpering and trying to talk at the same time, and Robert could hardly understand him. The slave started again.

"They said I couldn't do it—lift that wagonload o' corn.

... I done it, but it hurt me, Mr. Robert."

"Had the wagon turned over on somebody?"

"No, sir, Mr. Robert. We was puttin' a new wheel on it—the old one broke off—and th' other fellers said we'd have to put a prize under it an' I tol' I could lift it."

"You shouldn't have tried to do so much. And you're not as young as you once were," Robert added, not really knowing how old the Negro was.

"It don't help me none to know hit now…I'm a-dyin' for sure. That doctor, he wouldn't tell me nothin'—just let me lay here."

Robert was satisfied that the slave owner had done all he could. Neither did he doubt the doctor's prediction that slow internal bleeding and infection would kill Big Edmund in two or three days, at most. The pain came and went in cycles. When Robert decided to bind the sick man's belly with a long cloth, to relieve the pressure and, hopefully, the pain, Big Edmund said: "The doctor done that before. I took it off so's I could breathe a mite better."

Throughout the night Robert was torn by the groans of pain. By morning he himself felt a bone-deep fatigue.

The slave held on through the day, weaving in and out of consciousness. The slave owner's wife brought bread and soup, but Big Edmund refused to open his mouth, though he watched Robert eat with a glassy-eyed interest.

"You must eat, Big Edmund," Robert said again. "Let me help you eat."

"It don't make no matter to a dyin' man…don't make no matter a-tall."

Robert tried with conversation to comfort the man. They talked of the days they had both known at Colonel James White's house in Abingdon and the work and fun and laughter that had been a part of it all.

Robert had talked to the slave about his soul's salvation the previous day, when Big Edmund had spoken too convincingly about his preparedness. Robert had not forced the pursuit of the subject then.

Now: "Mr. Robert, I'm in need to ax you about somethin'," Big Edmund said between grimaces.

"Yes?"

"You never knowed about me when Colonel White done bought me?"

"Uncle James never told me anything about your purchase."

"I was a whupmaster—what the other slaves done call flogger man er whupmaster. I worked for a county man down in Alabama."

"I don't understand … "

"That county man got paid for whuppin' runaway slaves when they was caught."

"Did he *make* you help him?"

"Not exactly," Big Edmund said and stopped, his face contorted again with pain. Robert waited.

"No, he never made me do it, but he give me some pay if I would."

"And you whipped and flogged your own black brothers, is that what you're trying to tell me?"

"Yas, Lord!" Big Edmund cried out in pain and remorse that seemed to strike him simultaneously.

Robert moved his chair closer to the bed and wiped the tear-swollen eyes of a dying man. "God will forgive you for that. And when you get to glory every man you flogged will forgive you."

"No, they won't do it. I whupped some of 'em until their eyes done rolled back in their heads."

"God can, and will, forgive that." The black man shook his head, but Robert insisted. "Yes, He will. All of us in some way have beaten the helpless and betrayed our brothers."

"Oh, lordy, I don't feel it!" Big Edmund cried out his anguish.

"The greatest Christian who ever lived participated in the stoning to death of one of Christ's own servants. And he whipped and gouged and imprisoned hundreds of others. He cursed the name of Christ. But he saw a blinding light and he was a changed man after that. He himself felt the stripes of the whip on his back and the damp loneliness of the prison cell."

He went on with the story of Paul until Big Edmund seemed to be seeing a profound vision. "Oh, lordy, it must be so!" Big Edmund cried. "It must be so!"

"Have you ever been baptized?"

"I don't know. I don't 'member my mammy, but I know I ain't been since I'se a man."

Robert asked the slave's wishes and, in conformity with them, brought a cup of water from the watering trough in the barnyard and sprinkled the dying man's head. They talked in quiet tones after that, and finally there was an unmistakable peace in the fading voice of Big Edmund.

By dark Big Edmund's body started to stink, and he raved fitfully throughout the night. At dawn the giant of a man made one attempted leap from his pole bed of cornhusks and fell back wide-eyed and dead.

Robert returned home after Big Edmund was buried and found there a message to pay a call on one Martin Ingo. He did so, and after returning from the visit he burst into his cabin, as excited as a schoolchild at Christmas.

"Mr. Ingo and some of his neighbors are thinking about building a new church at the foot of Henley Mountain! He's asked me if I'd consider pastoring the church if they built it."

"It would be close home for you, but looks like to me there's churches enough around here," Elizabeth said.

"Some of the mountain families want a church nearby, and I'm not real sure but I think there is a serious division under way among them."

With a feeling of exhilaration Robert made his way the next week to the presiding elder of the Wytheville district to obtain his license to preach. He was questioned at length and some of the questions and the tone of the questioner gave him cause to wonder. In each case, however, he answered as fully and patiently as possible. Finally he was told to come back in a month.

He returned to the home of the presiding elder when the time was up, only to confront an evasive churchman who obviously had the backing of the examining committee.

"Mr. Sheffey, I'm afraid your application for a license to preach is not in order. We must in all cases determine the fitness of an applicant for licensing. As you know, one of your duties would include the performance of legal marriage ceremonies. The suitability of a candidate is not so much in question when he is a graduate of a divinity school or comes with the recommendation and endorsement of a church conference. In your case you are an unaffiliated itinerant."

"That doesn't mean I can't serve my blessed Lord with love and faithfulness, and minister to His people."

"No, not if you're qualified," the elder said. "Many itinerants are licensed and perform an honorable service to the state, the church, and the people. There are also those men who never bother to get a license, but of these, everyone must of course, be suspicious."

"Do you have reason to believe I can't honorably serve?" Robert asked, catching the inference.

The elder paused for a long while. Finally he cleared his throat and looked down at the floor. "Frankly, Mr. Sheffey, we asked you to wait a month to allow us time to do some asking around, and, more specifically, to discover if some of the things we had already heard were true."

"And what did you find out?"

"We learned that you are a man of some ability and piety—maybe too much piety. There are those who think you cannot properly see the real world for walking around in a heavenly one of your own invention."

"I make no apology for seeing the fruits and evidences of a blessed earth and acknowledging a merciful and benevolent God."

"What about some of the other things that have come to our attention? What of your throwing cold water into the face of a pupil? What of wrapping your arms around a tree as though it were a sleepy child? Do you really believe tearing off tree limbs is like tearing the limbs from a person?"

"I have done these things, and believe in what I have taught."

"Then, too, Mr. Sheffey, all of us pray, but do you not consider it strange that you are known to pray for three and four hours at a time and in the most unusual places? In the rain too, sometimes, I understand. You frighten the children with your prayers. I'm sure you know that. They say you do not pray but that you talk to God."

"Good sir, whom do *you* talk to when you pray?"

"Be that as it may, men should not act in peculiar ways. It unnerves others."

"But it is said that God's people are a peculiar people," Robert said.

"When they get queer enough to hug the sugar-maple trees and pray out loud for the honeybees—why, we can't help taking notice of that," the elder said gently.

"Yes, I do those things," Robert said. "And I have shouted among the bee gums also. Can you grasp what a wonderful thing it is that the little bees gather the sweetness of God's beautiful flowers and work like tiny soldiers to make the sweet honeycomb? Why, it is a most wondrous thing!"

The elder appeared unmoved by Robert's simple defense. "I'm sorry, Mr. Sheffey. Your application has been fully reviewed and I cannot give you a license to preach."

"I have been preaching already," Robert uttered in disappointment.

"With all due respect, I'm not sure that your wanderings and exhortations over this state and into the border counties of others could be considered 'preaching.' they certainly aren't done with the sanction of the state or any religious body that I know about."

"I don't need the sanction of anyone to proclaim God's loving-kindness," Robert said.

"No, no one can stop you from being an unlicensed itinerant. And I did not mean to imply that you have done no good. Your kindness to the lowly and the high-bred alike has reached my ears—and I understand that your testimonies are quite eloquent. Mr. Sheffey, if you got the recommendation of the Holston Conference on Methodism or the bishop perhaps—"

"I need no recommendation to speak what is in my heart," Robert interrupted. He thanked the elder and walked from the room.

He returned from Wytheville in a state of such dejection that he avoided even his wife until she discovered him seated, unmoving, in the comer by the fireplace.

"Why, Robert, I thought you were still in Wytheville. When did you return?"

"I've been home for about an hour."

"What is the matter?"

"They refused to issue me a license to preach. They think I am 'too peculiar' to be trusted with one."

Elizabeth listened while he related the rest of his story, but she did not seem fully to share his disappointment.

"I hope you'll still stay home in the summers anyway, Robert. I'm not feeling so perky yet; the baby is past three months old and I'm still not doing right."

He visited with Martin Ingo the following Sunday and told him of the failure to get a preaching license.

"Don't worry none about it. We'll all go over there and sign a petition when the time comes. Actually, some of our folks have cooled off a little on the new church idea, so I don't know what'll happen," Martin said.

Robert rode down the mountain so low in spirits that he did not even wish to go home. The children would miss him, for they would be looking forward to their Sunday-afternoon ride in the saddle behind him, and they would not take kindly to his breaking the tradition.

At the bottom of the mountain he got a piece of chalk from his saddlebag and drew a landscape scene upon a flat rock. The picture depicted a small mountain church of log and wooden shingles with a horse tied to a nearby tree and a man kneeling on a sheepskin prayer mat near the front door.

When the sketch was finished to his liking he studied it for a few moments, smiled, and got to his feet. He placed the sheepskin on which he had been kneeling back on top of the saddle, climbed on, and headed for home—in plenty of time to give horseback rides before dark, he thought.

But when he reached his home Elizabeth was complaining of an abnormal blood issue and he sat by her side until his oldest boy could fetch a neighbor. The temporary care arranged for, he rode to Austinville for the doctor.

The doctor stayed the night, and between frequent trips to Elizabeth's side Robert slept in the rocking chair beside the fire. He fixed breakfast for the physician before the children were up.

"Your wife has not made a normal recovery from her last delivery," the doctor said between gulps of coffee. "I would suggest you keep her in bed until the bleeding stops fully. After that she should do no lifting, nor any strenuous work,"

Sarah and Leah took turns staying with their sister until the first of December. Robert thought all was normal again and took his wife and family to his school Christmas program where Elizabeth sang the Christmas carols with all the gusto demonstrated by the other participants. The next day, however, she was compelled to return to her bed.

"I may as well move in," Sarah said the next morning, trying to add a note of cheer to the depressed household.

"Either that or you do the teaching and I'll stay home," Robert said.

"I'd like that," she said and hurried the two oldest boys, who now numbered among their father's pupils.

Elizabeth's constant need of care continued as January passed and February came, contributing even more height to the unmelting snows of January. By the second week in February half of the class—including the two Sheffey boys—was out of school with mumps. Parents came frequently to take ill children home from school, but the appearance of Melville Catron, a neighbor and father of two of Robert's students who had been out of school two or three days already I with the mumps, seemed unusual.

"Robert, you'd better ride home—and hurry," Catron admonished. "I'll look after the children and send the oldest boy there for the doctor. It's your wife, I might as well tell you that… "

Robert rushed home, and when he got there. Sarah sat by her sister's bed, weeping. As though a dam had broken, a flood tide of blood saturated the feather tick of Elizabeth's bed, and no color at all was visible in her face. About their mother's bed, the older children, eyes terror-stricken, looked up at their father for an explanation.

"I did all I could, but I couldn't stop the blood." Sarah sobbed. "It just kept coming and coming till I knew there wasn't any left."

"You did the best you could, I know that," Robert comforted her.

"I had to send James Wesley—and him with the mumps!—after a neighbor. Poor little feller, I hope I didn't do him permanent damage in his condition."

"They've gone for the doctor, but it won't be any use now. I don't believe there's a drop of blood left in her."

With this pronouncement and its ringing finality invading his very soul, Robert's own tears joined the chorus of those young and older who knew that a beloved mother, wife, and sister was no more.

Robert was given a week off by his employers. This time was not spent in planning for the future or staying with Sarah and Leah who lovingly looked after his children. Instead he wandered from neighbor to neighbor, dazed as a man hit on the head with a heavy rock. He rode the length and breadth of Cripple Creek, from Bertha Kincannon's burned down house in the west to New River in the east. The further he rode, the more relentlessly his sorrow bore down upon him. Would it never go away he asked himself and other friends who listened so lovingly, so patiently.

Robert did not return to his class room on Monday; he had to be reminded that it was time that he goes back to work. After that he did so instinctively, but as days turned to weeks he knew not in the slightest what he had taught, if anything. Sometimes the students would ask him a question and he would hear it as an echo in the farthest reaches of his brain, but he could no more answer than he could fly. In his mind he was making trip after trip to the Peters cemetery, where snow lay upon the clay-covered ground of a fresh grave.

Mercifully, March passed and his students were gone. He had his children, but he felt that if God were just, He could not have left six motherless youngsters in the world. How in the name of every holy thing could God in His abundant lovingkindness deprive a helpless baby of his mother's arms? He prayed to understand and could not. With vision blunted by his anguish, he was not comforted to read in the Scriptures time and time again that the rain fell upon the just and the unjust alike. That did not apply to seven-month-old babies, or two-and-one-half-year-old babies or ten-year-old children either. "My God!" he prayed. "Mercy! I never knew my mother's arms but for the shortest while, and I can't remember sitting on my father's knee. Must *my* little ones feel Thy wrath!"

Like a caged animal, he paced back and forth from his cabin to the mountainside, where he used to pray in the rain and the snow and on the hot nights of summer, when the fireflies cast an eerie light upon his face.

Even when he was with his children a terrible inadequacy overcame him that he could not explain, and he felt helpless. On warm spring nights he would wander from the cabin to the creek and back, trying to shake from his shoulders the millstones of grief and doubt. He could hear the dulcimer music of Leah as she sat on the porch, playing, when the younger children had been put to bed. He both wished her to stop and throw her goose quill in the creek and, at the same time, to continue and play louder and longer.

"Is there anything you want to hear?" she said one night as he came back from the creek.

"No, just keep playing," he replied and seated himself on the front steps.

She stopped to rest her fingers after a while, and he looked in her direction, but could see her form only by moonlight.

"Leah, I don't know what to do. My faith is shaken, and I cannot believe my God is just to me. I would be His advocate without pay or praise and He smites me down like I would swat a fly."

"I have heard Absalom Fisher preach on our trials and the strengthening they bring all of us. I don't know if that thought'll help you any, but I've been pondering on it."

"Thank you, Leah. Brother Fisher has come to see me twice since the funeral and he has comforted me some with those ideas."

"Robert—I don't know very much except how to play the dulcimer and look after children and keep a house, but I've been wondering if I couldn't help in your work... There's all kinds of ways to serve."

"You help me by taking care of the children—You and Sarah both."

"But that's what I mean. Couldn't I serve the Lord by taking Elizabeth's place? That way you can go on with your missionary work like before."

His eyes grew moist then. Others around him evidently looked for better ways to serve, while he wallowed in self-pity and felt as if everything he had once believed now rang with hollowness and sham. So many times he had comforted the doubtful and the bereaved with words he now wanted to deny, for they seemed a mockery where his own life was concerned.

"You shame me, Leah. You put me to the most humble shame."

She was standing now with the full light of the moon on her face, and he could tell that she did not understand what he meant. He walked away from her toward the creek and called over his shoulder for her to go to her bed.

The moon shone mirror-like on the water, seeming to creep from one bank to the other. Then he could see it no more, and a fiery red ball in the east winked across the mountain. With the first rays of morning sunlight on his face he fell to his knees, thanking God for Elizabeth and the fruit of her womb and for even the short time they had shared together. "And never let me doubt again, dear Lord … Thy will be done on earth as it is in heaven."

That summer he cleared more land and worked his corn crop, anticipating staying close to his children. Also, Sarah finally convinced him of her desire to be a mother in the stead of her dead sister and she reassured him that she and Leah would work out a system even if he had to be gone. He listened to the plan the women had worked out, but thought little about it, for this was one summer when he did not propose to go riding off to the farthest reaches of the state.

Twice he preached for Martin Ingo's people on Henley Mountain—in one of the mountain homes—and noticed the number of worshipers dwindling. "You don't have enough here to justify the building of a church," Robert observed, and Ingo conceded that they had all come to the same conclusion. During some of the summer days when his crop work was done, Robert would ride alone to the mountain cabins of Ingo's people and visit with them. Most were dirt-poor and wore rags or cheap jeans cloth dyed with walnut hulls for their better clothing.

For those who still wanted to worship among themselves Robert suggested a Sunday or midweek prayer service, alternating the location from week to week. Once, during a time when his blind brother Daniel had dropped in from his wanderings, Robert took him up on the mountain to help get the home meetings going. He found out quickly that Daniel would not be welcome anymore. The mountain people did not approve of fiddle music during worship, even if soul-stirring hymns did come from the crying violin strings. That seemed to suit Daniel just fine. He'd rather play for his nephews and nieces; they appreciated him more anyway, he said.

Daniel was off again when school started in the fall, and Robert went to his work with a dread he had not experienced at any time before. He longed for a church to serve, and deep down he knew that word of the refusal to grant him a license had gotten around. He wanted to do it the right way. He did not want to give up his work as an exhorter, but neither did he want to forgo the duties and privileges of a legitimate preacher. It was almost as though God himself were against him—that he was condemned forever to be a wandering, unlicensed itinerant whom people would laugh at and point to and call "preacher" in the most derogatory fashion.

Shortly before school was to let out in March, Sarah met him at the back door of the cabin one day and told him that a Reverend White awaited him inside. The man introduced himself and gave a quick resume of his background.

"I am presently a conference-appointed pastor on the Wytheville circuit. Long before I came here my fellow members of the Holston conference and I agreed we had a serious and unusual problem to combat in some of our territorial areas if the Christian work is to proceed as we would have it."

"And in what way can I help?" Robert asked.

"Many areas of the Wytheville circuit are infested by the whiskey makers, and intemperance infects whole neighborhoods. Young men and old alike abuse and starve their families while under the crazed influence of drink. We want to shut down these stills—or as many of them as we can—and see if we can't do something about this problem. You know the territory and many of the mountain people. Will you help us?"

"I am aware of this problem, but I have already looked into the matter and found there is no law saying that these men can't make their whiskey. As I understand it the law against manufacturing it without first paying excise taxes was taken off the books before 1820."

"We know this, but we are more interested in pursuing God's law than man's law. These men may have every legal right to make all the whiskey they want, but they do not have the right to corrupt young men and women. Some of our circuit ministers can hardly hold a meeting for the rowdy crowd of toughs and troublemakers who get their courage from the demijohn."

"I understand. I *have* exhorted and preached to the folks around here some, but I haven't been able to get a license. I guess you already know that, if you checked enough on me to find your way here."

"Yes, we do know about that," Reverend White said. "If you will help us, I believe I and other conference members can aid you in obtaining a license. You come well recommended enough that your work will consist of more than just trying to eradicate stills… And you will be paid—not much, but I suspect we both believe in the same Provider and don't worry a lot about that."

Robert looked to his sister-in-law, who, he guessed, had already anticipated his next question. Sarah gave an affirmative nod and smiled.

All that summer of 1855 he worked with the Reverend White, or, as he came so easily to call him, Ben. The Wytheville circuit covered hundreds of miles of main roads, side roads, mountain roads, and settlement footpaths; in all, the equivalent of more than six counties.

Ben White was a small man like himself, but not lacking in drive and determination. He was a dark-haired, dark-eyed man, animated of face and with a gentle disposition.

"Perhaps we're both *too* gentle," Robert heard him say at the end of summer. They had traversed the territory, met and pleaded with many a whiskey maker, and preached and conjoled in every village they came to on the evils of making whiskey and drinking it, but their accomplishments fell woefully short of hoped for results. They had not even scratched the surface; if anything, they may have increased the tempers of the toughs and rowdies against them.

It was not a totally wasted summer for the true magnitude of the work to be done was spiritually uplifting. There was yet another bonus: when Robert returned home from his and Ben White's last foray before the starting of school his preaching license awaited him.

He taught that winter, but the way was now open for change. He and Ben White both agreed that if they were to affect even a slow-down in distillery building and its consequent evils, it would be a full-time job. Robert agreed to give up his school if Ben wanted him full-time and could arrange it with the conference officials.

By the New Year Ben White had made all the arrangements. When spring came Robert did not leave the school teaching profession with a great deal of sorrow. He now felt that he was not directing his own path but that he was being led by a much higher authority.

His one reservation concerned the long absences from his children.

"Far as the youngsters know, Leah and me have been part mother to them as far back as they can remember." Sarah said. "Elizabeth would want me to do this, and she'd know I'm happy doin' it."

"I thank you for that. Pray for me while I'm gone, and that I might be doing God's will," Robert said.

She promised she would and he rode away on the most beautiful spring day he could ever remember.

The first route taken after he joined Ben White was along the base of Cove Mountain for several miles, then eastward toward the adjoining county line. They were riding single file when suddenly Robert stopped. "Ben, I want to pray before we go any farther," he said. He left his companion sitting astride his horse, took his sheepskin prayer mat, and climbed halfway up the side of Cove Mountain, where he knelt upon a rock.

After a while Ben's calling brought Robert to his feet, and he descended the mountain. Ben sat in the shade of a large poplar tree with an embarrassed look on his face.

"I was worried about you, Robert. You've been up there for over two hours."

Robert made no apology and said, "I have sought the will and the companionship of God. Unless He be with us our missions will surely fail."

Numerous mountain streams provided a choice of inevitable distilling sites, and along one flush stream they found two stills. Robert volunteered to go pray with the owner of one and Ben took the other.

When he told the proprietor his business Robert felt certain that he was about to be set upon. With generous oaths the whiskey maker told him he'd make and sell what he pleased and the Methodists and the Baptists could be damned. In the very midst of this tirade Robert dropped to his knees. "Lord, make him stop…and if he does not, remove him from the earth that he may not corrupt Thy people, and cause his evil machine to be dislodged from its foundation with a crowbar and destroyed forever if it be Thy will…."

When he rejoined Ben White, Robert could see that he was not alone in having suffered rough treatment. Ben's nose bled and his neck was red and bore scratch marks.

"Did John Wesley ever have to go through anything like this, do you suppose?" Ben asked.

They rode eastward for several miles and took their dinner in the home of a widowed woman with five sons and from whom they learned of the biggest distillery operation in the valley.

"That poison put the devil in my husband, God rest his soul, and if those snakes of iniquity ever give my boys as much as a smell, I'll blow that still outta that meadow with gunpowder!" she exclaimed.

It was not difficult to find the stillhouse. The large copper boiler and worm box could be seen easily from the buggy road. The unit sat on the edge of a meadow under an open stillhouse by a clear stream that wound its way into the eastward-running creek along the base of the mountain.

"I don't believe there's anybody around!" Ben called out as they circled the apparatus without dismounting.

"You better think agin', neighbor!" a growling voice from the nearby woods called out. Presently a squat, red-faced man with powerful arms emerged.

Both of them dismounted at the approach of the distiller.

"I was just sittin' around waitin' for the corn mash to work off. What's your business here, anyhow?" the man asked.

Ben asked first who the still belonged to and was told by the speaker that it was his own. He then informed the man of their business; before he could finish, the owner became incensed. "Git your hides back out in that road and keep a-goin'!" he said without further hesitation.

"Not before you have heard the will of the Lord," Robert said. "It is not His desire that you should turn good men into wife-beaters and hatemongers who abuse their children and take food from their mouths to buy your devil's nectar!"

"If you won't git, then I'll gitcha," the distiller growled before he landed a swift kick against the calf of Robert's leg. Robert dropped to the ground because of the pain, but while there he implored his Maker to destroy the evil apparatus. "Make a mighty oak to fall across it and break its back," he prayed.

"Now that's a plumb funny request." The distiller laughed. "As you can plain see, the nearest tree is thirty yards from this branch."

Robert waited out the interruption and resumed praying. "We ask it not for ourselves, Lord, but for Thee who said: 'All things whatsoever ye shall ask in prayer, believing ye shall receive it'."

Robert looked up to see the rage-filled face of the distiller. With a powerful fist he struck Robert flat to the ground.

When Robert's eyes focused again he was sitting under a tree by the creek and Ben was carrying water in his cupped hands to pour over his throbbing head.

That night they stayed in the home of a chair maker near the road fork leading southward to Newbern. "You ain't seen one-tenth of the stillhouses there is around here," the aging householder told them when advised of their adventures.

They journeyed on to Newbern anyway, knowing that they would need to make the same trip over again and do the job better. The Methodists of Newbern gave them a good reception and showed a healthy enthusiasm for several sermons on intemperance that Robert and Ben preached.

Returning to Wytheville, they made visitations along the route to pastors of all denominations, inviting help and pulpit orations against this growing menace.

Before parting from Ben, Robert confirmed the date of their next rendezvous.

"I'll be ready for another foray in a week or so—say the beginning of May. We'll make it the first Monday," Ben said.

"I'll meet you at the courthouse," Robert agreed.

The ride from Wytheville southward to Cripple Creek had never been more beautiful. Profuse moss along the mountain trail punctuated by wild flowers and ornate fern seemed a Persian carpet of welcome as he wove in and out among the dogwood and blood-red Judas-tree blossoms. He inhaled again and again until his lungs cried for relief.

When he reached his cabin he found that somebody had already plowed his garden. Sarah and Leah were bent low, carrying stones from the newly upturned soil in their aprons. The three older boys were assisting their aunts by raking the rich earth in preparation for the seed. One whistle and they all ceased their labors to run and welcome him home.

Before they left the courthouse he and Ben decided to strike out in new directions. Ben's reasoning was simple and wise, Robert concluded. If they spent their time traveling to many areas and as far as the conference officials would authorize, pretty soon unscrupulous distillers in every neighborhood would know of their efforts. Admittedly they could not stop the practice as a whole, singlehandedly, but pointing out the evils of the practice to men who otherwise might never have stopped to think about the matter was the first step.

Being of one accord, Robert and Ben rode north, with the intent of working around Stony Fork, from whence they would journey across Walker Mountain, traveling still farther north until they came upon many east-running streams. Where the fertile valleys and cool limestone springs were found, there would the whiskey maker be also. Robert reminded Ben that they would not find the distillers as active in the spring as in the fall. At this time of year they would be using last year's corn, while in the fall, at corn harvest and when the fruits were plentiful for brandy, they would be out in full force.

"It matters little whether they're makin' or not," Ben said. "We can see the stillhouses anyhow. Portable stills along the streams can be traced to the owners, and we'll certainly know a man's intentions whether we see him at work or not."

They spent two weeks in the selected territory and decided to spend a third. They had learned early during this foray that it would be best not to separate: Robert had been badly beaten by two young toughs and Ben told of being switched like a disobedient schoolchild. Now they stayed together not so much as a fighting force, for defensive violence was out of the question and self-defeating, but for the benefit of attending each other if hostile treatment was inflicted. There was another realistic point; as Ben said, "Both of us put together hardly make up one real good fighting man."

"But we can run fast"—Robert grinned—"and a little man can get through the brush like a rabbit."

"We may have to try that out if we get amongst too rough a crowd. I heard some tragic news from North Carolina before we started on this journey. One of our Methodist brothers got tied to a tree in that state by a bunch of toughs who thought that it was time to close down a prayer meeting. They tied the brother to a tree and poured molasses over him. We don't have to guess about what the ants did to him, but a bear interrupted the proceedings and mauled him to death trying to lap up all the molasses from his body."

Robert shivered a little, for he'd never made a trip across any of the mountains without having seen at least one of the muscular beasts. "I'll try to remember my Lord and His decree when Daniel found himself in the lion's den," he said self comfortingly.

If they had received harsh treatment in the first two weeks of their foray, the remaining week proceeded toward the other extreme. They found an entire family along Kimberling Creek distilling liquor with such fury and friendliness they could only watch in amazement.

"Sure, we're God-lovin', God-fearin' Christians," the head of the clan informed Robert. "But you see that wash – poor new ground on the side of the mountain? We're nigh about to starve to death, and can't make a dollar nowhere. There was a bunch of surveyors from some land company working through here for a few weeks and they said they'd buy anything from me I could make with any kick to it. I've already run out of corn, but those wild berries you see a-fermentin' ain't goin' to be in good supply for very long, and you better bet I'm a-squeezin' out every drap of brandy there is in 'em."

The family paused long enough for group prayer and went energetically back to work.

Robert had not encountered quite this situation before, and he puzzled over calling down the wrath of God or exercising restraint in the light of economic necessity. The family worked on, but he called to them, "I will pray that you may be shown a better occupation so you needn't make your living from the misery of others!"

"I'll do it, preacher, and I ain't particular what the Lord sends if it will fill our bellies."

Ben brought up the horses with a grin.

"What's the matter?" Robert asked.

"That oldest boy walking toward the worm box… he said those fellows they'd been selling to weren't the least miserable the last time he'd seen them… said they were downright happy, in fact."

"Whose side are you on?" Robert exclaimed. "One day you might just buy one of those tracts of land, and I'll bet the lines are as crooked as a dog's hind leg."

The final two days of their journey found them crossing still another mountain to Bluestone Creek. They were immediately discouraged from spending more time along the meandering waters of that stream, for here problems of another nature became known to them. The disease of milk sick ran rampant along the valley. That night they circled back to the base of East River Mountain and spent the night with a non-English-speaking German family. Robert read his Bible for them anyway, and the young German man got his own Bible when Robert had finished and did likewise in his native tongue.

At dawn they were saddled, well fed, and ready to head south for Wythe County.

"Lebewohl!" Friendly faces and waving hands gave a last salute.

"Thank you and may God be with you!" Robert called to them in return.

In contrast to what Robert had experienced along the westward-running roadways, travel across the mountains going north was infrequent. During their return journey only a few loaded wagons and fewer than twice as many buggies met them, heading north. Mounted riders were plentiful, but it was hard to determine whether they were long- or short-distance travelers.

Finally Walker Mountain alone remained to be crossed before the lush green bottoms of Wythe County would be not many miles in the distance.

"It won't be long now until you can take that sheepskin from your saddle and shake the dust out of it," Ben said jovially.

"And it won't be long getting dusty again. Between the trips with you I want to do some pulpit supply work close home, and before we get tied up full time this fall with the whiskey makers I want to join with the workers at some of the camp meetings. I've been invited to go to the Dismal camp ground and I'd like to attend."

"I don't see why you can't make your own arrangements between our trips. I do think you ought to keep a good record of the free-will offerings you are given. You don't have to, since you're not officially with the conference, but as long as we're working together I'd like to give a report when I am called upon to render my own accounts."

"That hasn't been much of a problem so far, has it?" Robert said.

Ben laughed and said that nobody could ever accuse them of being in a money-making business.

A heavily loaded wagon crested Walker Mountain at the same time that they too approached the summit. Robert threw up his hand in greeting to the wagon driver and his family, but instead of waving back, the squat little man stood up in the wagon and whipped his horses unmercifully.

"What do you make of that?" Robert said.

"Don't we know that man?"

Robert turned in his saddle to get another look and saw the wagon picking up speed as frantic horses started downgrade. At the turn the speeding wagon wheels careened in the loose dirt and the rear of the wagon smacked broadside into a hickory tree, flipping on its side into the opposite ditch.

Both Robert and Ben pulled children from under furniture and house hold paraphernalia before the young ones knew what had happened. The stocky strong-armed little man came from under a burst feather tick, cursing loudly and apparently not in the least grateful that the soft protector had saved him from a broken neck. The mother was bleeding about the forearm, but she could walk. She moved to stand quickly beside her children.

"Get away from us!" the man screeched when he came fully to his senses.

"Who are you? Your face looks familiar," Robert said.

"You ought to remember me—you put me out of business."

Robert had to follow the man's back-pedaling footsteps to keep up the conversation.

"This is one of the distillers," Ben said in a flash of recognition.

"I don't want nothin' to do with you!" the short man trembled. "I seen it happen with my own eyes!"

"Saw what happen?" Ben asked.

"It started to rain and lightnin', and afore I could get to the woods the wind laid me flat on the ground… and I looked up…and like a feather in a whirlwind a white oak tree as big around as that wagon wheel came dancin' down the hill and squashed my stillhouse like a stepped-on chicken egg!"

The little man stood panting for breath and his muscular arms flexed and unflexed as he relived the unbelievable that he had seen with his own eyes. Ben looked at him strangely, but Robert said nothing.

The wagon horses were unhitched, and, with the aid of a chain, they righted the wagon until all four wheels sat on solid ground.

"God be with you, my brother!" Robert called earnestly.

"He already was," a fearful voice shot back from the disappearing wagon.

CHAPTER XI

During the fall of 1858 Robert concluded his last attack against the whiskey makers in the company of Ben White.

"We've done all the good we can do for now," Ben said. "The conference officials agree, and they know as well as we do that if we don't let up for a while we'll just get ourselves killed."

"Tell Bishop Andrew when you see him that we gave the call 'to godliness' whether anybody heard it or not."

"They heard it all right, and thanks to you our work has been ten times more fruitful than any of us ever dared to dream. The church will work harder and harder to effect laws prohibiting the sale of liquor to any person, you can count on that."

"I take no credit for the workings of my divine Lord."

"Nevertheless, we thank His servant Robert Sheffey also," Ben said with a final handshake. "Robert, I must confess my own faith and dedication to purpose has been immeasurably strengthened and blessed by this experience we have shared over the last three years. I must confess, also, that in the beginning I couldn't understand your need to spend a third of our time in prayer, and you must forgive me for my impatience and lesser faith."

"In time we will both gain more patience in waiting upon our blessed Lord."

"May God's hand be upon me as I know it is upon you," Ben said reverently. "I have seen things that fill me with awe to prove that He has touched you. I will not soon forget you, Robert Sheffey, nor will the world."

"To God be the glory," Robert said humbly, and the two of them shared a parting prayer.

That winter passed slowly and bleakly. What money he earned was dependent upon what people were disposed to give him as he preached here and there: for a sick minister unable to perform his duties or a congregation who had lost their minister by death and awaited another conference-assigned replacement. Once during the winter he served a breakaway faction of a congregation in Grayson County and found himself in the midst of a bitter controversy.

Even more rarely did a pittance of his livelihood come from the sympathetic and grateful homesteaders along the less-traveled backwoods who were the object of his home evangelism during the cold months of winter. Empty pockets alone were not the badge of his status as he trudged from valley to valley and mountaintop to mountaintop with snow filled shoes, only to return home to find that, were it not for the grace of family and concerned neighbors—even those who did not always believe in his works—his own children would have been hungry and cold.

Not entirely in the back of his mind was Ben White's suggestion that he affiliate with the Holston Conference on Methodism. There would be advantages to having an assigned charge if they now felt him qualified, but there were disadvantages also. He could not reach the people who most needed reaching if he were confined to one small geographical district.

There was another factor that had long been present in his mind and was in fact the final element in his decision not to ally himself with the church conference. It was the issue of church politics and organized religion. He questioned God's approval of churches' conducting themselves like county courthouses, with church politicians gathering once a year to divide up the territory and the spoils, and to determine what policies would officially be sanctioned in the heart of every conference member for the next twelve months. He could not justify this feeling of voluntary alienation entirely, for he had been a part of the conference for the last three years with Ben White, and the results had been good. He also held many of the conference members whom he knew in highest regard, and they had told him of mission work and of the efficiency of organized effort through which much more was accomplished than could be done by a solitary, unaffiliate. But every argument with which he assailed or supported his position could not supersede the final one: Jesus Christ had for a short while been an independent man on earth, wandering about the countryside, giving voice and comfort to people wherever He found them. Where Jesus had been the voice of His Father, now Robert in like manner would be the unencumbered voice of Jesus, moving in the same atmosphere of freedom among all of the people, wherever he found them. A Methodist, yes, but an independent one.

By spring he was bursting with such vigor that he worked from daylight until dark getting the garden planted, in order that such duties would not deter him from what he considered his real work. This year he decided to look for completely new territory—places he had never visited—where he could serve with a missionary zeal even more dynamic than any he had ever experienced before.

The night before he was to leave, the children gathered about him, and he told them of lands flush with cool springs of every variety.

"There are springs of limestone, freestone, Sulphur, mixed minerals, and all kinds of funny-tasting water," he said to his giggling offspring. "If I follow the New River to the northern most part of this new country—Monroe County, by name—I will come to a new river of which none of you has ever heard before. It's called Greenbrier River."

He did not hurry his journey as he left Cripple Creek, and when the roads permitted he kept to New River as much as he could. He felt a sense of peace riding along the river that he did not experience elsewhere. But this peace did not always go unpunctuated by sound. A new age had dawned, and during those three years he had spent in the far-off mountains and valleys with Ben White a puffing locomotive had steamed down the track from Lynchburg to the Tennessee line. It was the thing his uncle James had dreamed about and never lived to see. This country he had known for so many years would never be the same again, of that he was certain. Without really knowing why, it made him a little sad. He swung his horse northward, away from the new and shiny tracks, which stretched as far to the east and to the west as he could see.

He found soon after arrival in Monroe County a sincere interest in and receptivity to his Christian work. Before the month was out he had covered the remotest areas of the county and used everything from a one-room school to a hay barn in the course of services that could not be held in a regular church. Too soon the services were over. Other areas remained, virgin ground for the Word, and he must be on his way. He would leave these new-found friends with reluctance, for they had demonstrated a dynamic spiritual hunger and vitality for life that included an interest in all things both far and near. In particular the new railroad far to the south of them was still a matter of fascination, although it was now more than three years old.

"Is it true *that* puffin' steam engine knocked down a thousand people when it turned around in Dublin—when the tracks ended there?" a lanky black smith asked him as Robert prepared to leave the county.

"It's only partly true." Robert smiled surprised that the story had been circulated so widely.

"It's been about three years ago I heard about it," the smithy said while he worked on Robert's saddle. "There now, I've fixed it. That bellyband ought to hold the saddle on your horse for a few hundred miles."

The blacksmith puffed on his pipe and shuffled his feet for a minute while Robert searched his pockets for money to pay the repair bill. Finally he found some coins in his bandanna handkerchief. He handed the larger one to the blacksmith, and was surprised to have it refused.

"You don't owe me nothin', preacher, and looks like you'd just be givin' me back the same coin I give you in the collection at the house-raisin'."

"I didn't remember you being there," Robert said, startled.

"I was there measuring for some door hinges I'm makin' for my part of the house-raisin'. I never heard a man preach at a house-raisin' before, but it meant something to me—meant a lot to them burned-out folks too. Never saw nobody happier. And now they got a new house almost under roof and preacher blessed before it's ready to move into. Are you goin' to preach in some more of the churches around here afore you leave?"

"Not this time. Three weeks might be enough for me—I don't want to wear out my welcome. I've been asked to come back."

"I'll be lookin' for you, and I'll not soon forget your face."

Before nightfall of the second day Robert passed southward, through Salt Sulphur Springs, Peterstown, and Pearisburg; turning from the turnpike road, he finally gave rest to his horse a long Walker's Creek, near to a village in the county of Giles, known as the Irish Settlement. He led his horse from the road down to the creek.

"Take a long drink, Charles Thomas Robert, you've earned it today," he said to the animal, who recognized her wrong gendered name with a whinny.

He took off his own shoes and dangled his feet in the cool May water, then got up and knelt so as to wash his face and hands. "We'll sleep in the house of good Methodists tonight if they'll have us," he addressed his only companion again.

He had stayed in this friendly village before when he had worked in the western end of Montgomery County and had ferried the river into Giles. It was with the same family whose hospitality he had enjoyed previously that he hoped to spend the night.

When he stood in the yard of Ed Stafford's two-story log house the dogs no sooner had called a greeting than their master stood at his door in night clothes. Robert could tell that the man was ill and did not recognize him so he reintroduced himself.

"We've all got the sickness, but I know you were counting on spending the night."

"I'll find someplace else. Now don't you fret about it, Brother Stafford. Providence be with you, and I'll see you on another trip," Robert said.

Ed Stafford thanked him and was touching in his apology. He added, "Go to the house of James and Margaret Stafford and tell them I sent you. They will make you feel at home."

Robert did not wait for the directions to be repeated. It was now nearly dark. Aside from James and Margaret Stafford, the household consisted of one unmarried daughter approaching middle age and one unmarried son who appeared to be in his mid-twenties. The Stafford's had other sons not living at home, Robert was told, but the truth was, he anxiously awaited a taste of the food he could smell much more than additional information about the family tree of his host.

Before he had washed his hands and bowed his head at the Stafford table his host and hostess had made him feel so much a part of the house hold that he could only marvel at the experience. It had long been dark and yet the aura here was one of perpetual sunshine.

Margaret Stafford had the rosy cheeks and alert cyanic eyes that, added to her cheerful disposition, made the Irish housewife beloved wherever she was to be found. Although moderately tall, her movements were quick as she served at the table. When all had been done she brushed back her chestnut-colored hair and joined her guests.

The other younger woman of the household remained standing until all plates were served.

"Why don't you sit down, Elizabeth? I think we can all make do," Margaret Stafford said.

Robert took special notice of so beloved a name, and stood to seat her. She sat down gracefully, thanking him with a demure smile, accentuated by pretty teeth and a glowing countenance.

"And where have you been on your rounds this time?" James Stafford asked.

Robert looked startled, and Margaret Stafford said, "Your name and work are not unknown to us, and there can be nothing but right in telling you that prayers in this very house have been uttered on your behalf."

Robert thanked them and told them from where he had just come and something of the day-to-day details.

"I've never been to Monroe County but once in my life, and I accidentally met a man there I'll never forget," James Stafford said. "He was a most interesting fellow—name was Dr. J. J. Moorman—and he was traveling through that section, taking samples of all the Sulphur water in the springs there. I remember him telling me that the water might have powers to cure sick people and that more hospitals and rest homes ought to be built in that area. You suppose there's anything to that?"

There was a mischievous grin on James Stafford's genial face, but Robert was only partially conscious of it or the need to answer the question: he had his mind on the attractive younger woman at his side that exuded a delightful presence even in her silence.

"I don't know," he said finally when the table had grown completely quiet. "What do you think, Elizabeth?" Elizabeth smoothed her honey-colored hair and tucked at the bun on the back of her head. Her posture was straight and her manner attentive. "Would Sulphur water cure my headaches, broken bones, or sour stomachs?" Robert enlarged on the question.

"I don't know about others, but I can be perfectly well and that water makes me sick just to smell it!" Elizabeth said, blue eyes dancing merrily.

The youngest at table advised them all that such mineral water must be good for some ailments, for a man in the nearby village of Pearisburg was selling bottles of it, and so successful was it that all sorts of miracle cures were claimed.

"That might be so, Jimmy," his father said, "but my guess is, knowing the man you're talking about, his 'mineral water' is about nine-tenths apple brandy and the Miracle cures are dreams of his patients after they've had a three-or four-bottle dosage!"

The laughter became even jollier with James Stafford's thin-skinned; ruddy face turning redder and Elizabeth's and her mother's cheeks getting an even rosier glow.

Too soon time came for a pre-bedtime snack of pie smothered in honey and a tall glass of buttermilk. The early hours of night were gone, passing so swiftly, so delightfully, in the company of new friends who were a balm to Robert's soul. When he went to his bed he knelt on the floor, resting his elbows on the sun-cured, crisp bed linen and the white counterpane for which he had asked and received, and marveled to God at His genius for the creation of life and the gift of human fellowship, especially as it was manifested in these new people.

He fully intended to leave the next morning, but at breakfast Margaret Stafford said philosophically, "But Mr. Sheffey, the body needs rest if the soul is to be penetrated to its greatest depths."

"Stay on with us a few days," James Stafford suggested, "and if we don't send you away in better shape than when we found you, then you can dishonor our name all the way to Monroe County the next time you go."

Elizabeth said nothing, but her alert eyes seemed to say to him, "Stay."

He did stay, and learned that the Irish Settlement of which he was very temporarily a resident had been settled by Staffords in 1785.

"And we didn't get chased out of England either," Elizabeth said with even more joviality than she had shown the previous day. "The tale has been handed down that our people had great sympathy for the colonists in the Revolutionary War. A new land, a new independence to worship and believe as one pleased, and a chance to be a part of a fresh new movement of self-government seemed a paradise compared to what our forefathers in Ireland must have endured."

"God has given us a great new land. It has long been my prayer that we use only what we need and protect the rest of it with the passion of a mother for her suckling baby," Robert said.

He detected her looking at him oddly then, and he rethought his words and knew that they must have sounded excessively solemn. Before he could explain himself in greater detail, she said, "Do you always take everything in life so seriously?"

The question caught him off guard, for it had never occurred to him that one could take life too seriously. One either understood life or else lived in the chains of self-deception. He still paused, partially because in this woman there was a gregarious bent; her mind seemed always two jumps ahead of his.

"I suppose I see the serious side of life because it's the side I want to see—or the part I'm exposed to most often. No, I should go beyond that and say it is what my Lord has picked for me to see."

"I didn't mean to make light of you in any way. Many of my people were converted by John and Charles Wesley before coming to America. We are not unmindful of the need for spiritual obedience, but neither have we forgotten the need to laugh at ourselves on occasion."

She said no more then, but her face was bright and expectant. The very essence of life seemed to swirl about her, and Robert was conscious that he had never known a woman quite like this one.

"It is good I have met you, Miss Stafford, for God does truly reveal himself in wondrous ways. Yes, I am glad I stopped in the Irish Settlement..."

The next morning his horse was saddled and made ready by his host, but the animal only nipped at the ground, oblivious to everything.

"You see, even Charles Thomas Robert does not wish to go. She believes, I think, that the sweetest of spring clover grows in this valley, and I believe she is right," Robert said as he mounted.

Like stair steps in height, the father, his wife, and Elizabeth stood side by side, waving to him. "Come back, Brother Sheffey, come back any time!" James Stafford called in a tenor voice. Margaret Stafford repeated the invitation, and Robert promised that he would. There was no doubt that the promise would be kept as he gave one final wave of his hand to Elizabeth.

Charles Thomas Robert moved sideways along the road shoulder for one final mouthful of grass before she picked up her normal traveling gait.

"It's not easy to leave, Charles Thomas Robert. The grass is sweet and the food is savory. But maybe that's the best reason of all to leave—maybe we would nourish ourselves to excessive contentment...."

Even as he spoke the words to the animal and his voice trailed into silence, the eyes of his mind did not want to wipe away the picture. There was a glow in Elizabeth that made his pulse quicken and his heart race shamefully for a man almost forty. He suspected that she was very near the same age, but he hadn't dared ask. His aunt Elizabeth would surely turn over in her grave if he had done so. No sooner did his aunt rise up from out of the past then his deceased wife, Elizabeth, did also. There was really no question. From the standpoint of physical beauty, Elizabeth Swecker held the honors. And in the oft-remembered eyes of Elizabeth Swecker there was still the vision of something he had not captured… something that was mysteriously beyond his reach and was now forever lost.

It was the opposite with Elizabeth Stafford. She had not the slightest aura of mystery about her and her entire being pulsated with an extroverted vitality that seemed never to run down. This fresh openness gave rise to feelings of delight but feelings of disloyalty and betrayal as well. He had not been a widower long enough to shed the instinctive loyalty to his dead wife.

"But every man gets lonesome, wouldn't you say, Charles Thomas Robert?" he said in defense of his own heart. "When we get back to Cripple Creek you will have forgotten the clover and I shall have forgotten such sweetness that I must surely be imagining it."

Bad news awaited when at last he was on home ground again. Sarah reported that James Wesley, the oldest boy, had run away from home and they had been frantic, without a trace as to his whereabouts, until his uncle James in Marion had reported the arrival of the unexpected guest.

"His uncle in Marion sent him back to Wytheville on the train, and when Papa went to Wytheville to get him the boy was so excited from the train ride, Papa liked never to have got him home," Sarah said.

"To tell you the truth, I'd like to ride the thing myself sometime," Robert said.

"You'd better straighten that boy out or he'll be doin' the very same thing the next time you're gone. He's gettin' too big for me to handle. And I don't mean he's not a good boy—it's just that he's old for his years and he's gettin' restless."

Robert promised to talk to his son promptly. He could tell that Sarah felt he was not as upset as he ought to be regarding the matter. The truth was, he remembered with delightful clarity when he himself had taken flight and how it helped him to grow. Still, his son was four years younger than he had been at the time. In spite of the boy's actions Robert brushed aside Sarah's and her father's urgings to deal harshly with James Wesley lest he do the same thing again and perhaps encourage his brothers to do likewise.

Robert let the matter rest a few days, and when the time came that he worked alone with his eldest son in the garden he gently confronted him with the worry he had caused his aunts and grandparents by his actions.

"I did it 'cause I'm gettin' too big to stay around here and be bossed by grand folks and old-maid aunts!" the boy said.

Robert was taken aback by this hostility, but he kept his patience. "But, son, you are not old enough to leave home and earn your own way, and you know your mother' s people need you here to help with the smaller children…"

"So you can chase off and ride all over creation! I don't want to stay around here anymore!"

"Your words pain me deeply, son, but that's not so important. Do you believe I 'chase all over creation' for my own pleasure, or would you guess it's for some other reason?"

The boy rested his chin on the handle of his hoe and lowered his eyes.

"Well? Have you forgotten our family prayers together when we have held hands and asked God to keep us together even when we're apart? And can't you remember anything I've told you of what our sweet Lord had done through me?"

"Aunt Sarah and Aunt Leah have talked to me about it—but I don't see the matter of it!"

"It counts more than anything in the world, son. And bless the sweet hearts of your mother's sisters for the good help they have been to us. They serve their Lord in a special way when they keep our home and make it possible for me to tell others of His wondrous love—others who might not hear it at all unless somebody trudged the ridges and hollows and told them."

"*You* don't have to do it all, and now it doesn't matter anyway—I'll run away again when you leave. I'd like to work around the trains. I asked Uncle James if he would help me get a job—that's why I went up there."

"Your uncle would not aid you if your behavior didn't make you deserving."

"He said he would," the youth said defiantly and rose to his full height, which now exceeded that of his father's.

Robert stepped over a row of vegetables and placed his hand on the boy's shoulder and looked into eyes that could never belie that he was his mother's son. "Tell me one thing before we go any further," Robert insisted. "Do you believe what I am doing is honorable and right—that I walk in God's glory and not my own?"

The youth's eyes were brimming and he did not answer.

"Is it that you are ashamed of me—that you look upon your uncle's wealth and position and wish you were his son…?"

"No, Father." The tears in the boy's eyes spilled over and ran down dusty cheeks. "I'm not ashamed, but I want to earn some money and pay my own way. And I'll send some of it home." Then he added belatedly, "Uncle James said he'd help me if you'd agree when the time was right. Said he'd help me get some more schoolin' at the academy, and maybe work, too. He said he thought that was the best thing to do."

Robert put his arm around the shoulders of his son and saw that the boy was relieved by his outpouring.

"I know it's heavy on your heart, son, and I won't put it out of my mind. Let me talk to the Lord about it first, though."

He prepared to ride out again the first week of June, but before he did he called James Wesley to him and walked with his son along the waters of Cripple Creek.

"Son, I have wondered as I talked to the Lord about the thing which is on your mind whether or not you have ever talked to Him about it."

"Yes, Father, I have. Every night when I say my prayers."

"But did you pray that you could do as you want or did you pray that God's will be done, whatever that is?"

"I—I guess I prayed to have my way… but I want to go so bad." The boy's chin dropped to his chest.

"God is very near to him who seeks divine guidance. Wesley, I want you to pray that God's will be done in this matter, for the rest of the summer and winter and spring. I will add my own blessing then, if our Father has not shown His will to the contrary. It is understood, of course, that you will be in the earthly keeping of your uncle James."

Robert saw disappointment in his son's face but without argument the boy agreed to the terms.

"You are a good boy, Wesley. Your blessed mother and her sisters are to be thanked for it, but now that you are becoming a man never go so far or rise so high that you do not ask your Maker as each day dawns what His will for that day might be."

"I can't hear as you do, Father. I've thought about that."

"The hearing comes after the listening. What do you hear right now?"

The youth paused, smiled, listened, and said, "Why, it's just some kind of bird callin'."

"Listen again."

The boy did, longer this time.

"I guess it's two birds callin' to each other and a rain crow across the way."

"Listen again."

The youth added the braying of a mule somewhere in the distance and showed his impatience in the tone of his voice.

"You have not heard one one-thousandth of it. You have missed the buzz of the bees behind you, the ripple of the creek, the whisper of the breeze as it passes through the pines, the sound of water being drunk by *that* milk cow, the chirp of the insects in the grass, the hammer of the wood hen's beak against the tree—I could go on and on until we stood in darkness and still newer sounds invaded our ears."

"Yes, sir."

"Do you understand what God is saying?"

"Yes, sir."

"Then all is well, but there is one more thing I want you to think on while the time is coming: whatever your work, make it also your prayer. Come now and help me ready my things, for I wish to be gone before sunrise."

The summer did not go according to plan at all. Robert intended to make a return trip to Monroe County in July and work throughout Mercer County, adjoining it, in August, after he had spent time at home. He had been certain that the chance for resting from his travels with the Stafford family for a few days would come, and long before his thirty-ninth birthday had been very long gone.

It hadn't worked out that way, though, and the month was late October before his travels took him through Giles County again, preparatory to excursions into new sections of Monroe and Mercer counties.

"We thought you'd forgotten us," Margaret Stafford said when heavy footsteps resounded unannounced on her front porch and she had identified Robert.

James Stafford put down the paper, which blocked Robert's view of the eyes he remembered as friendly and azure. The older man stood and accepted the offered hand. "You have not been so far back in the wilderness that you haven't heard about the raid?" James Stafford asked, pointing to the paper.

Robert pleaded ignorance and said indeed he had been in the wilderness.

"Well, it may not amount to anything, but a fellow by the name of John Brown led a raid on a federal gun house and armory at Harpers Ferry—way up in the north tip of the state near to Washington."

"Is that just lately?" Robert again pleaded ignorance of current affairs.

"On October sixteenth!" a feminine voice called from the doorway.

He turned and smiled at Elizabeth, who looked a little heavier than when he had seen her in the spring. She had, however, held the delicate balance between a healthy, well-fed look and that of actual plumpness. Her cheeks were tanned somewhat, but the affect was one of heightening her prettiness.

He took her outstretched hand and said how impressed he was that she knew all about current affairs. This in turn made her face bloom.

"It's all the talk at the county seat," she said. "Some of the people who've gotten a copy of city papers say that John Brown was trying to capture federal guns to give to the slaves so they could free themselves."

"Well, *this* paper says he was just a crazy man from Kansas who'd stirred up trouble out there also, and, 'The sooner he is hanged, the better'," James Stafford quoted.

Throughout the supper hour Robert listened to father and daughter discusses all they had heard of the uprising, how some of the papers were saying that John Brown had more sympathizers in the extreme northwestern part of the state than was being publicized.

"I don't think our frontier counties are as up in arms as some of the papers are saying. Up around Charleston they've been complaining for twenty years about the distance to the capital, also that they're not getting their fair share of revenue and attention. Things will quiet down after a while, though. You mark my word," James Stafford said.

Finally Robert was alone with Elizabeth, and she repeated her mother's words: "We thought you had forgotten us when all of summer passed."

"How could I forget something… someone… that has been on my mind all the sunny days of summer? I went to Russell and Scott counties after they sent for me, and thought I'd be there just a short spell."

"I'm glad they treated you so well that you were encouraged to stay on. I know you were thankful for the spiritual hunger," she said.

"Well, the situation wasn't quite like that when I got there. It was a camp for a state and county road-building project along the Clinch River. They were a rough gang of men, and when they weren't working they didn't have anything on their minds except fighting, card playing, and drinking. Thank the Lord they couldn't find any women—or the women couldn't find them. It was pretty barren country. We had prayer meeting on Thursdays and preaching twice a day on Sundays. I spent part of the summer in one county and part in another. And I was sure there wasn't any spiritual hunger when I first got there and saw people more like animals than men and women."

"And you found out differently?"

"Before the fifteenth day of September I sprinkled or baptized every man in camp who hadn't been converted, except for eight men."

"Robert, can't you return to our church before the weather gets cold and tell us more about your work?"

"Yes. I'll do it on my way back from Mercer County. Now I don't need an excuse to stop at your home, do I?"

"You don't ever need an excuse, Robert. I thought we'd all made that clear to you. Our home can be your home just as your God is our God."

"I have never heard simple words sound so dear, Elizabeth—"

"I would prefer that you call me Eliza; all my friends do."

Eliza's brother Jimmy came in before bedtime and gave them additional news. A traveling drummer from Baltimore had told at the neighborhood store that John Brown had massacred people in Kansas and has said, "God told me to do it."

Eliza shivered a little. "Massacres are not very pleasant to think about at bedtime, Jimmy," she said.

Nevertheless, they all did retire, but not before ominous eyes had exchanged glances with other ominous eyes, Robert noticed, and he tossed in his own bed long after the household was quiet.

At breakfast he was the last to come to the table, and before he was seated he could not help noticing furrowed brows and questioning gazes upon him.

"What's the matter, Robert?" Eliza rose halfway out of her chair.

"I don't know what you mean," he said.

"It's your face, Robert," Margaret Stafford said anxiously. "Your countenance is lamping."

He felt with his hand. He knew he must speak, must tell them now…

Eliza was quickly at his side. "Are you sick, Robert?"

"No. I'm all right. Just let me think a few minutes…and get me a glass of water—would you do that, Eliza?"

He sipped it slowly, but his eyes looked across their heads until his vision affixed itself upon a dying oak tree through the window.

"It was the dream…"

"What?" Eliza whispered.

"The dream...," he said absently. "...the dream. But I don't know what it means."

"Can you tell us about it?" More than one voice reached him.

"I had the most vivid dream, but I don't understand it. A young mother was standing in a meadow of tall grass, nursing two children at her breasts. They were not babies, but rather young sons. They broke away from her while the milk yet poured from her breasts and picked up swords from the grass. After each one struck a blow she fell to the ground, split in twain. When the sons stood in their mother's blood one was laughing and the other was crying."

He could speak no more of it, for he did not know what he had envisioned or why. He ate his breakfast in solitude and departed the house.

Robert's first knowledge of the Civil War came two weeks after the firing on Fort Sumter in April 1861. The news, coming from so far away, caused little commotion and he trudged off to the wilds of Lee County where, he was told, territory existed: "Too rugged for a bear and too scary for an Indian."

"Charles Thomas Robert and I don't believe God ever made any territory the devil could chase a man into and be safe in hiding from the Lord," Robert declared.

The separation of the northwest territory of Virginia and the impending convention, meeting to make that separation permanent, plus the secession of some states and talk of doing so by others, began to make up for turmoil and strife originally lacking.

By 1862 the spirit of his work had begun to suffer. The world seemed a mass of confusion. The northwest territories of the state, according to the newspapers, had repudiated secession and were calling themselves West Virginia. The call to arms invoked sorrow throughout homes of the ridges and plains alike, until he felt that not a word of comfort he offered, or a prayer he uttered, or a sermon he preached, was being heard. All ears seemed to hear only anguish, and eyes seemed only inflamed with anger or tears at the departure of loved ones who might never return. The God of War was now the great Presence.

"They need you more now than ever," Eliza would say encouragingly as he crisscrossed the territory, taking only occasional rest in the Irish Settlement.

"They don't seem to be listening, and I talk to the Lord about it until my prayer mat runs of my sweat."

"They are listening more faithfully, perhaps, than you realize. In these troubled days they wear new faces. Maybe it is this which you have not taken into account."

The first snow fell on October twentieth, and if there was ever a fall bleaker than this one Robert could not remember it. For almost three years John Brown had lain rotting in his grave, and now, from northern Virginia at Bull Run, and Murfreesboro in Tennessee, and Mill Springs in Kentucky to the west, the news and sounds of war came ever nearer. McClellan's moves on Richmond had brought the war still closer to home, but it was not necessary for guns to explode along Cripple Creek as a reminder that devastation crept toward them with every passing day. Robert found himself kneeling in prayer with his oldest son as the youth prepared to make his contribution to the defense of his home country.

Hugh Trigg, his second son, took his older brother's job and schoolroom chair, and Robert found his household reduced to four children. In addition, Sarah and Leah were now suggesting that those remaining be allowed to move back with their uncle and grandparents, to whom they were so close. Robert would not consent to such an arrangement at that time, but promised to think about it and make a decision later.

His ministry now began to take some new turns. He did not discontinue the personal evangelism and the home visits, but increasingly he found himself a part of prayer groups who, he believed, would gladly have stayed on their knees forever if that would bring their sons and husbands home and peace again to their land. He found himself preaching to units of home guards and local encampments of soldiers who were organizing to move out and into the heat of the battle in some distant location.

A week before Thanksgiving, at Eliza's invitation, he rode to the Irish Settlement and saw for the first time, Eliza's household in the grip of a most painful sadness. War had come closer to home for his dear friends also, as they prepared to give up their brother and youngest son.

"Brother Robert, we will organize at Pearisburg on Saturday. I will be in Captain Andrew Gott's company of the thirty-sixth Virginia Regiment, and I'd be obliged if you'd say a prayer over us," Jimmy Stafford said.

Robert did as he was asked, and returned home with the Stafford family, whose sorrow he shared in the same manner as that which he had felt at his own son's departure.

"We are not prepared for this!" Eliza wept. "What senseless men have brought this terrible thing upon us!"

He tried to comfort her, but she grew quiet and remote from him. Every member of the house hold found a favorite corner in which to grieve, but he prayed with each of them until faith emerged victorious over unhappiness.

"I don't know how we could have faced this without you, Robert," Eliza said. "You have been such a help to us, and there is such strength and conviction in your prayers."

"Whatever the decree of our divine Lord, we must accept it. Do you believe that as strongly as I do, Eliza?"

"Yes, I believe it. I'm not sure I can be as strong in that way as you are … perhaps as I grow more, spiritually. Maybe through you my own faith is deepening…"

"I would be pleased if I could be instrumental, if you saw in me some gift, some closeness to God that shines of His glory—"

"I think I believed in you long before I ever met you, Robert. Now there is no doubt."

He reached for her hand then, and she gave it willingly.

"If I could ever give you back six-fold the love that has been shown to me in this house I would still feel indebted. I've often thought of the happy times that Jesus enjoyed in the house of Lazarus and Mary and Martha. How much this house has been like that for me when I grow weary of my travels. With all of God's blessings to me I think none is greater than the arms of my children and the sweetness of this house."

He rode back to Cripple Creek still savoring the sweetness about which he had spoken. There were few days now that Eliza's loving face and kind blue eyes were absent from his thoughts. But accompanying the beautiful was the ugly, and fears about the war invaded his senses by every route.

"Don't any of us know what's goin' to happen," Wendell Swecker said, "but if them Yankees swoop down on us they'll take everythin' we got. Some of us'll be lucky if we have enough corn left for seed. What I'm sayin' is, why don't you rent out your place to a hustlin' family that can raise all that the ground will stand? You don't have the time to plant much more than a big garden."

"If those Yankees do swarm down I'd rather have these children closer to my kin." Sarah added fuel to the argument of her father.

Later in the week his brother-in-law also approached him. "I'm not sayin' I always believed in your callin', but Leah and Sarah changed my mind," Ben Swecker began. "And there are some sayin' you're just too lazy to tend your land. I stood up for you and told them that the Good Book pardons a man for leavin' his family if it's for the purpose of doin' the Lord's work. Anyway, with you being gone so much I'd like to keep Daniel Winton with me a while. The boy is gettin' close on fifteen, and he can be a lot of help—and he's takin' a real likin' to me. I don't aim to steal him from you, and I'll honor your name, you can count on it."

"I'd thank you for that," Robert said.

"Way I see it, there's no reason we can't both be a daddy to him. I'm as stuck on him as he is on me. I'll be good to him, and, when he gets older if he wants to leave I won't make any claim on him. I might as well tell you, John Robert wants to come with him."

At first Robert could not bear the thought of his youngest child's—hardly ten years old—leaving home. Sarah scoffed at this, saying, "They won't be goin' anywhere. They'll be where they've always been—just sleepin' in different beds, that's all. They'll be in one house as much as the other. If it'll put your mind at ease any, neither one of the girls can remember her mother. I am their mother as far as they're concerned, and I don't have to prove it to you that I've got a mother's love for them."

"No, you don't, Sarah… and God bless you."

It all made sense. Why not turn over his land to someone who could have food growing on every cleared foot of it? Indeed, the whole county might be laid to waste within twelve months. If devastation came upon them God would need him more than ever to weep and pray with the bereaved, the hungry, the poor and suffering.

It all made sense, really. Nothing was changing very much—and yet it was. Division would be taking place, and in a sense he would be relinquishing his role as father, albeit a part-time one. The other reason for his reluctance was one which he was afraid of putting to the test. If he asked Eliza to marry him and she agreed, would she accept his children? Would she truly want them?

He held back on an answer to Sarah or Leah, and likewise he held at bay his brother-in-law. Finally he told Wendell Swecker that he would give them his answer by the beginning of the New Year.

After spending Christmas Day ·with his own family and in-laws, he headed for Giles County and, specifically, the quiet valleys of the Irish Settlement, where frame, log, and stone houses seemed literally to exude a refreshing serenity. There was no snow, and for that he was thankful, but no puddle remained unfrozen, and the slow-moving streams were frozen solidly enough for a horse and rider to cross in some places. The trip was a full day's ride in summer, and the shorter days of winter would mean leaving before daylight and riding after dark.

This time the trip was a special one, with normal duties and routines in the background of his mind. In his saddlebags a very modest gift was safely tucked away. Eliza had wanted this, a book, but he could not wholeheartedly approve of it or of most modern novels.

He dismounted as the dogs announced his arrival. His legs were stiff, partly from the day's ride but also because he wore the new broadcloth trousers his family and in-laws had given him for Christmas and they were not yet broken in. His nicest frock coat complimented the new black trousers, and Sarah had pressed his jacket with the flatiron and dusted it. He knew that his sister-in-law sensed that something was afoot, but he had told her nothing.

Eliza met him at the door, ready and expectant, for they had agreed on this day. He handed her the book, taking note of the high-sounding name of Nathaniel Hawthorne at the bottom.

"A happy Christ's Day to you," he said.

"*The Scarlet Letter*! Oh, thank you, Robert! You could have kept me in suspense a while longer."

"I had no place to hide it; your father has put my horse in the barn."

"I shan't be so impulsive. You will have to wait for my gift. Come on into the parlor and warm your hands—they feel like gnarled icicles—and your feet must be frozen!"

He sat down by the lamp, and she looked more closely at his gift to her. "All my friends have been talking about this book. You are thoughtful to bring it to me, Robert.... Here I stand chattering and you have not had your supper. I made you some vegetable soup today—that will take the chill out of your bones."

He took the soup and sipped a spoonful of it noisily ("Forgive me, Aunt Elizabeth"), but his lips remained cold. Eliza watched him with an amused look; her eyes seemed to be twinkling like the winter stars he had ridden under. Only then did he notice how nicely she had dressed for him—how everything about her seemed to fit and make her handsome of gown and pretty of face. The ribbon-trimmed dress of amber with large over sleeves hung loosely on her body, and her hair fell down and over her ears and was pulled back into a high bun at the back of her head. She projected poise and confidence in herself, and he liked it.

"You look like some of the advertisements we used to get at the dry-goods store. You know drawings of models and women's clothes?"

"I wasn't sure until you got to the second sentence whether I was being complimented or not!"

"You are like a flower, Eliza—a flower that has drunk of God's sunshine and sends the rays back to where they came from."

He did not get to ask Eliza the question he had come for until the house was quiet and they sat alone. If it were possible he felt much more frightened on the occasion of his second proposal than he had on that of his first.

Eliza listened to him without showing surprise, nor could he observe any new flood of happiness. Her face was deadly serious, and she looked almost like a different person.

"Robert, I can't say that your proposal is a total surprise. I don't mean that without humility, but we're both old enough to know where we were heading—and where I have reason to believe both of our hearts were leading us."

"There is reservation in your voice," he said.

"Robert, your possible offer to me has been discussed in this house long before you made it—but don't think the discussion has been disrespectful to you or an undue prying into our affairs," she added, moving closer to him.

"What is it you're trying to say, then?"

She looked away and then back to him. "My parents and my two older brothers strongly oppose our marriage."

Her words shook him, and his head dropped. "I didn't know they were thinking like that," he said without looking at her.

"It isn't *you*, Robert. You know how fond they are of you. You can't disbelieve that. Mother even forgives you for the time you asked her to change her dress because it had a grease spot on it. Do you remember that? It was the second time you stayed here."

Her attempt at lightheartedness did not bring back the confidence he had held onto even above his fears.

"They object to my calling, then?"

"Not your calling—to the way it would affect me. They believe in your work, but they also believe that I would suffer from it—your being gone so much and everything."

"Part of that is true," he confessed, "but you'd be dear to me whether we were separated or together."

"They think our life would be mostly apart. My older brothers feel even more strongly about it than my parents."

"Maybe if John and David would tend to their own affairs—"

"Oh, Robert! Don't show any wrath toward them. If I were your sister and you loved me, wouldn't you be anxious for my happiness?"

"Yes. Now that we've been around the horn with the family, I'm more interested in what your feelings are."

"I wanted to get to me last. I wanted you to know how the family felt and why—and to have you know that none of their fondness for or belief in you is one trifle less. They simply cannot rid themselves of seeing me sitting by the fire alone on a cold winter's night and you miles and miles away somewhere in the wilderness."

"I can't deny there would be times like that."

"Now we have come full circle. What did you ask me in the beginning?"

The obliquity of her words caused him to frown a minute, until he understood, and he said, "I asked you if you'd marry me."

"And I accept your proposal. Days ago I came to my own decision."

"Well, you certainly went around the cow shed about it."

"I wanted you to know everything and where we've got to start from."

"Now I feel like the bishop loves me and nobody wants me in the church."

"Don't be like that. I want us to live in a way that will give them something to remember—not to prove them wrong but to give them the joy of finding their error for themselves."

He kissed her cheek then, feeling all the while a new and urgent nearness.

"Robert, I think I made this decision even farther back than I'm admitting. It goes deeper than just loving you. I have told you before that I believe in you, but I want to contribute more than that. I want to give something to your work, and I have long known what it is."

This part he was unprepared for, and instantly, he wondered whether he wanted to hear it or not.

"What I know of your ministry, dear Robert, and what I know of you lead me to believe you are truly God's servant, possessed of a magnificent and unshakable faith. No man's heart could hold any more hope than I believe yours does—but I believe that you are lacking in sufficient warmth for your charity. It is not wrong that the face reflects the love and happiness of the heart, and I have already prepared evidence from the Bible to support me."

Somewhere in the distance Charles Thomas Robert whinnied. Could it be that my blessed Lord has sent a warning to me through the lungs of my animal about this woman? Robert thought.

His continued silence seemed only to spur Eliza onward. "There is not one argument in favor of long-faced Christianity or the withholding of one speck of the humanness that Christ Himself exemplified."

Charles Thomas Robert whinnied again.

"It's hard to smile sometimes, Eliza…"

"Not if your face reflects what you believe."

He conceded that she must be right, though he had thought little of such reasoning.

"I can bear the loneliness we both realize that I'll have to endure if I know I'm contributing something. By giving something and believing in what you are doing, it will all be more bearable. We love the same Lord, Robert, and I love Him no less than you do. We must be partners in faith as we will be in life."

"If you can add new humanness to an old soldier, God be praised, and I have no doubt that you can. You have made my heart new already… But all of our problems are not solved," he added. The worried look on his face came suddenly, for, in her anticipation of loneliness, he realized that she had not even entertained the thought of having his children live with them. He approached the matter and saw that she could not conceal the degree to which the question had thrown her off guard.

"You had not mentioned this possibility before, Robert, and I suppose, in all honesty, I'm not prepared to deal with it." It was true, he hadn't. In one way of looking at the matter there was no reason he should have—he had not asked her to marry him before this night. Still, he had given her reasons to believe…

"I guess I hadn't thought it out either," he confessed. "Everything has been one way for so long—"

"Maybe each assumed things that really hadn't been settled. Those times you have mentioned your children, they seemed so content and attached to their aunts and grandparents…"

"They are, but I hope they're still attached to me too. I don't want them to forget who their real father is—you understand that."

She said she did, but the anguish on her face grew deeper. "Do you think I could be a mother to them—and handle them like I'd need to? I'm over forty-two years old, as you well know, and this would be a new experience for me. If I had known motherhood—"

"Nobody would be a finer mother than you, Eliza. All four of the children are almost big enough to take care of themselves."

"How old did you say the biggest boy is?"

"He's almost fifteen, and the youngest will be ten this summer."

"Would this be fair to the children's aunts and grandparents?"

"They'd miss the youngsters, I know that. But they can see my side of it."

"I wonder if we wouldn't be tearing people away from each other who want to stay together and who belong together." She paused in thought then, looking at Robert searchingly. "I'm not just saying that. I don't know what to say. It isn't a question I can answer so quickly. Let me think about it until tomorrow. I will give you my answer then."

At breakfast Eliza's eyes looked red and swollen and she nibbled at her food. His own looked no more alert, for he had spent a fitful night also. In spite of her obvious fatigue, Eliza tried to be bright and cheerful, but her mother and father both eyed her suspiciously, he noticed.

Finally, when the two of them were alone again, Eliza came to him and took both of his hands. "Yes, I'll help you raise the children. They're part of you...I had forgotten that. You will need to be patient with me. I am ashamed of myself. Here we are in the midst of war with each of us having a loved one away from home, and the sure knowledge that hundreds of children will be homeless, and I have paused in a decision that should have been made without so much forethought."

He thanked her, but somehow there was no joy in the victory he had won.

Returning to Cripple Creek, he had only to announce his decision, and he did so the next night after he arrived. It had been Sarah's week to stay with the children, and she gathered them around their father as he had asked and cast an ominous glance toward him herself.

"Children, only two of you—you, Daniel, and your sister, Sarah Louise, can barely remember your natural mother. I have met a fine lady who wants to become a part of our family, and you will come to love her very much ..."

He continued until he had told them everything about Eliza that he could think of; then he invited their questions.

"When will our new—when will the lady be coming to live with us?" the oldest girl asked.

"I don't think she will be coming here, Sarah Louise. We will probably rent our house and land and move to Giles County. But we'll come back real often," he added, to offset possible objections. "You see, your father's work has always been where other preachers are not so plentiful and in sections of the country where there are not many people. Part of my work will be in what will soon be officially called West Virginia—our thirty-fifth state. Giles County is much nearer to that section."

As silence reigned, he continued. "Our Cripple Creek valley has such a busy iron-and-lead industry now that it's no longer like it was when your mother and I were first married. All the mines and forges are working day and night to help us win the war. We must do our part, and I feel that God leads me to other pastures. And so many of the places I have served before have grown and have their own regular ministers now."

There was still silence. He could give them many more good reasons why things must change, but he noticed misty eyes; even Hugh Trigg fought back tears. He joined in their silence, but tried feverishly to think of a different approach. Was it possible for them to understand his need for a wife and the depth of his love for this woman? He had new thoughts in order when the two girls broke from the group, no longer holding back the flood of tears, and ran outside into the cold of December. In seconds the boys followed, hiding their sadness no better.

He asked Sarah to have them come back in, for he could not stand to cause them heavy hearts. If they would listen to more information about their new home site they would feel differently, he believed.

"Robert, for over nine years my family and I have helped to care for these children. You and I have had few cross words, but this time I think I'm going to speak my piece. If you want the children, you get them."

She stalked into the kitchen, and only a belated concern for the children dislodged him from his temporary immobility. They were weeping pitifully when he rounded them up from under a barren walnut tree whose limbs swayed in the icy wind. He got them back by the fire, but Sarah stood her ground in the kitchen and he went in to her.

"You are wrong, Robert," she said, as though her speech were rehearsed. "You, who holds love for the smallest blooming flower—*you* would hurt your own children? But you're not even knowing it, are you? That's the sad part—you really don't see what you've done."

Both her temper and her flow of words confused him completely.

"There's no wrong in a man's wanting a good woman by his side, and she's a fine Christian woman who believes in the Lord's work," he said.

"I have no doubt of that, but she couldn't be a mother to your children for years, if ever—not at their ages. Can't you see it, Robert? This is their home and we Sweckers are the only family they know or want to know."

"So that is why they weep?"

"Robert, I don't condemn you for the part of their lives you've missed—the souls you've helped to save for the Lord's kingdom speak for that—but you sure know a lot more about sinners than you do children!"

"Sarah, I think I'm just now realizing how much I owe you and Leah and the others—"

"Forget about me, but it's like tearing my own children away just to think about it. Lord knows what it would do to Leah and Mamma and Papa."

"I haven't meant to cause you grief. Looks like I didn't see all the picture for looking at just a part of it."

"Can't you see the answer?" she said. "It's as plain as the nose on your face. Go on and marry this good woman. If you want to live in Giles County nothing very much is going to change if you'll come and see the children regular. You are always gone anyhow, and not one of them will notice much difference. Things can be like they always have been and nobody be heartbroken or separated."

"Let me think about it overnight. You've pointed out some things to me I hadn't seen before. Let everybody get to bed now. We've got ourselves in a lather, and a good night's rest and a little praying is what we all need."

When he and Sarah came from the kitchen four nightshirt-clad bodies scrambled away from the door. Sarah scolded them for eavesdropping and sent them to bed, but the youngest girl held back and asked her aunt to sleep with her.

"All right, Margaret, get in my bed and I will be there directly."

"The boys will have it tough in the garret tonight. I guess they wish I hadn't come home so they could have my bed." Robert poked at the fire and added more wood. Sarah had something else on her mind, and he could sense it. "What is it, Sarah?"

She started at his perception. "Did Miss Stafford think your plan was a good one?"

"We talked about it, and she mentioned some of the things you called my attention to, but she agreed to it."

"She must love you a great deal to think of taking on that kind of load. I can't believe she believed it sensible—she would know too clearly the picture here—yet what a great trust in you. I can't make up my mind, Robert. She was either very foolish or very wise to say 'yes' to everything you apparently asked of her."

"Now that the night is almost over and I think back to being with her, I think she was wiser than I have realized until just now."

Sarah went to her room, but he sat by the fire and penned a letter to his older boys. He thought over all that had transpired and within the hour he sank to his knees until at last peace came to his soul. All was well with him now. If only the war was over, and if James Wesley were only home… But another prayer of thankfulness crossed his lips: battle had not yet come very near. In a few days a new year would be beginning. Perhaps the coming of 1864 would see an end to the national tragedy.

The next day he agreed to leave matters at Cripple Creek as they were. Shouts went up as if the war itself had ended and Cripple Creek had been victorious.

In a few days he rode back to Eliza and told her of the decision he had made. Relief was visible in her face, but he made no mention of it. They announced their final plans and wedding date to Eliza's parents, who, though still opposed to the marriage, offered their congratulations in good grace.

"I have no misbelief about how your life together is going to be." James Stafford spoke with a seriousness Robert had not before seen. "For that reason I hope you will make your home with us. When you are gone, Robert, at least our daughter will have someone to look out for her."

On January twenty-seventh, serenaded by a powdery snow falling through a bone-chilling rawness, they repeated their marriage vows.

Robert made no attempt to move his belongings to Giles County until the winter was over. By the time spring came he had rented his land and log house on a yearly basis and settled his family with their kin in a manner that was pleasing to all. Most of his household belongings were loaned to his sisters-in-law against the day that he and Eliza would set up housekeeping in their own home. What personal belongings he required rested with ease across his horse's back; tied in sacks and in saddlebags. He made no special ceremony of saying good-by to the children, saying instead that he would be gone about the usual time and would see them again before they missed him.

He was out of sight and headed north toward Wytheville before the tears flooded his face.

James Wesley had had no furlough in months, but he had written to say that his company would pass through Wytheville the weekend of April twenty-second, on their way up the Valley of Virginia, and that if his father could meet him there they would be able to spend perhaps an hour or so together. This Robert would do, and then he would be free to leave Wythe County for another place and another life.

CHAPTER XII

Robert left his bride of three months and journeyed toward a conference district meeting at Grayson Sulphur Springs on the Grayson-Carroll county line. There were those who still insisted that he become a full-fledged conference member and Reverend J. W. Whittington—from whom the invitation to attend the conference meeting had come—was one of these. A district meeting would draw only one or two of the higher ranking conference officials, the presiding elder, and not more than a dozen or so ministers, but Robert's old friend Whittington insisted that he come and observe the organized clergy in action and see if he liked the "tone of things" while in the throes of debating "on-trial" conference membership.

Robert started on his way to fulfill the appointment with a great deal more vigor than did Charles Thomas Robert, whose years and worn-out teeth were beginning to show. Though he had let the animal take her head and ease during the journey, and, in addition, stopped to water her more frequently than usual, it became obvious that long-distance trips were now beyond her capacity.

In Hillsville he inquired of a reputable horse dealer, and, being told of the demands of the war and of a reluctance of the people to dispose of animals they might need in time of hardship, he was not encouraged.

Finally he was given the name of a local farmer who occasionally had surplus animals to sell, and he headed in that direction not at all sure that Charles Thomas Robert could keep her belly off the ground long enough to get him there.

In just an additional mile of travel the animal was exhausted again, and Robert dismounted and led her rest of the way. "I won't add misery and sweat to your faithful old bones," he said, and she answered the words of her master with a whinny. "What you need is a field of clover and somebody who'll just ride you to church on Sunday and let you rest the other days of the week."

He repeated those same words to Brother Alderman—as he came quickly to call the man—whose integrity seemed beyond reproach. "She's well over twenty years old, and she's covered many a mile. Feed her three ears of corn twice a day about *this* long"—Robert demonstrated on his open palm and forearm—"and let her drink her water slowly." He talked further of the animal and kept his cheek against her nose and stroked her neck for what he knew would be the last time.

Brother Alderman said that he appreciated the honesty of the information about the animal and, after taking a routine look into the horse's mouth and questioning Robert more about his occupation, he offered a proposal more generous than Robert had anticipated.

"I have told you my animal is worn-out and old," Robert insisted.

"She'll do some good for a while yet… and I've got the man in mind who needs a good Sunday horse."

The trade was made, but only then did Robert realize that he had insufficient money with him to complete the transaction. "Brother Alderman, I can't pay you much of the difference today. I haven't come prepared. Would you be trusting of God's servant until I can make arrangements?"

Mr. Alderman began to transfer the saddle from the aged horse to the young one. "Any man who considers himself a good judge of horses ought to try out his judgment on men every once in a while."

Robert thanked him, and asked him what the name of the new horse was.

"You wouldn't let another man name your boys, would you? You put a name on him and he'll learn to answer to it."

Robert positioned his sheepskin prayer mat on the saddle and climbed upon the back of the sorrel horse with some noticeable apprehension.

"Looks a little farther down to the ground than before, I'd say," Mr. Alderman said.

Robert knew that his small frame looked dwarfed upon the larger animal, but he said, "I always did hate to get my feet wet fording the streams. Looks like I won't have that problem now."

Just before he arrived at Grayson Sulphur Springs he eliminated all the tentative names for the animal he had thought about during the ride and announced the selected one to its recipient.

"I will call you Gideon. Gideon was a deliverer of God's people and so will you be as I ride the trails of the wilderness upon your back."

Robert settled in the Reverend Whittington's house for the two-day meeting, but after one day of it he had had enough.

"The brothers spend too much time searching for straws in the whirlwind, and some of them like to keep their nostrils warm with their own breath," Robert said.

"But Brother Bob"—Reverend Whittington shortened his name affectionately—"they don't get away from their circuits very often, and we must forgive them for coming out of the harness a little bit."

"There is a lack of godliness at the meeting. They sound like a gaggle of politicians sometimes, and long-winded politicians at that."

"I know you're out of our district now since you've moved to Giles County, but let me put in a word for you. Let me be instrumental in having you placed on trial as a conference preacher. After that it will be only a matter of time until you will be admitted to full membership."

"I won't change my notion now, but if I ever do I'll write you about it," Robert said, declining.

"We're not going to give up on you. You'll be made a deacon one of these days in spite of yourself. If we can't tie you to the conference one way, we'll do it in another."

The next morning the two men rode in opposite directions, Robert northward toward Wythe County and a visit with his children before heading back to Giles County.

He journeyed slowly, stopping frequently to talk to wayfarers or to speak to a farmer or slave across a split-rail fence. Gideon gave him no trouble and Robert shouted happily into the treetops, "Thank you, Lord, for honest horse dealers!"

As he approached the valley to the south of Iron Mountain his stomach began to feel the pangs of hunger. There had been few cabins along the trail until this fertile bottom land was reached, and if he was to get his dinner before he crossed the mountain it would have to be soon. This reasoning had no more than cleared his brain when a small cabin appeared in view. A Negro man and woman of middle age watched his approach from their garden.

"Would there be food enough in your house to share with a servant of the Lord?" Robert asked.

"Lawsy me, yes, if the Lord's man ain't particular!" the woman called out joyously. She paused only long enough to hear her guest's name, then filled her dirty apron with fresh lettuce and spring scullions and made for the cabin.

Promptly a meal of scalded lettuce and scullions with generous slices of fried side meat was ready. The corn bread was hot and emitted a pleasant aroma, but there was no buttermilk to go with it. Robert drank the cool spring water instead without question or comment.

When dinner was over his host asked him to pray again, and though he thought the request a strange one, since he had asked a blessing over the food at the beginning of the meal, he did as he was asked. After finishing he said, "Are you hungry for the Word, my brother? Is that the reason you asked me to pray a second time?"

"None of us ain't heard th' Word since last fall and Jason is dead. Hard times is come and we is scared—ain't no need, fer none of the othern's a-goin' run away."

None of the statement made sense to Robert, and he questioned his host until he discovered that Jason had been their Negro preacher, and "hard times" represented both the fear of the war creeping ever closer and the fear of local slave owners that all the slaves might attack their masters or at least make a run for freedom. His host and hostess were free Negroes, Robert learned, but they assured him that the slaves in the surrounding area did not plan to run away in spite of hardships.

The more time he spent with the man and woman, the more Robert realized that the frightfully deep and paralyzing fear that gripped the Negro people made them sure of approaching death, whether there was any real basis for it or not.

"We all want to get baptized again before we go to glory," the woman pleaded.

"I don't believe any harm will come to you, and if it be God's will the war will not come to this valley. We must trust and pray."

"Jest the same, we all wants to get baptized," the man said.

"Do none of your people sit in the balcony of the white churches?" Robert asked.

"Ain't done it lately. Some of th' white folks turns around and looks up at us 'culiar-like—and they ain't smilin' neither," the woman said.

These people with whom he shared bread finally asked him more emphatically to baptize them, and further, that new baptism was the desire of all the local black people.

"For the sake of my sweet Jesus I'll baptize you one and all if it is your wish."

They said it was, but sprinkling wouldn't do. They wanted to be immersed until they could neither see nor hear another sound except the frantic fountain of their sins being washed away.

This presented complications, for by sprinkling Robert could go to the individual penitent's home and render his service. The alternative was to gather them all together by a nearby stream.

Rounding up this particular congregation would have posed no problem in ordinary times, but these were not ordinary times. No groups of slaves moved freely out of their masters' sights, he knew. He would be compelled to go to each individual slaveholder and ask permission for the slave to attend and participate in the mass baptism, plus give his own assurance that the slave would be returned to his master.

Robert explained this to his host, but the spirits of the other were not dampened. "I'll help you and show you where they all live." It was two days before Sunday, and his bed for that time would be on the floor of the couple's cabin. There would not be time for much sleep anyway. There was work to be done.

Before the sun went down he was confronting his first slaveholder.

"You mean to tell me you would baptize a nigger?"

"I'll baptize anybody my blessed Saviour died for," Robert replied.

"I don't abide that brand of Christianity, Brother," the farmer said, "and if you'd stop and think a minute you'd know that a few hundred runaways like that ebony bastard beside you helped cause all the war news we're hearing."

"I can't do a thing to bring the killing to a halt, but I can prepare a man to die if it be God's will."

"You'd better get them ready good, for if those Yankees come sneaking down this valley and my slaves get any ideas about running, I'll shot them before I get my first Bluecoat."

Robert pleaded again for the freedom of the slaves to attend the Sunday service. "You are welcome to come and sit on the creek bank with us," he said, to try to assuage the slave owner's fear.

"No, thank you. I can't stand the smell of three of them in the field together, much less be around two dozen."

Two dozen was a close guess. Robert counted twenty-nine, including the women and children, both slave and free. The May day was warm but the mountain stream still held the chill of winter. But from the baptized, chattering teeth registered far below their shouts of praise and hallelujahs.

When the visit with his children on Cripple Creek was over he returned directly to the Irish Settlement. Eliza reclined on the front steps of her father's house, the late afternoon sun playing reflectively on her hair. She walked to meet him with an open letter in her hand and a smile of sweetness upon her face.

"For me?" Robert said as he started to reach for it.

"For both of us." Eliza jerked the letter back playfully before she relinquished it.

"I wish James Wesley was as close as Camp Princeton," he said, noting the return address on Jimmy's envelope. He read his brother-in-law's letter and handed it back. "Sounds like Jimmy will have to tow the line for his Captain DuBall."

"What did you learn at Cripple Creek about James Wesley?" Eliza said.

"He's still in the area of Lynchburg. They have not been to battle, but he writes that an attack down the Valley of Virginia is expected. God be with him if it comes. We can do nothing but pray."

They talked about the news of the war they had both heard independently and Robert's spirits began to dampen. Eliza entwined her arm into his own and said, "We won't speak more of it now. You are hungry and tired, and when you have eaten I want to hear about the horse trader you apparently overtook somewhere on your journey. Did he get the best of you?"

"Yes, but only with his integrity, which is not a virtue often to be found among horse traders. Don't let me forget to take him some money or send him some."

Miraculously, a beautiful and lush spring was over and no sounds of a major battle had echoed from the mountains and valleys of Robert's territory. The war still seemed very far away when the newspaper reported, almost a week after the event, one of the bloodiest battles yet, fought in Gettysburg, Pennsylvania. General Lee's retreat there had begun on July Fourth of 1863, Robert's forty-third birthday. The paper carried few details of the battle, but it was evident from the meager information that George Pickett's valiant efforts to charge through the enemy lines had been a horrifyingly bloody disaster.

When Robert returned on July the eighteenth from New Castle, in Craig County, where he had opened the doors of an independent mountain church, Eliza passed on the fearful news.

"Word was received at the Dublin train depot that Colonel Toland and his federals raided Wytheville yesterday."

"Do you know how extensive the battle was? Did a column go down Cripple Creek to destroy the lead mines?"

"We're not sure. All we heard was that some young girl rode in ahead of the federals and warned the town. Home guards and a few local troops outfought the Yankees and drove them off," Eliza said.

"And oh, yes," she added, "Colonel Toland was rumored to be killed in the fighting in the streets."

"I must go see about the children," he said, anxiety mounting in his face and manner.

"I expected that, but I hate to see you be off when you have just come from a long trip—and it won't be but a few hours until dark."

"I can get part way before I wear out, and Gideon has lots of pep left in him yet. Now, fix me some biscuits for my saddlebags, Eliza. I know I can get to Bland and I'll eat as I ride along."

"I've already got your supper packed," she said dutifully.

"Then I will have a glass of spring water before I go, and if the Lord be with me I'll rest in the home of a gentle widow woman who will feed me a good light bread and honey when the morning comes."

His weak attempt at levity to appease his wife's mind did not show at all in his face. The crow's-foot lines about the corners of his eyes and the deep etched wrinkles of his forehead continued into his hairline on each side until they were hidden by strawberry-blond hair now tinged with gray. Upon his face was implanted much more than his own private agonies of heart and mind.

When Bland courthouse was reached a violent rainstorm overtook him and he discounted riding very much farther toward Wytheville. Only one other man whom he chanced to meet at a crossroads seemed as foolish as himself to ride in the rain. That chance meeting, however, was the source of his bed for the night.

His host was a man well balanced in intelligence and friendliness, and Robert found himself enjoying the conversation of Allen Newberry, who revealed his own connection to Methodism.

"My father was a Methodist circuit rider licensed to preach in eighteen-twelve. From what I hear of you, he traveled almost as much territory—from Saltville to the west, to New River in the east."

They talked of many matters later than Robert's usual bedtime. They had fully discussed the war earlier in the evening, but Robert found the subject hard to push from his mind, though he was becoming relieved somewhat, the more Allen Newberry elaborated on events.

"I'm sure the federals' plan was to destroy the Virginia and Tennessee Railroad tracks and to raid and destroy the lead mines in the bargain," Newberry said. "I think your worries can end right there. They never got any farther south than Wytheville, where they got a dose of hot lead, and retreated back over the mountain. The mines and all the Cripple Creek valley are intact, and not a hair on the heads of your children could have been touched, if I get the story right."

"I'm sure you got the correct information, and thank God for it," Robert said.

"The Wytheville people said Colonel Toland had over one thousand troops, and they whipped them with a bunch of old men, young boys, and some of the women. There wasn't a handful of Confederate troops there. This will go down in the history books, and so will little Molly Tynes. We've got our own Paul Revere. You've heard of him?"

Robert said he had and asked if it was true that Colonel Toland had been killed during the raid.

"Yes, it's true. He was shot on Tazewell Street in front of the residence of Captain William Giboney. Some say he was killed by a boy, but I've since talked with a man who says it was a young woman who shot him—and right through the heart."

"May he rest in peace," Robert said sadly. The dead man was first of all a fellow human and only second, the enemy.

"However he rests, that's one less Yankee brigadier," Allen Newberry said. "It'll make you a little less sad when you stop and think what our troops and your own children would have done without the salt and lead we've been getting delivered up and down those train tracks."

Allen Newberry's reasoning didn't help Robert's sleep that night, for the Bible still said, "Thou shalt not kill," and the commandment did not make any distinctions that might ease a troubled mind. Yet other biblical words said there would always be wars and rumors of war. There was no answer to that dilemma of the heart, and he knew it.

When the rooster crowed the approach of dawn he crawled from his bed unrefreshed. He ate well in spite of his unrest and asked

Elizabeth Newberry if he might take a honey biscuit along with him in the saddlebags. She fixed him three and he thanked her but added, "Next time, Sister, if you'll cook the biscuits a little longer I'd like them better… they'll get a brown crust on top that way." She promised she would but Robert doubted her serious intent toward his instructions for a partially subdued smile crossed her face.

After breakfast Allen Newberry saw him to the barn, and, when the horse was saddled and the rider mounted, he asked Robert to come back again, adding, "Even an itinerant should have a better suit of clothes than you're wearing."

"I like to stay clean, but I don't care about being fancy."

"I'll be going back up to Baltimore in the fall, and I usually bring back some bolts of English broadcloth to my liking. You happen around and I'll see if I can't spare a little of it to make you a suit with."

"You're the Lord's helper and I thank you for thinking about me. Of course I'll stop again, and not just for the suit either."

A light drizzle started when he reached the Raleigh Grayson Turnpike, but he did not stop for shelter. His mind was considerably at ease now after what Allen Newberry had told him, but the last lingering doubt would not be erased until he saw his children's smiling faces.

The rain had ceased by the time he reached the crest of Walker Mountain, and he tried to sing but discovered he was getting hoarse. "I can't do it today, Gideon; that dampness is getting through the sinew."

Although the sun had come out as he descended the south side of the mountain, surface water ran profusely down the wagon tracks. A terrapin crossing the road was caught in the miniature flood and washed farther along until the water thinned out. There the creature found itself safe from drowning, but just as helpless, on its back with legs thrashing frantically.

Robert stopped his horse and dismounted. "God bless you, old fellow, we'll get you on your feet again. We'd better make it snappy too, or you'll be feeling that set of wagon wheels coming yonder across your back."

He carried the terrapin across the road and saw that its stubby legs were on firm, level ground again. He waited for the oncoming wagon to pass before he remounted, but it stopped short. An attractive middle-aged woman whose black hair showed tinges of gray called to him. Her young male companion sat rigid and held the check reins taut.

"Did you kill it? Was it a rattler or copperhead?" she called.

"No, it wasn't a snake. It was a terrapin. He was over on his back and helpless."

"I was sure it was a snake," she said, unsmiling, "and of all things, I couldn't afford to have the leg of my mare bitten in *this* country."

Robert caught the inference but didn't know what to make of it. He moved closer to the woman, whose lips had added special vehemence to her expression. Anger contorted her face, and bereavement showed clearly in her reddened eyes.

"I don't understand," Robert said. "Has someone borne you ill will?"

"Has someone borne us ill will?" she said. "Would you listen to that, Jacob! Has someone borne us ill will indeed!" The woman wept and then tried to laugh.

"It's all right ma'am, you just lean on me," the young driver said.

"No, Jacob, I won't lean on you or anybody else. I'll sit with my spine straight and my head high. I will not let these southern scum have one last laugh at our agony—"

"Please, ma'am, we're not out of the territory yet," the driver said.

"Then let them kill me too—what have I to live for now, anyway?"

Robert started to mount his horse but got no further than putting his foot in the stirrup when he saw into the back of the wagon. What the conversation had not revealed came perfectly clear when he saw in the wagon a man-sized coffin.

"You are carrying one of the dead from the battle at Wytheville?" Robert asked.

"Yes, I'm bringing home one of the martyred dead who would die willingly again that all men might be free," she said calmly, but tears still streamed down her f ace.

"Would to God that this terrible thing had never come to pass—the war—the killing. It is not right. We must change men's hearts with the love of God, not his politics by the slash of the sword and the fire of the cannon."

"How noble, but how historically naive!" the woman said. "But I do want you to know this terrible tragedy is a little more bearable if I have met one more person who believes that as long as one of us is slave, all of us are slaves."

"The God I love makes no distinction between men by the color of one's skin; it is the color of his heart that my Lord shall judge."

"Don't tell that to your southern brethren very often or you too will be sent home in a pine box."

"All who know me know my heart. I can do nothing for you now except to offer my prayer in your presence and over his casket, that you may be given the strength to bear your bereavement and suffering."

"I will not add hypocrisy to the humiliation and sacrifice I've already suffered in this godforsaken land!"

"Look into my face and tell me if there is anything there except the love of God for this one who has been so dear...."

"Yes, there is kindness in your face, and if we were in West Virginia—"

"Is that where you are taking him?" Robert asked.

"Yes. And we had best be on our way. Other wagons are coming, and soon the smell of death will settle on your countryside."

Robert reached onto the saddle for his sheepskin and knelt on the road. "Dear Lord, give her the strength to bear this terrible burden and bring peace to this torn land...," he prayed as he heard the wagon wheels start to turn. They stopped when they came abreast of him, and he finished his prayer. When he raised his own tear-stained eyes the heads of the others were yet bowed. He walked to them and grasped the trembling hand of the woman. "God bless you, my beloved sister. You will meet him again."

"Yes, yes!" she cried and leaned from the seat until her head rested upon his neck.

"This will not be the only prayer I shall say for you. I will keep you in my thoughts and hope that your good courage will help others. I have not asked you your name, but I should like to know it as the sorrow of your face comes to my mind."

"It is not important that you know that," she said softly.

"You would have me pray for a face but not a name?"

"No. I will be grateful for your prayers. I am Mrs. Toland."

For the remaining distance into Wytheville wagons and surreys and buckboards came one after the other, driven by grim-faced women or teen-aged boys and old men who had come to claim the bodies of the fallen federal dead and take them back into West Virginia, where loved ones could make the disposition as to their final resting place.

As the months wore on, war news came with increasing frequency. The Battle of Chickamauga Valley became news in September, and by November the battle at Missionary Ridge overlooking Chattanooga saw the creeping take-over of eastern Tennessee by federal forces. The war closer to home took the form of small skirmishes. With the coming of 1864 new major battles of the war still had not come to southwest Virginia. Colonel Milton Ferguson's sixteenth Virginia Cavalry, or a detachment thereof, captured a steamboat on the Kanawha River in West Virginia. Aboard the boat was Brigadier General Scammon, who was captured and sent as a prisoner to Richmond. When Robert had read all the details of this to his father-in-law the older man made one grim-faced prediction: federal activity and the buildup along the Kanawha River valley had ominous overtones for the New River valley, which was a natural outlet.

The prediction came true when Confederate scouts sent advance warning along the New River valley that Union Army forces under the command of General Crook were on the move. This word was received in the Irish Settlement on the third day of May, and daily reports thereafter on troop movement of the enemy left no doubt of the direction of their travel. Robert made no trips away from Eliza and her family that week, for he now found himself in the same grip of fear spreading over the entire valley.

For the next two days the troops from Giles and Monroe counties moved southward, to where, Robert surmised, the battle line was being formed. When these activities ceased there followed a long two days of haunting silence until scouts reported that General Crook was marching by way of Raleigh courthouse and Princeton in West Virginia, through the break in the mountains at Rocky Gap. From there the enemy would either move by way of Abbs valley in Tazewell County, Walker's Creek valley, or continue on the Raleigh-Grayson turnpike toward Wytheville.

On May eighth the direction of movement was certain, and the enemy forces were reported split; some were coming down the Walker's Creek valley via the Holston turnpike, and others were going by way of Abbs valley. On this same day Robert and his people of the Irish Settlement were informed that the federal columns had passed by the Shannon farm at Poplar Hill, where the Holston turnpike intersected with the Pulaski-Giles turnpike—scarcely eight miles to the south. When Thomas Shannon's Negro brought the word he also carried stories of atrocities committed by federal troops as they moved down the Holston turn pike.

The breathless Negro, whom Robert already knew as Pinkney, related the atrocities in detail. "Mr. Shannon says the bluecoat soldiers are workin' their way to the railroad at Dublin and Central depot," Pinkney said.

"Did Mr. Shannon say how many of our troops were at Dublin and Central depot?" someone standing next to Robert asked.

"He never said nothin' 'ceptin' the Yankees would swim through their own blood before they got to the railroad," Pinkney reported.

Robert and the other residents of the Irish Settlement were aware of the earlier troop movements of the home guards and regular troops to some point to the south. That region was pinpointed the following day when the roar of cannons could be heard faintly in the distance, somewhere between Cloyd's farm and the village of Dublin.

The distant sounds of battle did not cease until midafternoon, but by dark casualty reports began to filter back along the turnpike road and the byways to the Irish Settlement. Some reports Robert heard said that less than three hundred and fifty Confederate troops had been killed or wounded but the federals had given up nearly seven hundred men. Not until the next day were Robert and Eliza aware that her brother Jimmy had been in the battle and had been wounded.

"There wasn't any braver men in the battle than the men of Captain Gott's thirty-sixth," the messenger said.

It was learned further that Jimmy had been wounded in the legs and was being attended in Dublin, as were the other casualties.

By midmorning of the following day Robert and his father-in-law, along with one of Eliza's brothers, joined the long train of wagoneers who now traveled the turnpike road to view the site of the battle or to bring back the dead. Confederate wagons and Union wagons alike would be taking the same road, and nobody asked whether the dripping blood from a pine box was from the body of a man who wore the blue or the gray.

The battlefields in the meadows and woodlands of Cloyd's Farm yet had the aura of horror. The bark and leaves of every tree seemed to hold captive the smell of battle, like water soaked into a sponge. It was a sickening odor of gunpowder, dust, and the sweat and manure of both animals and humans. Bloodstains colored the grass and trees, and along the crevices of fence rails the trail of crimson could be followed.

A growing but nearly silent crowd continued to linger on the battlefield, awed by the eerie stillness that hovered over them. Slowly some of them began to filter away. They were misty-eyed and quiet, a few weeping openly. One lone grave had been dug on the battle field and a makeshift tombstone of oak inscribed in chalk marked the site. The epitaph read: *Capt. Christopher S. Cleburne, C. S. A. He fought with the 2nd Kentucky Cavalry and asked to be buried where he fell.*

As they left, Robert could see the path of retreat the Confederate forces had taken through the tall meadow grass, and the pursuit of the Union forces, which had trampled the earth. The trail of wagon wheels and artillery pieces, and the digging cut of horses' hooves could be detected as far as the eye cared to follow.

Jimmy was in good spirits. The depot and numerous buildings in Dublin were serving as temporary field hospitals.

From Jimmy, who had heard sketchy information here and there about the significance of the battle, they learned that Confederate forces had been badly outnumbered. The enemy, General Crook, had better than six thousand men, while the Confederate General Jenkins had fewer than three thousand.

General Jenkins himself had been wounded, Jimmy reported, and was replaced by Colonel John McCausland, who had retreated by way of the railroad bridge to the east side of New River.

One of the attending doctors brought more news to Jimmy's bedside. "We've received word that the federals have lost their nerve and retreated across Salt Pond Mountain into Monroe County in West Virginia," he said.

Robert breathed a sigh of relief and left Jimmy with his kin. He then wandered from bed to bed, offering a prayer for every wounded man who would let him. There were no refusals.

His own son, James Wesley, did not experience pitched battle until the invasion of Union General Sheridan down the Valley of Virginia in the fall of 1864. James Wesley wrote that in spite of his war experience he had lost only part of his left ear. Valley farmers and residents were less fortunate, however, he told them—they had lost all their crops and granaries. General Sheridan seemed bent on destroying these in order to starve as many Confederate troops around the area of the state capital.

By spring two glorious things had come to pass. The war had come to an end and Eliza was pregnant with their first child.

"I wonder what kind of world our baby will be born into?" Eliza said. "We are a defeated people in a torn land."

"He will be born into a world not without hardship. It's always like that. Maybe some good will come from the defeat our Lord has allowed us to suffer. I can't believe He has not used the folly of men to His grand purpose."

Robert held his newborn son in his arms on November twelfth, 1865. They named the child Edward Fleming, and Robert thought that the infant and his mother were the most beautiful people a loving God had ever made. In spite of Eliza's having her first childbirth experience much later in life than most women, she made a quick recovery under the skilled hands of her doctor brother.

When Robert was sure she was well he made preparations to be off to the wilderness, which would as yet not have recovered from the scourge of war and the losses of brothers and husbands and fathers. Even those who hobbled home minus a leg or arm would not find their houses and communities as they had known them, Robert surmised.

"It won't be the same as before, will it?" Eliza said perceptively.

"No, but the Lord never threw a man in deep water to drown him. Maybe a lesson has been learned and spiritual hunger will grow rampant throughout the land. There sure isn't much of anything else growing."

"They do need you now, Robert. They're weary and defeated and hungry and tired. I expect if the truth were known they're still a little scared too—some of them, at least."

"You think, then, I can make them believe: 'Whomsoever the Lord loveth, He chasteneth'?"

"We'll leave that up to you." Eliza smiled at him from the porch as he mounted. She held up the baby so he could see the miniature face of his son.

"You look after Eddie now!" he called.

"You think he'll *really* want for anything?" she asked, glancing from right to left.

Robert took note of his father-in-law, mother-in-law, and his recuperating brother-in-law looking down at him and said, "Looks like he'll be pretty well taken care of."

The route he had planned to take was the one that roughly paralleled the route of the Union soldiers when they had swept down upon southwest Virginia. Along this way the people seemed more despairing and downtrodden. There were families who still had not recovered from having all their grain stolen, their fences destroyed, and every farm animal, including the family milk cow, stolen. Those people who had not suffered from foraging enemy soldiers had, on occasion, suffered at the hands of marauding bands of scavenger troops.

"We'll cheer them up, Gideon," Robert said to his animal as they turned west along Walker's Creek and up the Holston turn pike. "You move along gently now while I study Acts. We'll preach to them about Paul's sea journey to Italy—when he went to appear before Caesar. Why, Gideon, that whole shipload of people were nearly torn apart by the tempest upon the sea, and they thought themselves lost forever, or certain to starve to death. But Paul told them to be of good cheer, for God was with them in their moment of despair. That's what we've got to do, Gideon, tell them all God is with them and to be of good cheer."

He had gotten nearly to White Gate when his reading was completed. "You let me down a minute now, Gideon. I have read too much and I'm a little swimmy-headed. Now, let me wash, Gideon, and we will be on our way."

On the opposite side of the road Walker's Creek meandered slowly eastward down the valley to a rendezvous with New River, many miles in the distance. Robert stepped down to the edge of the water and noticed the shallowness of the stream. He stooped to wash his hands and dried them on a handful of leftover winter leaves. He cast the leaves adrift and watched them float downstream like little boats making for a distant port.

"Hey there, you a-messin' up the water!" A youthful voice came from a nearby point.

Robert stepped downstream and apologized to the young fisherman. "Are you catching anything?" Robert added.

"Got a whole string," the boy said and held forth a forked willow branch heavy with fish from the size of a man's foot down to fish as small as the palm of his hand.

"Why do you keep the little fish? You have plenty of bigger ones to help feed your family," Robert said.

"If I kotched 'em I got a right to keep 'em."

"But the little ones should have a chance to grow, and they are too small for your ma to fix."

"She just always throws the little'uns away," the youth agreed.

"I want you to promise me that from now on when you fish you will keep only the bigger ones and catch only what you must have for your family. It is not God's will that we waste and abuse the bounty He has so lovingly provided us. Do you understand me?"

"Yes, sir." The boy answered with a new respect and attentiveness.

Robert did not ask it, but as he left the creek and walked toward his horse the boy was taking the small fish from the willow branch and throwing them headlong back into the water.

He mounted Gideon and rode to the edge of the road nearest the creek. "God bless you, my son; and it is to your credit that you are obedient. If it were dinner time I would go home with you and help you eat those fish."

"It ain't dinnertime and I'd have to kotch twice this many to go around to you—there's seventeen of us'ns."

He spent that night in Bland with his friend Allen Newberry. The biscuits of his first meal were well browned, and he gave praise to the good sister who had prepared them.

Newberry told him that the damage done by Yankee troops was not nearly as extensive in some places as had been rumored. "When the enemy columns came out of West Virginia they split: some of them went by way of Abbs valley, some by way of Rocky Gap and down the Holston turnpike, and some came this way, foraging, and on down the creek. They did dirty deeds, all right, but the farmers who were hurt the worst have since been helped back on their feet."

"The Lord bless all of you who've had a part in it," Robert said.

"There's no time to nurse our wounds now," Newberry said. "The country will never be the same as we knew it before, and we might as well get down to the business of building back better than ever."

From Bland, Robert rode to Rocky Gap and turned west up Clearfork valley toward Tazewell County.

"Carry me easy now, Gideon, and let me study my text. We're preaching first at the Ebenezer church, and I want to get my thoughts in the right order. I'm going to pay back a debt, Gideon. I'm going to preach Brother Alex St. Clair's favorite sermon. The sweet Lord put in his head to buy me a new pair of boots the last time I was here at the camp meeting. Now you walk steady. I don't want to skip anything, and Brother St. Clair knows this scripture better than I do."

It was after the supper hour when he rode into the St. Clair residence, followed now by dozens of youthful followers to whom he had called out a greeting as he entered their neighborhood. He climbed down from his horse and embraced them all with a strong arm and a "Bless your little heart," or a firm handshake and a heartfelt, "It's a Lord's blessing to see you again." They all followed at his coattails, except for an older boy entrusted with the care of his horse.

Free of Gideon, Robert wrapped each arm about all the children his short arms would reach. The joyful entourage brought Brother Alex St. Clair to his front porch. "Brother Sheffey! Bless the Lord you got back to us safely. Come in! Come in! My good wife has your bed ready, and the pantry is filled with huckleberry jam and good honey. Have you had your supper yet?"

"No, but let us have family devotions first and thank our dear Lord that He has brought us together again."

Robert sent a child to fetch his Bible from his saddlebag, and when the boy came back Robert gathered the neighborhood children and his hosts about him and read from *Psalms*, "O come, let us sing unto the Lord: let us make a joyful noise to the rock of our salvation..."

When he had finished he blessed all the children by name and asked them to go back to their homes, for it was beginning to get dark.

"I can't even ask Brother St. Clair to sit with me while I eat tonight, for though I have studied my scripture the Lord has not made clear to me all that He wants me to say tomorrow. I must think about it a while until His will is made known to me."

He was left in solitude and did not see his host and hostess until the next morning, which was Sunday.

"I hope you slept well, Brother Sheffey," Alex St. Clair said at breakfast.

"Not so well, with such an aggravating pillow on my bed."

His host's wife turned from her stove, inquiring of the difficulty.

"Could it be, sister, that you have goose feathers in the pillow? They poked and stabbed at me all night. The quills are as long and as stiff as a corncob. I want you to empty them out and fill the pillow with pinfeathers from the chickens. I'd be obliged if you'd do that for me.

She promised she would, and he went out of the house for his morning walk before the church hour drew near. He set out down the road from the direction he had come the previous day. Two tumblebugs pushed laboriously at their little ball of dirt until they traversed the roadway onto a path at the roadside. He followed them until their way was obscured by a fallen tree limb. He took away the obstacle to their travel and went on ahead, removing anything that might further obstruct a continuation of their journey. When the way was clear as far as he could see he squatted down on his heels and watched them pass him.

"Be on your way now, little creatures of God, and do the tasks set before you."

"Ain't you got nothin' better to do than sit around talkin' to bugs?" a deep voice called out from immediately behind him.

He turned to face a bull of a man whose homespun clothes were rigid with grime and dirt.

Robert introduced himself and said that God would not like him to make an apology about talking to the tumblebugs.

The man's face had a look of puzzlement upon it then, and he started to back away. Before he got far Robert asked him to attend the nearby church service for which he would be the guest preacher.

"You think they'd take kindly to me comin' lookin' like this?" the woodsman said.

"It's true the Lord does look kindly on cleanliness. You've got plenty of time to go back to your cabin and change your clothes."

"Ain't got no woman to wash these, and I ain't got no other'ns."

"I'd give you mine, but it looks like you couldn't get more than one leg in them."

"Ain't no need in worrying about me. Nobody ever has. Hell's got to have somebody to fill it. Looks like it's bound to be the likes of me."

"God has made me a judge of men, and I am not hearing the voice of a man who is reconciled to that awful outer darkness just yet. It's a path no man need even think about if he knows where to place his trust."

"I tried to read the Good Book, but I can't hardly sign my name, much less make no sense out of it."

"That is what our churches are all about—a revelation of what God's Word means for us and the words of the promise—"

"I ain't goin' to church like this, I told you."

"What's that building I see there in the edge of the clearing?" Robert said.

"That's my cow shed."

"Then we'll have preaching there. Just you and me."

He returned to the house of his host to find Brother St. Clair frantic with worry that some harm had come to him.

"Harm? Oh, no, Brother St. Clair, not harm. A great blessing—another soldier for the Christian army has been found and signed up. Let us go now. My heart is full and I must get to the pulpit and let my joy flow over your people."

When the services were concluded at the Ebenezer church he journeyed on to the furthermost regions of Abbs valley. From there he would work his way back home over the same route he had come, but not before he had visited every war widow and bereaved mother and father along the way.

He was three weeks in carrying out this task to his own satisfaction—and, he believed, that of God's—and he was back at Bland again before he felt a terrible loneliness for Eliza and little Eddie.

"The Lord will forgive me, Gideon, if we rest at home a few days and then return to our task."

CHAPTER XIII

In 1870, five years after the end of the war, heavy migrations northward from the Carolinas and other southern states continued unabated. Robert was particularly aware of this, for on his journeys he saw houses and cabins being built on land that had been formerly vast and uninhabited, or that had held only an occasional dwelling.

As he traveled about the hills and hollows of western Virginia and into the fringes of other states, he learned the reasons for the migrations were both practical and political.

"Ain't livin' under Yankee rule," he was to hear time and again, or, "We had to move somewhere—our old place didn't have house nor barn nor mule left on it. We was starvin' to death."

Whatever the reasons, more people meant more opportunities for service. By spring he had a loosely organized circuit of his own that consisted of a few churches, but mostly schools and houses where prayer meetings were held. Even in the most thinly populated areas, if he could get the smallest nucleus of Christians about him, a future church building was a certainty. His fellow preachers who were conference members still called him a "local preacher," but if his ministry was "local" it certainly covered many places and great distances, he thought with a chuckle.

Mail came to him now in increasingly heavy volume, and Eliza became efficient and enthusiastic about taking care of it. "This is the 'request-for-prayer' pile, and the 'requests-for-help' pile, and these are letters asking you to come to churches both distant and near," she would say.

He read the letters carefully each time he returned home, always taking the "request-for-prayer" set first. After that was finished he would walk from the house, get his sheepskin prayer mat, and go to the hill behind the house or into the woods nearby. Little Eddie now followed him faithfully, if allowed, but sometimes, as he went to pray, Robert would not take the child with him from the house. On these occasions, however, he would sometimes look up from his prayers and find the child sitting upon a tree stump or rock some distance away.

"Lord bless you, son," he would say, running and clutching the boy to him. "I can talk to you now. The Lord and I have finished. Come with me and let's read our other mail and see who needs us."

Back at the house he would continue to hold Eddie while he asked Eliza to read the other letters.

"Well, here's one from a woman who says she is sixty seven years old and doesn't have clothes to go to church. She wants you to mail her one dollar for calico."

"Send it to her," Robert said. "Tell her that if she can't get to a store I'll fetch it to her the next time I pass."

Eliza noted the dispositions he made of each letter while he read the final pieces. "You can't go to all those places," she would say when he was hardly more than half-way through.

"No, but here's one or two that I especially want to visit." He handed her the letter with the explanation, "I always feel like I'm going home when I have a chance to go to Ivanhoe. Besides, it's been a few weeks since I've seen the children, and I'll just make one trip out of it."

"And here's another letter that says you promised to come to Fancy Gap last fall and didn't get there," Eliza read.

"I'll make that trip too," Robert said. "Matter of fact, I'll just leave a week early and go there before Ivanhoe. I can backtrack through Hillsville and cross the mountain to Ivanhoe. It's not so far out of the way."

Within the week, on the second day of June, he was gone. The little mountain church at Fancy Gap was still new enough so that the fragrance of oak from the sawed board siding had as pleasant a smell from behind the pulpit as from the churchyard.

After he had been introduced there was much commotion in the congregation, and he pointed a finger at some young boys with the admonition that they respect God's house with their obedient silence. He started his sermon, but the boys still had not quieted to his satisfaction. He stopped for a moment, and then bowed his head abruptly. "Oh, Lord, we know that we have to watch out for the big devil. He is everywhere, playing at his mischief and plotting his evil. But we find we are also surrounded by little devils. Now, Lord, if all the devils could be sent on back to hell we could get along with worshiping Thee."

When he opened his eyes deathly silence prevailed and young hands were folded motionless in laps.

There were sixteen converts at the end of the service, but he had already been warned by the regular pastor of the church that six expected converts—and six of the sixteen who now stood before him—were one family who became converted at every special meeting of the church. It never quite seemed to "take," however. This dilemma was in his heart as the service closed and he beseeched his God: "Oh, Lord, we have those among us whose souls flit around like bats in a darkened cave. We fear they will never make it to Thy eternal kingdom if Thou does not take them away right now."

Early on Monday morning, he prepared to leave the Fancy Gap community and his young pastor host. "You've got some good people in your church, Malcolm, and some that have a ways to go. Keep at it and know that my prayers are with you. God's silver cord connects us all together to Him so we are not really so far removed from each other as we suppose ourselves to be."

Hillsville lay only ten miles north of Fancy Gap, and there was no hurry to get there. The special meetings at Ivanhoe didn't start until Saturday and would end with a class meeting and preaching on Sunday. Robert rode along at a leisurely pace, which Gideon seemed to be enjoying as much as he did. Sometimes he would let Gideon stop and nibble at a particularly flush outcropping of clover or he would halt the animal to converse with a man on foot or on horseback. Occasionally he would stop only to look at a well-tended garden or healthy corn crop, marveling at the wonders of nature.

"Do you know, Gideon, that God's hand is as surely upon a full corn crib as it is on the beating heart of a newborn baby?"

As he neared Hillsville he climbed from Gideon's back and picked a handful of meadow flowers. "There's a little old wisp of a woman in this town, Gideon, who lost her husband and all nine of her children. You and I are going to ride up to her front door, and before she knows it every corner of the house will smell as if she is tiptoeing through the meadow. She has told me many times that her dearest memories are of playing in the field with her children. She will cry a little, but we mustn't mind that; I have to confess that I weep with her sometimes."

By midafternoon he was headed toward the center of town, where he hoped to find a tailor who would patch the pants he had ripped upon mounting Gideon earlier in the day.

He found one who did the job, but expressed dismay at the fact that his customer had no money.

"As surely as the Lord watches over me I will send you a dollar or bring it the next time I pass," Robert said.

"Do you have anybody to vouch for you?" the tailor asked.

Robert said that he would try to find somebody. In the meantime he left his coat for surety.

He watched people pass him in the street for almost an hour without recognizing anyone. Finally one man came down the street, with a team of horses and wagon, whom he thought he knew, but he couldn't be completely sure. He asked a passer-by who the man was, and when he heard the name Alderman he remembered that this was the person from whom he had purchased Gideon.

Excitement overcame him, and he ran, shouting, toward the wagon. "You must help me get my pants paid for! You must vouch for me, Brother Alderman!"

When the neighborly deed was done Robert thanked his benefactor and told him in parting what a fine animal Gideon had turned out to be. "And I hope the good brother who got Charles Thomas Robert got some service out of her," Robert added.

"Your old mare died in less than a year after the trade."

"Then I owe your customer some money," Robert said.

"No, it was a fair swap. Your animal could drop dead on you tomorrow."

"I will talk to the Lord about it," Robert said, "and whatever He tells me I should do about it I will do."

"Well, if the Lord gets into it we sure can't argue with that!"

All the way to Cripple Creek a Voice seemed to tell him that he should indeed give some money back since his old horse had died.

Three of his children remained contentedly at Cripple Creek now, and the younger of his first marriage, John Robert, was almost seventeen and towered a head above his father. Wendell Swecker had lain in his grave for almost six years, but otherwise all things were about the same.

Again he picked an armful of meadow flowers and laid them on Elizabeth's grave before he rode eastward down the Cripple Creek valley toward Ivanhoe.

The meeting at Ivanhoe was being held at the Forest church and greeting him immediately were visiting officials from both the Holston conference and the Baltimore conference. Most of the time was spent in an open discussion of regional level business with a night preaching service. He was not asked to preach, pray, or exhort either during the day or at the conclusion of the Saturday-night service.

He rode his horse back to Cripple Creek to spend the night, with second thoughts about returning for the Sunday services if they were going to be led by those pompous dignitaries whose ecclesiastical propriety hung over the gathering like winter fog. He decided in favor of participation, for most of the clergy fitted no such mold, and they could all, he supposed, allow the visiting hierarchy one final day to show their superiority of intellect and piety.

The day progressed with meetings, wherein the participants recounted their individual spiritual experiences, followed by a morning preaching service. Dinner was served on the grounds—and *still* Robert had not been asked to preach, pray, or exhort. As an invited member of the clergy such a state of affairs was discourteous if not downright insulting. He could not help noticing that all the others had had at least a small part in some phase of the two-day meetings.

The Sunday-night service was all that remained. Not one message from the pulpit brought one healthy Methodist shout—much less a convert—and finally Robert was asked to close the meeting with a short prayer.

He stood, lifted his sheepskin prayer mat from the chair on which he was sitting, and walked to the front near the altar. There he knelt facing the congregation and lifted his voice.

"Dear Lord, a chill wind seems to imprison our hearts; and the brothers and sisters sit about as rotting tree stumps; and even the mouths of Thy servants who have spoken seem cold with formality and aloofness. These brethren who call themselves preachers and who by divine calling should let Thy lovingkindness shine from them like the light of the sun do not know what the trouble is. I think *I* know what the trouble is. Thou are not with us. We have not invited Thee. They will not like Thy servant Robert Sheffey for asking you this at so late an hour, but, Lord, come quickly, like a descending dove. Forgive them, Lord, for their stiff shirt collars and brand-new suits make it hard for them to look down from the pulpit to see if anyone stands at the altar. Forgive them, Lord, they are small potatoes, and very few in the hill..."

The service continued by lamplight that night. It was nearly midnight when he took his arm from around the shoulders of the last petitioner who sat hunched upon the bench, a radiant peace at last coming upon him.

Upon returning to the Irish Settlement he found that his mail was again heavy, but only one letter spoke with any urgency, and that urgency seemed camouflaged with understatement. The letter said, "Brother Sheffey, come and talk to my man. I'd be obliged if you'd get here straightaway. If I'm departed give my children to my sister. Here is a map." The letter was signed by a Mrs. Beamer.

Robert was not sure he remembered the woman, and the approximate place from which the letter came had been visited by him only two or three times over the past ten years. The area lay in the Bear Wallow section of West Virginia, and the ride would be a long one.

"That's ranging out too far," Eliza said when he told her the location of the place he was going.

"No place is too far to go to spread my Lord's lovingkindness."

"This letter has the aura of danger about it. The letter seems like an unusual distress call of some kind," Eliza said, frowning.

He placed his arm around her waist and spoke calmly. "Now, Eliza, you know my sweet Lord would not let harm come to me unless it be His divine will. And if so, so be it."

"The simplicity of your rebuttals leaves me defenseless, Robert. I always end up saying, go do what you must do."

"And that is the thing you want to hear yourself saying."

"And how did you know that?" she asked.

"Because you're all a part of it now—such a vital part, I'm obliged to say—and thank God for it."

The population growth here had been rapid, he noticed as he rode along the turnpikes until it was time to turn onto the spur roads and then the still narrower mountain and ridge roads. After crossing into West Virginia he rode until he had reached Slate Creek. The territory looked more familiar to him now, for he remembered staying in the village of Harrisonville on a previous trip. He continued riding west to Bradshaw's Creek, where the woman's crude map directed him. Only an occasional cabin appeared in view and there were almost no travelers.

By midmorning of the next day, when Bradshaw's Creek was reached, he saw a young mountaineer lounging on the creek bank and, further beyond him, a larger group of men who seemed to be participating excitedly in some enterprise out of his view.

"Can you tell me where Mrs. Beamer and her man live?" Robert asked.

"I'm new in these parts myself," the younger man said. He pointed and added, "Maybe some of them yonder can tell you if they can get their minds often that gander-pullin' long enough to answer you."

"Off of what?" Robert asked.

"Gander- pullin'. Ain't you ever heerd of gander-pullin'? That's the funniest game around."

He rode up the creek to the gathering and watched for a few minutes until he understood exactly what was going on. A large male goose hung from a low tree limb by his feet, which were tied with rawhide string. His long feathery neck glistened with bear grease, and the mounted riders were thus far unsuccessful in stretching the helpless bird's neck until it broke. After further passes of mounted riders, unmounted participants made runs, jumps, and stretching lunges, which as yet were unsuccessful.

As the bird honked pitifully from pain and fright, Robert could stand the cruelty no longer. He rode into the midst of the men and boys, near to the hanging gander, and blocked any further passes at the defenseless fowl.

"Who'll be man enough to cut the goose down—in the name of the Lord?" he demanded.

"If anybody does, *you* might just get put back up in its place." A bearded older man spoke up.

"A gander exists for two reasons," Robert said. "He is to be eaten or used to help bring other little goslings into the world."

"Now you ain't exactly right, are you, mister?" A youth stepped forward. "A gander is fer a gander-pullin'. You're a mighty brave man a-stickin' your nose in other folks' business."

"That is not my intent, my brothers, but our Lord does not sanction the use of his creatures for cruel sport. 'Thou shalt not muzzle the ox when he treadeth out the corn,' the Lord said, and He does not smile upon you as you stretch the gander's neck until in great pain it breaks and he dies. If you are killing the goose to eat; do it quickly and without any greater pain than you yourselves would want to bear."

There was a hushed silence then, but nobody moved to free the gander from his captivity. Finally a stout redheaded man of middle age stepped so close to Robert that he could smell the pungent odor of fermented corn upon the man' s breath. "You want him down, mister, you take him down."

"My Creator has seen fit to make me a man of small stature. I don't fight because I can't do a very good job of it and because there is not use for it. I want you to cut the gander down because the love of Jesus has spoken to your hearts and you know it is God's will."

Nobody in the group spoke for the longest while; each man seemed to be pondering the arrogance of a stranger who would ride in their midst and interrupt their sport with no fears whatever.

The first man who had spoken to him got up and moved a distance away, motioning his companions to join him in an encircled conference. When the ring broke, the same man acted as spokesman. "We ain't goin' to cut the gander down, but we'll let you do it."

"Without harm to me or my animal?" Robert asked.

"We won't lay a hand on neither one of you—you got our word."

Robert rode over and untied the rawhide string, handing the bird to the spokesman. "I want to ride back this way sometime. I will be anxious to know what you do with the gander."

"Well, we sure ain't goin' to waste our time a-teachin' him to lay eggs!" an old-timer called from the back of the group.

The humor broke the tension, and Robert had the feeling that this particular gander would live to an honorable old age and boast of more ancestors than any gander in the settlement.

Before departing he asked the men whether or not they would come to a revival service later on in the summer—if he could find a place to hold it. Each man to the last said he would.

He rode away from them then with clear directions to his destination and new warmth in his heart. "Oh, Gideon, the Lord be praised. Truly His gifts are boundless. It could have worked the other way, old friend, and I rather suspect the inhabitants of this wilderness do not really approve of us. Perhaps they would like to believe that they are so far removed from civilization that they need not give account to men or God. But we have spoiled it for them, Gideon; we remind them that no man hides from God, no matter how deep in the wilderness he may be."

The Beamer cabin lay still farther west along the ridge, and when Robert got there the problem immediately became self-evident. The young mother of three looked not a day older than seventeen or eighteen at most, but new bruises and old ones covered her head, neck, and arms, and scrap cloth hid her leg wounds.

Robert did not recognize her and was sure now that he had never before seen her. In spite of this, she knew in the briefest moment who he was, and as she fell upon his neck her anguished sobs carried down into the narrow valley and back again.

"Tell me more about you, child?" he asked when she had stopped sobbing. "We've never met before, have we?"

"I was just a little girl when you prayed for my mamma and papa at camp meeting. My father was Josh Pickle, and Mamma used to laugh and say you prayed to the Lord that their hearts were not as sour as their name. They're gone now, and I married and moved here in the mountains. Mamma said if I ever needed any help to write to you and no matter how far away I was, you'd come."

"I'm glad she told you that, child. My sweet Lord sends me where He wants me to go."

Her sobs overcame her again and her body shook so hard that she could not talk.

"Is it your husband? Did he put those bruises all over you?"

She cried louder and nodded in the affirmative. In that moment he felt that he himself had been the victim of a brutal blow.

"Where is your husband now?"

"I don't never know where he is. He comes and goes. He's not a bad man when he's not drinkin'—honest he's not, Brother Sheffey."

"I just came from a gander-pulling a few miles back at the creek. Would he have been there?"

"He might've been, if he was sober enough to walk."

When the woman was quiet and her most recent wounds dressed he left her and went to Gideon for his sheepskin prayer mat.

He climbed the peak behind the Beamer cabin, and his voice was troubled. "Oh, Lord, it's a tall order I'm asking you for today…"

He stayed with the beaten woman throughout the hours to follow, and while he sat at her table, having a meager and late dinner, a lone rider stopped near the open door of the cabin. He waved back and forth in the saddle, and his long coal-black hair fell over his face and obscured his eyes.

"Woman, get me out of this saddle—fer it's turnin' round and round and round—you be a-hustlin' or I'll box your jaws this time—"

"That's him, and he's stone-drunk. He makes me help him off the horsc when he gets in bad shape."

"Help him down," Robert said, "and then I have an errand for you to do before it gets dark."

Robert tied the drunkard's horse as his wife guided his tall and staggering frame through the narrow cabin door. Mr. Beamer would have been strikingly handsome had he been clean.

When Robert re-entered the cabin, the young woman appeared to be concluding an explanation of her visitor's presence. "Uncle Robert was just passing by this part of the country"—she was lying nervously, Robert could tell.

"Then give him his supper and tell him to be gone—and be damn quick about it."

"You'd better get somethin' in your stomach—," Mrs. Beamer started to say.

"I got my supper right here," he said and added an oath. Robert then saw him teeter backward onto the straw tick of their bed and reach under it for a small demijohn.

The couple's oldest child climbed upon his father's bed, only to be met with a backhanded slap that landed him halfway to Robert's feet.

The mother picked up the screaming youngster. "He's not like that if he's not drinkin'. You've got to believe that."

"No man's past saving, I grant you that, sister. But right now your man is not fit for the kingdom or the devil either. We need to point him in a certain direction and help him make up his mind."

Suddenly, a loud thump from the bedroom sounded, interrupting their conversation.

"He's fell off his bed, I know he has," she said, startled. She pushed the door open hurriedly, and an empty demijohn came rolling toward them. "All his liquor is gone and he's passed out. He won't bother nobody now," she said.

"How long will he be sleeping?"

"He won't come around until midnight, and then he'll rouse up and make me wife him or whip me. About then he'll drink some more if he's got it, or go back to sleep and sleep all the next day."

"It'll be dark in three or four hours, and I want you to go on some errands for me before then. And you must not ask any questions."

With childlike obedience she promised she wouldn't. He gave her two five-dollar gold pieces and several pieces of silver. "Go buy all the liquor and brandy this money will buy. You'll have to make several trips to different places, and try not to raise suspicion. You've done this for your husband before, haven't you?"

"Yes," she said, "plenty of times, and sometimes very late in the night."

"Go now. I'll look after your babies… There's one more thing I'll be needing. Do you have a large tub or soap making cauldron'?"

"We've got a wooden tub we take a bath in sometimes, and a little cauldron I boil fat in."

"The bathing tub will do. Where is it?"

She told him and started on her way.

When she returned with the final load he asked her to take one of the demi johns and spoon-feed some of the liquid down her husband's throat.

"What do you want me to do that for—he's dead drunk now!"

"This is one night we want him to have all the liquor he wishes."

He instructed the girl to put the children to bed as soon as it got completely dark. He then lifted the large bathing-tub onto Gideon's back and hooked it over the saddle horn.

West of the crest where he had earlier gone to pray was a small clearing of land, most likely used, he guessed, as a corn or potato patch during years when young Mr. Beamer had felt the inclination to work. In the midst of this small clearing he sat and leveled the tub.

When all the details of his setting were as he liked them the task of gathering pine-knots and green pine boughs was all that remained. Having accumulated a large pile of both, he broke them down into smaller piles and placed these three or four feet apart in a complete circle around the tub.

By the time he had delivered all of the liquor and brandy to the clearing, and placed it about the tub, night had come and a full moon and a clear sky cast an eerie light by which to work. Lamplight now shone in the cabin window far below him, and he hoped the children were asleep.

When he returned quietly to the cabin the woman put her fingers to her lips as he entered. "One more to go," she said, peering from the room where all three of the children slept. In moments she came from the room and closed the door. Her small body trembled, and she made no effort to hide her fear or her anticipation. "I know you won't hurt him, Brother Sheffey, but I'm scared just the same. I don't know what you're going to—"

"Have no fear, my child, the Lord watches over us. After this night you will never again feel the drunken wrath of your husband."

She looked at him questioningly but made no further protest and asked what other things she was to do.

"Do the babies sleep soundly? Will they be all right?" he asked.

"None of them ever wakes during the night unless their pa is raisin' Cain with me."

"That won't happen tonight," Robert said. "Now help me lay your man across my horse's back."

An occasional groan came from the man's drooling mouth, but otherwise there was no sound except that of the powerful hooves of Gideon digging into the mountain soil as they climbed upward.

When they stood beside the tub Robert asked the woman to help him lower her husband and then to break branches from the low-hanging pine trees that enclosed the circle. When she was out of sight Robert removed the man's clothes, lifted him little by little into the large wooden tub, and sat him upright.

He was pouring the liquid from the demijohns first over the man's head and then about his body when Mrs. Beamer came running back. He could not see her eyes clearly in the moonlight, but her voice cracked with apprehension, and she gasped as she saw her husband reposing motionless in the half-filled tub.

"Won't the liquor burn him? Oh, Brother Sheffey, if you'll just take him home he won't beat me no more, I'll promise you that... Let's just take him home...he's a good man."

"No, child. Nothing for you will be changed unless we complete what we have come to do. A little hurt is sometimes good for us."

"But the liquor will sting—"

"Yes, but hell is a place that will surely sting. He'll be lucky if the pain only lasts for one night. Would not God be merciful if He allowed your man only one night of hell and then opened the way to His glory?"

He could see the girl nod in the moonlight. "But why must he be naked?" She was whimpering a little now.

"Hell will have no clothed people, of that we can be sure. There will not be even a garment to hide behind for those who will forever live in shame and hopelessness."

They waited together in silence until the man showed signs of emerging from his stupor. He settled back with his head resting on the tub rim and did not groan or attempt to speak.

"It's time to light the fires now," Robert said.

She helped him, but by the firelight he could see the tears running down her face. Soon the entire circle was ablaze.

"Now, go get me some of the green branches you broke off," he said. "I want there to be smoke enough that he cannot recognize the setting even if he were sober—which, believe me, he soon will be!"

It was almost an hour before the weaving, groaning head snapped to horrified attention in the smoke-filled firelight. At first the man seemed paralyzed in utter terror; then his head and neck began to gyrate wildly and without control. His eyes became enlarged mirrors of firelight and appeared to be bulging from their sockets. Finally there was a guttural scream choked off by smoke. The man flailed his arms wildly in an attempt to rise out of the stinging liquid surrounding him.

Burning pine cones whistled in the consuming heat, and crackling branches echoed in the stillness of night. From out of the shadows where they stood, the woman started to break away from Robert and run to her husband. He grabbed her at the outer circle of the fire before she could run farther.

"No, child! Let him be cleansed," he whispered.

Almost immediately the man's feet began to gyrate in time with his thrashing arms and he leaped from the tub. Seeing his own nakedness and the encirclement of fire about his liquid tomb, he began to run in a circle around the tub, looking back periodically as he ran and giving a repentant shout each time the tub was rounded. He continued to run in this way until his panting cries echoed into the night. As he stood silhouetted against the firelight, every hair upon his body seemed to stand upright and there were visible welts on his body. Finally, with both hands, he tore at his own hair and made a wild leap through the outer circle of fire. A quick burst of flame, like a lamp that had been lighted and quickly blown out, consumed the last bit of alcoholic vapor that hung near to his naked body.

Straight ahead in the running man's path were groves of yellow pine, and it was as if he could see neither light nor darkness as his head slapped dully against a small sapling. His body sprawled helplessly.

"Oh, lordy, you said you wouldn't hurt him," the young woman moaned.

For a moment Robert too was frightened, for he had not anticipated this fall. Kneeling by the man's side, he examined him, and then stood confidently. "He's only knocked himself senseless for a little while, and perhaps it is the Lord's blessing. I hoped to preserve the illusion just long enough for him to see what his eternal future might be like. Now we have time to make the experience even more effective. Bring me that last demijohn and help me get some of it inside him. I want this to be his last dose of liquor, and when he wakes up do not be surprised if he never mentions this strange 'dream' he has had. You will be wise to ignore the singed hair on his body, and he will never know for certain what really happened."

She sat holding her husband's head in her lap, but Robert left them at peace for only a moment. "Let's get him home now. Daylight will soon be coming and I must first take our equipment home and cover the ashes here. I have to leave after it is done—it will not be well for me to be around when he awakes."

When all was finished the woman filled Robert's pockets with cold biscuits and a goose egg she had hurriedly cooked. Daylight began to come upon the ridge, and a first groan could be heard from the adjoining room.

"I had best be on my way now. I will ride west through the clearing and see that none of my work in the moonlight remains to tell a tale."

"I'm glad we did it now—but when we was up *there*..." She halted.

"I know, child. May the Lord's blessing be upon our deed. It was the only way. Write to me if all is not well."

By the full rising of the sun he had crossed two more northward-running ridges and, at the crossing of two more, the settlement of Shack's Mill lay in the distance.

When he came to the first house in sight he dismounted and knocked timidly at the door. A skinny woman in a bonnet answered promptly and he said, "Would there be any food in your house for a servant of the Lord?"

"Indeed there be. Are you more than a mite hungry?"

"More than a mite," Robert confessed.

"You look like a traveling man. I always pack a traveling man's pockets when he leaves from my house."

"The good sister where I stayed last night did that, but I met a friend. The poor thing looked like he hadn't had biscuits nor bone for a host of Sundays."

"Are you talking about a man or a dog?" the woman asked.

"A bluetick hound," he said, "and it would've done your heart good to see him gobble those biscuits and gnaw into that goose egg..."

By the following midday he had ridden across the state line and far into Virginia, but an hour after dinner had been taken with two elderly sisters a summer downpour threatened to engulf both him and Gideon if shelter could not soon be found. He traveled somewhere between Millstone and Elk Garden in Russell County, but no house appeared in view. As his eyes swept across the terrain he detected several sheep entering a limestone cave at the base of a steep cliff.

"It'll keep us dry, Gideon, and it's tall enough for you to get your head in. Looks like there's a shelf above it that will keep you dry anyway."

He stood in the opening of the cave so the sheep would not be forced, by fright of him, back out into the heavy downpour.

"Your kind doesn't mind water so much, but sheep do not like to get wet. They don't object to snow, but when rain soaks their wool—"

"Are you talking to me or that animal that shuts out the light with his head?" A voice boomed from further back in the cave.

"I was talking with my animal, but it's the Lord's blessing that we can share this house of nature until the storm passes. I'm Robert Sheffey."

"I know who you are. I knowed you when you stepped in out of the rain."

"Then come closer, brother, so we can get re-acquainted."

A one-eyed man stepped nearer the light. Robert recognized the face, although he did not remember his name. The man wore a rawhide jacket and pants, and he was tall and lean like a hunter.

"From where do I know you?" Robert asked.

"It was at the revival at Elk Garden. You done everything but twist my tail to make me go to the altar."

"God be praised if I succeeded."

"You never had no luck with me."

"Have you since made your profession and been baptized?"

"No. I ain't ready, but I'm interested."

"Well, that's a start," Robert said. "Only problem is whether you've got the time to wonder and wait or not."

"It's not time wastin', it's trying to figure things out. Don't nothin' about religion makes sense. Why be born in the world if we got to change our ways… and why do we have the will and the way to do bad if we're not supposed to be that way?"

"My brother that is not a new question. Since the very presence of our Saviour in the world Christians have had to fight all reason to serve Him."

"I'm not ready for another sermon," the man said curtly, "and this place is not exactly lined with pews."

"It wouldn't make any difference if we were in a cow shed. I've felt the presence of my sweet Lord there just as surely as I have felt it in the finest of churches."

His listener towered over him and laughed. "Why, we'd both be run out of Russell County if the word got around we were holdin' preachin' in a cave."

"Religion is a divine force that a man can find on the back of his horse or with a hoe in his hands. The great cathedrals of the world give no more guarantee of finding God's promise than the dripping walls of this cave. Oh yes, my brother, it is quite possible that the closest either of us shall ever come to our God is right here."

"Just the same, I think I'll study on it some more and maybe I'll see you at revival time."

"I won't be there this year, but another who loves the sweet Lord as I do will be, and he'll do just as well."

"It's stopped raining now—least the sheep have left us for the outside and your horse is getting his bridle wet, nipping at the clover. Those sheep going out—it's something like the dove that left Noah's Ark after the Flood—you know, to see if the land was dry?"

"Yes, I know." Robert smiled a little at having the passage explained.

"Well, so long, preacher."

"Tell me one thing before you leave, my brother: do you *really* search for God?"

"I haven't tried to fool you."

"Then if you really search for Him, you have found Him already. When you discover this for yourself, make your surrender."

The sky cleared and Gideon took his head.

"That's it, old friend, let's not tarry. We've miles yet to travel, and I would like to go by way of Marion and see my boys and my brother. I miss them all, Gideon."

The sky was overcast when Robert reached the Irish Settlement at last. Little Eddie sat perched upon the lane gate, as he often did, and Robert called a greeting. The child scampered down and ran toward Gideon until he came abreast of the animal. In their usual manner, Robert removed his foot from the stirrup and lifted his son until both of the boy's small feet rested securely in the relinquished foot hold. Then, with an exaggerated grunt, Robert lifted him the rest of the way into the saddle in front of him.

"There's no sunshine; you don't never come home when there's no sunshine, Papa!"

"Then why were you waiting for me at the gate if you didn't think I'd be coming home?"

"The sunshine came out for a little while."

"I've come home many times when the sunshine wasn't out. Can't you remember back in the winter when the snow covered the ground?"

"Uncle Johnny and Uncle David said you've been gone too long."

"Uncle Johnny and Uncle David don't understand everything, son."

Robert released the boy and helped him slide to the ground. The child's joyous shouts soon brought Eliza to the yard gate, and Robert removed his hat and inquired politely before he dismounted, "Does a Mrs. Sheffey live here?"

"Yes, but we're beginning to wonder about Mr. Sheffey."

He slid to the ground and embraced her. Then it started to sprinkle, and Eddie ran ahead of them into the house.

"I wanted it to be a pretty day when you came back. It usually is."

"All my days are sunny, Eliza. If they are not, all I need to do is look at you."

Chapter XIV

"There comes a time when things must change, Robert," Eliza said one day before the winter of 1871 was hardly over. "It would be best if we had our own home now. Eddie likes to frolic, and young and old do not always blend well."

"You cover great troubles with small explanations, dear wife."

"Not great troubles, Robert. Only a time of trusting and trials. Eddie and I will not always have the shelter of family. It is just as well that we face that now as later."

"We are not to worry about the future, Eliza. My sweet Lord tells me that as plainly as any message He has placed upon my heart. I may not always be able to supply your needs, but by His grace He will place the joy of so doing on the heart of someone else and make them all the richer for it."

Two days after Robert's fifty-first birthday he moved Eliza and Eddie into the community of Sugar Run, only a few miles from the Irish Settlement. It was a beautifully lush valley of rich land and bold springs, inhabited by people long known and loved and previously ministered unto. For the most part they were simple farmers who tended their crops and meadows with loving labor. They possessed no great herds of livestock and those they did have responded to individual names spoken with affection.

He had preached many times at Eaton's chapel, a picturesque little wooden church nestled along the valley, and had been deeply fond of the community and its people for as long as he had known them.

Eliza, after a trip with him to Cripple Creek, had made the observation that a great similarity existed between the two valleys.

"Why, it *is* so," he agreed. "And little Eddie will be happy here. I never knew of more contented children anywhere in my travels than those on Cripple Creek. Sugar Run looks like the same kind of delightful place."

Their rented home sat near the gristmill on the farm of Francis Farley and was modestly furnished by some of Eliza's personal things plus some of his own furniture that he had stored for years at Cripple Creek. It was an odd-shaped house, with the front door and windows out of balance, as if the carpenter did not know what he was doing or had partaken of refreshments before he had worked enough to get thirsty. German siding covered the outer walls, with curly oak shingles comprising the roof. It was set in an open field and had no trees except numerous fruit trees toward the rear of the house.

"What an assortment of odds and ends we have!" Eliza said good-naturedly when after a week she had not arranged their things in a manner which seemed to suit her.

Neighbors filled their pantry, and before long Robert could wander about the small four rooms and be assured that Eliza had not once again changed everything completely around.

"It's the bestest house we've ever lived in, Papa," Eddie said from the very beginning.

The boy could be observed enjoying the simplest of pleasures as he sat by the groaning waterwheel of the gristmill, hearing the grating mill stones pulverize ton upon ton of grain; or, when new adventure called, exploring the home of lizards and crawfish in the brooks and branches that ran close to every side of the modest house.

One day he and Eliza and Eddie climbed the field to the rear of the house, and as they surveyed in wonder the patchwork of meadows and mountains stretching as far as they could see, a speck of activity around their own premises could be observed.

"Eliza, is that a horse at the back of our house?"

"It's a man and a horse and plow."

"Did you ask him to come?" Robert said.

"No. I believe we are seeing a neighborly kindness. Robert, have you been down on your sheepskin since we moved?"

When they descended the hill, Forrest Farley, Francis's son, had already turned the first furrow of garden sod. Eddie immediately waded into the fresh dirt and picked up the fat white grub worms that had been unearthed.

They had to make Farley stop the horse in order to thank him for his kindness.

"You're gettin' your garden out too late as it is," he said dourly. "The old folks say if you plow early you can still freeze out a lot of the cuttin' worms and bugs. Makes sense to me."

Robert followed the plowman completely around the garden on the next furrow, thanking him profusely at every corner.

"By the way, Mamma sent you a pound of honey," the man said. "It's on the front steps."

Robert went straightway through the plowed earth toward the front of the house.

Summer came, the garden matured, and Eliza and Eddie dined many times on fresh vegetables before Robert planned any prolonged trips away from home. He would not be traveling alone this time, for a new experiment in Christian outreach was being tried with which he was in accord.

At the urging of conference officials, preachers of the district had been asked to work in groups of two or three and make home visitations preparatory to the August camp meetings held annually in several locations within the conference's jurisdiction.

Robert waited at home for the arrival of one Reverend Jordan; the two of them would meet Reverend Maiden in Pulaski County, the starting point for all of them.

Reverend Jordan arrived the first week of August. "I had not expected you this early, Brother Jordan," Robert said. "I'll get my affairs in order as quickly as I can and we'll leave."

He went over a few things with Eliza, demonstrating frustration with the volume of mail. He held two handfuls of letters, first looking at one and then the other.

"Tell that girl who wants me to pray that she can have the man she wants…tell her…tell her I want to wait and meet her friend. I want to know what I might be praying that young man into. Send the money to old Mr. Collins for the bushel of cornmeal. Write my friends at Smyth County—Spratts Creek—I'll come in the fall. Tell them all to pray for the success of the camp meetings. Say, 'The prayer of a righteous man availeth much.' That's all now. Everything else will have to wait."

It was dark before they reached Pulaski County and met Brother Maiden. They were to stay the night in the spacious O'Dell home, Robert and Reverend Jordan were informed, and both men confessed to being ready for both bread and bed.

The O'Dell family was large, and Robert sat thinking with some apprehension as to whether the table, as big and laden with crockery as it was, would accommodate them all.

"There's plenty of room and a whole lot more chicken when we need it," the master of the house said as his perspiring wife lowered the final plate of chicken and dropped into her chair.

"I don't see the dumplings, sister. Have you forgotten the dumplings?" Robert said.

She had already lowered her head for the blessing of the food, but she raised her eyes with a startled look and told him that she did not often make dumplings. His host asked him to pray, that they might get on with the meal.

Robert bowed after all of them had. His pause was prolonged, and feet started to shuffle. He prayed: "Oh Lord, we thank Thee for this good man and this good woman and their sweet fine children. We thank Thee for this good chicken, but even Thou knowest how much better it would have been with dumplings. Amen."

The next day all three men began their visitations in the Newbern section of the county. There was hardly a Methodist family who did not already plan to come to the Wabash camp meeting, located only a few miles from the Irish Settlement, or to some other camp meeting within the district. Presbyterians, Baptists, and a mixture of others soon let it be known that they too would attend as they had in past years.

After a week of hearing this same good news everywhere they went, Robert suggested that they have a special Saturday service of fellowship and dedication, wherein the "good Methodist brothers and sisters can come together and pray about what they plan to do to keep the fervor of godliness alive and growing until the camp meetings actually begin."

The Saturday service Robert proposed was arranged at the Thorn Spring church near the village of Pulaski. What had been planned as a one-day service of prayer and unity-of purpose meeting, evolved into a spontaneous revival to equal the fervor of any camp meeting, though on a much smaller scale.

A nightly service continued on Monday after the successes of Saturday, Saturday night, and the three services on Sunday. Word of these spread rapidly throughout the county and adjoining areas.

"Praise my sweet Lord, if they keep coming we'll be needed here another week," Robert said to his two friends and the church's regular minister, who himself had enlisted two more preachers of his district.

"What has caused it?" each asked of the other.

"They are earnestly preparing for the camp meetings," Robert said, "and their souls beg of their ears not to close."

"If hunger anticipates bread, my brothers, we had best get better-organized," their host pastor suggested. "They almost overran us last night. I'm going to ask Brother Bob Sheffey to work at the altar and exhort from the aisles. Also I want his prayers to open the service. Brother Jordan will preach first tonight, followed by those remaining. I will ask Brother Maiden to lead the singing."

Not one-half of the assembled crowd that night was able to crowd into the small church, but it was warm and the pulpit and pews were moved outside so that there would be no separation of the congregation.

The penitents were many, some even starting their journeys to the front long before the call had come. The conviction of the penitents was so profound that Robert marveled at having seen it only five or six times during his entire lifetime. The most hardened of known resisters to spiritual conversion now sat at the mourners' bench unashamedly tear-soaked and submissive.

Robert stayed on his knees at the bench until the last of the mourners was either soundly converted or had retreated to face the haunting knowledge that he had been so close and now stood so far away.

One of the deacons came to Robert after the service had ended, and reported that a woman had watched from behind an apple tree to the south of the church yard. In fact, the deacon added, the same woman had been seen listening through the open church window on the previous night as well.

"Who is she? Perhaps she is feebleminded and fears us," Robert said.

"I don't know her, but I'll try to find out."

The woman did not appear the next evening, but by then her identity had been established.

"She is the wife of a prominent merchant and one of our members works on her husband's plantation. Our church treasurer says that the family is very wealthy and owns property down in North Carolina."

Robert wiped his tired and perspiring brow but said nothing.

"Do you think I ought to go to her and ask her to come and be seated with the congregation?" the deacon asked.

"Yes, but something is amiss. If she desired our fellowship or our sweet Lord's saving grace she would not tarry behind the trees. We must not be surprised if she comes to poke fun at us."

"I will watch out for her tomorrow night then," the deacon said.

After services the next night the deacon reported back excitedly, "She came, but when I started to approach her she moved quickly away from me."

Robert remembered her in his prayers then without really knowing why or what specific thing he might ask of a loving God on her behalf.

The following night he gave instructions that he was to be signaled if the woman appeared and he would have another of the preachers take over his duties.

Before the service began, the woman was spotted, but Robert purposely left her alone until things were well underway. Quietly he slipped outside the island of light provided by hanging lanterns and pedestal-supported lamps. She stood behind the same tree, though unhidden, for the whiteness of her dress by moonlight outlined her perfectly.

She started to turn as he got near, but he asked her to please wait. "My sister, our fellowship would be richly blessed if you would sit among us."

"Sit among you! I don't see a soul who looks like they have retained a shred of their dignity. Why, they have yielded themselves completely—"

"Yes, they have got in a good way, but only because they are confessing their unworthiness, their sin—and they love their Lord so much—"

"I don't care to come and sit—that is—I just heard about the meetings and I was curious."

"But you have been with us before and we do not honor our sweet Lord when you are outside our fellowship."

"Yes, I've been here before, but I was—I'm just curious," she repeated.

"Is there anything the sweet Lord has laid on my heart that I may tell you?"

"No. Nothing. There is nothing I wish to hear."

"Will you come back tomorrow night?"

"No."

"If I hadn't come to you, would you have come back?"

"I will not tell you that," she said.

His eyes adjusted to her young, pretty face in the moonlight, and he expected to see her smile in her defeat of him but she did not. Nothing at all in her face supported the imagery by which he had characterized her.

She excused herself then and walked from him. The swish of her dress could be heard long after she disappeared from view. Presently the sound of a galloping horse could be heard traveling southward toward the village.

The woman appeared no more and on Saturday night the meeting closed.

After the camp meeting at Wabash was over, the last of August, Robert was free to journey to Smyth County at Spratt's Creek and assist the pastor there in a two-day service.

He rode from Sugar Run joyously, for the successes of the meetings at Wabash still warmed his heart. Only during the war had he personally witnessed an equal fervor, but those had been troubled times, when the pressures of war might have driven some people to a place of collective worship. But at Wabash the conversions were more spontaneous.

Passing through Bland, he learned that an old friend had died in the community of Ceres, to the west of the county seat.

"We can go by that route just as well, Gideon, and it would do my heart good to walk with Monroe to his last resting place. The tragedy of his life is yet so near to me. But he won out. Bless Jesus, he won out. I have preached at the Red Oak church many times, Gideon, and there were times when the hearts of the people were so cold. I'm going to ask the Lord to shake up that place."

When he reached Ceres the funeral was almost over, but he took a seat on the back pew as the casket lid was being closed and the minister stood at the feet of the family, ready to utter the final prayer of the service.

As the preacher followed the coffin out, he motioned Robert to follow him.

"Brother Sheffey, I didn't see you back there or I'd have asked you to pray," he said. "I know how long it took you to deliver the soul of this brother into the keeping of our Father—Monroe told me before he died and he also told me the story that you heard from his own lips years ago. He died a good man, and he would be honored if you would lead his burial procession with me."

Robert willingly consented, and the two men walked along the dirt road ahead of the casket. Only a few hundred feet after the procession had started, Robert lifted his hand and asked everyone to stop while he knelt beside a deep wagon track and lifted from its dirt-walled prison a tumblebug that lay helplessly upon its back. He delivered the insect to safety on the opposite bank, but, rather than returning to the procession, he sat there remembering the man whose cold corpse they now carried to the cemetery.

The bug, the creature of God's creation that he had just rescued, was walled in by its helpless position. Mankind, he thought, was subject to the same imprisonment—symbolically speaking, at least. It had been so with the dead man. He had cut his own groove and made his own prison walls that few others could see.

"Brother Bob… we are holding up the procession." A gentle hand touched his shoulder.

He stood and walked, and the creaking wheels of the horse-drawn hearse moved the procession forward again.

"Dust thou art, to dust returneth," he repeated to Gideon when they were on their way to Smyth County again. "These words ought to make a man honest, wouldn't you say? Monroe wasn't always honest, but he died honest. Would you like to hear about it, Gideon? Would you like to hear about it, old friend?"

The animal whinnied.

"Well, it was like this: I knew Monroe for ten years before I ever got close to him, or before he'd even let me pray with him, for that matter. I could tell the first time I met him that he carried a terrible burden on his heart, and one day I told him so. He laughed at me, and it was another seven years before he wrote me to come to his house—that we had something to discuss. I went, but he wouldn't talk in his home; we went to the barn instead. He didn't speak a word; he cried as if his heart would break, and I gave him his time. There in the straw he revealed to me that in his youth he had burned down a man's store and his house—everything in the world the man had, Gideon. He did it for pure meanness! He told me with his own lips that the storekeeper had never even been unkind to him. For pure meanness, Gideon! Everything in the world the man and his wife possessed—and they were old, he said, and had neither son nor daughter to go to. Oh, yes, I asked him why he didn't go to them when he could stand the burden of guilt no longer, and he said that he had, when a number of years had passed, but that both of the old folks were dead. Even after that first trip he went other times to Mercer County where he had done the awful deed and stood tearstained in the ashes of the house and store he had destroyed.

"In all my years, Gideon, I have not met a man so racked with guilt and regret. But he and I and the sweet Lord found peace together and he was ninety-four when we put him under the ground today. I do not know whether my sweet Lord gave him so much time to remember or so much time to forget, but he did die in peace. Of that there is no doubt."

The next day Robert stood in the pulpit of the Spratt's Creek church and made it clear that he was in no hurry to begin the services.

"Smyth County is too dear to me to hurry away from this place," he said. "I like to ride here from any direction, for the good handiwork of our God is everywhere. Pray with me that we may preserve it and cherish it until the smallest black ant is safe within our care. I stayed with a dear sweet family in Chilhowie last night, but I was not treated so well. My bed linen was not crisp with fresh sunlight, and the good sister did not keep her children clean. I think I am in better quarters here in your community, and if my hostess tells you that I drew a picture around the knothole in my bedroom door, she tells you no falsehood. I did it. I was lying upon my bed and I said to myself, 'Sheffey, what does that knothole look like?', and after a minute it came to me. It was the mouth of a great fish—perhaps like the one Jonah was swallowed by—and I drew the body of a fish around the mouth that was already there. You have been slow to notice that I am wearing a beard since we last worshiped together. It will be a blessing to you to know how I happen to have it. I was riding down East River Mountain last winter and got caught in a hailstorm, which cut up my face tolerably bad. My sweet Lord said, 'Sheffey, if you would grow a beard the wind and hailstones would not hurt your face.' How many times does our sweet Lord tell us what to do to ease our pain and we don't listen? Well, today I am going to tell you about a man who was told by God but would not listen..."

When his sermon was over and the invitation given, no converts came forward. He showed no disappointment and began his final prayer.

"Oh loving God, we thank Thee for bringing us all together and may it be so again, soon. Now bless Sister and Brother Summers. They are having trouble and they do not love each other enough. Brother All's still loves his liquor, Lord, and I want you to turn it sour in his mouth like pig slop and make him spend his money on his dear little girls. Make Brother Sid and Amos stop fighting over what their dear father left them. How sad he would be to know that his land, which he had sweated over for so long, now causes brother to hate brother. Make our young brothers and sisters to be pure of heart and character. And finally, Lord, watch over Brother Barnard, sitting *there*, who has never asked me to his house since I've walked over the sweet soil of Smyth County. Put it in his heart to let me eat at his table sometime soon and partake of the good honey Thou does so bountifully give us…"

"Well, Brother Bob, I know I can't talk you into moving back to Smyth County, but I realize that you want to go and see your brother and your sons. Perhaps they *can* do what I *can't* do," his host pastor said as Robert prepared to leave at the closing of the last service.

"I'll come back every time you'll let me, but Eliza thinks the heart of Giles County is the next thing to the Garden of Eden," Robert said.

"Good-bye, old friend, and may God's light shine upon you as it has for all of our days together. The children await you now, and you'd better hurry if you want their sendoff. They will be going home soon."

As he climbed upon Gideon's back all the children rushed toward him, some hanging onto his pants leg or the stirrups on both sides, still others onto Gideon's tail. They ran along in front of the animal until finally he had to stop and tell them to move back.

"Pray for me, children, our dear Jesus loves the sound of little prayers."

The following day he sat in the Marion law office of his brother James. He was shocked at how much his brother had aged and told him so.

"You're no spring chicken yourself," James shot back. "Why don't you get a nice little church or two to serve somewhere and stop this ridge running?"

"Why don't you lock your desk and make the front-porch rocker *your* home?"

"I guess I'll stick around a while unless my son and law partner decides to retire me for inefficiency. I must admit he knows more about law than I did when I was twice his age."

"I'm no more ready to retire to green pastures than you—and besides, I'm younger."

"You don't look it. You're burning your candle at both ends. You're doing what a younger man should be doing. You've served your time as a mountain evangelist. Besides, you misunderstood me. I didn't say quit. Just stay in one place and make it a little easier on yourself. If you did you might find your congregation upgraded a little—and the collection plate likewise. You can't tell me that the work shouldn't pay a decent living."

"The sweet Lord will take care of us. Have no fear about that. If it be His will I'll be riding the mountain trails as long as I can crawl upon the back of a horse."

"Do you honestly believe that even half of the people you serve have the brains to know what you're doing and why? I know it isn't true of most of them, but some must be so illiterate as to make communication near impossible—"

"You ought to get out of your law office more often, James. People in the remotest mountains might not have changed much, but along the byways they're not like we knew them a few years ago. The coming and passing of the war has made a difference. Anyway, it is through the heart that every man is really reached."

"My point is, a man has to understand before you can touch him even *there*."

"Understand? It would take me a week to tell you how quickly they 'understand,' dear brother. I have never met a man who didn't 'understand' already, no matter how ignorant. Even in the most hostile of feuding clans there is the instinctive knowledge that sin is being committed—that a human being's real duty to love God and his neighbor is being violated."

"I have not meant to degrade your work or some of your people, but some of the poor wretched devils would surely drive off an undertaker—"

"You're still behind the times, James. It was a whole lot like that twenty years ago, but now I ride among clean little villages and well-kept farms as much as I ride among the smelly trappers' cabins and the gully hovels or tenant shacks."

"Well, it's your life. Live it as you please. If it were me I'd find a little more comfortable ground," James said.

"What could be more comfortable than loving my sweet Lord's people, both rich and poor. But you know what? If I had to make a choice I'd take the poor. There's something beautiful about a man who hasn't one single defense left to prevent his seeing the real meaning of the cross. I have never felt that you or any of my brothers have understood or have been in real sympathy with what I try to do in the Lord's name."

"Now, Robert, that isn't true—"

"All right, I'll take part of it back. Perhaps Lawrence does, for a doctor and a preacher have something in common, but the rest of you are just as convinced that my life has been as wasted as if I were a beggar!"

"I can't say that's not partly true, but I must confess that my mind has been changing on it lately."

"Well, praise God that it has. It's been long enough in coming! Still, I can't say you haven't been wonderful to me—the help you gave Lawrence and me and the good help you have been in assisting and guiding my boys. I have been too hard on you, James."

"No, you haven't. No harder than I deserve. Come on home with me now and we'll get a bite to eat."

"I'm obliged, but I want to see the boys and get on to Cripple Creek for a day or so. The old life there has all but passed away. The children are grown now, and I fool myself if I think they need me."

The uttered statement, ringing with haunting finality, gave them both pause and Robert started to leave.

James extended his hand. "Good-bye, Robert. Take care of yourself."

"Good-bye, James. It's a little sad, our shaking hands this way. At our ages and as the years pass by we are always conscious that each time we say good-by could well be the last."

From Cripple Creek he decided to go through Wytheville and back over Walkers Mountain to Bland. The route was more picturesque than going by way of Pulaski and Dublin, and perhaps a little shorter. The next day Gideon moved briskly along the Raleigh – Grayson turnpike through Kent's Mill and began crossing Cove Mountain. At the foot of Little Walker Mountain a fast-moving rider turned onto the turnpike from a side trail. In a moment the frothing horse and his rider were at Robert's side.

"Have you seen 'Aunt Sis'?" the young man said.

"Who?"

"'Aunt Sis' Umberger—the midwife. She's supposed to be working around the mountain here today."

"Don't know her and haven't seen a woman on horseback," Robert said.

"She rides a mule, and we got to get 'er. My sister's in bad labor—real bad."

Robert volunteered to ride alternate trails with the young man in the search for the midwife. An hour later she still had not been found, but they learned specifically where she was.

"I'll go get her," the young man said. "You listen to what I'm saying and then ride ahead and tell the folks I found her and that we'll be along shortly."

Robert did as requested and found the young girl in agonizing labor with no one in attendance except her mother and a neighbor woman, who was some distance from sobriety.

"Has her husband been sent for?" Robert asked. "That might ease her a little, if she knew he was around."

"She ain't got no husband," the mother said. "The baby is a bastard, and if I'm guessin' right about the daddy the same word fits him."

"Let's just make her as comfortable as we can then, until the Umberger woman gets here," Robert said.

"We ought to call in the whole county seat—'specially the young girls," the mother said. "Maybe if they saw the agony side of it they'd do some two-way thinkin'."

"That may be so, but our dear Jesus didn't revile the worst of sinners while they were in their agony," Robert said.

The girl's cries reached intense proportions and there was little he could do except to continue to bathe her sweating forehead with a damp cloth. The girl's mother held her daughter's twitching legs apart and as steady as possible.

"It won't be long, child. 'Aunt Sis' will be here directly." The mother's voice softened as her child's pain deepened.

"Oh Mamma—oh, Mamma—oh, Mamma!" the girl groaned pitifully.

The braying of a mule rushing faster than agreed with his constitution announced the coming of "Aunt Sis" Umberger. The tall mannish-looking woman strode into the room and took instant command. She greeted Robert by name, which surprised him, and went about her preparations. Her back was ramrod-straight, her face and hands leathery but seemingly gentle.

"Be gone with ya!" the midwife said through taut lips set above a twitching chin with an occasional wild black whisker. A sweep of her arms indicated to the onlookers that she meant "now."

Robert sat in the back yard with the girl's brother, who seemed unusually quiet. Finally the young man said, "I never figured who you was until Aunt Sis' called your name."

"I don't remember any of your family either," Robert said.

"You wouldn't. A long time ago our pa said a crazy preacher came by and prayed with him to destroy his still and quit making liquor. Pa said he laughed at the man and 'whopped him a little'; said the man prayed then for his whole stillhouse to be prized out with a crowbar. About a year after that our family fell on hard times and had to sell off over half our farm. Pa happened along a few days after the sale and saw the new owners and his boys tilting the stillhouse over with their crowbars. Pa said he never made a drop of liquor after that and he was a changed man. You are the man he talked about, Brother Sheffey. You are that man."

"God be praised that your father was changed by my prayers or those of any other man," Robert said.

"It didn't change Ma any. She's had it hard for too many years and she wakes up hoping every day will be her last."

"Would you go bring me the sheepskin on my saddle, son? The sunbeams are coming through that elm tree at the top of the hill like the very gates of heaven were open. Do not come and get me. I will be down when I am through."

When he descended the hill all the rest had eaten their dinner and the newborn baby boy lay in his cradle, giving a low, trembling cry.

"Is the girl all right?" He directed his question toward the midwife.

"O' course she is. The young ones make a lot of noise, but they're tough as a pine knot."

He asked if he could have something to eat as soon as he talked with the new mother. As they fixed his plate he went to the young woman's bedside. She was still panting from her labor, and her sensitive face was pale, but she smiled broadly.

"He's a pretty baby. Have you seen him, Mr. Sheffey? Big feet like mine and all… I want you to baptize him too." Her chatter seemed endless and evasive, but he sat with his comforting hand upon her arm until her voice was quiet. He said nothing then, for he knew by experience what the second phase of the conversation would be.

"Brother Sheffey, I know I have sinned. Will God forgive me—and use my son and not curse him?" she began, in the same manner he had heard countless times across the years.

He heard her out and went to his food. "As soon as I eat we will have a family service around the bed of the new mother," he said to all.

It was clear when he began that nobody in the household was accustomed to family prayer. He could always tell. They squirmed and shuffled and played with their fingers and picked at a thousand pieces of imaginary lint upon their clothing.

"The young sister has confessed her sin to me already," he began, "and she prays to a loving God to forgive her and use this child. Human mistakes can be turned around and proved a blessing to God, though we must always bear the scars of our failures. I have prayed about this once already today. I asked my dear Lord to make this little one a blessing in this house. I asked the Lord to make this mother a good mother and for this grandmother also to feel a new burst of life and strength as she comes to love the little one. I'm going to ask for more than that, for the storehouse of our Lord is surely bountiful."

He grasped the infant by the foot before he prayed. Timidly, they bowed as he spoke.

"Oh Lord, we have not loved Thee enough. We have not trusted Thee nor called upon Thee enough, for surely Thy gifts are ten thousand times more generous than we have ever asked. Lord, we ask of Thee a mighty thing today—not to our glory but to Thine. Take this little infant boy and make of him Thine advocate who will stand in a hundred pulpits across this land and bring a thousand souls into Thy kingdom. And, Lord, Thy servant Sheffey would like to know what dispositions are made of his petition and, if it be Thy will, tell me before I join Thee in heaven Thy plan for this little one's life. Amen."

Swiftly he got up and moved away through the front door and out among the trees. They would not understand why his very soul cried out for him to shout, why in loving and serving his God and His Blessed Son the joy so warmed and overpowered him....

"Aunt Sis" sat astride her mule when he came back to the house.

"If a mule can walk beside a horse and a midwife can ride along with a preacher I don't see any reason why we can't leave together. Do you?" he said.

"I've rode off with worse characters," she said unsmiling, and took the lead.

By the middle of the next afternoon he dismounted at the home of his good friend, Josiah Bruce in Bland County. Hardly had his feet touched ground when Bruce—his senior by a dozen years—met him at the yard gate.

"Brother Bob, old friend. It's not our regular preaching day. What are you doing here so soon?"

Robert told him of the trip he was now concluding and said, "The sweet Lord has not seen fit to make a great preacher out of me, but those things He has had me experience in this life can be retold to His glory. I have much to tell you and our little congregation."

"It is well you came a day early, for storm clouds now gather closer home. I had best warn you of the danger so you can be prepared. But there's no rush about it. Come inside and rest yourself. My good wife has made some damson pies and now you can eat them sooner than she expected."

In minutes Mrs. Bruce began whipping the rich cream she had skimmed from the milk-filled crock of her springhouse.

"Sister Bruce, you know how I like it now. Spread a thin paste of honey over the pie crust before you put the whipped cream on—"

"I know how you like it, Brother Sheffey. I've fixed it for you before, you'll remember."

"Some of God's people preach a better sermon with their kindness than I ever did in the pulpit, Sister Bruce. You are one of those because of your tender care of me across the years."

"Maybe you'd better wait and taste the pie first," she said. "Go on back in the parlor now with Josiah and I'll bring it to you."

He did not obey her immediately, for he felt a giddy anticipation that compelled him to stay and witness the whole process. Josiah called to him, and reluctantly he left the room. In seconds he stepped back through the door.

"Sister? Be sure and use a clean knife to cut the pie."

That evening before bedtime Josiah Bruce outlined to him what "storm clouds" he had referred to.

"Some of the toughs in the neighborhood are out to get you, and they're not holding their tongues about it. My guess is we can expect the service to be interrupted tomorrow. From what I've heard they're not as mad about you praying against their liquor making and drinking as they are about you calling them lost souls and praying for them by name."

"We'll go about the Lord's business on schedule, Josiah. If they come tomorrow it may mark the very day when we can rescue another soul for the kingdom."

The next day he preached and prayed with the small group of worshipers without interruption. There seemed visible relief among the people as they departed the Bruce home. "Josiah shouldn't pay any attention to those roughnecks. They've got more mouth than muscle," Robert heard somebody say. In a way he was also relieved, but it was not a comfortable relief. How could he effectively fight God's foe if there was no confrontation?

When Josiah brought his horse around to the front, this impending confrontation still rested on his mind. "Josiah, before our next meeting date get word to those who have fought against me and tell them I will meet them wherever they want. I believe I can stand at the whipping post and show them that they cast more darkness than light. There are many roads to Christ, dear Josiah, and we will keep the byways open."

He positioned his sheepskin upon the saddle and tied his saddlebags securely before mounting Gideon. The animal seemed fidgety, but in a moment Robert was on and seated comfortably. "Be good to Sister Bruce, Josiah. The sweet Lord has given you a pearl of precious worth in that woman, and bless your whole family."

"Come anytime, Brother Bob. When you are here our house is especially blessed."

Gideon started down the dusty road in a spirited trot. Robert began to sing, for the spirit of the service he had just finished was still very much with him.

At about the same time he heard the voice of Josiah Bruce call out to him a shrill warning, bushes parted on each side of the road, and a tan muscular arm wrapped around his waist before he was aware that anyone was behind him. The grip tightened, dragging him from the saddle and flinging him onto the road. The fall stunned him, but he did not lose consciousness.

"Stomp the life out of the old devil!" someone called from the shoulder of the road.

The command was obeyed, for next he felt a heavy foot upon his leg and then upon his stomach. On instinct, he tried to stand, and a fist from another direction crashed into his jaw. A handful of dirt and gravel peppered his mouth and chin but was soon washed away by his bleeding nose.

"Let him go!" He heard Josiah Bruce's voice shouting. Robert raised to his elbow and saw his old friend fire a warning shot into the air. For a moment the attackers paused, but from the bushes other men converged to overpower his gun wielding rescuer. He tried to sound the alarm, but all the air seemed to be stomped out of his aching lungs.

With the lightning move of hounds on a rabbit Josiah was thrown onto the dirt and his gun taken from him.

"We ain't got no fight with you, Josiah," a man Robert recognized said, "lessen it's because you open your doors to that little weasel there."

"Leave him alone!" Josiah called. "He preaches the Word of God, and you know it and I know it. If it causes gravel in your shoes, maybe it ought to."

"He can shout and preach and pray all he wants, but he'd better stop callin' me and the others by our names. And while we're at it, he'd better not be seen down on the creek anymore, nosin' around our stills. We got troubles enough without him prayin' for floods and lightnin' strikes. He's got half the county scared to death, tellin' around that what he prays for comes to pass."

Robert got his breath back momentarily and sat up. "Woody"—he addressed the hostile spokesman—"I bear you no personal harm, but it is not God's will that you—"

"Shut your mouth!" Woody shoved him backward with his foot. Josiah started to lunge at Robert's tormentor but was restrained. "And you too, or I'll crack your own gun barrel over your head!"

"I won't stop praying for your soul, Woody, nor those of your friends," Robert said.

Woody made no effort to strike him this time, but a terrible fury shone from black eyes set in a massive head. "My 'soul' ain't botherin' me none, and I don't figure it's any worry of yours. And don't think there's not all kinds of ways to stop you. I'm not the only man whose got it on his mind either. Why, you can't hardly hire a decent still hand no more. They're all scared to death you'll pray 'em into hell or cause a tree to fall and bust their skulls open."

"If I was a younger man I'd do some skull busting of my own," Josiah Bruce said. "Now leave us alone and go about your evil business if that's the only thing you've got brains enough to think about."

"This ain't the end of it," Woody said and motioned his followers away.

Robert could not stand without his friend's help.

"Just put your arm around my neck, Brother Bob. We'll get you patched up. You'd best stay the night. We're not going to send you home to Eliza and Eddie until you're in good riding shape."

The soreness in his body had not left him when a week passed. He was, therefore, at home when a messenger of the Bland county court advised him that his assailants had been arrested and would be tried. Furthermore, his testimony would be needed to insure the conviction of the guilty men.

"It's not in my heart to testify against them," Robert said.

"You must, or the court will have you summonsed."

"Is there no other way?"

"I can't answer that. You will have to speak to the judge beforehand if you don't want to go."

On the trial date he went to Bland, and when he got there the court was already in session, dealing with another case. He sat on the hard seat for only a minute before he crept forward to the bench and grasped the arm of the presiding judge.

The judge turned his eyes from the papers before him and put his left hand over an ear, shutting out the raving of the attorney for the Commonwealth. He leaned forward as Robert stood on tiptoe, the better to show himself to the judge.

"Reverend Sheffey, you are interrupting a court in session," the judge whispered. "Your case is not yet to be heard."

"Let them go," Robert said.

"I beg your pardon?"

"Let them go."

The judge quickly ascertained that Robert meant the men who had attacked him, not the criminals presently at the bar.

"Do you mean you will not press charges? You will not testify?"

"The only testimony my heart would leave me free to give is that my sweet Lord loves them. Let them go, Your Mercy, and I will praise your name."

The judge studied Robert's eyes and gave his head a slight, reluctant twist. "Are you sure you don't want to testify against these men? Their actions and general reputation indicate that sentences are in order."

"They meant no harm—it was the devil acting in a moment of their weakness—"

"The court cannot look at things in quite the same way, Reverend—"

"Now that my sweet Lord has let me think upon the matter I might have to testify that I provoked them—"

"Very well then. It seems that the case for the Commonwealth is weakening. I just hope you have an end figured out for this episode."

"Men do not write an end to things, Your Mercy. Would you not agree to that? Have you not sent a man to prison who came back a saint, or met a saint who fell from grace into the dungeon?"

When he returned home Eliza appeared to be watching him suspiciously for the first few hours. Her alert eyes seemed always to pierce him like steel, which never failed to delight him, but when he kept something from her they would light up like fireflies.

"Robert—look at me. You let the men go free, didn't you?"

"Now, Eliza, we don't question the other days when God is so merciful—why should we make mention of it today?"

"Oh, Robert! May heaven protect you. You are certainly incapable of it yourself."

"Don't fuss with me now. I've got to put my thoughts in order and make some arrangements about winter wood."

"John Frank has already brought a load and a neighbor you'd never guess is bringing another."

"What would I do without you, dear Eliza—and without them too? But do they all look after you and little Eddie out of pity or because they believe the Lord sends me?"

"It is not well that you know all the answers to that question just now, my husband. Just trust and go about your work. There seems plenty to occupy you for a while."

He glanced toward the desk, which Eliza always kept in immaculate order, and noticed the usual three stacks of letters.

Commanding his attention first, however, was a letter placed alone on the desk.

"Why is this one by itself?" he asked without bothering to read first.

"It's from an old friend of yours on Cripple Creek—John Simmerman, I believe his name is. He wants to know if you will sell him your Cripple Creek farm."

Robert sat and read the letter, fingering his beard in deep thought.

"Well? Are you interested?" Eliza said after a while.

"I don't rightly know on such short notice. There's some good judgment, and some bad too, that runs through my head. There's no hurry, and I'll want to talk to the Lord about it…"

CHAPTER XV

Robert held up under the persistence of John Simmerman's annual offer to buy his farm until the year of 1873; the same year, ironically, when he learned that his brother James was slowly dying. By this time Eliza felt that the final offer was a gift from heaven and said so.

"We are getting no younger, Robert, and I don't believe we would be selfish to want a modest home of our own in which to grow old."

He agreed that the farm sale would provide that. Also there was something more it would do. Two of his older children needed financial help and he had long wanted to give each and every one of them something from the land they had known as children.

"We'll sell it then, Eliza. All things seem to be working together for good. Write Brother Simmerman and tell him we will accept his offer and meet him at his convenience."

The new home they decided to purchase was a small two-story white frame house with an acre of ground, perched on the side of a grassy hill and overlooking Walker's Creek to the east. The location was in the village of Staffordsville—the so-called Irish Settlement had spread both eastward and westward with the advance of time—and located only four or five miles away from Eliza's girlhood home. The term "Irish Settlement" was one now used primarily by the old-timers, as adjacent villages continued to grow and be recognized in their own right.

Robert still liked the connotation the term "Irish Settlement" held for him, but Eddie would frequently correct him. "Grandma says you're supposed to call where she lives by the name of Trigg, Papa," the boy would say.

"Well, as long as we all know we're talking about the same place, I don't guess it matters," Robert said.

But it was an ever-changing place at that, one could hardly help observing. Their new home village seemed to be attracting more than its share of the population growth to the area, and not without reason. Staffordsville boasted a picturesque setting along a wide and beautiful stream with mountain gaps on three sides. For such a small place, Staffordsville enjoyed a bustling commerce. Very near the half-way point of the village a milldam spanned the creek and the giant undershot waterwheel was fed by a long millrace of double-thick limestone rocks, piled ton upon ton.

Eddie was quick to tell his father that he liked the smaller and older waterwheel of his former home much better.

"I want the water to spill over the top, Papa," the boy explained before Robert realized that his son knew the difference between an overshot and an undershot waterwheel.

"But as long as the big wheel turns—," Robert argued.

"But it turns backward, and I want the water to spill over the top," the child wailed almost their entire first week of residence.

Soon Eliza diverted the boy's attention elsewhere. Their new community of residence had in addition to the waterwheel a mill complex that formed a part of it, a modern blacksmith shop, a large general store and post office, a sawmill, a small tannery, and a boat landing.

Robert watched the boy grow between his absences from home and saw, gradually, the pride Eliza had instilled in the child about his new community.

"Not every boy can live in a village named for his own ancestors," Eliza said proudly.

"Whatever he amounts to in this life will be because of you, Eliza. Does he think ill of me that I am gone from him so much?"

"He's getting along fine, and his teachers brag on him just like he was a scholar. Why, Mrs. Jones said he was quicker to catch on than any child she'd ever taught."

He could not help smiling, for this was the kind of pride of which even his God would approve.

"Could we possibly be more richly blessed than this day finds us, Eliza?"

When Eddie reached his tenth birthday they allowed him to walk alone the four -mile distance to his grandmother's house. Robert trusted Eliza's judgment in these matters, but he could tell that there were times she agonized over the roundabout routes the boy would take, making him hours late in coming home.

"I was at the mill, Mamma," he would explain when Eliza insisted on a reason for his tardiness. "I like to stand on the mill floor and feel the boards tremble when corn is being ground and the waterwheel groans. And the fresh cornmeal smells so good, I stick my hand under the hopper sometimes and eat a handful."

Eddie seemed always to be dirty, Robert noticed. He was always covered in cornmeal, axle grease, mud, or ashes from the bellows of the blacksmith shop.

Robert commented about it to Eddie's new teacher, Kemp Miller, who said, "You don't know much about little boys, or you've forgotten what you did know."

Robert conceded that that might be so.

"Why, a boy is like a hound dog, Brother Sheffey. He's got to sniff around a whole lot before he knows what he's looking for."

One day when the child was dirty and disobedient at the same time, Robert attempted to switch him and then bathe him. The whip broke and he could hardly see what he was hitting at, for the flood of tears in his own eyes. Thereafter he put the vigor of a switching into a soap-filled washcloth and scrubbed the child nearly raw. He thought he had done an excellent job of it, but the act brought forth slightly more than the mild wrath of Eliza.

"Robert! You'll have the child bleeding at that rate. Sometimes I think you are obsessed with cleanliness!"

He gave up trying to keep his son spotless after that. Then, shortly before Eddie's twelfth birthday, in 1877, he was offered a part-time job that found him coming home as dirty as a European chimney sweep. Staffordsville saw the start of a newspaper entitled *The True Flag,* and editor-owner Charlie Meadows used Eddie for two hours in the afternoons to clean around the type cases and help agitate the ink on printing days, and, at other times, for general sweeping and cleaning of the presses.

"Look Papa, my first wages!" Eddie cried out at the end of the week, and proudly displayed the half-dollar that paid him for ten hours of labor.

In 1878 Robert returned from a revival meeting in Washington County to find that Walkers Creek had been on the rampage, as a result of a freshet, and much of Staffordsville had been washed away. The dam and most of the mill were gone. Many buildings he had grown accustomed to had simply disappeared—washed completely from the face of the earth. Barns and houses along the creek both above and below Staffordsville were also gone.

Eddie wept bitter tears, for the newspaper office, as well, was lost, and all that had been salvaged was a little paper and most of the type. It had all happened so quickly that there had been no time to save the press.

"Mr. Meadows will build it back, Eddie," Eliza said consolingly. "I don't have a washhouse either, so I lost something too."

It was true; Robert hadn't even missed it until Eliza called it to his attention. One or two old cabins by the creek had been used by the village women as washhouses and now only the foundation stone remained to give evidence that they had existed.

Buildings were not all that had been lost. A kindly old Indian man and village resident had been swept away along with his barns, and Eddie had lost a friend of long standing.

"Papa, there'll never be another man like Old Wallace—I used to go up in his barn loft where he liked to sit and smoke his pipe and he'd tell me stories about Indian lore."

"Yes, I know, son. Every life is made from a different mold, and if we see that life in the right light it tells us something of the blessedness of human fellowship and the genius of a loving God. Just be thankful for the time you had with Old Wallace."

Within a few weeks *The True Flag* was back in business and Robert rode away from Staffordsville leaving a contented son. He also was contented, and even Gideon moved along with extra spring in his step.

They were soon nearing the county seat of Pearisburg.

"Gideon, we are in no hurry today. The service in Bluefield is still two days away and our dear friends in West Virginia will not expect us very much ahead of time. Let's just take our time and enjoy our journey."

He took a deep breath of September air and held it until his chest ached. Slowly the oxygen escaped between his teeth, and he laughed a joyous laugh.

"Oh, Gideon! God is so good to give us such a beautiful day. Have you ever seen a lovelier day! Good morning, Sister Morris!" he called to a passing buggy. "Gideon, there is a nice flat rock up ahead that I've never drawn a picture on, and it's so close to the road that it's odd I never paid any attention to it until now."

Out of the saddlebags came the chalk. The horse nibbled at the clover by the roadside. "Gideon, I've decided not to draw a picture. I am going to pose the most important question a man can ever ask of himself."

He sketched away in bold letters until the writing was done. The letters pleased him, and as he backed up the road the words were still clearly distinguishable. WHAT SHALL I DO TO BE SAVED? they said.

"That ought to do it now. Come along, Gideon. I want to get to Pearisburg before the sun gets very high. By the time I climb a ways up Angel's Rest Mountain the sun, if we look to the east, will stare us straight in the face. It's a wonderful place for morning prayers, Gideon, and you know how much you like the good spring water. Come along now."

They got no farther than Narrows when midday came. There had been so many people to stop and talk to; the turnpike roads were unusually full of travelers who seemed as willing to talk of God, politics, or the weather as he was.

"Our sweet Lord never meant for us to rush through life, Gideon. People who do it remind me of a dog with its tail in its mouth, trying to catch itself. Be still and know that I am God—that's what our sweet Lord tells us."

The route he decided to take to Bluefield was by way of Wolf Creek to South Gap and across East River Mountain.

"We could go by way of Glen Lyn and Princeton, Gideon, but if we go up Wolf Creek, Sister Wheeler will have some fresh apple pies for our dinner."

He ate, had family prayers for his hostess and her invalid husband, and was shortly on Gideon's back, riding westward along Wolf Creek. He liked to sing going this way, the route held so many memories for him. There was another reason: his voice sounded different here, due to the acoustical peculiarities of the region. He'd discovered that years ago when he was singing "Twilight Is Stealing Over the Lea," and it was that very song that he sang now.

Above the sound of the song's chorus, galloping hooves approached from behind him. He guided Gideon to the road shoulder so as to allow the speeding rider all the room he needed. Rather than passing, however, the young boy reined to a halt by Robert's side. Momentarily a dust cloud engulfed them, but the boy's staccato words kept pouring forth.

"My brother, George, got bit by a rattlesnake this mornin'. We're afraid he's goin' to die. Pa just now seen you passin' and said for me to overtake you and get you to pray for George."

"Do I know you and your family? Your face is not familiar," Robert said.

"No, you don't know us, but Pa and Ma both knows of you. Pa said if you'd pray for George the Lord would let him live."

Robert followed the boy home, where George lay on the grass in the back yard. A solemn-faced woman who refused to meet the inquiring gaze of her visitor attended the wounded man, and presently the father came from the kitchen.

"Reverend Sheffey, call upon the Lord so my boy will live," the father said.

"Have *you* ever called upon the Lord's name, my brother?"

"No, but if you'll do it the Lord will surely hear our prayers. It is said that many things you pray for come to pass even after many years."

"And you have a wife and children, I see. How many? Do *they* ever call upon the name of the Lord?"

"No, I guess not." The father hung his head. "There's—there's three boys and us."

"Son, would you fetch my sheepskin from my saddle?" Robert said to the boy who had overtaken him.

He started to kneel, and all of them had bowed and closed their eyes before he got both knees on the prayer mat. The wounded man put his hands over his face.

"Oh Lord," Robert prayed, "please bring Thy healing to this young man, and Lord in the same breath we thank Thee for snakes and pray that there be many of them. It is because of a snake that this family calls upon Thy holy name today. One of the sons has been bitten, and they call upon Thee. Now, Lord, get the picture: except for the snake they would perhaps never in their lifetimes have turned to Thee. What a blessing this lowly, crawling thing has been! Lord, I want you to send lots of snakes. Send another one to bite the youngest boy here, and send still another to bite this woman who never had her boys kneel by her chair, that they might hear the prayers of their mother. And, Lord, above all things send a great big rattler, a really large one, to bite the old man so that he may call upon Thy name fervently and much. Amen."

Bluefield was a growing little town that had changed greatly since the first time he had seen it, nestled in a bowlike enclosure of nature on the north side of East River Mountain.

The church to which he had been invited was one of the nicest Methodist churches in that part of the state, and he looked forward to the engagement.

He was asked to preach at both the morning and afternoon services, and a large crowd greeted him for the first one. He felt warmth from the congregation, and though there were no converts, he was certain that the night service would find resistance crumbling like air-dried bread and those penitents by the score would come forward.

However, when night came and the last word of his sermon had been uttered, and the tears of love had dribbled down his wrinkled and whiskered cheeks, not a convert came forward. He could have consoled himself by the thought that all in attendance had been previous good Methodist converts, but his host had told him otherwise. Not even half of those in attendance were baptized Christians, and he knew it.

Nevertheless, he continued the altar call, and one or two people came down for rededication but not conversion.

"Well now, we're all dressed up and seated comfortably here together—so, let us not waste the night. Somebody should gain from our effort. I think we ought to pray for the devil. If the sweet Lord can't make any headway, there's no reason a-tall why old Satan can't have a good night of it. Bow with me now:

"Oh, Mighty Satan, giver of power and god of lust and pride, look how many of us await your next command. There are all sizes and shapes and varieties of us ready and obedient. Notice the fancy-dressed lady near the back pew with the hat that looks like a dead chicken. She's not close to the Lord at all—her pastor told me so. I believe she's already in your camp. Now the old man sitting next to the aisle—you'd think you didn't have a chance with him but he's been hiding from the Lord for over seventy years. And he's been hiding right here in the church! He's yours; you can put him on your roll and add some more fuel to the lake of fire. Now, we don't mean to be giving you the old cast offs, Satan; there are those in their prime who will spend eternity with you. Notice the young unmarried girl with straw-colored hair hunched down almost out of sight about half way back. She has been eating too many green apples and her belly is swollen powerfully bad. She must be infecting herself, Brother Lucifer, for the same thing has happened to her four times before. But we won't send her alone. The father of one, or maybe all, of her children is sitting on the opposite side like he didn't know her. They've been so close in life it would be a pity that death would separate them. Oh, mighty Satan, there's so many we could point out to you, but you have them all down anyway. You must excuse us for being poor losers tonight. Somehow our hearts are not as happy as when one lost soul—one baby lamb lost sheep—comes bleating into the fold of *your* adversary."

From Bluefield he and Gideon retraced their journey back as far as South Gap, then traveling southward toward Bland courthouse and Allen Newberry's home.

"Gideon, I don't know what I would have done if the sweet Lord hadn't put it in Brother Newberry's head to give me all those good suits, and now he tells me I am too slow getting another one he has ready for me. Of course I'm not saying everything is altogether to my liking at that home, Gideon. There's a new Sister Newberry now, and it took me the longest kind of time to get the old one to fix my biscuits the right way. Now I suppose it'll be like starting all over again. Bless their sweet souls, though—I've missed them all so much."

Allen was absent from home when Robert arrived. The second Mrs. Newberry—whom Robert called Car-o-line, in long syllables, just as her husband did—informed him that her husband and two of his sons had gone to a neighbor's house.

"They've got a tough job to do. Our neighbor was bitten by a mad dog and by this morning he was worse off than the dog that bit him," she said.

"I'll ride over there and see if I can help in any way," Robert said.

"You can go, but don't expect to do anything. Allen and the boys came back for rope. The poor man has to be tied to his bedstead."

Robert had not thought for a moment that Caroline Newberry exaggerated the situation, yet still he was shocked at the sight that awaited him at the stricken man's house.

Allen and his sons had nailed an upright board to the head of the sick man's bed, to which the man was secured by ropes around his chest as he sat in an upright position. His arms hung free except for a rope knotted about his wrists to prevent flailing of the arms.

But the tied wrists did not stop the man from beating his own stomach in his crazed agony. He was young, and the muscles of his arms looked powerful, seeming even more powerful than normal, for in his ravings he was seemingly given a superhuman strength.

Robert helped the Newberry's thread another rope around each elbow and took care not to get too close to the man's snapping teeth. The additional rope rendered the gyrating arms almost immobile, but as the man's wildness increased, so did his strength. He wrenched at his anchorings with frenzied, animal-like grunts until the board nailed to his bedstead almost broke free.

After a while the man was still, and Robert went to his wife who sat wet-eyed but silent in her kitchen. She was a pretty woman, but her face and slender arms were gaunt from hard work and worry, which left hardly enough flesh on her bones for survival. An infant nursed at her breast, and she seemed embarrassed that life and nature had to proceed in spite of the circumstances.

"You just sit still now," Robert said kindly. "All I want is something to give him to eat. He's almost exhausted, and he must be hungry."

"Doctor said he wouldn't eat anything and for me to stay away and not get close enough to get bitten. There's nothing to do, Doctor said, but wait. There's nothing any doctor around here can do," she said. She pointed to a pot of soup on the stove and he asked her where the spoons were kept, then chose the longest spoon he could find and went to the stricken man's bed with the bowl.

"Stay good and clear of him, Brother Sheffey," Allen Newberry warned, but the man seemed exhausted and almost docile now. "Here, my brother, have a little soup and maybe you'll feel better," Robert said, extending the half-filled spoon.

Sick, fiery eyes returned Robert's compassionate glance but there was no offer to cooperate.

"Just a few spoonsful will help, my brother, just a little nourishment now—"

Without warning the stricken man lunged at his ropes and with one convulsed snap of bared teeth, bypassed the spoon, and locked onto the rim of the soup bowl, shattering it. In a matter of minutes, his condition seemed to worsen. One of the Newberry sons took his wife and baby to his stepmother's when it became evident that she could stand the scene no longer.

They could do nothing now except wipe the sweat from the man's face. Finally the tortured body went limp and lifeless. He pitched forward and his head dropped.

"Let's cut him loose and cover him up," Allen said.

The ropes around his wrists and arms were cut first; then Robert rolled him over upon his back and lay the bed quilt over the body.

"Go ahead and get the undertaker, son," Allen whispered.

"Do the woman and child have a place to go when this is all over?" Robert said.

"Yes. Her family are people of property, and though they didn't approve of her marriage they won't turn her away. Her husband wasn't a bad sort of fellow; he just didn't have much 'get up and git.'"

Suddenly, without warning, Robert saw the quilt on the bed quiver, and before he could call out to Allen or his son, the supposedly dead man rose from his bed with a paralyzing shriek, and running, slammed into the west wall of the bedroom with such force that the whole house shook.

Robert was not the only one whose hands trembled, as, once more; they lifted the dead man upon his bed.

That night Robert tossed restlessly. What he had this day seen turned over and over again in his mind. Here he had been witness to a man's suffering and death, and there had been the feeling of helplessness—he was not the right hand of God, but instead merely a useless bystander. It was not the first time he had felt his own inadequacy, but on this occasion the sense of loss and mystery simply would not leave him. Why couldn't he understand the strange workings of life? Wasn't he God's man under the guidance of the Holy Spirit? Where the special gift of understanding now was needed so desperately?

The more he thought about it, the more the very thought itself condemned him. What a sin it was even to entertain the idea that he, a humble servant, might be given such wisdom as to understand the workings of the Divine Creator.

"Forgive me, Lord, that I would dare to question," he prayed.

The prayer did not satisfy his need of obedience, ·and he searched the Scriptures by lamp light until he found in Corinthians that which he sought: "For who hath known the mind of the Lord, that he may instruct Him?"

Robert preached at Newberry's chapel and at Byrne's chapel, in Mechanicsburg, before he left Bland County and returned to Eddie and Eliza at Staffordsville.

October activities were confined to the circuit, but in November an invitation had come asking his participation in a revival at the Rehoboth church, in Monroe County, West Virginia, near the village of Union.

"I want to go, Eliza," he said. "Is there anything I need to take care of before I leave? Are we still solvent?"

"By the grace of my brothers, yes. Is it my imagination or is the time between your collections getting farther and farther apart? Perhaps if you had more frequent services and visited the remote sections less…?"

"Now, Mrs. Sheffey, you don't mean that; don't you know without asking that my sweet Lord sends me where He wants me to go?"

"No, I guess I don't, even now. But I do want you to acknowledge the help my brothers have given me."

"'I will if I think about it, but it never comes to mind at the right times. Besides, they're just doing as their sweet Lord asks them to do—just like you and me."

"They might not see it with quite that degree of spiritual maturity, Robert. I should like you to thank them."

He promised more seriously that he would, and he thought upon the matter still further as he rode away.

"Gideon, it is a funny thing, but those closest to us do not understand sometimes. Our blessed Christ was a pauper, and He didn't ask even briefly what he could earn from life…. He wanted us all to spend our time examining our hearts and not our purses. But even that isn't all that matters, for our sweet Lord knows that when we are poverty-stricken, and not a whiff of the haughty spirit abides in us, then we are most beautiful to Him."

He had half decided to preach his first sermon along the lines of such thinking when he left the West Virginia line behind him.

"Maybe I will make *that* sermon number two, Gideon. I will preach first on the stewardship of a good church. There are good churches and bad churches. I'm talking about the people now, Gideon; I want to preach this good sermon to these good people. This church has been a blessing for such a long time—thank God for the souls who have found rest there. It was dedicated by Bishop

Asbury in 1786, and I've heard that Indians were still about when that took place."

Robert kept up the chatter even as he allowed Gideon to stop by a road side spring.

"Do you always talk to yourself like that?" a voice inquired over the swirling water around Gideon's legs.

Robert lifted his head and saw no man, mounted or walking.

"Over here—against the tree trunk."

"Why, my brother, I didn't see you," Robert called. "Are you tuckered out? Have you walked far?"

"Not far a-tall. I'm not a traveler. I've just come over the hill from salting my cattle and decided to rest my bones."

"And what a glorious bed of rest you have! As far as the eyes can see, the painted leaves and the smell of autumn give testimony to our God's handiwork. And for a pillow there rolls the fertile hills."

"Who are you, some roving minstrel?"

Robert moved Gideon closer to the inquirer and said, "No, I am Robert Sayers Sheffey, a servant of the Lord."

"There is something about you that told me I should recognize who I was talking to. Guess most everybody in southern West Virginia knows you."

Robert said he couldn't vouch for that, but if such was the case then the Lord was to be praised. "And the Lord be praised for our fellowship today… You have not told me your name," Robert added.

The man gave no answer and Robert asked him if he would be coming to the services at the Rehoboth church.

"I reckon not."

"Why not? Do you not pay homage to our Master?"

"I don't have anything against the Master."

"What is it then?" Robert said.

"Well—from what I've heard I'm not altogether sure I'd like your ways exactly—"

"Neither does the devil!"

The seated man rose to his feet with the faintest grin upon his face and started to walk away.

"Just a minute," Robert said. "It's near to mealtime and I think I'll have supper at your house."

"My God," the other said. "Everything I've heard must really be true."

A great deal of that winter was spent in southern West Virginia. Once he timed his return to Staffordsville so closely that he rode up to his own front gate and called Eliza out without so much as dismounting. She hardly had time to dry her hands on her worn apron before he had inquired, "How're Mrs. Sheffey and Eddie?" and, "I must be going now," all in the same breath, then rode away.

In the spring Robert came home from an engagement in Montgomery County to find that his son had taken a new job without consulting him.

"You weren't here, Papa, and I needed the work."

"I'm partly to blame, Robert," Eliza confessed. "I don't think my saying 'no' would have mattered anyway, but I didn't say no."

"It's a good job, Papa, better than the one I did here for our little paper. I'm going to be a printer's devil at the *Pearisburg Virginian*."

Eliza gave aid to her son. "Our little Staffordsville paper can't survive longer, Robert."

"But it's a big ride to Pearisburg ... and you've no horse... and school and everything...," Robert objected.

"Uncle John will give me a horse or help me find a ride with somebody else. I'll just work on Saturdays until school is out, and when summer comes my wages will really fly high and I can start paying Uncle John and Uncle Dan back regular—"

"So that's it," Robert said sorrowfully.

"No, that's not altogether 'it,' dear husband. The boy is smart and industrious and he wants to work and help himself and to pay back some of what we owe my brothers. It's the right thing to do and it needn't make you feel any shame."

"There's no call to soften it, Mamma. I can't sit at my desk in school without the other boys, and girls too, pointing at me and saying, 'Eddie Sheffey's uncles have to keep him and his mother from starving to death because his daddy is so crazy on religion he won't ask for money and he won't come home because of chasing sinners up every hollow.'"

"Eddie! Not in front of your father," Eliza pleaded.

"Why not? It's the truth, isn't it?"

Robert did not even debate the point but tears spilled down his wrinkled cheeks.

"He didn't mean it, Robert," Eliza said softly when her husband had gone remorsefully to another room.

"Yes, dear Eliza, he meant it. It is the thing I could expect to hear. But it will not alter my course, for that course is so clearly set before me that my sweet Lord Himself holds the torch that lights my way."

"We have made out fine. Now don't you be worrying about anything, for whatever we need, somebody will provide," Eliza said.

"Bless them all. I do know about the whispering, but I know about the joys too!"

Robert rode away in June to attend the affairs of his circuit and Eddie took up his full-time job at the newspaper office. The boy had left with a countenance shining with challenge, and Robert admitted for the first time that he himself was growing old. And, for the first time also, he admitted to a bone-deep tiredness; in spite of it, there was something renewing about seeing his son so young, so full of hope and energy, go riding off into the world. How strange that God would let the old siphon strength from the young. It was not the first time he had felt this way. The same feeling had come hundreds, and perhaps thousands, of times when he had held a newborn baby or a little child, whether in a ramshackle mountain hovel or a rolling plantation farmhouse.

"Yes, Gideon, renewal comes with holding onto another human being, even if he is the smallest squirming thing."

They rode along back toward Pearisburg again for a service there; and, for a week after that, no engagements would prevent his going to Independence, in Grayson County, to help out an old friend in a series of services.

"It's been a while since we've been to Independence, old friend," he said to Gideon. "You will like it there when the time comes for us to go. The water is cool and the clover is tasty and green, and, for me, my sweet Lord has provided me with so many dear people—so my pastor friend has told me."

The twisting road into Pearisburg finally straightened, and the edge of the village came into view. So did the rock on which he had chalk-sketched that commanding line which hopefully had caused many a passer-by to stop and ponder on.

At least the words still stood out boldly in glistening white against a dark gray background. But what was this! Something new had been added in smaller letters that he could read only as he came very close to the rock. *He* had written WHAT SHALL I DO TO BE SAVED? And under it a man whose occupation was self-evident had added, USE HITE'S PAIN CURE.

"Well, Gideon, the sweet Lord never objected to a little humor, and Eliza tells me that I'm a regular smiley compared to when she married me. Bless her sweet soul, Gideon; she's all the world to me. Now what was I going to say? Oh yes, we had best not let that medicine salesman get the best of God's message."

He dismounted then and added a third line: AND PREPARE TO MEET THY GOD.

Two days later after reaching Independence, Robert removed the letter of his host from his pocket and reread the instructions. "Well, Gideon, he says for us to go to the Lundy home, and we'll do just that."

When the house was reached he asked to have family prayers.

"We'd be blessed; we've looked forward to this moment for a long, long time," the mistress of the house said.

His prayer was long, but his audience showed no impatience and he got up from his sheep skin fulfilled. The smallest child of the household, six or seven years old, ran to him immediately, all timidity banished.

"Brover Sheffey, Mamma and Papa told me you would sit down on a sheep and I wish'd you'd give it to me."

"Bless your precious little heart, son. One day I'll give you my sheepskin when it's worn out, but I don't have another one right now. My first one was very dear to me, and when it was too old I buried it in a place that I'll not tell to any man.

I've gone through three more, but I've given them all away—I wish I'd saved one for you."

The child whimpered in disappointment. Robert paced across the floor, for he was as helpless observing the discomfort of another's child as he had been with all his own. "I don't know what to do to pacify him," he said helplessly.

"Pay no attention to him," Mrs. Lundy said. "I don't know what made him come up with that anyway."

A quick summer rain started and the child rushed to the window.

"Now, Brother Sheffey, I'll bet you can't turn off *your* problems like that," Martin Lunday said and pointed to his son, completely absorbed at the window.

Robert gave a thoughtful nod of his head.

"I'm getting chilly," Martin Lundy said. "I'll just strike a match to that trash in the fireplace and knock the cold out of the room... Been replacing some of the boards on the front porch before somebody breaks a leg. There's something like ants that've eaten plumb through the old boards."

The fire blazed and Robert moved closer.

"That'll warm your outsides, and I'll get the wife to heat you some cow's milk to take care of the other side," Lundy said.

In his host's absence Robert watched the dance of the flames. Suddenly, from the burning wood, dozens of black ants began making a fast exit out upon the hearth He began scooping them up with a piece of newspaper, and when he had most of them captured he headed for the front door.

"What's the matter, Brother Sheffey?" Lundy called, glass in hand, from behind him.

"The little ants are about to get burned and I'm going to take them out to the woodpile—"

"But we'd be well rid of them. They're nothing but a nuisance."

"The sweet Lord didn't think so or He wouldn't have made them. Did you ever think of that?"

No one was more surprised than Robert himself, that, when in the pulpit for the first service, he suddenly cast aside that which he had prepared to say in favor of a sermon on the lowly ant. Perhaps God had even willed it so, when out of the fireplace the crawling black things had come to attract his eye and provide his object lesson.

"Some among us would not believe that the lowly ant has for us a spiritual message," he began. "What? You do not believe me? Then you do not know the Proverbs:

> Go to the ant, thou sluggard; consider her ways, and be wise:
>
> Which having no guide, overseer, or ruler, Provideth her meat in the summer, *and* gathereth her food in the harvest.
>
> How long wilt thou sleep, O sluggard? When wilt thou arise out of thy sleep?"

That night when the service had ended and the converts came in unexpectedly large numbers for an opening service, he marveled not so much at that but rather how God could use the simplest things to teach the most profound messages. This was still on his mind when he said good night to the pastor and returned to the Lundy home.

"Brother Lundy, the mystery of our divine Lord is an awe-inspiring thing. If we could but grasp it our bodies and minds would surely explode with joy."

Robert could tell that Martin Lundy was not seeing the vision his guest was seeing, but he talked on, and his listener sat patiently.

"I preached a sermon on the tumblebug once, Brother Lundy, and brought a dozen souls to Christ. I didn't invent the lesson of the sermon; the sweet Lord showed it to me, and every word I needed was there. Why, it's as plain as the nose on your face! Two tumblebugs push a little ball of dirt to and fro, back and forth, with great labor. They travel for miles with this little ball of dirt, and sometimes they come up against a rock or a fallen tree limb and backtrack all the way home. If that's not like a man being pushed by the devil and pulled by a martyred Christ, I don't know what is."

The services at Independence ended on Sunday afternoon, and Robert rode toward Speedwell and Marion. It was the third anniversary of his brother's death, and a full day's ride lay ahead.

"We did not get to place flowers on James's grave the first year nor the second, Gideon, old friend, but another year will not escape us. And this time we're going to take time enough to ride every one of my grandchildren upon your back, and if you do a good job of it I'll slip a lump of sugar into your box."

Gideon whinnied and shook his head with animal understanding.

With stops at Marion and Cripple Creek behind him, one more stop, at the Wytheville train station, yet remained. He had missed seeing John Robert, his youngest boy by his first marriage, who had ventured to Salem by train in search of a better job. If his son returned on schedule as expected, he would be able to see him for at least a brief while.

Arriving at Wytheville station, he hitched Gideon to the public hitching post among a baker's dozen of other prancing, sweating horses and went inside. This stop was a thrill to him, for only once before had he met someone traveling on the belching iron monster that thundered across the countryside.

Gideon still flinched at the sight and sound of a train whenever they, together, encountered one. If the truth be fully known, he also had both a fear and a fascination for the puffing locomotive whose mighty mouth sent sprays of hot cinders into the air and made God's good earth tremble. Today more than ever he wanted to ride the mechanical beast, for though he had promised himself for years to do so, he never had.

The train schedule, scribbled in chalk in an obviously unsteady hand, indicated that the westbound train from Salem would not arrive for another hour. So be it. He was in no hurry. He positioned his sheepskin on one of the hard benches and sat down. Other passengers waited in the sweltering heat. They all seemed remote and unfriendly, and it gave him a feeling of loneliness.

Presently an unfamiliar rattling sound caught his attention and a gangly pack peddler invaded the train station. Around his body a canvas-like jacket, similar to an oversized cartridge belt, hung loosely, and every pocket seemed to contain a different ware or trinket.

"Amuse yourself while you travel! Here, here!" he called. "Trinkets for sale—and corncob pipes with tobacco pouches, or New Testaments to read while you ride! Hurry, hurry before the train is due! Ladies, your attention! I have a few small looking glasses. Primp your best; you may be meeting your next husband on the train!"

The overzealous sales man walked about the waiting room, giving his pitch, until finally he stood in front of Robert. "Old-timer, if I ever saw a man that one of my corncob pipes and a little of the devil's weed would cheer up, you're him."

"I don't get any pleasure out of breathing anything but the good air or the purest aromas of nature," Robert said.

"I might have known it," the peddler said, bending low to Robert's ear. "I can spot a man who likes a whiff of something really good every time. I've got a little homemade peach brandy out back in the bushes," he said, whispering still lower. "Follow me out back and—"

"I'm not traveling by the train; I'm just waiting for somebody -"

"In that case, my brother, you ought to be reading the Good Book and worrying about your soul while you wait. You see this leather-bound New Testament? Only a dollar, and if I ever saw a man that looks like he needed to be saved, you're him."

"What makes you say that?" Robert said.

"Why, it's as plain as day—the hardness of your face, the guilty eyes—and your back looks a little droopy to me. Probably been deep in anguish, haven't you? Insides burned tee totally up with guilt, I'd say. The book says, 'Though your sins be as scarlet'—Read it for yourself. Think you'll find it in Genesis, about page one hundred forty two."

"It's in Isaiah, Chapter One, verse eighteen. Since Genesis is the first book of the Bible it couldn't be on page one hundred forty two, could it? And by the way—how did Genesis get in the New Testament?"

"Yes, sir. If I ever saw a man lost to the ravages of mortal sin—what did you say?"

"I said the scripture you quoted is in Isaiah," Robert said, Chapter One, verse eighteen."

"You know any other scriptures, old brother?"

"Yes. 'The getting of treasures by a lying tongue is a vanity tossed to and fro of them that seek death.' Proverbs, Chapter Twenty-One, verse six."

"I don't believe—I don't believe I have anything else to sell you. Good day sir."

The departing back of the peddler passed jauntily through the door, and Robert could hear the jingle of wares moving farther down the street. When his eyes were refocused on the people sitting about the waiting room a middle-aged man with a scholarly aura about him looked toward him and smiled. Robert stroked his coarse beard in surprise, for he did not recognize the friendly man.

"Don't we know each other from somewhere?" the stranger said, standing and closing the distance between their two benches.

"Not that I know of."

"I couldn't help overhearing that super salesman giving you his pitch. Don't take him seriously. If it'll help any, I see nothing hard about your face at all. The fact is, I see there an infinite kindness that draws me, and I cannot understand it unless we have met before. Is it possible you could be wrong? I feel a strong sense of brotherhood that can't be explained any other way."

"I've never been introduced to you on any of my circuit rounds that I can remember, but my name is Robert Sayers Sheffey," he said, extending a hand.

"So that's it. At last I have met the renegade Methodist evangelist whose converts march like an army across this land. You are right, we haven't met, but it seems I have known you all my life and I feel no less a stranger shaking your hand at last. I'm F. G. Richardson, a member and temporary secretary of the Holston conference."

"I guess that explains part of it, then. There *should* be a recognition among all men who serve as soldiers of the cross."

"Yes, except that we have not been privileged to include you in the full fellowship of our fraternity."

"We are joined by the common good, Brother Richardson, but when the time comes that I can serve my sweet Lord better by full connection with the conference, I'll let you know."

A train whistled in the distance and the passengers began picking up their suitcases.

The better part of the afternoon was spent with John Robert, and the sun was low in the west when each of them went their separate ways. No more stops at all could be made if he was to traverse the obstacles of two mountains and get to Bland before night.

Both he and Gideon had gone through the Little Walker and Big Walker mountain ranges so many times across the years that Robert thought that his animal understood the twists and turns of the Raleigh-Grayson turnpike as well as he did.

"Take your head, Gideon, I want to read from the Psalms.

"Waste no time now."

The blistering heat lingered on even after the sun was half hidden, and Robert mopped his brow frequently as he read. The squeak of the leather saddle and the rolling motion of Gideon's steady pace began to make him sleepy, and he raised his eyes for a moment. Visible heat waves rose up from the dirt road, and no air seemed to be stirring.

"This is the kind of day to breed a thunderstorm, Gideon, but I think we can get to Bland."

He was reading again when Gideon stretched his neck and whinnied loudly. The bray of a mule called back, and Robert looked up to see in the distance a form that could have but one identity.

"Nobody in the world can ride a mule sidesaddle with the dignity and regal posture of 'Aunt Sis' Umberger, Gideon. Look at that stiff spine and jutting chin, would you! I never spent much time reading the classics, but if she doesn't have the form of a queen of the Nile I never saw anything more like it. Bless her sweet life, Gideon;

she's served her blessed Lord almost as long as I have, though in a different way."

The queenly woman upon the mouse-gray mule continued along the side road until it intersected with the turnpike.

"Be glad to have you ride over the mountain with us!" Robert called.

"Not goin' over both mountains. I'm turning off halfway up the first one. There's too many babies comin' this week. I can't get around fast enough."

"Well, maybe you'll get a rest by the time the cool weather comes."

She mopped her brow with a sleeve-covered arm and blew a wisp of graying hair from in front of her eyes. "What are you talking about? You don't know much about the baby business! Have you forgotten what a bad winter we come through? You think the sorry menfolk of Wythe County was layin' around the barn whittlin' during them snowdrifts and zero weather? If you think they was, you follow me around nine months from January, February, and March. That's not to mention the scoundrels that didn't have enough to do with spring chores and run me back out in the dead of winter."

Robert tried to suppress a smile. "I know you have a thankless task sometimes, but look at all the good our sweet Lord has let you witness to."

She ignored this. "Childbirthin's not exactly like having the hiccups, much as some men folks would like to think so. Why, if one man could ever have a baby and tell his kind about it there wouldn't be more than one urchin in every household, you can bet on that!"

"Do the best you can, Miss Umberger!" he called as she turned from the main road. "Sometimes the Lord works His wonders through the humblest of His flock."

The almost eerie wilderness between the two mountain ranges was negotiated and they started up the last mountain as dusk began to fall. Gideon whinnied again, but this time Robert had seen what provoked the warning call of his animal.

"What do you make of it, Gideon? Looks to me like that family is in trouble."

Closer up, the problem became clear. A loaded wagon stood by the side of the road, and one horse of the team lay dead. About this animal stood a man and four children, and when Robert dismounted, two more little ones craned their necks from beneath the household goods. The wife and mother were unseen until she moved from the back of the wagon and lifted the patchwork quilt on which she and her infant had been resting.

"What do you think happened?" Robert asked.

"I can't tell you that, mister," the pleasant-faced man said. "The animal just dropped dead like he'd been shot. It's been so hot. Maybe that's it."

"Do you live around here?"

"No, we left Ada, West Virginia, and were goin' to North Carolina."

"My people are there," the man's wife added, "but looks like this is as close as we're goin' to get to them."

"Keep heart now," Robert said. "We're a long way between villages, but somebody in one direction or the other should have a horse for sale.

The stranded man—whose mood previously had been almost jolly under the circumstances—now took on a look of defeat, and his wife's gaze shifted to the ground.

"It won't do no good to find a horse dealer. I don't have but four dollars and a few brownies. That's the reason we're goin' south. Maybe things will be better there."

Robert felt in his own pocket before he remembered that the collection he received at In dependence had been given back to the church treasurer for application toward the debt on the new church.

The hopelessness of their situation seemed to silence the entire family of travelers and Robert wandered from them to the shoulder of the road. He sat on his heels and rested his elbows on folded knees until guidance and inspiration filled his heart and head to overflowing.

"My dear Lord, would You require *so* much?" he whispered.

"What did you say?" the man asked.

"Unhitch your animal and drag the dead one off the road and down into the hollow. You will need the harness to put on my animal."

"*Your* horse? But we haven't any money to pay. And how would we get him back?"

"You need no money to pay. My Lord has told me that we are all of one family and what each of us has belongs to the other. This is your hour of need and all of the earth and the fullness thereof is the Lord's. Take God's animal and be kind to him. In the same way the Lord has called me to befriend you, so will He call upon another to befriend me."

The harness of the dead horse fitted Gideon to near perfection, but he pranced discontentedly in the confines of his work suit.

Robert outlined his horse's feeding instructions to his new owner and asked to be alone with his animal before they should all part company. Little heads peered around the rear of the wagon long before he had finished his farewell, but he delayed no longer and bade them leave.

"But how will you get back to your place?" both the man and woman inquired belatedly.

He shouldered his saddle and bridles for the long walk to Bland and made light of his predicament. "If a black bear gnaws at my heels I'll feed him the saddle first—then he should be too well filled to growl for dessert." The humor of his voice belied the welling up in his eyes.

The wagon started a crawling, turtle-like motion of creaking weight and groaning wheels.

"God be with you, my friends!" he called before his throat seemed to close. Lips that had shortly before brushed against the bone-hard cheek of a much-loved animal began to tremble. Gideon bucked in his harness as the wagon moved along and fitfully swayed his head to the right and left in display of his rebellion.

Robert took one final look. The animal flung his head so violently to the side that his neck nearly paralleled his body, and one screaming whinny echoed through the trees.

Robert forced his vision northward toward Bland. "Goodbye, dear friend. Our sweet Lord does indeed require much."

Long after dark Robert trudged, exhausted, into the little village of Bland. Only the saddle, carried at times upon his head, kept the smallest part of him dry from the torrents of water that seemed to have been dumped from the heavens during the last two miles of his trek.

The crossroads trading store was open and he could see the faceless forms of men sitting on the open porch and outlined by the lamp lit windows. The men talked in mumbling, low tones as he approached, but he could identify no one by voice. With a sigh of weariness, he cast the burden from his back upon the store porch and sat down to rest.

"Brother Sheffey—is that you?" a voice called from the store porch.

"The sweet angels are not out tonight. It is me in the flesh."

Harmon Newberry, the son of his dear friend Allen, stepped out of the shadows. "I was sure that was you coming up the road when the lightning lit up the sky. What are you doing out in the rain and the black of night without a horse?"

"Did lightning strike him dead?" an unidentified voice inquired. "That'd really be something if the lightning struck *your* horse dead."

Robert told Harmon Newberry and the others the background of his horseless condition. They all listened patiently until he finished, and, for good measure, added a short sermon.

Then Harmon Newberry said, "You've got no worries about another horse. There's a drove of unbroken western horses here in Bland right now. They came in by rail car to Wytheville yesterday, and one of my men helped the auctioneers drive them over the mountain. They're slick, fat, and frisky, and the auction block is going to be busy tomorrow. Come on home with me now and I'll give you a bed and some beans… and so you'll sleep better, I'll see that you get the best horse in the bunch tomorrow."

Before Robert could show his gratitude a man name Nye Finley stepped to his side and said, "And I'll pay half the bill." The next morning at the auction square, Finley was already waiting when Robert and Harmon walked over to the split rail enclosure. Finley retracted his propped-up foot from the second rail and pointed to the horse he had judged the best.

Robert chose otherwise, and Harmon backed his judgment. When the large bay horse stood before the auctioneer Harmon and Nye Finley were not alone in the bidding; they were alone, however, when the hammer crashed down and "Sold!" reverberated around the ring.

"Well, he's yours, Brother Sheffey," Harmon said. "I'll get one of my men to break him for you. None of these horses has ever been ridden before. In the meantime I'll loan you a horse to ride."

Robert shook hands with both men and said, "May the Lord bless you both for your kindness and listening hearts to His will."

They all watched the buying and bidding continue, but Robert was soon anxious to go.

"Would you get my saddle and bridle?" Robert asked Harmon.

"You didn't understand me, Brother Sheffey; I said I'd loan you a horse when we go home for dinner. You can't ride your new horse until he's been broken."

But Robert insisted. When the saddle and bridle were brought and put on the new animal, it pranced wildly. Robert placed his hand upon the animal's nose and rubbed his own cheek against the larger, coarser one of the animal. Only then was he conscious that silence prevailed all about him; that to every bystander and auctioneer it was obvious what he was attempting to do. Quickly he closed his eyes and muttered under his breath a prayer. Nye Finley held the bridle rein with the same frozen stance that stilled his voice. Robert mounted and asked Finley to relinquish his hold on the horse's bridle.

For the space of a long moment the horse did nothing. Then slowly, deliberately, the animal turned his head backward and looked at the fixture upon his back. He stared still longer at the little man upon him, then straightened his head and gave a contemptuous snort.

"Give us a little room now!" Robert commanded as he started from the auction square.

"You'll kill yourself, Brother Sheffey!" Harmon Newberry called frantically.

Robert leaned forward and patted the animal's neck. "By all rights, new friend, I should call you Gideon II, but there's no use in being fancy and the Lord has rid you of your fanciness already. I will just call you Gideon, the same as always," he whispered.

The way was clear for the strutting animal now—all the way out to the turn pike road.

"I think it's all right now, Brother Newberry—Brother Finley. Let's be easy now—move along, Gideon. We've a lifetime to spend together, big fellow—no hurry. Take your time. Take your time."

"Where do you want us to bury you?" one of the auctioneers called.

"That time has not yet come, my brother," Robert shot back, "leastways, I hope not. I've got a preaching engagement at the east end of the county, at Mount Zion church."

"That's the place you ought to be then, I reckon!" the still-dumfounded auctioneer called back. "You've got to be a saint or the worst kind of fool to try what you're trying."

"Good-bye, Brother Newberry!" Robert called at last. "The auctioneer may be right, but if he isn't I'll be by the waters of Walker's Creek at nightfall and eating from the table of Aunt Julia Bogle."

As long as he stayed in sight of the auction ring, figures there were still motionless and the vibrato outpourings of the auctioneer still silenced. "Why should they be amazed, new friend," he said to Gideon. "Isn't it a simple thing to know that the same sweet Lord who holds dominion over them also holds dominion over the creation and actions of His animal kingdom as well? It is the simplest of truths, new friend, and perhaps it is well that they think upon it until they have provided their own answer."

By the time he had reached Aunt Julia Bogie's house near the Giles-Bland County line, Robert was sure that Gideon II would soon be an obedient and gentle friend. The animal had not been completely mastered yet, but before long Robert would be riding upon a disciplined back so gentle and trust worthy that the Psalms could be read with no fear of less important things.

"And now, new friend, I will turn you into Aunt Julia's pasture lot, abundant in clover and good limestone water. Look around now. We will be here often and just as surely as I eat Aunt Julia's good honey and bread you will find yourself in a garden of grass."

He rested the next day and prepared his sermon during the evening hours. He loved to preach at Mount Zion church, and he loved the people that he preached to even more. Their kindness never seemed to waver as it did on occasion in other localities. And here too was a hunger not just for the Word but for Christian fellowship of the purest strain.

"I told my beloved Eliza once that her girlhood home was as dear to me as the home of Mary and Martha and Lazarus must have been to our blessed Saviour. At the time, that was true, but we can't go back to our younger years, and now I must say that *this* home has taken on that meaning for me."

Tears came to Julia Bogie's eyes, and she managed only a muffled, "Bless you… and thank you." In this sensitive woman, so generous with unlimited love and unselfishness, he expected no more acknowledgment than that. Perhaps that's why he loved her so—for her unobtrusive presence, the busy hands that rushed to serve another first and the sense of loss that reflected in her kindly face when fellowship of any sort needed to be broken because of too rapidly passing hours.

"Brother Sheffey, you have just given my home a new name," Julia said. "Now we will hereafter call it the Preacher's House."

The church on Sunday was packed and many stood at the open windows. He opened the service with impromptu remarks to the effect that "the blessed Book says, he who is first shall be last, and he who is last shall be first. I'm thinking as the sweat runs down my neck and under my shirt collar that the late comers are better off outside in the shade, looking in."

In spite of the swelter of a hot June day, he gave them his message, and it was two hours later before he stepped down from the stained-walnut pulpit and wandered into the oak-shaded church yard.

"Well, you said in *there* that we are all strangers in the world—and short-lived ones, at that—so where you gonna find anybody that knows you, so you can go home to dinner with him?" a Brother Warner chided.

The cluster of old and young around him laughed, and the sound of it was good.

"I'm going to disappoint you all. I'm fixed up already. Your good brother Aurelius Vest has asked me home with him. Pray for me now until we're together again—and pray for our loyal old friend, Mr. Barbee, who couldn't be with us today. I'll stop on my way down the valley and rub the rheumatism from his aching old joints. He will cry a little, but I'll tell him that you all love him and he'll be all right. Don't you worry any now. I'll borrow some of Aurelius's pine-oil-rheumatism-chaser to rub in, and by next service time Brother Barbee will be sitting in the front pew."

Chapter XVI

In the fall of 1883 Robert concluded one of the most extensive evangelistic campaigns of his career. The age of sixty-three hardly seemed a stage of life to be taking on so much new territory, Eliza had argued, but he went, nonetheless, and came back triumphant.

"Eliza, the Lord be praised! I knew it was going to be a good trip the day we finished the service at Oldtown in Grayson County. We kept moving south and west after that and made a circle of three hundred miles, I'd judge."

"I've missed you, Robert. You've been gone over a month on this trip, and Eddie and I have been worried, to say the least…"

"What need to worry? Everywhere I met God's children, and it was no different than our own little church here at Staffordsville. There are no strangers, and certainly no harm doers to a carrier of the Word."

Eddie stabled his father's horse and returned to the house with a glow of excitement in his blue eyes. The youth was now a head taller than his father and reflected the lean masculinity so prevalent on the Stafford side of his parentage. The boy's handsome face had the same look of bright expectancy so characteristic in his mother, and it was with the full impact of this engaging personality that he approached his father.

"Papa, has Mamma told you about me yet?"

"No, but if the sweet Lord has blessed you like he has me over the past few weeks—why, we've been into North Carolina at Skull Camp and as far west as Blountville, Tennessee. Came home by way of Scott County in western Virginia—"

"But Papa, you must stop and hear me first—mine won't take so long," Eddie said.

"Tell me, then," Robert said, "but I'm suspicious already, for you and your mother have both bright *and* secretive countenances."

"Papa, I have been offered a job in the city of Lynchburg, and I will earn almost twice the amount of wages I'm earning."

"That's nearly a hundred miles away from home—," Robert began.

"Hear the boy out, Robert. Don't be sure it's not a gift of Providence—it's worked out almost like that."

"About the time you left on your trip, Papa, a drummer I saw in Pearisburg told me of a job with the Nowlin Brothers grocery company. I wrote to them, and he vouched for me—well, they're willing to give me a chance on the job."

"Eddie would work six months on trial and then the position would be his, *if the company liked his work,*" Eliza added.

"But, son, you're only seventeen years old, and it's not like I had a brother there to look after—"

"Papa, it's been like I was on my own since I was fifteen. The drummer says this work will lead to a white-collar job and a whole lot bigger responsibilities."

The boy gave all the additional verbal ammunition he had, Robert suspected, and it was rehearsed to perfection.

"I make no decisions in this life without talking to the Lord about it first. You know that, son, and I hope if it be His will, as well as that of your blessed mother, I can add my blessing also."

In every private moment they had together it was evident that Eliza favored her son in the matter.

"There should be no cause to ponder the matter for even a week," Eliza said. "The boy has a healthy ambition and a good business head. All of his uncles think so."

"That's part of the reason for his wanting the job? The need he feels to pay back his uncles for the help they have given us?"

"Yes, Robert, but there's nothing wrong in that. I can't disagree with you that God privileges many to help us while you're out laboring for Him—nor can I disagree that being God's helper is reward enough without the expectation of being paid back, in some cases. But it doesn't *always* work that way, dear husband, and when it does, it should always be a voluntary act on the part of the giver."

"You keep me humble, dear Eliza, and in touch with temporal man—"

"Look at it this way: if Eddie feels the need to pay back much of the financial help my brothers have extended me, this very desire can be the seed of his ambition and an important stepping-stone in his character growth."

"I'd have to concede that's true," Robert said.

"I'm proud of him, Robert. We've raised a fine son. I know he's young, but I sense a rightness in what he is asking of us."

"Well, maybe it will work out all right. My brothers-in-law might even smile at me more often under the new arrangement," Robert said jovially.

"And you know the answer to that too," Eliza said. "There might have been a day they thought ill of you for giving preference to your work rather than your family, but that day is no more. 'The tree shall be known by its fruits,' or something like that..."

Somehow there was a joy in losing to Eliza. At least he would let her think so.

With his parents' blessing, Eddie took up residence in the Virginia city of Lynchburg by Thanksgiving of that year.

In early December, Robert rode off, leaving Eliza alone for the first time in her entire life. The same sparkle in her eyes which had been his buoyant send-off across the years bade him farewell again, but he could not help noticing that this sparkle was obscured by the faintest mist.

Montcalm, West Virginia, was his destination and there he would be for a week of revival services. It would be hard not to take detours all along the journey, for almost every ridge and hollow were familiar ground to which, at some time across the years, he had carried the message of the Christian gospel and witnessed the first fruits of the miraculous power of its doctrine. But his blessing had not ended there: in some families he had assisted in the conversion of three generations from the same household.

It was a pleasant December day when he reached the small West Virginia village and he rode to the home of the Ellis Bailey family, with whom he had been invited to stay.

"The Lord has certainly smiled on us this year," Ellis Bailey greeted him. "The weather is little worse than early fall, and the extra room on the schoolhouse gives us more space than we've ever had before."

Robert felt uplifted by the enthusiasm of his friend, and with a happy heart he sat at the generously laden table and there held a devotional service before anyone took the first bite of food.

There was no less enthusiasm demonstrated when he finished the final prayer and piled spoon upon spoon of honey on the freshly made bread.

"Brother Sheffey, why do you eat so much honey all the time? Every time you're here you put honey on your bread and even on your vegetables," the youngest of the children present asked.

"Bless your little heart, child. No one across all these years has asked me that."

He took another bite of the honey and bread and let it roll across his tongue before attempting to answer her. His dancing white whiskers soon slowed from chewing and he patted the girl's hand.

"Child, a long time ago I had a taste for sweet things, like all children; but I love honey in particular, for it is a balm to my soul of another kind also. When I was growing up I used to drink a lot of whiskey and brandy, and when I came to love my sweet Lord so much, I could still taste the ungodly nectar in my mouth even years after I no longer touched it. The honey in my mouth takes the old taste away and helps me give testimony."

This one answer seemed to give birth to other questions that, before long, were coming in all directions from his host family and other guests who honored him with their presence each time he came into the community.

"The most unusual worship service I've ever had, you say? That won't take much thinking on," Robert said, stroking his white beard. "I can't remember the year it happened for sure, but I'd say about eighteen-sixty. It's funny how the sweet Lord shows us a need sometimes by the oddest sequence of events."

"Where were you at the time?" one of the guests asked.

"I was traveling through Tazewell County and I stopped at a plantation home and asked if there was food enough for me to share. The lady of the house smelled of perfume and her hands showed the whiteness and tenderness of disuse, but she started telling me all the food she didn't have. It was in the final weeks of winter before garden time and she kept complaining that she didn't have fresh asparagus and snap beans and that she was sure I wouldn't like dried apples rather than fresh applesauce."

"And did you finally eat there anyway?"

"No, I didn't," Robert answered his hostess. "She did not seem thankful at all for all the food she did have, and I rode away up the road a piece, and went into a house that I later found out was the plantation owner's tenant house and ate there. The tenant family didn't have anything except potatoes, but when the woman of that shack asked me in, she was more thankful for those potatoes than any king has ever been over his banquet table."

"Did you ever go back to the plantation?" one of the children asked.

"No, and I found out later I wouldn't be welcome. But anyway, I'm getting away from the experience I wanted to tell you all about. The woman at the house where I did eat had a husband and several children. Her man had never accepted Christ—and had no intention to, she said, until a goiter he had on his neck grew bigger and bigger, so he could hardly breathe. If you could have heard him wheeze you'd have thought what he was thinking: it was doubtful whether he could live out the winter.

"In any event, the sinner wanted to be baptized before he was to trod through the great beyond. The rest of his family were Baptists, and when he said baptized he didn't mean sprinkled on the head: he meant under the water."

"But how could you submerge him in the cold of winter?" Ellis Bailey said.

"That was part of the problem," Robert replied. "The man insisted on immersion, and he seemed to have no doubt that he would die before spring so there was no putting him off, in spite of the fact that there was ice frozen over the creek from one bank to the other."

"You could have cut a hole in the ice with an ax," an older child said.

"That's what we did finally do—but not right then. We hoped it would warm up a little the next day and make it easier on the poor brother.

"That night two old Indians who lived nearby brought the family some deer meat and were told by the sick man of his conversion. I've never heard a more touching testimony, and right under my nose the man converted those two heathens and they too wanted to 'go down with the fish and be clean for the Great Spirit.' I couldn't understand the Indians well, but I was convinced of their sincerity and knowledge of what they were doing. The Lord be praised. We all knelt there on the floor together with our arms around each other and the sick man's wife and children crying over him so happily. The Lord may never show me for certain, but those old Indians were just as much a part of that fellowship as any man who ever stood at the altar."

"Did you baptize them all together?" an anxious child tried to speed him along.

"Yes, but let's not get ahead of ourselves," Robert said. "We agreed that the baptisms would take place the next afternoon at the creek below the house, and the Indians promised they'd be there. They not only showed up on time but each one had his squaw, and one of them brought his two daughters. We chopped a hole in the ice about the size of a washtub and baptized the white man first. He wouldn't go back to the house—he wanted to honor his red brothers with his presence—but we wrapped him good in a quilt. The strangest thing of all happened when I baptized the first old Indian. I let him down through the hole in the ice while holding onto his hands in the same manner I'd submerged the white man. When I got the Indian under, hands and all, he wrestled free from me and disappeared from view under the ice. I was beside myself to know what to do, and I'd about made up my mind that trying to save him was futile. However, I grabbed the ax and started chopping a bigger hole to find him and effect a rescue. The white man, his family, and I seemed the only ones upset, for the Indian families showed no fear or excitement."

"I'll bet the old Indian thought it was time to die, and he figured that going through the hole in the ice to the Great Father was as good a direction as any," Ellis Bailey said, half seriously.

"No, they don't think like that," Robert said, "but you're nearer right than you think. As I chopped away at the ice I heard a gurgling sound to my rear and the head and body of the old Indian popped up out of the water behind me. I couldn't understand his chattering words but the tenant family said he was asking me if he had stayed down long enough to please the Great Father. I still didn't understand, until they explained to me that the Indian had thought the longer he could stay under the water the better baptized he was, and that it would be more pleasing to our sweet Lord that way. Well, we got them all to understand that endurance had nothing to do with it and baptized the rest of them quickly and wrapped them in blankets they had brought. It was a grand and glorious day to bring seven new sheep into the fold, and not a one of them suffered any sickness from the cold!"

The next evening at the appointed hour the Bailey family and a handful of friends accompanied Robert to the school building for the opening night of the revival. A half hour after the announced starting time, only two additional people had come. Robert, in his sadness, asked those present if they would join him in prayer and then go out with him to visit some of the people whose hearts had obviously hardened since his last visit.

The reception each received and reported on was a remote one.

"Why have they grown so cold?" Robert pleaded for enlightenment.

Not one could tell him for sure—other than to guess the recent prosperity of the area had something to do with it—and he insisted that the school doors be opened again the following night anyway. But the result then was no different. Robert stood before the improvised altar and pulpit with tears streaming down his face. He looked out over the handful of loyal friends without really seeing them, for his heart was so heavy and his eyes burning with disappointment. He spoke more to himself than to his meager audience, but they came closer to listen.

"It is an abomination to the Lord, their disobedience," he whispered intensely. "A great calamity will befall this community. I will pray God's wrath upon these people who turn from their Creator. Deliver my sheepskin to me, Brother Bailey, and depart from me—all of you—and I will join you for family prayer at home when I have finished."

At daylight the next morning, with a winter fog obscuring the rays of the morning sun, he and Gideon left the village.

"It's a sad day, Gideon, but somewhere else our sweet Lord will have a job for us. Perhaps we shall never know whether our prayers were heard or whether they are in accord with our Father's will. But woe unto these people if their disobedience is untimely in heaven."

Not until the year of 1885 did he hear of the smallpox epidemic that had a few months earlier engulfed the village, taking entire families in its terrible wake. For days upon days, he was told, stricken people had lain undiscovered until the spreading stench of the village became so widespread that travelers would detour for miles. He told Eliza about the background of the matter, but he found his real peace alone down the hill from their home, by the waters of Walker's Creek. When the power of God seemed especially manifest, he felt both an inward peace and an awesome fear at exactly the same time. He sat on a creek rock near the edge of the stream, with some of the villagers watching him, and raised his eyes to the heavens.

"Dear Father, we will never know, for it will not be Thy will that we know, whether this scourge has come because Thy servant asked it in Thy name. Whatever the true answer may be, let this and all things be to Thy honor and glory, that we, Thy people, may not shut out the presence of Thy Holy Spirit ever again."

In the four years to follow, the spirit of religious revival, and particularly the camp-meeting variety, seemed to be dying away. Robert witnessed this with a heavy heart, but fought back with an increase in personal activity to do his share in trying to overcome such spiritual apathy. The people alone could not be blamed, he learned, for some presiding elders and some conference officials in league with them had spoken openly against the continuance of camp meetings. How blasphemous they were in even suggesting that "The church had now come out of the mountains and it was time both dignity *and* piety joined hands for the ultimate good of the whole church"! Couldn't they see that a love of education and culture was becoming the fraud of the age! The very word "dignity" was an abomination in the sight of God! Nothing on earth was really important except the extension of God's kingdom by loving one's neighbor and meditating on God's Holy Word both day and night.

"Eliza, if the camp meetings are ever done away with, may the wrath of God fall heavy upon our heads," he said tearfully. "So many have been reached in this way, and how much poorer will heaven be if we miss one soul who might come out of the mountains repentant, only to find the log pews empty and the altar rotted away."

"The world is changing, dear Robert. It is not the same world you knew fifty years ago. Haven't you been telling me that many of the mountain cabins and the trappers' camps that you served so many years ago now stand deserted?"

"Yes. The people have moved from hacked-out clearings and ridges to cleared fields and white houses below. They're a different generation, but it will be a pity if they do not remember their humbler beginnings."

"Perhaps we can't prevent change. Maybe we shouldn't try. We might even be acting contrary to God's will."

He did not often find fault with the dear wife, whose aging eyes seemed to get kinder with the passing of the years, but such statements left him shaken and sad.

"If I must do it by myself, Eliza, I will keep the camp meetings so full that not one man who dares to call himself a servant of God will raise one finger to do away with them."

In July of 1890 Robert prepared to set out, more than one month ahead of the scheduled Wabash camp meeting, and do the thing he had vowed to do. He would take care of his circuit, but after each engagement he would comb the hills and hollows. Then, when the last week in August came, there would be the equal of a long wagon train from every conceivable direction to the Wabash camp ground. But he would do more than that. When his travels took him too far out of range, he would send wagon trains of God-seekers to other camp meetings both within and without the state.

"Help me get my affairs in order, Eliza. I am off at daylight."

Together they went through his mail, Eliza commenting now and then, and making note of his special instructions. When she was done, he told her that he was tired and asked that she sit down on the wicker couch so he might lie there and rest his head in her lap.

"Sing to me, Eliza, for in the morning I will be gone." He closed his eyes, and from her body, grown heavier with age, the strains of her voice with new mellowness reached the depths of his soul: *Twilight is stealing over...*

His plan was to make a complete tour of his regular itinerary, which consisted now of fourteen counties. First he would go to Mercer County and work his way northeast until all his West Virginia territory was covered sufficiently well to spread the word. From there he would make a circle to the easternmost counties in the Virginia territory, and, afterward, work west.

"Well, Gideon, Bluefield will be our starting point," he murmured to the animal as they passed through the village of Narrows and turned up Wolf Creek. Quite contrary to his usual practice, he made no stops along the creek, for he would spend more time with these good people later.

Suddenly he did stop Gideon and dismounted. After he had removed his hat and begun the task for which he had stopped, a man he recognized as a lawyer by the name of Staples reined to a halt beside him.

"Brother Bob, what in the world are you doing? The way you passed me up and some of your other old friends along the creek, we thought you must be in a hurry, and here you are dipping up water from a mud puddle in what looks like a brand-new hat?"

"It's the little tadpoles, Brother Staples. You see, the water has receded and they are isolated. The hot sun will have them cooked like stewed chicken in a puddle as shallow as *that*."

Robert continued his task until all the tadpoles had been moved to less isolated, though still shallow, water. As a final act of tidying up he rinsed his hat in the waters of Wolf Creek.

"Brother Staples, it's a Lord's blessing that you happened by, and I want you to ride along with me. You are going to Bland to court, no doubt, and I want you to advertise the Wabash camp meetings everywhere you go. Do better than that, even. Catch the people inside and outside the courthouse and implore the judge to do the same and tell the people there are those among us who would do away with the camp meetings, and we must fight them with all of God's might!"

The other man promised he would, but there was lack of conviction and enthusiasm in his voice.

When the two men parted company at Rocky Gap, Robert felt that a bad omen might arise from his solicitation.

"Gideon, can it possibly be that all the world is right and I am wrong? Has my sweet Lord changed His face and I alone cannot see it?"

On August eighteenth his circle ended at the Bethany church on Pilgrims Knob in Buchanan County. Even there, so distantly removed from the Wabash camp grounds in Giles County, he found eager hearts awaiting the days until the camp meeting began.

From there he rode straight toward home, for the camp meetings were scheduled to start August twenty-third; and by August twentieth he was back at Staffordsville. The wait to see the fruits of his labor was a short one. The thrill of this occasion had never failed, and every year the sheer joy and challenge of it seemed to grow in magnitude. Periodically for fifty years he had attended these meetings, and for twenty five of those years he had been, by the grace of God, a cornerstone. Two dozen other ministers had been faithful workers as well, and their joint efforts and dedication, second only to a genuine spiritual hunger and need of fellowship on the part of the people, told the real story of the camp ground's success.

The Wabash camp ground lay only three or four miles southwest of Staffordsville, and Robert wanted to be there two days early, as was the custom, to help with the numerous arrangements. Eliza would come with members of her family on the opening day, and this year Eddie would be home visiting, to worship with his mother and kin. Eighteen to twenty preachers, both local and regional, would be in attendance; the local ministers were always expected to make ready the tents of the brethren traveling from a distance.

Robert hoped that eighteen or twenty preachers would be enough for the five-day meeting. He could recall two or three years in the past when more than that number had worked themselves to exhaustion during the spontaneous outpouring of faith.

When he reached the Pulaski-Giles turnpike leading to the camp grounds he looked with amazement upon the endless train of human and animal flesh. They also were two days early, and there would be droves who had come even sooner and who already would have set up camp for the duration of the meeting. The toll gates along the turnpike would have their coffers full this day, and nobody knew any better than he did how much the money was needed for road maintenance. The churning wheels and animal hooves turned the hard clay and creek gravel to powdery dust. The young women walked along barefooted, carrying perhaps their only pair of shoes, keeping them clean and unscarred to wear at the meetings. There was a time he might have frowned upon this little vanity, but time and God's love had mellowed him. He had seen many happy and fruitful marriages result from the courtship phase as well as the worship phase of the camp meetings.

Eliza also had helped to enlighten him on this delicate subject. "Is there any better place for the young to discover the young and to fall in love than in our Lord's holy presence?" she had said.

How right she had been, he thought, riding along and passing children and grandchildren by the score who had been the offspring of camp-inspired marriages, and the generation after generation of converts who kept the fires of the camp grounds alive year after year.

He went past what he knew would be the last melon and candy wagons. They were doing a brisk business, as was the picture-taking wagon, covered in black canvass. None of the hucksters would be permitted nearer than two miles to the camp ground, he knew, for he had helped to make such rules. For any who chose to abridge such rules the camp officials had also made provisions each year to appoint camp constables to augment the county sheriff and his deputies who normally kept an eye on fringe activities. Such surveillance had been fruitful on a number of occasions when profit-minded mountaineers came to camp with knee-deep straw in their wagons, which provided a cover for the squeezing of corn and the stronger-than-cider apple juice. The constables did a good job of peacekeeping and noise suppression, but the one thing they reported being unable to stop was the horse trading that flourished at the very edge of the camp grounds.

A few of the women each year had been not unjustly accused of "fashion parades," for he had witnessed this himself. He had preached against it also, for if the camp meetings succeeded as God would have them do, excess attention to what other women wore and the fashions of the day defeated that purpose.

The camp ground proper lay to the northeast of the turnpike road. It covered the space of five or six acres offering a variety of terrain from flat land to grassy knolls, with both open space and some ground well shaded with white oak and poplar. The area was a complementary annex to the little village of Wabash. (Still further back in history, the name of the village had come from an early settler, who started a wagon journey to join his son on the Wabash River in Indiana and broke down on the present village spot. Having to spend the winter there, he named the place Wabash.)

In physical appearance, Robert had often marveled at how much the campsite looked like the most perfect nature-carved amphitheater. It was a place where he could almost whisper from the top of one grassy knoll and be assured that his voice would carry without loss of volume or tone to the more distant hills.

The scene that had been so vividly in his mind now appeared before him in reality. He relinquished Gideon to one of the stable boys, admonishing him to listen carefully to his instructions for the animal's feeding before turning him out into the pasture meadows along with the animals of all the other camp participants. Nowhere was the grass greener and thicker than the silt-rich bottoms of Wabash; the bubbling fresh-water springs fed with abundance both man and beast.

He had hardly dismounted when hordes of little children who were offspring of the early arrivals rushed to be the first to hold his hand or coattail as he made his way along the dusty road to the preachers' tent.

"Brother Bob, it's going to be the biggest crowd we've ever had this year!" an elderly resident called. "Wouldn't surprise me none if we had four or five thousand."

"God be praised if you are right, Brother Frank. Pray for the meeting now. I'll see you a little later."

The preachers' tent was a large but temporary cloth edifice placed near the worship shed for the benefit of all participating preachers, and used as sleeping and eating quarters as well as a quiet place for sermon preparation, prayer, and meditation. The worship shed—or simply shed, as it was more commonly called—was precisely what the word implied. It was simply a huge wood-shingled roof supported by vertical log posts. Neither the sides nor the ends of the building were enclosed. The openness was welcome during the summer months, and even if the nights turned cool, he had witnessed the heat of religious fervor so great that the ventilation was greatly appreciated. Thick oak slabs with pole backs provided seating, and sawdust or straw lined the aisles.

The shed seated less than a thousand people, but there had been few camp meetings during the fifty-six years of its existence when many more had not stood outside and around the shed than those under its roof.

Robert placed his own belongings within the preachers' tent but did not stay inside. He loved the activity of seeing the camp come to life and the hustle and bustle of joyous people already filled with the spirit and eagerly awaiting what was to come. Some had set up their homemade tents as much as a week early. It was not necessary that they all stay in tents, though, for the village of Wabash had grown enough over the years to provide, now, a small hotel and two inns. Although the inns were annexed to the homes of permanent residents, they commanded an eager clientele from the cities of Roanoke, Lynchburg, and West Virginia cities to the north, who came by train as far as they could and the rest of the way by hack.

Most of the families of the region set up tents year after year, or occupied the numerous cabins that sat at the far fringes of the camp ground. Some occupied the same cabin or campsite year after year and provided food and lodging for distant travelers and/or relatives. The camp cook took care of the needs of the preachers and visiting dignitaries, who had been by no means infrequent across the years. Wabash camp ground had been host to the most eloquent orators and highest ranking personages the Holston conference—and those of her sister conference as well—had to offer. It was not unusual at all to have speakers from four or five conferences at one time.

Just as Robert started to leave the preachers' tent and make his customary journey to the top of the hill, Reverend Tyler Frazier, a county minister he knew, arrived with his own belongings. "Brother Frazier, I was just ready to go to the hill for my prayers about the meeting. Would you join me?"

The other agreed but begged time to spread his bed linen for airing, and Robert waited patiently. There was increasingly more to see. Children busily traversed the footpath to his left, carrying bucket after bucket of cool water from the bubbling spring in the distance to their family cabin or tent. Without looking in, Robert felt that he could visualize the activity inside the family enclosures. In the cabins the men would be preparing bedrolls in the loft and the women would be hanging sheets as partitions for dressing areas within the cabins. Other family members would be unpacking wagonloads of ant-proof locker boxes of meats and vegetables, which would fed all of their family and twice as many more.

The packing would not have been so hurried that the family's dog-eared Bible was forgotten, nor would they neglect the camp custom of greeting other participants with short Bible verses, long ago committed to memory.

"I am ready, Brother Bob!" Tyler Frazier called from inside.

A young woman walked by Robert and greeted him with, "'Lo, I am with you always, even to the end of the age.'"

"'He that believeth in Me, though he were dead yet shall he live'," Robert returned the greeting.

The two men walked away from the tent together, Tyler Frazier's arm upon Robert's back. "Brother Bob, you don't seem so talkative today."

"I'm doing too much thinking, I suppose. I look about me at the precious joy of human fellowship and the raptured faces of those who know they are as close to God in this place as they'll ever approach Him in this world, and I wonder what the hearts of those who want to bring it all to a close must really be like? God forbid that they do away with such joyous times!"

"We won't let them do it," Tyler Frazier said with an affectionate pat on the back of his elder.

On the crest of the hill they knelt and prayed together, first one aloud and then the other, until they had implored all the forces of heaven to invade the hearts of the unsaved and send them home victorious and reborn.

"Let's not hurry back down," Robert said, arising. "I need to stretch and rest a minute. This old earthly body has been around for seventy years, and it balks on me now and then." Tyler Frazier helped his elder be seated again and sat beside him. "Brother Bob, I remember a few years ago you prayed here at the camp meeting for our Father to 'make this world a little heaven to go to big heaven in.' I've never forgotten that, and I'm reminded of it as I sit here looking down over this beautiful valley. As far as I'm concerned, this is as near to heaven as any spot we'll ever see."

"Amen. And it gets prettier every year. I first saw this camp ground in eighteen-forty and there was little here. Look at the village now. I am told Brother Cecil's gristmill runs day and night and there are three or four stores and blacksmith shops, not to mention an iron foundry, casket shop, sawmill, harness shop and stave mill. Look all about you, Brother Frazier. Could there be a more perfect and peaceful place to live and die?"

They walked down the opposite side of the hill, past the Wabash Academy, where within weeks high-pitched voices would echo about the classrooms. From there they could see only the top of the gigantic waterwheel that was the power source of the mill complex, but the splashing water from the millrace could be heard with stair-stepping splattering's, as earthward over the wheel the water fell. The big wheel squeaked as it turned, and Robert opined that, rather than being an annoyance, it had probably become a welcome melody throughout the valley and would be missed when it did stop for the Sabbath day.

They returned by way of Dr. Anderson's residence and paid their respects but were not allowed to leave until the good doctor had shown them his latest telephone equipment. Robert looked with interest at the thing called a switchboard but could not understand how it operated. Dr. Anderson spoke with pride of how he had installed it himself—even making part of it with his own hands—and said that he hoped to run lines in every direction from Wabash.

At the post office they encountered Reverend William Bailey, who would be another occupant of the preachers' tent. With him they returned to their temporary quarters to find the place invaded by four more clergical brethren.

After the passing of another twenty-four hours, camping areas and all cabins were filled to capacity. Equally good reports came from the hotel and the inns. Participants from local churches and not-too-distant villages and towns would come and go, but at any given time they would be the groups which would swell the camp-ground ranks.

That night by the light of the moon Robert walked alone to the shed. It had always seemed such a holy place to him, and there were so many memories attached to it that one now overlapped another. The hum of human voices could be heard in every direction, still exuberant. That too would change when the meetings actually got under way. The spirituality of the occasion would demand a different kind of exuberance. Strollers crisscrossed the fields and moonlit woods alone and in groups, while still others could be seen by lamplight through their cabin windows, studying the Book of books.

The shed stood ready for the morning service at nine that would formally open the camp-meeting session. The oversized Bible with large type lay closed on the crudely built rostrum. Behind it, a dozen hickory-bottomed chairs rested in soldier like alignment toward the back of the platform. Lanterns and homemade wooden candle holders were strung about the support posts of the shed, while still larger candles lined the rostrum area, hanging above the long slab of wood supported by hickory or sourwood legs resting on straw, and known to saint and sinner alike as the mourners' bench. None of these items of illumination had yet been lit; they stood virgin-like before Robert's searching eyes as poised and ready as his colleagues who paced the preachers' tent, waiting for morning to come.

For years the routine had been the same: the bugle was blown by the camp bugler at precisely six am., which meant that all arise, wash, have breakfast, tidy up, and, if there was time left over, study the Bible diligently. The bugle sounded again at nine a.m. for the beginning of prayer service in all tents and cabins. Again it was blown at eleven am for the first worship service of the day. Twice more the bugle would be heard: at the three pm service and again at seven pm for the final night service. The early evening service did not assure an early departure from the shed, however. On the contrary, it was not unusual for the service to continue until ten or eleven o'clock at night; Robert personally had stayed down on his knees in the straw with mourners until daylight had come once again. Just as readily would he do the same with new converts, until he was sure that the conversion was genuine and that those converted had felt the full impact of the new life chosen.

Little sleep was had that night in the preachers' tent, but the wakefulness produced well-organized plans and prayerful humility in the outlining of what needed to be done for the success of the days to follow.

The first day of services produced the usual "settling-in" process and organizational confusion, but even these were happy times. Converts had come forward—not in the large, fevered numbers to be expected near the middle and close of the meetings, but all things considered, it was a good beginning. There had been many years when the first day and night had been simply a "warm-up" time for both preachers and congregation.

Robert lay on his bedroll in the preachers' tent, satisfied, and took note of the quietness of the night. That in itself told something. The exuberance of the people had quieted, and he knew that they had begun their worship in earnest. Gone for the while were the boisterous social overtures, for now it was time for every man's confrontation with his God. There seemed peace even among the animals, which, sharing a mutual pasture and strange surroundings had whinnied mournfully in the beginning. Cows brought along to camp as a fresh supply of milk mingled their bawling among the prancing horses and braying mules, until; at last, they too had found a compatibility of sorts. They were almost quiet now, and Robert pictured them lowing by the Wabash branch, chewing their cuds and feeling the same peace he himself was feeling.

His feeling for and about animals was as well-known as he was. This he knew without immodesty, but even so he had never discussed the subject in the depth he felt at times almost compelled to.

The following day's services began in earnest, and by midday of still another day, which was Friday, a vast influx of foot and wagon traffic converged upon the already crowded camp grounds. There could be no policy other than welcome and yet Robert was aware, as he knew his colleagues were that at least a small part of the latecomers were freeloaders who would partake of the food and shelter of friends and relatives with no thought at all toward contributing to the work and purpose of the camp meeting. But sometimes the problem had a happy ending when an unsuspecting freeloader would fall victim to the spirit of the meetings, or the pleadings of a friend or relative who showed genuine concern for his soul, and leave the camp ground a new person. For that reason no one was unwelcome, no matter how suspect such a person's motives might be.

By Saturday night the crowd had swelled even more. In his rushing about, Robert would be stopped by first one and then another who would request of him special prayer, or unrelenting pressure on a family member or spouse who remained, year after year, unsaved.

"Yes, brother, I'll ask it of the Lord," Robert repeated as one last man held onto his coattail, delaying him from going under the shed and opening the night service with prayer, as was the tradition. "Tell me again what your name is?"

The man repeated it, but Robert felt it flee from him as he made the journey up the straw-covered aisle to the preachers' platform.

Even before his opening prayer, Robert felt the air about him electric with spiritual obedience, but he prayed no less fervently and he did not forget the little things that were important to the humble people, and, he was sure, to God, also. "… and Dear Lord," he concluded his prayer, "bless that man standing at the back who asked me to pray for him and whose name I've forgotten. From the cut of his coat and the way his pants hang, I believe he's from Grayson County."

Robert relinquished the rostrum to Reverend Dill Strader, the youngest preacher on the platform and a man who had been licensed to preach at the Wabash camp meetings only two years previously. The young man admonished his listeners not to let the fervor of the camp meeting die and to take it back to their individual churches. Having reiterated again the purpose of the camp meetings as was the custom of the leadoff preacher every night, and the citing of the innumerable army of converts that the Wabash camp ground had produced across the years, he launched into his sermon.

Robert sat on the platform with the five remaining ministers who would in turn follow the younger man. He would not preach, but when all the others had finished he would make his way up and down the aisles, exhorting, walking with the timid and fearful toward the mourners' bench, or kneeling with a spoken promise to spend unlimited time with a would-be penitent until peace came to his troubled heart. Sometimes he preached or gave testimonies, but his preaching did not move the crowds as did his prayers and exhortations. Each man knew his place—or, as all the assembled ministers had discussed—God's place for them: the special talents and gifts that each possessed individually and the best ways each could utilize them. Not only had Robert seen them all find their special niches of service across the years; he had seen most of them perfect the role, until the most devout of personal belief and faith, coupled with repeatedly practiced effort, had produced a core of the Lord's spokesman, hard for the most unrepentant soul to deny.

One after another the platform preachers took their turns, resting only between songs and intermittent lusty Methodist shouting. The crowd grew as the service progressed. There were late comers and those who habitually waited for fevered shouts of victory to move them from their own tents to an empty seat under the shed—if one was to be found. The latecomer was lucky to find a place, and most times found himself standing outside the shed, where, during years of good attendance, three-fourths of the crowd heard the gospel messages. That too had advantages, depending on the individual point of view. For the "talkers" and "sparkers" the opportunity was greater at the fringe areas, but an attentive camp constable would often put a stop to anything above a whisper or the most unobtrusive of movement.

When the service ended that night, one hundred sixteen converts had been counted. Participating and non-participating ministers alike reassembled in the preachers' tent, as was the yearly custom, to rejoice over the repentant souls who had made their professions. There was an extra measure of joy in the repentance of those who year after year had resisted, and on this night had succumbed, tearstained and humble, to accept a way of life Robert knew no contrite heart could any longer deny.

The camp cook entered the preachers' tent and set their fourth meal of the day before them. Exhausted bodies were replenished, and conversation continued.

"Do you think Lady Nick will come into the fold this year?" Reverend W. N. Wagoner asked Robert.

All heads came to attention, for each year this woman whom Robert had first met as the "night visitor" at Thorn Spring church in Pulaski County had never missed the camp meeting services. In the same manner with which she observed from a distance the Thorn Spring congregation, so did she watch during sessions of the Wabash camp meetings. Robert had named her (not altogether aptly, he realized) Lady Nick, in reference to Nicodemus the Pharisee who came to Jesus by night, inquiring.

"But Lady Nick has heard 'Ye must be born again' so often it can't be continued sermons on regeneration she's waiting for? I think she's just got the hungriest curiosity of all the camp followers we've ever seen," Reverend John Perry said.

"No, Brother Perry, that isn't it," Robert said. "She knows the way, but like the rich young ruler who was instructed to give up his wealth by our blessed Jesus, she has much to give up."

Reverend J. R. Walker, who now served the Staffordsville· charge, asked to be given more background on the subject at hand and Robert did so, concluding, "The woman's social position and her dependence on family wealth, among other things, represent a great chasm she must cross. It is not hard to see that she resents the obstacle. She has felt the presence of the Holy Spirit. It is that against which she is really in rebellion."

"A heart feeling the gentle nurturing of the Holy Spirit on the one hand and all the enticement of worldly pleasures and comforts on the other?" Reverend Tyler Frazier restated the universal problem of their profession.

"Exactly," Robert agreed. "And maybe she does have a greater gulf to cross than many do. If it be so, may the ever-present sweet Lord extend His patience a little longer."

Reverend P. L. Cobb had been the quiet one, and still he looked worried. "Brother Sheffey, do you feel that we have come no closer to winning this woman than we were this time last year?"

"I don't know, Brother Cobb. I have talked to her and I get two impressions. I feel, in spirit, she is already a part of us, and yet there is resentment as I talk with her and try to pray with her about her deliverance."

"Brother Bob, there is no offense meant—you know that without my saying it—but what about Brother Bailey and myself approaching her? I mean, if somebody new to her...?" Tyler Frazier said.

"By all means. The Lord be praised ... be it none of us," Robert agreed.

The lady in question did not stay in the camp-and-tent area each year, and the following morning, a warm but overcast Sunday, Robert directed his colleagues, Frazier and Bailey, to the proper inn. As he watched them walk from the preachers' tent onto the turnpike road and turn northward he had a sense of foreboding that they would be unsuccessful in their mission. Their pleadings and personal testimonies would live and die as unfruitful as the little clouds of dust at their moving heels. He watched them moving farther and farther away as if the unspoken benediction he sent with them was being lost also.

Presently several children ran after the two men, one or two of them searching for an older, guiding hand, but they did not stop as they might have done had not their hearts been, Robert suspected, as filled with higher purpose as was his own.

In his fifty years of being God's advocate the current problem was above all others the most unexplainable and perplexing. How could any person, having reached the stage in life of knowing God's truth and experiencing the visitation of the Holy Spirit yet stand stubborn and unreceiving? The very patience of God must be strained at such times! Stubbornness itself was a grievous sin. Did not this woman and all mankind know that now was the day of salvation and even God's patience would not rescue a soul gone beyond redemption from tardiness of action and coldness of heart?

Before his two colleagues, returning, had gotten closer than hollering distance, he knew that their mission had failed. It was written in their posture, the gait of their walk, and in their downcast heads.

"She does not wish to give her life to Christ," Robert ventured matter-of-factly.

"No," Tyler Frazier said. "Not in the morning service, night service, or even next years' service', to put it in her own words."

Robert lowered his head. "She comes for more than curiosity, I know she does," he whispered.

"She mentioned that." Reverend Bailey whispered also. "She said she likes to come and 'watch the parade of fools.' She said we all 'look like a circus act' she saw in Philadelphia once, and she missed 'seeing the monkeys jump around and hug each other.'"

"I will go to the hill and pray for her again. Will you fetch my sheepskin, Brother Bailey?"

"Brother Bailey did not tell it all," Tyler Frazier said. "She walked out to the yard fence with us—she is an intelligent woman, you must admit, even if she does have the bite of a viper about her—and plucked *this* flower and asked me to give it to you."

Robert held the crimson flower his hand. "Is that all?" he said. "Just a flower and nothing else?"

"She said for you to look at the red flower carefully and smell the freshness of it—she said to tell you that red means life and beauty and vitality, and what you want for her is death and sorrow and drabness so real to her that nightmares invade her sleep."

"Could you not tell her, my brother, that death to self is the pathway to the most magnificent of life?"

"I told her that and she laughed at me," Tyler Frazier said.

Robert took his sheepskin and walked alone to the north hill behind the camp ground. Far below him, hurried movement gave the appearance of a busy anthill. Within the hour the eleven am service would begin and only one more day of the camp meeting would remain. From the north streamed long lines of buggies. He could not see far the other way, except for the southern end of the turnpike, and from there came horse and buggy traffic from Dublin. Dust clouds indicated that worshipers from still other directions also were on their way. Sunday was always the biggest day, although Monday, the last day of the meetings, often times saw the largest number of converts come forward. It was a sort of "last- chance day," and for those who had resisted the call to conversion throughout the session it was "now" while the spirit was soaring or go back to one's home church and hope that the local preacher could build the same fire in one's heart that the camp ground evangelists had—that, or wait until next year's camp-ground session. Robert knew all the strengths and evasions of mind, and this year there had been a large number of "holdbacks," in spite of the collective work of all the ministers and his own exhortations.

Time slipped up on him as he watched, godlike, the scene below. He had not yet prayed for Lady Nick, and he repositioned his sheepskin on flatter ground and proceeded to do so. The prayer would be another of many he had uttered in the same cause. He felt that he knew an answer that none of the others had mentioned—and certainly one that the woman in question had never thought of—God did not save a person against his will. Still he prayed over and over again: "For the sake of our blessed Jesus, dear Lord...for Jesus's sake."

Four unexpected visitors came to the preachers' tent only moments before the eleven am service was to begin. They introduced themselves quickly, and Robert took note that all four appeared to be conference officials from four separate conferences. He, like his colleagues, bade them welcome and asked if they'd like to have a part in the worship service (already two more conference officials were scheduled to preach during night service). They declined, saying that they would not interfere with plans already made and that they would be leaving after the night service.

"You can at least sit on the platform with us," Tyler Frazier said. "Our camp-ground participants are not always accustomed to the mightiest of our Christian army during the sessions, and we will give them something extra to remember."

Four extra chairs were hurriedly placed on the platform and clergy and guests had already seated themselves before Robert had them on their feet again for his opening prayer.

"Our dear Heavenly Father," he began, "we have many worshipers on the grounds and some mighty men on the platform today. But it has come to our mind that Thou art not mindful of mighty men—it is humble men on the plain order who are nearest to Thy heart. These of high rank do not come this great distance today altogether for the purpose of worship. They think we do not know it, but they come to sit in judgment—to decide whether Thy children do truly worship Thee when such happiness fills their hearts that they surely would burst if they did not shout. They disapprove of the camp meetings, dear Lord, for it is rumored that they have invented a new word—ee-motional-ism, I think they call it—and You can see that in their hearts they want to smite this holy place. Don't let them do it, Lord; some of the most precious souls in Your kingdom found Thee here at my feet..."

He continued his prayer, disregarding the anxious shuffling feet behind him. When he had finished he had covered the most inspiring highlights during twenty-five years of the camp-grounds' existence.

That evening at the night service, when the visiting dignitaries again took their chairs, Robert thought he sensed a change in their countenances. Desperately, he hoped there was. All the services on this Sunday had been spirit-filled and fruitful—an example, if the observer were looking for any, which could not help but inspire: the early-morning love feast, the singing and shouting, the morning communion that witnessed the partaking of the cup with the reverence that the very blood of Jesus glowed red therein.

The flood tide that Robert knew had been building began to break when the third speaker had finished. That speaker was Tyler Frazier, whose eloquent and impassioned pleadings had started such a fire in the hearts of his listeners that their raptured faces shone with the glow of winter frost by moonlight. No words had been minced as to humanity's low estate and the blackest of sin that reigned in every individual heart, and God's redeeming love that was, for every man, the only cure.

Before his colleague was seated, people were standing and crying, "Mercy! Mercy!"

The next speaker, a conference official previously scheduled to speak, began to take his turn at the rostrum and Robert waved him back.

"Let them shout, brother—give them all the time they need to shout, and then you can speak! It is a glorious time! They have got in a good way! Praise God!"

The tempo from the crowd rose higher and Robert left the platform and stood in the aisle at the base of the rostrum. Suddenly a man ran to Robert and shouted, "I want to forgive my neighbor of a wrong he has done to me!"

"Thank God." Robert called back, and his own heart was so overcome with love that prostration before the throne of God seemed the smallest gift he could give in return.

In the heat of a continuing aura of spiritual servitude and Christ like humility, the next speaker poured forth more of the food that would satisfy the hunger. The big, rawboned man who was first a preacher and second a conference official, towered over the crude rostrum and dwarfed it. His voice and manner of delivery were reminiscent of a man esteemed by Methodists everywhere, but particularly at the Wabash camp meeting grounds. Robert had never seen the coming and going of a camp-ground year without hearing mention of William Elbert Munsey's name; he had more than once been witness to the dynamic power of this man who had often prefaced his sermons with the story of his own conversion and ministerial calling. Munsey was converted while in his teens. He had taught school after that, until he became twenty-three years old, at which time he felt the call to the ministry. "I was not sure God wanted me to leave my widowed mother and little sisters and brothers," he had often said, "for they were completely dependent upon me. But I decided to ask my Lord if His calling to me was real, to show me in some powerful way. Shortly thereafter, at a meeting at Rocky Gap near my home, I became so filled with the Holy Spirit that I could neither speak nor move. I was carried from the altar as one dead."

Dr. Munsey had been gone now for almost thirteen years, but he had attained a generalship in the Christian army during his short forty-four years of life, and had in the process served some of the most influential Methodist churches in America. Robert again looked at the speaker and listened; then he turned his eyes away and listened only, for the two men looked nothing alike in stature. Dr. Munsey had been thin and delicate, with small eyes and a fragile face, but the voice of the two men sounded remarkably similar, Robert thought, unless his memory was failing him completely. How much he hoped it was not! How much he hoped Elbert Munsey could be born anew again and again and manifested in a younger body for every new generation!

The present speaker had not the perfection of thought and elocution that Elbert Munsey had used to crown his own mission and faith, but the former was not lacking in effort of delivery. Once during the Civil War years Elbert Munsey had preached a sermon on "Hell and the Lost Soul" at the Wabash camp meetings, and Robert had seen with his own eyes worshiping women tear at their own hair and men rise groaning from their seats to parade the aisles in combat against the graphic realism that God's spokesman had presented for their consideration.

It was that fervor which was now being reached. From all sides men, women, and children pressed in against those under the shed who had gotten seating early. Truly the crowd did number well over three thousand, as Robert had learned from the camp constables, and now all of them seemed to swamp the worship shed like drifting snow. He loved their raptured faces, and as he sat waiting for the final speaker to conclude, the desire was in his heart to go down among them all and to caress each one and simply say, "My brother—my sister."

"And now the hour has come," the speaker concluded. "Has God's Word convinced you that you are blind to pin your hopes upon this wicked world? Christ is the only King whose Kingdom never dies! Live, starting tonight, as if you will be dead tomorrow! And neither, my brother and sister, have any fear of death, for it is the final and absolute freedom! Christ lives!"

With sweat-bathed face and heaving lungs, the speaker relinquished his place to the song leader.

"We will close the service with the singing of 'Shall We Gather at the River,' but before we do I feel it upon my heart to remind you that tonight and tomorrow are all that remain of this year's happy time together. We have no assurance that we will live to see each other again next year. Life is uncertain and death is sure. Tonight may be your last chance to make a decision that presses heavily upon your heart—or perhaps you, the baptized, have fallen from grace and wish to rededicate yourselves anew. The time has come. The time is now."

"Oh, what joyous times, Lord!" Robert said aloud. All the others were already singing, and his colleagues started making their way from the platform to stand together at the head of the aisles. He did not join them, though he should have gone first to his place of exhortation farther down the aisle.

The music drifted out upon the hills and valleys until there was a second chorus: an echo that was sweeter still. How they loved to sing! How joyous and harmonious their God-filled voices!

"Last verse!" the song leader shouted, straining to be heard above the others. "Soon we'll reach the shining river, Soon our pilgrim age will cease; soon our happy hearts will quiver with the melody of peace. / Yes, we'll gather at the river, / the beautiful, the beautiful river, / Gather with the saints at the river / that flows by the throne of God."

A steady stream of penitents from inside and outside the shed wound their way down the straw-lined aisle. There was other movement afoot as well. Robert went about his exhortations, but he noticed that he was not alone. Spirit-filled people all over the shed were exhorting or pleading with uncommitted friends or neighbors. Some families formed a circle of their own, enclosing therein a rebellious father or brother to whom they were pouring out their earnest tears and supplications.

Some started to sing again, but Robert had lost sight of the activity about him as he knelt in the straw beside those who poured forth their doubts of pardon for their sinful lives. "Though your sins be as scarlet…," he repeated as softly as he could above the clamor of victorious voices and soft weeping.

Out of the corners of his eyes, the figure of a young man brushed past him. How familiar that face was! It was the face of a liar and a thief, expert at his trade, one for whom Robert had prayed countless times.

Robert stood up, unbelieving, as, tear-stained, the young man presented himself as a convert. There was a leap in his heart pulsating every fiber of his being as he viewed the newborn Christian. He deserted his role as exhorter for a moment to come to the side of his spirit-son. His arm about the reborn young flesh seemed electric, and so overflowing with joy was he that his lips could not be silenced: "Old Satan's mad and am I glad! He's lost a soul he thought he had!" He repeated the spontaneous rhyme until those about him stared in wonder.

There was no formal cessation of the service; the crowd slowly drifted out into the open fields. Groups seemed to form without conscious plan. Brother could be heard forgiving brother, wife reconciling with husband, father to son. From where had this outpouring of humility come? Robert marveled.

He was alone now. No man or woman, or even a child, seemed any longer to need him or the other camp-ground ministers. The strangest thing was happening. The worshipers stood by themselves in a glorified individual strength, which of itself generated an almost tangible, luminous energy. If it was indeed a spirit -filled awakening, as all evidence indicated, God had surely answered his prayers with overflowing abundance!

In his aloneness, Robert rushed back to the preachers' tent.

"Have the visiting brethren seen the fullness of our blessing? Can they feel the Divine Spirit hovering over us? Why have they not returned to the tent?"

"They have gone, Brother Bob," Tyler Frazier said. "You were alone on the grounds and they did not wish to disturb you with their parting remarks. They said to thank us all for the joy of worshiping with us."

"There's far too much of the Pharisee to be seen in them—"

"If you knew them better, I don't believe you would say that, Brother Bob. They are all good men, and they earnestly seek to guide the whole church in the way they think is the most far-reaching. It is not a responsibility I would wish upon myself or upon you."

"You are young, brother, and I am old, but if we do not watch out the virtue of humbleness will be lost and we will not see God's lovingkindness in all its fullness. We must not move away from this, nor from a just fear of God either. A righteous fear strikes dead the most wanton vainglory."

"I know time has brought change—and will continue to bring more change, but let us pray that it is for the best."

"For the best? Has my sweet Lord brought me through all these years to have me see a frivolous world seeking its own pleasures and becoming the destruction of our age? God forbid! Where are the heavens on earth that disobedient man has built and laid claim to? At Emory and Henry we were taught of Greece and Rome—and Egypt. Where are they now!"

Robert felt the arm of Tyler Frazier about his shoulders and heard his colleague's soft voice. "Brother Bob, each of us can only do the best he can during our own time. All the hopes and prayers of our voices will fade from hearing when new voices replace those tired and worn."

"Do you tell an old man that his time has come and gone, and that he doesn't use the sense the sweet Lord gave him to hear it?"

"Your voice will be heard and loved as long as you can speak, Brother Bob, and I am among those who thank God for it and pray that it may never die."

As the preachers' tent filled, Robert took his leave and walked out upon the open field. The night was hot, but the faintest breeze gave a kiss of welcome relief. The murmur of human voices seemed not to have subsided at all. In the distance, from every direction, low singing permeated the air. Candlelit windows from the cabins and tents gave a faint perimeter of light, and behind the structures, farther back in the trees, still fainter candlelight was visible. The groups had not separated. Their hunger had not been filled and they continued to feed themselves.

"Blessed Lord"—Robert lifted his eyes—"if it is not Thy will that I should ever see this holy place again, my soul is satisfied with what I have witnessed. Blessed be Thy name..."

The night wind gained force and the low rumble of thunder sent candle bearers scurrying back into their cabins and tents. Robert looked into the blackening heavens with a plea upon his lips. "Dear Lord! If the morrow brings rain the crowds will not come and there are so many who are only a step away from Thy fold!"

He stepped into the preachers' tent just long enough to retrieve his sheepskin. He was unnoticed; the other brethren ate and talked heatedly of the fast-changing church doctrines that seemed to be engulfing other denominations as well as their own.

The way to the top of the north hill was first dark and then illuminated brilliantly by the plunging tail of lightning. An angry clap of thunder seemed to shake the very ground beneath his feet, but the rain did not come until his knees had already become numb upon the prayer mat. Large, plunging drops of rain splattered upon his upturned face, and soon the tip of his white beard seemed a gully outlet for the downpour.

He always prayed aloud, but so heavy was the deluge that his words sounded garbled.

"Give us tomorrow filled with sunshine, Dear Lord. Surely it is Thy will that the workers have a good harvest on the last day. In Jesus's name we ask it..."

He had finished. Now he would wait for an answer. The rain slowed a little, but that was just the prelude to another down pouring. He kept his position, though little gullies of water now ran in front and behind him. At first he heard only the trickling water, but again the lightning silhouetted his tilted face and he turned long enough to survey the sod at his very knees being taken away.

Minutes after the rain stopped he leaped to his feet and went running down the hill. His descent was not complete when voices and lantern light sought him out.

"Is it you, Brother Bob?" Reverend Perry's high-pitched tones reached him.

"Brother Bob? It's Tyler Frazier. Call to us. Are you hurt?"

Robert waited until he got nearer the lantern light before he called back. "I'm here! I'm all right. What did you come out in the rain for?"

"What are *you* doing out in the rain?" another, unidentified, shot back lightheartedly.

"That's between my Lord and me," Robert said. He could see nearly all the faces of the smaller group now outlined by lantern light. They were concerned faces, and for that he was grateful. Only a short distance behind his colleagues was row upon row of candlelight, with an occasional lantern being taken up the hill.

Reverend Walker yielded his own light coat, but Robert refused it.

"Take it, Brother Sheffey. A man your age out in this downpour…"

"We were worried about you," Tyler Frazier said a little impatiently. "We were afraid maybe the lightning had—"

"I am much blessed but little harmed."

"There is more mirth in your voice than there would be in mine, had I been out in this storm," Reverend Cobb said.

"Let's get back to the tent," Reverend Wagoner urged. "Look! We're just getting ready to get the second wave of a worse storm. You might as well pack up your things tonight, my brothers. There'll be rain all night and all day tomorrow. It never fails the last week of August or the first week in September. You can watch it every time."

Tyler Frazier conceded that his colleague might be right. "I'm afraid our final day is doomed to failure."

"I would not count on that at all," Robert said, and with sprightly step led the way to the tent.

The morning broke fresh and clean and the sun rays danced playfully among leaves still wet with night rain. Robert had slept uneasily and his body felt drained and his temples throbbed. In spite of this, his head cleared quickly as he stepped from the tent into the fragrant morning air. The whole earth had the smell of having been swept clean, with the aroma of every blooming thing melting together and floating upon the gentle breeze.

He turned from the bath of morning sun coming from the east and looked about him. No family was packing, and though the hour was early he could hear the crunch of wagon and buggy wheels coming from the turnpike.

"Isn't it a beautiful day?" someone called from behind him. Robert turned to recognize members of a Baptist family, buckets in hand and heading down the path to the big spring.

"A glorious day!" he replied with all the benediction that he felt.

They passed on after he had thanked them for coming to the camp meetings. The success of the camp across the years was not to be credited to the Methodists alone, he knew, for every year faithful Baptists, Presbyterians, Disciples of Christ, Brethrens, Pentecostals, and a scattering of Episcopalians swelled the ranks. Even some of the black-hatted believers that he assumed to be Dunkards came in small numbers, and one of his colleagues called his attention to a handful of Jewish merchants from Bluefield, Pulaski, Pearisburg, and Roanoke who attended every year. No worshiper found anything but welcome.

"Oh, my sweet Lord! This is the way it ought to be. This is what Thy blessed world is all about—that we should all come together and acknowledge our brotherhood and drown ourselves in the joy of human fellowship."

"Brother Bob, what in the world are you doing out in the wet grass, talking to yourself? Breakfast is ready and the camp cook says when she has it ready you're never here and the minute she gets her skillets clean you're in the kitchen, wanting something to eat."

Robert took Tyler Frazier's smiling chastisement in good humor. "I will come directly," Robert said. "We'd best keep Aunt Rachel in good humor, or she might desert us next year."

He loved the black face of Rachel Hicks as if she were his own blood. Year after year she had been the faithful camp cook, and he knew that nobody loved the meetings any more than she.

Robert promptly entered the tent, where Rachel served his plate with eggs and hominy. Then she brought him a lone dish of hot applesauce. She always watched after him more devotedly than the others, and his colleagues had joshed him about it.

"Sister Rachel, how many souls will give their lives to the Lord on this last day?" Robert queried.

"All of them that's listenin'."

"Why, that would be most everybody," Robert said. "We can't ever hope for that."

"I didn't say everybody that was hearin'. I said everybody that was listenin'."

When the final day was spent and the last of the penitents had trampled the flattened straw still deeper into the mud and surface water that had invaded the worship shed by night, one hundred and seventy-one converts had "listened," their numbers exceeding the success of any day during the session save the previous one.

By daylight of the next morning pots and pans rattled noisily and balky horses neighed stubbornly at what Robert could guess was a preference for another day in deep grass and clover rather than the confinement of harness. Notwithstanding the reluctance on the part of both people and animals, camp broke, and by midmorning the long wagon train resembled a westward movement through the gap of the Cumberlands.

Robert stood watching, as he did every year, until the grounds were empty and the cabins stood deserted.

"I can hardly wait for the camp meeting to start next year, Brother Sheffey; I'm thinking about it already!" a young mother with babe in arms waved and called to him in passing.

He watched her husband's buggy join the train of horse-drawn vehicles and the young woman's arm slip shyly about her husband's waist.

"Bless you, my children," he said just under his breath, "truly you have stood on the threshold of true happiness...May it always reflect in your faces."

He remembered then that he had not said good-by to all his colleagues and returned to the tent to do so. When only two or three remained, Tyler Frazier asked if he might assist his elder by staying.

"There is nothing to do," Robert thanked him. "You know it is not that I'm needed—the camp constables will leave the grounds in order. Brother Frazier, I'd like for you to go with me on some of my travels. Would you do it sometime?"

Tyler Frazier assented and extended a final handshake.

Robert gathered his things and walked to the meadow gate with the local stable boy whom he had instructed to saddle and fetch Gideon. While he waited, a lone oxcart turned from a poplar grove that he knew had been used as overflow camping area when the regular grounds could accommodate no more. The obviously poor family of more than a half-dozen children, and the stout young mother whose childbearing years looked to have only just begun, were audible with their mirth, while the robust young father continually urged the slow-moving ox to greater speed.

"Get along now, Boaz! It's time we got home and worked as hard as we've worshiped! Get along now."

"Good-by, Brother Sheffey," all passengers seemed to speak out at once. "I said a prayer for you during the meeting… I'll do it again for next year!" the woman called over her shoulder.

"Thank you, sister. That's the most precious favor we can give to each other," he returned.

Gideon pranced with recognition as Robert opened the gate. The animal's hide was slick and shiny. Robert ran his hand over a well-curried hip and said, "You like this wallowing in the clover too much. You've gotten fat and sassy, but I'll unspoil you! We'll be on the road again soon, but in the meantime carry me back to Staffordsville. Eddie will be leaving us soon to go back to his new job and my sweet Lord won't mind if I take a few days' rest."

CHAPTER XVII

In the late fall of 1890 Robert learned from numerous colleagues returning from the Holston annual conference of the mounting sentiment against the historic camp-ground type of evangelism.

"What is being said?" he would inquire time and again, always receiving essentially the same answer.

"Brother Bob, the majority feeling is one that our very best thinkers believe in and have convinced us that John Wesley himself held dear. It is this: Wesley loved the early open-air meetings, but he believed that they were lastingly effective only when the church and its ministry were able to provide an intellectual base to go along with the emotional experience. Many of those who find precious the Lord's work earnestly believe that we have forsaken one goal in the overzealous pursuit of the other. It will surprise you to know that many of our lay people feel this too. To put it another way, what is the good of flooding our altar with those caught in the heat of religious emotion if we have not prepared them with adequate background to make their experience completely meaningful and long lasting?"

To each separate answer, framed merely in a different set of words, Robert could but stare, dumbfounded and unbelieving. How under God's heaven was it possible to fill His divine mission on earth any better than to send converts flocking to the altar by any means? That was the important thing! After that, visitation of the Holy Spirit upon the true convert would be eternally sustaining. The only precaution needed was the ascertaining of the genuineness of the conversion. It seemed he had spent half his lifetime in the straw upon his knees with converts, stressing repeatedly that very fact. Such was not to say one could not fall from grace, but in so doing the Christian would of his own evil, renounce the presence of the Holy Spirit. But even in the most rebellious denial, the true conversion could not be negated. The worst fallen Christian would need an obedient return to grace, and the watch care of the Holy Spirit, but his original conversion could not be held in doubt by even the most liberal thinker in Methodism.

As Robert pursued the matter further he had little doubt that the die was cast. As a matter of fact he found that to be true a long time ago in other sections, and what he was feeling in his own area was past history in many others. Two positive factors yet remained: no absolute church moratorium existed against the camp meetings, and, second, in his beloved domain there was still strong public interest. But this was temporary comfort, and he knew it. The continued life of the camp meeting would depend on continued support of all the circuit-appointed ministers. The church would never forbid the camp a meeting, of that he was sure. But such knowledge seemed an inadequate consolation. As the church thought, so would it move; as its architects planned, so would the structure be determined.

Nevertheless the summer of 1891 came, presenting a hot and dry August by which to worship along the waters of Wabash branch. In spite of Robert's fevered efforts, the number of participants was not impressive, but the religious fervor was high and the converts numerous. Even Lady Nick returned again to present him with the customary red flower by which to mock him. The small number of participating ministers seemed to foreshadow darker days ahead. But Robert pushed the knowledge from his mind and rode off after the camp meeting closed, and without rest, in the pursuit of the "hold outs" who had left camp unconverted.

"I'm going to get them while they're still warm!" Robert called a farewell to Tyler Frazier. "You go home and rest a while and I'll come and get you. You young fellows wear out easily. You should have had your training on the same trails some of us old clodhoppers did!"

He continued the pursuit of the "hold outs" throughout the fall, and on several trips Tyler Frazier rode by his side. He loved this dedicated man who was by twenty-five years his junior, and he loved

Frazier's camp-ground heritage even more. Tyler Frazier had first come to the Wabash camp ground in 1861 at the age of sixteen to profit by the selling of apples, melons, and candy to the great influx of people. His profit turned out to be more than he bargained for, when the spirit of the camp meeting possessed him and he was truly born again. With the seed of that rebirth, his life was henceforth dedicated to the ministry and service to the Holston conference, under which he served tirelessly and obediently.

"Brother Tyler, it gives my soul great comfort to know that a man like you follows in my footsteps as I grow old," Robert often said as they rode along together, and particularly when he remembered the younger man's story.

Robert's seventy-second birthday came and passed, and by late summer widespread interest in another camp session seemed woefully lacking. A few of the people he was sure could be counted upon to launch another camp meeting session hedged in the face of specific responsibilities and duties. He hid his heavy heart as best he could, but sometimes the flippant excuses of some hoped-for volunteers rang with hollowness when they would say, "Times are changing," or, more absurdly still, "I believe people are outgrowing that sort of carrying on."

Only slightly undaunted, he prepared to ride off the first week in August to start his annual appeals.

"Robert, please stay home this year. You are past seventy-two years old and you have no business—"

"I have no business, but the sweet Lord has business," he interrupted Eliza sharply.

"But, Robert, there are younger men who can do the distant riding," Eliza pleaded.

"Do not count too heavily on the younger men, Eliza. Some of them have been swayed from the true faith, and they seek to do the church more harm than good. I'm puzzled to know where they are learning some of the things they espouse without shame."

"But the world has changed so much since we were young, dear husband. The great war is twenty-five years past and even I can see dimly the new face our country is beginning to wear."

"It isn't splendor of a good kind you are seeing, Eliza. What you see is the germ of our destruction."

"Our destruction? You talk to me of riddles—"

"Yes, our destruction! You are seeing born the first fruits of our disobedience when we try to educate the head before the heart. The time will come when man will let the imaginations of his mind fly so free that he no longer holds dear any truth. Then he will have no place of refuge and no star to set his sights by."

"But, Robert, don't you think we must believe that as the people come out of the mountains and go to school and learn more they will uplift their country in the uplifting of themselves—perhaps even to a higher justice and love among men than we have ever known?"

"There will never be earthly justice. There is no such thing. Only God will work justice. His justice is for this world as well as the next, but it can't work if we hide it under a barrel in preference to some modernity that will be the destruction of ages to come. No, dear wife, we will not find our souls' best love by floating log like down a flood-swollen, raging stream. When we find ourselves there, reaching vainly for the solid banks to save ourselves, it will be too late; the current will be too swift and the logs we reach for will be moving just as swiftly as our own—not in the least able to deliver us to safe and dry ground."

Over Eliza's continued protests, he rode off at the coming of dawn. "Gideon, old friend, the sweet Lord has let us see another August, and I'm thankful for that, but as the sun shines over my shoulder like a great light I'm thankful even more that I have been shown a whole lot more about life than I can see on this earth."

He continued riding west and spent the first night of his journey with Julia Bogle at the "preacher's house" in the Mount Zion community of Bland County. Notwithstanding a sumptuous meal, his hostess and her family accused him of melancholy, and he could not deny it.

He went to his room early that night, for, although he sensed the disappointment of Mrs. Bogle and her children, he wanted to spend long hours in prayer.

At breakfast he was still tired, but something in his face brought a smile to those about him. Julia Bogle started to talk to him, but curtailed her words.

He took a few bites and looked across the table at her. "Why did you stop short with your words, sister?" he asked. "I didn't know how to say exactly what I wanted to say, but I guess it boils down to the hope that my children will find God's grace as you have found it."

He lifted his eyes from his plate and knew instinctively that her question had been prompted by his long night of prayer. "Sister Bogle—and children. God's grace hovers free for the taking above every man's head. But because it's there doesn't mean that every man can accept it. The man who would, must first prepare a container for it, and because there is only one kind: that container is each of *you*, prepared in a special way. The preparation begins by our self-examination—when we first realize that within the soul God has given us is not only the room and inclination to do the highest calling of His kingdom but the greatest evil as well. Acknowledging that, we have begun to shape the container."

His little unplanned sermon continued until, realizing the lateness of the hour, he hurriedly dispatched Julia Bogie's son, John, to fetch Gideon from the field and saddle him.

Presently he arose from the table, thanked his hostess, and gathered his prayer mat and saddlebags about him. The young man was unduly long in returning to the house, and when he did so, Gideon did not follow, bridled and saddled, behind him.

"The animal will not let me catch him;" the boy related. "He is frisky and playful and runs from me when I get near. The field is too big for me to corner him."

Robert dropped his sheepskin to the floor beside the dining room table, knelt, and called out his petition in low tones: "Blessed Lord, Thy servant must be on his way for the furtherance of Thy kingdom. The boy cannot catch the horse to saddle him and the hour grows late. Rest Thy hand upon this beast of Thy creation and still him."

Robert stood as quickly as his brittle bones would allow and faced the incredulous stares that reflected also some of the light his own face mirrored when he felt as close to his maker as he did at this moment.

"Go now, son, you will catch the animal without difficulty."

In little time Robert mounted his animal, affixed his saddle-bags, positioned his sheepskin upon the saddle, and rode away.

His intent was to cover first the entire community surrounding Mount Zion church—with the primary importance of boosting attendance at the Wabash camp ground—before it was necessary to ride on for a regular appointment at Wessendonck church, farther to the northwest.

In his haste, he crisscrossed Walker's Creek, visiting first a house and then a cabin until his very head seemed to be swimming. Perhaps Eliza had been right. Perhaps his stamina was not equal to the task, for as yet the whole territory had barely been touched.

He worked his way along the creek until the final house, that of Tom Whittaker had been reached and solicited. It was nearly dark then, and he hurried Gideon so that they might re-cross the creek before all vision was obscured.

At the west bank of the stream, where the water was shallowest and the green slime made the creek bed more treacherous, Gideon lost his footing momentarily and fell to his knees. In a split second Robert found himself pitched from the saddle, sliding awkwardly down Gideon's neck. Quickly his head slammed against the hardness of creek rock. Half conscious, he still held on to Gideon's bridle with one hand, and the animal continued moving out of the shallow water. Having reached a place well up the dry bank, Robert felt his legs fail, and shortly all his senses deserted him.

When he regained consciousness two men and several boys were bent over him, wiping the blood and creek slime from his face.

"You sure got a bargain in that horse," one of the men said. "I believe he's got some watchdog blood in him the way he stood over you with his mournful whinnying."

Robert tried to speak, finally responding by a painful nod of the head.

"We don't think you've broke any limbs, Brother Sheffey. Can you walk?" the second adult asked.

Robert mumbled that he thought he could. He tried, with some help, and found that he could not keep his balance. At last he asked those present to deliver him to the home of Aurelius Vest, who lived nearby.

"Aurelius will have some kind of remedy to make my head stop hurting," he said, blotting at the small trickle of blood above his left ear. He still did not feel that he could mount his horse, and even after assistance could not maintain his balance upon the animal's back. One of the boys offered to get his father's buggy.

Somewhere along the route blackness overcame him again, and when he awoke for the second time he lay upon a bed in the house of Aurelius Vest.

"Brother Sheffey, can you hear me?" Aurelius bent low over his friend. Robert nodded, and the expression on the kindly face changed from a frown into its normally bright luminescence. In minutes Robert raised himself and sat on the side of the bed.

"You'd better not get up for a while," Aurelius said gently.

"You are always good to me, Aurelius," Robert declared, looking into the eyes of the other.

The wife of his host cleaned his wound, and Aurelius soothed the bruise with ointment. After an hour Robert considered himself cured and attempted to walk from his bed to the kitchen, but his feet would not go where he directed them. How could any man walk in a room that moved around?

Never could he remember a better night of sleep, nor of sleeping until midmorning. His breakfast was taken slowly, and shortly after he finished Dr. Blackburn, who had sat before him several times at the Mount Zion church, made his way to Robert's chair and examined his head.

For all of the good doctor's gibberish, Robert could only surmise that his fall had shaken up his brains a little, and for such a minor occurrence being confined to bed seemed an unnecessarily harsh remedy.

He obliged with the obedience of a child, however, and Mrs. Vest put him into a bed where the crisp white linen smelled of captured sunshine and was crowned with a starch stiff white counterpane.

A neighbor was dispatched to tell Eliza of his incapacitation and that he would soon be home. In a matter of hours he felt no pain, but he still could not keep his balance.

Aurelius Vest, a farmer, carpenter, and country undertaker by trade, ceased his work often during the day to look in and offer comfort to his elder.

"Now, Aurelius, you go back to your casket making and don't worry about me. One of these days I'll want one of your best walnut coffins, but the time is not yet," Robert would say.

Before the week was out, Robert decided to go home. Dr. Blackburn agreed to such an arrangement only if somebody took his patient by buggy. Robert needed nobody to remind him that he couldn't sit upon a horse.

He departed the home of Aurelius Vest impatiently, for there was yet work to be done and the final week in August crept ever closer.

"You have been kind to the Lord's servant," Robert said to both his host and hostess, "but it is good that I can be leaving. Much is to be done. I want to tell you this before I go—if I'm ever sick again I hope it will be God's plan that I may do my suffering in your house."

Aurelius seemed so overcome with such a humble benediction that he pledged to Robert the watch care of himself, his home, and his prayers.

"It is not every man who can feel uplifted by caring for God's fallen. God bless you for your Christian heart, Brother Aurelius."

Eliza nursed him like a baby and he was ashamed that he should require it or even allow it. As the last of August drew near he wept at times that he could not be about his work, but Eliza kept referring to the "others" who were out in his stead. When he questioned her as to their names she could never remember, claiming that those ministers who had never been to the Sheffey house weren't in her mind identifiable.

One morning he asked his wife to assist him in his walking practice, for the time was near when he would need to stand upon the platform at Wabash and walk the straw-covered aisles in his exhortations. That same afternoon Tyler Frazier sat before him and told him that the Wabash camp meeting was being canceled. For the first time in fifty-six years candlelight would not flicker through the trees of the tent area at night and the sprawling worship shed would stand empty and desolate. All his practice had been in vain. There would be no one to exhort, and he need not have worried about kneeling, nor the difficulty of rising again: there would be no one so weighted and ashamed of his sins that Robert would need to kneel likewise, offering guidance and comfort. Such activities were unnecessary in a shed empty of sweating, breathing, repentant humanity.

Through bitter tears he listened to an explanation from Tyler Frazier as to why the campground committee had no choice but to call off the event. Robert had heard the reasons before, and he did not really care to hear them again. In his heart was the belief that he could have helped to turn the tide.

"As faithful as you are, Brother Bob, nothing would have been changed," Tyler Frazier said. "You are forgetting that our best years have involved the cooperation of dozens of ministers and scores of churches, not to mention the appearance of some of our most eminent divines who are themselves large crowd gatherers. Brother Bob, as much as I love you, you are wrong to think this vast undertaking can possibly rest on the effort of one man, no matter how dedicated. And last, do not forget the people. Where is the great out pouring of their interest that we have seen dwindling for two years?"

Robert could not ride his horse well until after Thanksgiving of that year, but he lost no time in being about his business and paying special calls of thanks on those who had helped him during his period of convalescence. From such an errand, and a still earlier preaching service at Bethany church in Bland County, he was returning toward Staffordsville. The late afternoon was exceedingly chill with a stiff wind, but the strongest inclination pressed him to stop at the Wabash camp grounds. The sorrow caused him by the camp's idleness the summer just past had not left him, but he could now accept it as fact. When he dismounted and wandered about the vacant cabins, seeing firsthand a splintered and vandalized rostrum lying in the mud on top of the upturned mourners' bench, a feeling of utter desolation overcame him. Wind whist led through holes in the roof shingles of the shed. They were small holes—either evidence of rock-throwing boys or just the faintest hint of deterioration.

The singing wind seemed to mesmerize him as he walked up, then down the dirt aisles. A stool of wheat sprouts grew wild almost in the center of the aisle. Perhaps it has seeded and reseeded itself since the last straw was put in the aisle, he thought.

Finally he wrestled the mourners' bench from the mud and sat it upright. With what dry straw there was to be found, he brushed the dust and mud from the crude furniture and sat upon it. The faces of those who had sat there over the past years came to him with starling clarity, and not alone the most recent ones. Those of twenty years' duration looked to him from out of the past, the depth of their convictions still showing hauntingly in their remembered countenances.

It was all becoming too real. He jumped from his seat and, tidying up, sat the battered rostrum back in place and sang to forms that shone with faintest outline against the pole-back seats. He reached the second chorus of "Blessed Be the Name of the Lord" before a broad-shouldered intruder of middle years glided effortlessly into one of the slab pews, appearing a great deal more real than those who Robert knew were only creations of his own reverie.

Robert stopped, but the visitor urged him to go on.

"These are only the foolish imaginations of an old man," Robert said inadequately.

"I was enjoying the singing, and I like the atmosphere, Brother Sheffey. If you are so inclined, preach or sing. I will be your appreciative audience."

"You call my name but I know not yours?"

"You will when I get closer. We've worked together too long for you to forget."

Robert met his visitor halfway and called out his name joyously. "Brother Bailey! Ed! My eyesight fails me, but my happy heart makes up for it. What brings you here?"

"I'm the conference-appointed minister for the Staffordsville charge now. After the fall assignments I knew I was coming, and

I'm on my way now to spend a few days with my predecessor. He'll introduce me around, and I'll count on you likewise."

"I'll do it. And thank God you've come."

"Brother Bob, I have not made this place my first stop without purpose. I didn't see you or your horse until I moved under the shed, but if I make my confession complete I wanted to do just what you're doing: to stand here and feel the spirit of victorious souls about me. This camp ground has been too great a witness to fall into ruin. If I must do it myself, I want it flooded with shouts and songs of praise when summer comes."

Robert was so overcome that he could not speak, and before his eyes spilled over he was holding fast the younger man in fraternal embrace.

Composed, Robert thought swiftly ahead. "It is the thing I have dreamed of. I will ride at your side, or alone, to put candlelight back at the altar again."

"I'll need you. We will have little help, but we'll have little opposition also. We are free to exercise our own consciences in this matter. Now let us see how the consciences of those in our territory are leaning."

The following summer, in 1893, candlelight flickered at some of the cabin windows but the camping population was small and the travelers from distant places almost nonexistent. Lady Nick was not among the missing, however—neither was she among a small handful of converts. Had not the influx of larger local crowds swelled the Saturday and Sunday services, the most optimistic of the small band of organizers could only have conceded failure of the whole endeavor.

"Never you fear, Brother Bob," Ed Bailey said. "We'll be cocked and ready next year."

"I've got a few ideas of my own to boost attendance then," Tyler Frazier added.

Robert felt that they need not encourage him at all. There was no need of it. Had there been only twelve people in attendance and one convert, to him it would have been a new beginning.

Other than taking care of his regular itinerary, Robert did not resume the more distant riding of former years until the coming spring. Even then, figuratively speaking, he had Eliza to fight. He could ride well now, and only when he became exhausted did the old problem of imbalance come back to plague him.

"Robert, it'll only take one more fall like you had before and I'll be spending my days and nights nursing you. I've got better things to do than that!" Eliza tried to sound harsh, but he knew her too well and for too long. Further, she made the fatal mistake of coming to him with a tender hand upon his shoulder as she scolded him.

"Now, Eliza—" he would say.

"Don't 'now, Eliza' me! You've got no business going. And we're not starving to death like we once were. Haven't you seen Eddie's letters lately? He sends us a check almost every time he writes. We've got enough to live on, dear husband."

"That part never did worry me, Eliza. It doesn't now."

The conversation was one repeated several times that summer, but, unfailingly, off he would ride.

He saw the fruits of his labors when the camp-ground season came around again. He had called upon churches, preachers, and people, both individually and collectively. Everywhere he had gone throughout the summer he had preached two themes: hold fast to Christ's love, for only in that way will you possess the strength to live life; second, while clinging to this love make it your highest aim to find God's purpose for you as an individual.

Having preached this, he would add that no better place on earth could be found to start this new philosophy than at the camp grounds. "If you have lived a hundred years and have not had a genuine encounter with the living God, then you have not lived at all," he'd add and ride away to any other place that provided listeners.

They had listened. To Tyler Frazier and Ed Bailey and others they had listened. Handbills had been sent out and notices posted. Advertisements were placed in newspapers. August of 1894 looked amazingly like the Wabash of an earlier era. Lady Nick was there, and two eminent divines perched upon the speakers' platform and confessed proudly their secret love for the humble Christianity of the camp ground.

Again Eddie had come home to worship with his family at the camp ground. He made clear to his father that he had come for another reason also. "Father, you are seventy-four years old, and it is foolish for you to be riding hundreds of miles alone. I want you and Mother to come back to Lynchburg with me to live. I can care for you there—there's so little I can do here."

Robert scoffed at the idea and sent his son home. Never had he felt better or happier. This year even the cold of winter would not deter him in his travels; he'd decided about that, Lord willing, months ago.

Eliza went into frenzy when he left on a December day that had seen her wash water freeze solid upon the ground as soon as she emptied it out.

"Don't you fret, Eliza, I'm just going to work along the mountain at Mechanicsburg. Some of the people there have written me—they get so lonesome when they can't get out to church and have the Bible read—the old ones especially. Don't you worry now—we'll be a blessing to each other."

The visits along the mountain range to the south of Mechanicsburg, some twenty miles from Staffordsville, were extended only to the known shut-ins, but each family continued to send him farther and farther west to visit some relative or personal friend who was in need of encouragement or visitation. He obliged joyfully, and often he would find himself doubling back to the same house to bring needed food to enable a family to survive the winter.

"Gideon, there is no *little* task for the Lord. Sometimes the smallest of them is the great link in some plan of our divine Maker."

Onward he traveled to Point Pleasant, and westward to Bland. Snow peppered down after he left the home of an old man who had lost a leg, yet farther still he rode.

He met a man walking and inquired of his destination. "I'm hunting a job. Going down toward the creek at the sawmill; maybe they'll hire me. If they don't, we may plumb starve to death this winter."

Robert looked closely at the young man, who hardly had enough clothes on his body to ward off the snow. While they talked the pedestrian kicked playfully at the road gravel. Robert saw that he had well-worn shoes and no socks at all.

"You've got no socks on, man? You'll freeze your toes off without socks!" Robert exclaimed.

"Ain't got none," the other said.

"Then you shall have mine."

"My toes might as well be froze as yours."

"The sweet Lord will provide my needs," Robert said and dismounted to remove his shoes so that the promised socks could be relinquished.

He did not feel numbness in his feet until he was a mile off from the home of Newton Mustard. The snow was still falling lightly.

"The snow will not stop us, Gideon, but we will impose on Brother Mustard for a little soup, and if he notices our condition we will not refuse a pair of his socks."

Newton Mustard did not answer the knock upon the door, but his wife did, and exclaimed, "Why, Brother Sheffey, I was just thinking about you this morning! I finished knitting you a pair of socks before the snow started and I was just wondering how I was going to get them to you!"

He put the love gift in his pocket and later slipped the socks upon his feet while his hostess prepared his soup in her kitchen. When she returned he sat upon the floor near the hearth.

"Newton is breaking open a new haystack for the animals. He says we might get two feet of this white powder—why, Brother Sheffey, why are you sitting on the floor? Sit in the rocking chair there by the fire. I thought I'd invited you to."

"You did," he said, taking the soup and spoon from her always-busy hands.

"Then why don't you sit there?" she insisted. "My cushion ought to be a great deal softer than the floor or hearthstone!"

He sipped at his soup and leaned his back against the fireplace wall. Her eyes still questioned him. "I have left the rocking chair for Jesus," he said.

The woman diverted her glance from him and when, with his toe, he set the rocking chair to oscillating back and forth, her face began to flush.

"I don't really mean I expected our blessed Christ to sit in the rocking chair, but I should be most happy if He would. No, I was just thinking that I would like to imagine Him there, resting here with us. To my knowledge, snow is not mentioned in the blessed Book but six or seven times, and it is hard for me to picture our Jesus plodding in it. We always think of Him in sandals walking in the sands and soil of the east, or along the blue seas of Galilee."

The woman still looked at him strangely, but the tautness of surprise had left her and her brown eyes were soft and receptive.

"I should like very much sometime to see my Jesus come in out of the snow and be able myself to brush His garments clean. I'd like then to watch until the heat of the fire steamed the moisture from Him as now it is doing to me. It is not hard for me to picture Him setting there rocking…resting from his labor…being one of us… smiling down on us."

The fire had made him warm, and he asked his hostess if he might lie down on the floor and sleep for a little while.

"Eliza says I am getting like a little baby, and I guess she's right. It's hard for me to get through a hard day with only the sleep the night has provided. You let me be, now—right here on the floor. When Brother Newton gets back we'll have a family prayer."

The letter that sent Eliza into the fury of a mother hen whose eggs had been stolen arrived in Staffordsville only two days after his return.

"Is it true?" Eliza demanded.

"I don't know *what* is true until you have told me about it, dear Eliza. What is it you ask?"

Eliza continued reading until, with a disapproving sniff, she cast the letter aside.

"This man is writing me with practically a demand to keep you at home during the winter months for your own sake. He says if you keep going around in the cold and snow we'll all find you along some mountain road, a frozen-to-death corpse."

"I wonder why the good brother should be concerned about me."

"I'll tell you why," Eliza fumed. "The man writing this letter said that you stopped at his home in Hicksville one night and that you were so frozen that he and his son had to lift you off your horse. Is he exaggerating?"

"No, he's telling you the truth. Bless their sweet life—they let me sleep there for the night and gave me fried mush for breakfast. I rode over that way after I left Brother Newton Mustard's house..."

"Robert, what am I going to do with you! Now strangers are writing me to keep you from killing yourself—they love you and don't want you hurt. Can't you see that?"

When the weekend passed and the bulk of the snow had cleared, he was ready to strike out again. He avoided Eliza, feeling as guilty as a sneaky urchin pilfering his mother's sweets. He left his wife a note and crept out the front door. When he reached the barn Gideon was gone. His alarm changed to contemplation and from contemplation to sadness. It was evident what had been done to him.

He went back into the house by the kitchen door this time. Eliza was already crying but his own tears did not flow until he sat in his chair and leafed clumsily through his table Bible. Eliza became silent after a while.

"Gideon is at Mr. Woodyard's. It was the best place I could think of until spring. Mr. Woodyard loves that animal like you do—he'll be well cared for. The neighbors will look after us and we'll make arrangements to have a boy with a buggy take you around your itinerary."

Robert did not lift his head, but out of the corners of his eyes he saw his wife wipe her face with her apron and disappear around the door.

Gideon was as slick and fat as a well-wintered bear when spring came, and to keep peace with Eliza he took only short trips during early summer. Always he left in early dawn and came home by nightfall. He visited Eggleston, and Pembroke; Little Creek and

White Gate, among other nearby villages. Whenever he ran out of Methodists to minister unto (or simply commiserate with) he would share his time and thoughts with Presbyterians, Baptists, Pentecostals, or the non-religious. "I love Baptists," he would say in an unplanned display of humor.

"I've lodged with a lot of Baptists and once, under a tree, I was talking with my sweet Lord and a dear Baptist brother saved me from a vicious dog. I told the brother I'd always remember that if Baptists were good for nothing else, they were good for keeping the dogs off Methodists so they could shout!"

The first week of August brought a restlessness that now came as regularly as this rising sun. "Bringing in the sheaves, my brother, bringing in God's harvest. That's what we are doing," Robert defined their solicitations during the weeks before camp meetings began. Planned for the following year of 1896 was a full five-day meeting as in the old times. Again, for this year, they would content themselves with the four days of Friday, Saturday, Sunday and Monday.

Robert's compromise with Eliza was that he ride alone no farther west than Tazewell County, and the northern, eastern, and southern limits of his missionary work were to be Mercer County, West Virginia; Craig County; and Carroll County, respectively.

"Gideon, no matter how old a woman gets she doesn't really mellow much. When I get to heaven I'm going to ask my sweet Lord why in His great plan of nature the heads of all the good sisters are shrunk last. It happens long after their bodies begin to wither, Gideon. Long after."

There was no way of condemning Eliza, singly, for the prohibitions and compromises. All his brothers of the cloth that he knew about had deserted him altogether and sided with his wife. Such a sorry state of affairs only underlined more fully the deterioration of the world and mankind's untrustworthiness. The Disciples only accomplished as much as they did by sticking together, and one Judas was one too many for any era.

Robert traveled his limited territory and covered it better than perhaps ever before. He found the district circuit ministers cooperative if unenthusiastic. Often they not only gave him the time for his announcement but asked him to pray or give a short exhortation. Between villages and churches he would visit as many homes as possible to spread the word.

The last week before the camp meeting was spent in the western-most territory. No people were closer to his heart than those in Tazewell. His final day in the area, before he had to rush back to Wabash, he spent with the worshipers of the North Tazewell Methodist church. His heart was happier than it had ever been. His nearly concluded work seemed like the great climax of a divine commission with which his God was pleased. The night's rest had been good, and he had shared the table of the Gussabus family whom he had loved for so long.

He came into the church expecting to hear the vibrant young minister he had met just the day before—a fine young man, Robert felt right off, so impressive, in fact, that Robert had had the spontaneous feeling of having come upon a modern -day St. Paul.

The same young minister, however, deferred to "an old soldier of the cross," and Robert found himself standing in a pulpit he had never expected to be in again (though it had been his pleasure many times during earlier years).

The congregation listened patiently as Robert told them from what heritage they had sprung and asked them to consider prayerfully where they were going.

In closing, he said, "Each year you seem to get a little further away from me, though I know the sweet Lord is not stretching the land. We will pray together once more, for we may never meet again in this world." A quickly muffled sniff reached his ears, and he looked up sharply. "Oh, no, we will not be unhappy. Never in all of the life my sweet Lord has given me have I been so blessed and joyous."

He asked the resident minister if a special song that he liked could be sung, and it was done.

Finally the prayer he had promised them emerged from his throat with great effort: "Oh Lord, when we come to die, grant that we may die shouting; and when soul and body are separated, may a covey of angels escort our blood-washed spirits to the skies where we may sweep through the Celestial Gates into the City of God. There we can dip our wings in the crystal waters of the Sea of Glory and then perch upon the Tree of Life and shout and sing evermore. Make us *then*, a sea of tree molasses, and a fritter-cake tree to grow right up through the middle. Send an angel up to shake the fritters down, give us a golden fork, and let us dip in and live forever."

No stops were to be made between Tazewell and Staffordsville. There was no time. One day stood in reserve until the camp meetings started, and that day could best be used in making advance preparations. Leaving Tazewell on Tuesday morning, Robert turned Gideon eastward down the Clearfork valley, the most direct route back to Staffordsville.

By midday Rocky Gap remained but a short way in the distance. "Gideon, I don't know about you, but I'm hungry. If it suits your fancy, we'll just stop and share the Lord's bounty on the table of Dr. Bishop."

Dr. William Bishop was more than a friend; Robert had long thought of him as almost a coworker. The two men were near the same age, Dr. Bishop being Robert's junior by four years. Sometimes in brotherly jest Robert would refer to his friend as "Dr. Moses," for the good doctor looked in physical appearance as Robert envisioned Moses might have appeared, plodding onward toward the Promised Land. Dr. Bishop wore a long white beard and let his silver hair grow long until it swept over his ears and neck with the symmetry of a turkey's wing. His eyes were steel-gray and clear, with a sharpness almost piercing to the onlooker—in the opinions of some, an expression of angelic sadness. He was a tall man but not big boned for his height, except for a large head and prominent nose.

The man was more than a doctor. He was a good farmer and a shrewd politician, with time left over to serve his fellow man. He was the founder of Bishop's Chapel Methodist church, where Robert had often preached. Robert, in brotherly jest, had often accused the good doctor of well-hidden aspirations for the ministry, but the accusation was never confirmed nor denied. Still, William Bishop had done his share of missionary work and doubly blessed it with his gift of healing.

Robert tied Gideon at the barn gate of the spacious frame home and was admitted by Dr. James J. Bishop, son of the elder Bishop by a second marriage.

"Tell your father I have not come with more paupers at my heel, Jimmy John; I only want a little piece of bread with honey on it and some milk if he can spare it."

"You're always welcome to that, and you know it without asking. As you can guess by my being here, Father is not well and he will not be able to sit at the table with us. I'm taking care of both our patients for the time being."

Robert went to the elder doctor's bedside and took his wrinkled hand and held it. Naomi Bishop sat beside her husband too while Robert admonished his friend to be out of his bed by the next day to attend the camp meeting at Wabash.

"I'll be blessed if I can walk to the barn by this time next week," William Bishop said with a weak smile.

"You're looking in good health, Brother Sheffey," Naomi Bishop said.

"Pshaw," William Bishop said. "He looks as withered as I am, and I could plant pole beans in the lines of his face. We're both two old nags too worn out to work and just don't have sense enough to know it yet!"

When Mrs. Bishop left them to start the meal Robert told of his experiences in Tazewell. Rather than eating at the table and leaving his ailing friend alone, Robert asked to be served where he sat, so the conversation being enjoyed could continue.

The two men talked on until Robert was aware of considerable time having passed by the coming and going of patients and the repeated striking of the grandfather clock in the parlor. Now it would be long after night before Gideon delivered him to Staffordsville.

"You have stayed too late." William Bishop guessed aloud at Robert's thoughts.

"I can still get home in time. I'd have missed a great blessing if we had not talked of our days together. I hope it's brought as much joy to your heart as it has to mine—and wisdom too. There is something to be learned of affliction of the body and the spirit, would you not agree? What is the one message that has come to you from out of the midst of it all?"

"Today of all days I'm not in the proper shape to philosophize. I'm not sure from *my* viewpoint I've gotten a clear-cut message. I know you want a better-defined answer than that. Maybe I could sum it up by saying that I have seen more than my share of human affliction. I suppose if every man didn't have his burden we wouldn't all be in the pond together. That would be bad. We all need to be in the same boat. If too many of us were on safe dry ground there would be no concern for the others. Human hopes and troubles are the things which nail us together and give us a common goal and bond."

Naomi Bishop went to the barn for Gideon, with Robert trailing behind her. His horse gnawed against his bridle bit as if the sweet taste of corn still played upon his lips, and Robert commanded the animal to stand still for mounting. Routinely he grasped the saddle horn, placed his fool in the stirrup, and swung upward. The pain struck him at the midpoint of mounting, and he called out with a little shriek before releasing his grip and falling to the ground. The feeling was one of having a knife plunged into his belly. He had fallen on his side, but he straightened a leg and repositioned his body until he lay flat on his back. His hand searched for the area of pain, and instead of finding a hole in his belly he felt a protrusion of soft tissue in the lower abdomen.

Naomi Bishop instructed him to lie still and he waited in no severe pain until the younger Dr. Bishop knelt at his side.

Robert had already figured out his difficulty as he had lain there and pushed his own intestines back into his body. Dr. Bishop confirmed the fact of his rupture.

Presently he was on a day bed in the same room with William Bishop.

"Now you won't be going to any camp meeting, preaching, marrying, or anything else," William Bishop said—with not enough sympathy in his voice, Robert thought.

"A little rupture is not so bad, you can live with it. You're just like too many people, Robert; you don't have enough respect for the infirmities of the body. You have pulled yourself into that saddle thousands of times and this time Robert Sheffey's body just said to Robert Sheffey, 'I'm not going to do it anymore.' Now, we're *two* old nags down and out, right here in the same stall!"

Robert was not in pain to any degree but tears almost came to his eyes anyway. There was almost mirth in the voice of his old friend at this unexpected misfortune, and for a moment Robert vowed not even to talk to William Bishop.

"Oh, Robert! Can't you see the lesson of it all? We both think we're so indispensable and that nothing should stop *our* plans, *our* work, and *our* particular destiny. The world will not miss us one jot nor tittle if we never get out of these beds. We are taught in our arrogance that we are just as subject to human frailties as any man."

And now it was insult to injury, Robert thought, but the idea lingered until it resounded with a most penetrating and profound truth.

He raised up on his elbows defiantly and felt a slight pain, which he tried to conceal. "I must leave in the morning," he said. "I have to be at the camp ground no later than the first day."

"You will lie on your back until my son goes to Bluefield on Saturday to get medicines. He'll measure your rupture and purchase a truss which will fit correctly. After that, I'd advise that you go to Richmond or some other medical center and have surgery to repair your wound permanently. That's being done a lot nowadays, but too few people are taking advantage of these new developments."

"Why can't we send one of the farmhands to Bluefield in the morning?" Robert inquired.

"If you don't get the right kind of truss you might as well have none at all. Besides, that same farmhand can be better used by sending him to the post office. That way, word can be sent to your wife by the various mail carriers. We'll let her tell your congregation that you will be resting during the camp-ground sessions this year."

Now the tears did flow, but Robert kept them silent and his face to the wall.

The truss felt like a miniature set of horse harness, but the soft kidney-shaped pad held his abdomen firm and, consequently, the mass of intestines remained securely in place.

Riding was not as uncomfortable as he'd supposed it would be, but the unfamiliar harness felt strange as he moved along on Gideon. What a bothersome catastrophe it was! No preacher he knew had such a malady. Ruptures were the disorder of men accustomed to hard physical labor, and not the least uncommon. But there was another way to look at his misfortune: wasn't he in a better position to sympathize with those who had similar ailments or worse? Then too, he felt humbled by the experience—and wiser.

He continued to ponder his state and to ask God to use it in some positive way.

Following the adamant instructions of the Drs. Bishop, he rode only a short distance on this day. The younger Dr. Bishop had returned from Bluefield with the truss too late in the night to start for home on Saturday, so he had left after breakfast on a beautifully warm and clear Sunday and now found himself almost halfway home. Lodging with one or two of the families he had in mind was not possible when he discovered that they had deserted home and barn to go to the camp meetings, but he soon found friendly people who knew him—though he did not know them—and offered him a bed for the night.

Long before dawn abdominal pain like a toothache surged through his body. Maybe he had ridden more than halfway—maybe he had ridden too far and strained his tender muscles.

He asked permission to rest the day, and kept his hostess busy carrying hot cloths to his room, where he bathed the area of the lesion made even more sensitive by the friction of the truss. He lay on his bed with dual thoughts: the pain of his body, which the doctors said would go away permanently after a few days if the truss was worn regularly, and the knowledge that by the end of the day the camp meeting would be coming to a close.

The following day, Tuesday dawn, he and Gideon were off while at least one rooster was still crowing.

While descending the incline of the road as it ran eastward from the Bland County line into Giles, he could see in the distance toward the village of White Gate a long train of wagons, buggies, and horses returning from the Wabash camp grounds. As the people drew nearer he saw a look of ecstasy and peace about them. Some of them hummed low and a few wept softly. He slowed Gideon as soon as he was sure that some trick of vision and rationalization was not being played upon his senses.

The train of travelers came abreast of him and began stopping one by one. Men, women, and children climbed down from the wagons and buggies and joined the foot traffic already rushing toward him.

"Oh, Brother Sheffy," an elderly woman literally cried out to him, "you should have been there—the angels sang!"

He explained his confinement and absence from the camp meeting, which he knew had been explained to them at the camp ground, but his words seemed to sail past the ears of all his onlookers.

"The angels sang!" A dozen voices echoed the original statement.

The ranks of faces, still enraptured, swelled about him. Some clung to each other; others chanted a barely audible ode of joy.

"Brother Sheffey, it happened when we were singing the closing hymn of the service last night," a faithful camp goer not noted for conversational enthusiasm reported.

"The sweet Lord manifests Himself in many ways, Brother Suiter, and I am anxious to hear that which you have all seen and heard."

As if their very souls bubbled over with joy, the front ranks of the small group of travelers tried to speak at once.

"Bless you for the testimony which you feel, but I cannot listen to all of you at once. Let Brother Suiter finish telling me what he has started," Robert said.

Suiter stepped forward a step or two, and at closer range the look of haunted sublimity was even more pronounced upon his face. "Brother Sheffey, I don't know whether you will believe me since you weren't there," he began. "It has been a glorious camp session, and the constables told us that over five thousand people were in attendance. It was the most spirit-filled meeting I've ever been to, and you know how long I've been going and taking my family."

Robert nodded and asked the other to proceed.

"On Monday—last night—the last night of the meetings, Dr. J. W. Perry from Abingdon was preaching from the eleventh chapter of

Hebrews. He read the fourteenth, fifteenth, and sixteenth verses, saying, *'For they that say such things declare plainly that they seek a country. / And truly, if they had been mindful of that country from whence they came out, they might have had opportunity to have returned./ But now they desire a better country, that is, an heavenly: wherefore God is not ashamed to be called their God: for he hath prepared for them a city.'* Before he finished reading I had a feeling I've never felt since I was born into this world. I can't explain it to you very good, but my wife and others around us felt it too."

Mrs. Suiter nodded agreement and several heads around her, both male and female, also nodded affirmatively.

Suiter continued: "We were sitting on one of the slab pews under the worship shed, near the north overhang of the roof. When the call to repentance and conversion came, numbers all around us started going forward, and those remaining started to sing 'Jesus, Lover of My Soul.' Before we had finished the first verse of the song a strange feeling came over me and I heard a high-pitched drone above my head—like a swarm of bees going by. I looked around me and others just outside the shed in the open air were gazing toward the sky and pointing upward with their fingers. The people under the shed kept singing, and when the second verse of the song was started, Reverenced Bailey, the leader, stopped singing and looked up toward the roof. Reverend Wagner, who had also preached that night and was still on the platform, called out in a loud voice above the singing, 'Listen! Listen! The redeemed hosts of heaven are singing! I hear the voice of my mother!' We all stopped singing, and one of your wife's people, a Mrs. Stafford, recognized *her* mother's voice.

"By then people were rushing out from under the shed, but some stayed and knelt in prayer. We could hear better out from under the shed, and there was a sweetness in the voices I couldn't explain if my life depended on it—they were much clearer and higher than human voices. The heavenly chorus didn't sound like it was right in front of us, but it didn't sound far away either. It lasted only a little while; then the angels' voices stopped just as quickly as they started. All the faces turned up toward the moonlight looked like mirrors reflecting moonbeams, but we waited in vain: no voices were heard a second time. Everybody in the camp stayed up all of last night—we haven't had any sleep since Sunday."

Suiter stopped, seemingly exhausted. Robert searched his face and saw in it the countenance of a man who had relieved himself of a great burden.

"Brother Sheffey, you must believe me, all that I have told you is the truth!"

Robert asked for no confirmation but every head was nodding agreement.

"Not for a moment do I doubt our sweet Lord's presence in a very special way," Robert said.

"It was a miracle," Suiter breathed reverently.

"Why do you say it was a miracle?" Robert inquired.

"I never heard the angels sing before, and many people felt things they'd never felt before. I did."

"There is so much for our hearts and minds to see if we prepare ourselves. Only our sweet Lord knows if it was a miracle that you saw, but I believe otherwise. I believe from what you have told me that this blessed camp session has been so spirit-filled that many of you have been able to humble yourselves to a level of spiritual obedience that has allowed you to see the substance of life with more depth than most men ever see. Neither can we forget the earlier happenings of the session: many were converted, no doubt, and this alone is cause for great joy. Do you not remember that our Lord has said that there is more rejoicing in heaven over one sinner that repenteth than over ninety and nine just persons that need no repentance? It is not beyond reason nor divine dispensation that we have been shown only the heights of a very great happiness."

"But it never happened before." A timid voice, more troubled than comforted, spoke out from the circle.

"Have you ever felt yourselves more humbled and yielding before?" Robert countered.

Suiter agreed they hadn't—and, furthermore, that this knowledge had been the main subject of the all-night discussion after the soul-shaking experience. Recounted also was a concern that if they had indeed witnessed a miracle, why had not all onlookers been aware of it.

"When we go to the well and lower the bucket, we are not surprised when the bucket comes up full merely because we have not seen the bubbling water at its beginning. When we go to the spring and kneel to drink, we can see the water only as it seeps out of the rocks; but the source is no less real because it is born underground, beyond our vision. Dear brothers and sisters, what I am saying is that you have seen for only a brief while what is all around us—what was already there. Bless you for your soul's vision, and may it always strengthen you, as I can assure you that it will. Do not allow yourselves to think of this experience as the supernatural, but rather as a ride to the bottom of your well, on the well rope, wherein you have seen the source of all that is outpouring for you. The Bible tells us that we, in our human frailties and arrogance, see only through a glass darkly. What will our vision be when *all* the smoked glass is removed from before our eyes?"

He stayed with the group, growing ever larger, until the noon hour and shared with them the sparse remains in their food lockers.

In a little more than an hour after eating he and Gideon stood on the soil of the Wabash camp grounds. Nearly all of the participating preachers had remained. He found them to be shaken and humbled men, and Tyler Frazier confirmed all that Robert had already heard. He wandered about the grounds and the worship shed and finally came back to the preachers' tent.

"Lady Nick? Did she find her peace in this great awakening?" he asked of Tyler.

"She left on Sunday before it happened," he said, reaching behind him and handing Robert the customary red flower.

Robert smelled it and dropped it to the ground. With the heel of his shoe he crushed it into the soft soil.

In a moment he was passing from view of his colleagues and climbing the hill laboriously—a sheepskin prayer mat in one hand and the other held firmly to his groin.

CHAPTER XVIII

The camp-ground sessions of the following year, 1896, were as successful—perhaps more so—than the very oldest participants could ever remember. Certainly Robert could recall none that had been better attended—nor more fevered. The phenomenon that had happened the previous year had much to do with this. That awe-inspiring experience and the resultant depth of vision were very much on the tongues of every man, woman, and child.

Such was not to say that every aspect of the sessions had proceeded without incident. Near the close of the meeting camp constables had to confront several young toughs who had invaded the tent area, harassing some of the campers and breaking strict camp rules. One of these rules was a prohibition against smoking within the camp ground proper. Smoking itself was not forbidden, but the smoker was required to go to fringe areas or out onto the turnpike road. There were times that the latter rule set Robert and other camp committee officials to scratching their heads as to its wisdom. Some campers had brought the new cigarette-making machines with them, and the excitement created when these were demonstrated, or when the machine operators and the "roll-your-own" experts started having speed and efficiency contests, caused worship attendance to suffer.

The incident of evicting the young ruffians was especially unpleasant, for it gave fuel to the fire of dissent from those who claimed that such excesses were fostered by large camp ground gatherings. It was an old argument, and one not altogether unfounded.

But the "no-smoking" rule was entirely defensible within the camp grounds on the basis of safety alone. The danger of fire had been explained to the hostile group of young men, but they had countered, "Push us around and you'll have a fire around here that'll toast chicken eggs a mile away!" Their threats were dismissed and they were evicted from camp.

Two other matters weighed heavily on Robert's heart, both of which had altered the habits and routines of the current camp-meeting season from those of recent years. Eliza's health was failing, and she could not attend; nor could Eddie with his wife and family, who elected instead to stay with Eliza. Lady Nick had not come at all this year, and for all his hopes and prayers, Robert knew that they had not won her.

Eliza rallied during the first week of September and left her sick bed, instructing Robert to send her volunteer visiting nurse away.

Robert stayed close home, for lasting strength seemed forever to have fled from Eliza. After seventy-six years all that seemed vitally alive about Eliza were the brightness of her eyes and a vivid alertness of mind.

One Sunday he rode to Eggleston and preached, having hopes of leaving Staffordsville on Monday for a short missionary trip toward Dublin. Many had offered to stay with Eliza, and fall—when the prohibitions against his travel (a renewal of his earlier agreement with Eliza) would again be in effect—would soon be over.

On Monday, with Gideon saddled and ready by the front gate, Robert went back into the house to tell Eliza and her companion good-by a second time. Suddenly a rider could be heard coming to an abrupt halt.

"Brother Sheffey! The camp ground is burning! It's all burning!" a teen-aged lad called as Robert stood dumfounded on his own front porch.

He looked to the west and could see the billowing smoke rising grotesquely against and above the mountain range.

Arriving on the scene later, all that faced him were smoldering ruins. The worship shed was gone, along with all the cabins and semi-permanent tents; even a number of the white pine trees had gone up like an oil-soaked torch.

"Who has done this terrible thing?" he demanded of the assembled onlookers.

"We don't know." Many responded with the same answer.

He wandered about the grounds, surveying the smoldering pile of gray-black ashes until his face was blackened and hot. Tears fell over his cheeks until his water-streaked face took on the frightening look of an Indian warrior decked in battle paint.

"Who would commit such an ungodly act to my sweet Lord's holy place?" he pleaded anew.

A Wabash resident he recognized, one who lived the closest to the camp ground, told all that any of them knew of the incident.

"Tell me again, Brother Eaton, I want to make sure I know everything."

"It's like I said: this morning just before daylight I heard two or three riders going down the road, and they were riding hard. I didn't think no more about it until breakfast, and then I heard my turkey hens stirrin' up a fuss. I went out to see about them and saw the smoke from the camp ground. When I ran down there the whole camp was ablaze. It was set. I know it was set. There wasn't just the shed burning—every cabin was ablaze."

A soft-spoken farmer finally emerged from the crowd and said, "It doesn't take much to recollect back about two weeks ago. All of you can't be forgettin' the threats made when that bunch of trouble-makers got booted out of camp?"

"And they said if we were worrying about a little old cigarette fire they'd show us a real fire. I remember that." another said.

There was nobody, then, who said he didn't remember the incident, but to what avail was the information now? A labor of love and a landmark and symbol of Christian work second only to the cross itself lay in the dust.

There seemed no reason to leave Staffordsville now. All Robert could do was wander from room to room and wipe away the tears of his terrible agony. He listened to the words of comfort his dear Eliza offered him, as well as those of Tyler Frazier and Ed Bailey and others.

"Eliza, you must lift the prohibition against me and let me ride out this winter. Perhaps I can get up enough interest to rebuild the camp ground by spring. That way we could have it finished by August in time for the sessions..."

Eliza would only look at him until the tears spilled down her cheeks. He did not make her say the words, "The prohibition still holds," for it would pain her terribly. These days the task of living agonized her very bones, for, she often complained, the withered body could not keep pace with a soaring, searching mind.

A melancholy so deep as to silence his voice descended upon him. The thought that the camp ground would never be rebuilt caused him indescribable despair. "Eliza, I have failed," he would whimper without control at the most unexpected times. "I have failed to live up to the great commission to the best of my ability. God has been so good to me and there is so much more that I should have done."

"You have not failed, dear Robert, and your stewardship will live long after we've both passed into dust."

Only if he could rebuild the camp ground could he live up to the assurances of Eliza. He told her so, and the weight of his sorrow now rested upon her shoulders as well as his own.

By the middle of September Eliza had taken to her bed again. On September sixteenth, a high fever invaded her body and Dr. Daniel Stafford, her brother, sat solemn- faced at her bedside.

Eight nights later, having fought intermittent fever, Eliza passed into the world of the dead. While Eddie and her nephew, Bowman Stafford, who had sat by her bed for over a week, and Dr. Daniel and others kept a silent vigil over the sleeping body Robert held the lifeless hand of his faithful mate and sang "Twilight Is Stealing over the Lea."

At her funeral he asked the indulgence of her family and neighbors to allow him to speak for a short while. It was his purpose to tell them how much Eliza Stafford had meant to him and to recount her virtues, which he wished not to be forgotten. They heard and they understood; their moist cheeks told him so.

Eliza was laid to rest in the Wesley's Chapel cemetery. He could not help remembering the first time he had attended church there. It was when he had first come to love Eliza, whom he now committed to the earth. It seemed such a short time ago.

He said no to Eddie and meant it, with regard to moving to Lynchburg.

"I'll find someone to look after me—now don't you fret. I couldn't be happy with city life, son, and you know it. I'm obliged for your loving watch care, but you've got your own family, and the sweet Lord will look after me. I'd a whole lot rather stay around the people I love and the hills and hollows I know, if you want the truth of the matter."

Eddie brought his father a distant relative for a housekeeper, and, hearing Robert's firm stand on the original proposal for the second time, he and his family returned to Lynchburg.

Robert had lived in his house under the new arrangements only a few weeks when a surprising proposal was made to him. The occasion was the funeral of an old friend at Poplar Hill, conducted by his undertaker friend, Aurelius Vest. The solidly built Vest, a head taller than Robert, had said with friendly, dancing eyes, "Brother Sheffey, we want you to come and make your home with us."

"Aurelius, God is good! I would never have told you, but you have answered my prayers! We have much in common, and you are good company and a fellow servant of the Lord. We will mean much to each other; I can think of no family I should sooner spend my remaining days with."

The agreement had been that simple. He turned his house and all but a few belongings over to Eddie, and then moved in with the Vests.

From the very first day of his new residence he felt a part of the little family he loved more every passing year since he had come to know them. He followed Aurelius about freely, sometimes watching him make caskets or do other cabinetwork in the woodworking shop. Other days he would go to the fields with him, or, if the occasion required, watch him prepare a body for burial. He loved Aurelius like a son, and there were those who told him that there was a great similarity between them, Aurelius and himself—in mannerism, godliness, and gentle temperament.

Aurelius Vest was a unique man; Robert came more and more to learn. Aurelius also loved and served the poor, and though Robert had rarely observed him do it, it was said that he could construct a man's casket, prepare his body, and preach his funeral with equal skill. Aurelius confessed readily that he had done it many times.

After Eliza's death Robert had given up any semblance of maintaining a regularly scheduled itinerary, but such a release from more formally scheduled duties did not stop him from riding out again in the spring of 1897 when the warm days of April came.

Gideon did not show the signs of friskiness that he had displayed in former days, but the animal still walked with a spirited step.

"You may be fading, old friend, but you'll still outlast me," Robert said as he rode toward White Gate.

Just south of the village he overtook a man walking whom he recognized. It was George Carr who lived still farther to the south in an ancient log house on the north side of Walker's Mountain. He was a great hulk of a man with large ears and work-swelled arms.

"Brother George, you're walking with a lot of pep this morning—would you be in a hurry?"

George Carr said he was and with good reason. It was the twenty -first day of April and that morning his wife Sallie had given birth to their fifth child, a boy.

"What did you name your son?" Robert inquired. "We're calling him Jesse."

"Much will be expected of him if he is to bear the name of the great King David's father."

"Maybe so, but I ain't worried about nothing now except feeding another little mouth. That's why I'm headed for the store—my hoe is wore out and I've got to get one and put out an extra row of potatoes and some corn."

Robert continued taking short trips until early summer. Then the air of the mountains swelled his soul and body with such an intoxicating energy that he planned still longer ones, over much of his old territory, for the remainder of summer and into early fall. Unless Aurelius restrained him he would continue riding on into the winter, or until he felt physically unable to do so. Aurelius had been so kind about that, advising him only to be careful and not overtire himself, but otherwise giving him his freedom. He did not feel for a moment that this vigor would pass from him in less than a decade. God was so good to him. His recovery from his sorrow was now as complete as it ever could be, and the time was ripe to solicit help and support for the rebuilding of the camp ground.

He came back from a trip one day to find a letter from Eddie, demanding that Robert come to Lynchburg on July Fourth for his seventy-seventh birthday. Inside the letter was money for a train ticket, along with the usual check that was sent periodically for some of Robert's needs and expenses.

At first Robert refused to go, but he later agreed to make the trip, looking forward to the train ride with a mixture of delight and trepidation.

He rode Gideon to Dublin, where he was to catch the train, and left the animal at the livery, with detailed instructions on how he was to be fed, thrice repeated (and with the additional admonition: "Put tree molasses on Gideon's corn—he' s getting old and he likes it better that way"), until he should return.

He purchased the ticket with a great deal of difficulty, and then stood by the track, trembling like a badly frightened child. Presently the fearsome blast of the oncoming steam engine quieted and the wheels squealed to a halt at the loading platform. He was taken to a comfortable seat by a uniformed man who seemed godly enough and who gave him much more attention than other passengers were receiving, even brushing a piece of lint from Robert's long white beard and smiling a friendly smile. Robert thought the act was one of fraternal charity and decided then and there to write the president of the railroad and compliment him on the courteousness of his employees; furthermore, he would declare that a prayer would be said on his behalf. He placed his sheepskin prayer mat upon the seat, sat back, and waited.

The start of the train snapped his head forward, and frantically he reached for the seat in front of him and held on. He did not release his grip until they came to the town of Christiansburg, some fifteen miles' distant and only then at the insistence of the conductor.

He started to get off the train at Roanoke, sure that such a sprawling collection of buildings had to be Lynchburg and that

Eddie waited to meet him. He was restrained with gentleness by the conductor, whom he liked better the farther the train traveled, but who in turn seemed to be showing a decidedly growing impatience with him.

With the outskirts of Roanoke behind them, he sat back and let his full weight rest against the seat. It was a wonderful way to ride; the movement was much gentler than that he felt when upon Gideon's cantering back.

Suddenly he was completely at ease. Then his eye caught a hanging strip of paper coming down from the ceiling of the coach. He studied it closely for a moment and squinted up his eyes, trying to make out what the black dots on the paper were. Reluctantly he turned and asked the well-dressed woman behind him what the strip was. She remained reserved, and her passive face seemed to be making a silent inquiry as to whether his question was serious or not.

"Good sister, I said I did not understand what the paper was hanging from the ceiling for!"

"It's flypaper," she said, with a friendlier look now.

"What paper?"

"Flypaper. It has sticky glue on both sides of it to catch the flies in the coach and kill them. They're such a nuisance, you know."

He observed the flypaper jiggle about in the breeze from the open window and dance to the rhythm of the rolling wheels. With close concentration he could see the flies soar up from the floor and become fastened by wing or leg to the quagmire of glue that would never release them.

The more he watched, the less he could stand the sight. He rose from his seat and picked off each fly as gently as he could, dropping them into his hat and taking care to cover the opening with a red bandana. He could not rescue all of them from their sticky grave, and sometimes they came off minus a leg or wing, but he finished the task and headed back toward his window seat to set the captives free.

When they got to Lynchburg he was the first one helped off the train, and if Eddie and his wife had not been waiting, he would have gone back on the train to thank the brother for the special care he was sure he had gotten.

Mattie Mahood Sheffey, his daughter-in-law of six years' duration, unveiled a birthday cake his very first night at their city home. Having shared it with his grandchildren, and making a sustained effort to reacquaint them with him, he fell into bed exhausted and still a little frightened at his new experiences.

After the first day he tired of staying in the house. He also tired of his grandchildren. "Then I will take you and show you how shoes are made," Eddie said to him. "That will get you away."

The shoe factory was noisy but interesting, and when he had had enough of it, he spoke to Eddie about taking him back to the train station so he could go home.

"What is it, Father?" Eddie's face reflected his concern.

"I feel closed up here. There is no space to breathe and walk, and the streetcars rattle a mile off and more."

But he promised to stay another day or more if he had some spacious place to walk. Eddie announced that they would leave him at the city park during the day and bring him home after work; in the meantime all the open acres that the city owned could be explored.

The next morning Robert, with sheepskin prayer mat and packed lunch in hand, took his first streetcar ride. The moving contraption sizzled like a swarm of bees and his ears rang until he could hardly hear his son's instructions to get off at the next corner—the site of the city park. He approached the partially manicured expanse of green with a great deal of caution. Young women with children and old men (much, much older than himself, he was sure) sat about in the grass or upon the benches. He wondered if one had to pay to sit there. It mattered little, for he had his sheepskin and he would recline on the ground. Eddie had offered him money but he refused all but enough to buy milk to have with his lunch.

Presently he placed his sheepskin on the grass under the shade of a large catalpa tree. The little children played with squealing delight, and he wondered what good man had given of his land so others might enjoy God's bounty even in the very heart of a great city.

At mid-afternoon some point of interest near the street corner at one end of the park seemed to attract the public attention. All the children went running in that direction. He paid them no mind until the tempo of excitement rose, and then curiosity overcame him. As he came closer to the corner he still could not see exactly what was exciting the large crowd. He gave a gentle poke to the back of an old man who seemed only able to stand with the support of a sour wood cane and said, "Good brother, can you tell me what is going on?"

"Eh?" The other cupped his free hand to his ear while Robert repeated.

"A bear, you say? I don't understand," Robert said with raised voice. "A real live bear?"

"The man and the bear come to the park every Fourth of July and stay a week—or as long as he can sell anything," the old man said.

Robert inched closer and got a good view of the street vendor and his chained pet. The owner of the pet was as roly-poly as his animal and though the vendor appeared to be jollier, the bear seemed a great deal smarter, judging by the tricks he was doing. The animal could roll over, end over end or a barrel roll; stand on his head; dance a little jig; and gnaw at an apple held with both paws just like a man. The more ingenious the bear's act, the more the children and adults seemed to buy of the vendor's wares.

Robert came nearer. He now stood only twelve or fifteen feet away. The bear pointed his nose skyward and sniffed loudly, swinging his nose from right to left. Suddenly a bloodcurdling growl escaped the open jaws and bared teeth of the animal, and he stood upright on powerful hind legs. The ferocity of the growl sent the crowd scattering and brought a look of terror to the street vendor's face. The animal now stood a head taller than his owner, and he faced Robert, who also was retreating backward.

Without warning the animal lunged forward until he was on all four feet and free of his master's restraining hand. The animal's chain dragged noisily along the sidewalk as he picked up speed. His obvious point of interest was Robert. Robert lunged for a tree, but all points of safety were occupied and instantaneously he was trapped in the open. The bear came on at full gallop, and with one final lunge snapped his jaws on the sheepskin Robert held in his hands. With crazed growls the animal sent wool balls and sheep hide flying, until the smallest shred of the mat that was left would not have provided comfortable seating for a bullfrog.

Having completed his apparent task, the bear's temper seemed slowly to be coming under control again. The street vendor yanked frantically at the chain he had managed to catch up with. All was peaceable and quiet again long before highly excited policemen with drawn Billy clubs and one ancient-looking gun appeared on the scene.

Robert assured them that he was unhurt and admonished "the brothers" not to do anything to the vendor or his bear. Soon the children were playing in the grass again and the vendor had his arm about Robert's aged, drooping shoulders, continuing to apologize in foreign-sounding, staccato words.

"Do not fret, my brother," Robert said. "There is a great lesson in a bear. I'd like to tell you about some scripture in Proverbs where the sweet Lord compares a sinner to a bear. Now it goes like this … "

A replacement for the sheepskin was not procured until he got to Dublin on the return journey. After taking Gideon from the stable he rode to the farm of a friend and part-time tanner and selected a well-tanned skin, lush with bleached-white fleece.

After he had told Aurelius and his family, as well as numerous other friends who had gathered, about his trip and the adventure of the bear he set immediately to work. His mail volume was still very large in spite of the curtailment of activities. He could no longer write well, for the joints of his hands, swollen and gnarled, would not hold a pen to good effect. Even his drawing, which was not as intricate as penmanship, was adversely affected. A neighborhood girl helped with his correspondence, but no one could help him put the visions of his heart and mind into pictorial form.

"My sweet Lord has not removed this talent from my mind, but He has taken from me my ability to perform," he would say; adding, "The loss is not a sorrow to my soul, for He blessed me for so long, as many rocks and trees still show forth with my illustrated testimony."

When the days became longer he would try to paint or sketch anyway, laughing at his awkwardness all the while. Many of his neighborhood friends liked to watch him. One Brother Warner seemed especially thrilled at seeing familiar scenes committed to paper or slate, and he often told Robert what a powerful man and famous artist he might have become had the vocation been pursued seriously.

"Why you mighta been a rich citizen and mayor of all New Jersey," Broter Warner would say.

"Brother Warner, the good Judge Porterfield once told me in Pearisburg that all the fruits of the world could be divided into two things: love and power. He wisely said that no man could ever have both. The sweet Lord has never let me be sorry for the choice I made."

During the winter Aurelius did not forbid him to ride out on short trips, with the understanding that the family was to be informed where he was riding to, and the approximate travel time required to go to and from the planned destination.

"Aurelius, you are wise. You know I could not live without my freedom."

When the warm spring of 1898 blossomed forth, the freedom was even more unrestrained. He felt younger than he had in five years, and he told Aurelius so. But his friend hesitated when Robert outlined his plan for a long trip to the town of Richlands, some hundred odd miles away.

"But Brother Sheffey, that's almost to the Kentucky border," Aurelius rebuked him gently. "You are nearly seventy-eight years old...you oughten to try a trip like that...the riding will wear you down."

In all honesty Robert had considered that possibility. Eliza had not lived long enough to make him go to Richmond for surgery on his rupture. But the reasons for making this trip were a great deal stronger than any combination of reasons for staying. He told Aurelius so.

"A dear old friend has written me to assist him in a revival at Richlands. I love him so much, Aurelius, and he needs me. He tells me that the country is booming with new riches and that the people have become ungodly and wild in their ways. I want to go to him and help him with the Lord's work."

But Aurelius did not give his consent. Then, in a few days, he asked Robert if the trip could be made by train. He told Aurelius that part of it could, but still, it was not his preference to go by that method. He loved the western-running valleys and mountains, and he longed to sit astride Gideon's back and watch the tilled and well-kept farms go by. And who could stop by a fence row or by a cool limestone spring while on a train? Even the nicest of conductors would not halt the train while he talked to the members of God's creation as they walked by. There was a more important reason still: if he was to effect the rebuilding of the Wabash camp grounds it would be necessary to visit many people and churches along the way, going *and* coming.

Robert urged Aurelius to come to a decision, for the planned revival at Richlands was to be held the third week of June and time was running out. His colleague would need to know Robert's answer.

Aurelius pondered the question for a fortnight, while there were hushed conferences of family, friends, and neighbors. Finally the answer and the conditions were out lined.

"Brother Sheffey, we know how much this means to you, but we all question the wisdom of it. We don't need to tell you that it is our love for you and the possibility of accidents that makes us hesitate. Maybe there is a solution. If you will promise to ride just a little part of the way per day, and tell us at the end of each day's journey who you will plan to stay with, you can go with our blessing. We will expect you to send us a letter every day so we will not be worried.

Robert agreed to the conditions and sent a letter of confirmation to his friend. On the eleventh day of June he pointed Gideon westward.

The first full day he rode as far as Bland, now only twenty odd miles from his new home.

"Gideon, we told Aurelius we would stay at the Allen Newberry house tonight. Sister Nancy is the third Sister Newberry, and she puts too much soda in the biscuits—far too much. The first sister, Elizabeth Newberry, never cooked the biscuits long enough, and the second, Sister Car-o-line, made them too flat—just like stepped-on mashed potatoes. Every time I got one of the good sisters' doing to suit me, they'd pass on and Brother Allen would get another. And Brother Allen is gone now too, Gideon. Bless their sweet lives—I love them so much."

By taking short jaunts of a few miles each day to scheduled stops and familiar places, the communities of Ceres, Broadford, Claypool Hill, Cedar Bluff, and a host of much smaller villages were traversed.

He arrived at Richlands on the last possible day. He had not planned it thus, but time had run out so quickly as his visits and appeals for the camp-ground rebuilding stretched from minutes to hours and from hours to days. And how much the world was changing! Places he had visited just five or ten years previously now swelled with people and changing terrain. Wherever he went—to church or home—he met with politeness, and often in the house of a really old friend or former coworker the spirit of welcome was one reminiscent of the happiest of former days. The business of the camp-ground restoration was another matter. The people west of Ceres reminded him how far removed from the camp grounds they were, and though their ancestors had journeyed the long distance, there was no longer need of it with modern churches now at their doorstep. He couldn't dispute this. He had seen a dozen churches built within the past five years of his absence. He refused to be discouraged, however. The real support for the camp-ground rebuilding would be in areas immediately surrounding Giles County, and he would work that territory later. Ed Bailey and Tyler Frazier were doing part of the legwork at this very moment, and he would soon join the effort.

Richlands was a hilly town of diverse businesses following the terrain of the land, located less than twenty miles south of the West Virginia border and not more than forty miles southeast of the Kentucky border.

As he rode through the town he felt a strong sense of the rampant gaiety that obviously pervaded the area. The dirt streets were crowded even at midday, and merchandise stores were doing a bustling business. Voices were frequently at high pitch and humor crackled back and forth between horseman and pedestrian. The staggering form of a drunken man was seen more than a dozen times: twice in a matter of half an hour he had lifted the body of such a man (unable to walk at all) out of the street and saved his skull from being crushed by the hurried and frequent wagons of commerce.

"What has happened here, Brother Bandy?" Robert asked when his old colleague had been located.

"Half of the county has become drunken with prosperity, Brother Bob. To start at the beginning I guess we'd have to go back to eighteen-ten. A mighty freshet exposed a seam of coal in this area, and the influx of people started from that. Anyway, by eighteen-seventy a blacksmith named Jordan Nelson opened up a commercial mine not many miles from here, and before long he had cheap coal—at a penny per bushel, mind you—going in every direction. They were using the stuff for glass making, iron forging, and even to heat the kitchen stove with. To make a long story short, the mule trains got longer, came more often, and used the light of the moon to stretch the work day. The railroad wrote the rest of the story all by itself."

"And now prosperity takes the place of godliness and the tavern replaces the church—"

"And in not a few cases, the brothel has taken the place of the home."

The following morning Robert accompanied his host to the site of the planned revival. His colleague's small mountain church at the fringe of the town was being augmented with a large tent to be used in conjunction with the main building.

"We'll use the regular pulpit, but the big double doors at the back of the church will be removed and we'll look from the pulpit directly into the tent."

"I'll be in prayer that we can fill it," Robert said.

"I'm worried about that now. I'm afraid it's too ambitious. A few months ago I wouldn't have said that."

They returned to Reverend Bandy's house then. An early meal had been placed upon the table by the only daughter of his host, but there seemed no happiness in the girl's face. Before the meal was over he had learned that her mother had been dead less than a month.

Four hours later the two men returned home, crushed and despondent. The first six rows of pews had not been filled, much less the whole church and tent area. Robert tried to comfort his friend by relating his experiences of a similar nature. The other was inconsolable, however, and doubly sorry that Robert had been summoned such a long distance for nothing.

The next morning after breakfast Robert asked to be excused so that he might walk about the town and develop a feeling for the area and its people. Brother Bandy acceded to his request, saying that it would be an opportune time for him to return to the church and attend to routine matters.

Before riding into the town Robert walked into the hillside orchard of his host and knelt beneath the apple trees. He had not finished his prayer when apples began to fly fast and furious over his head. Looking up, he saw three boys, arms cocked again to hurl apples into the next tree. He couldn't finish the prayer now but maybe it was useless anyway: he seriously doubted whether any people of the community would hear the soft voice of the Holy Spirit even if he prayed to that end the live long day.

"What are you doing, boys?" Robert called before they had seen him.

They looked up in surprise and started backing away. "We're tryin' to knock down that hornets' nest," a lad of sixteen or seventeen said, pointing upward, "but we ought to be goin' on to town now—we're running late a-gettin' there…"

Close up, the town reeked with more debauchery than had been observable at a distance. People used obscene words openly, and there seemed as many taverns as stores. Intoxicated men could be seen planting kisses on painted women when a saloon door opened near the street.

Robert walked on until the area of commerce was bypassed. He stopped outside a house that echoed alternately with high-pitched laughter and boisterous male voices. He listened by the open window near the sidewalk but could make no sense of the festivities. He stood there a moment until a man nearly black with grime and coal dust passed him by. Before he disappeared around a corner Robert called to him. "What business is conducted in *this* place?" he asked.

"Nothing you'd be interested in, old-timer. I 'spect your beard might get in the way."

Robert insisted on being told, and, most abruptly, he was.

The very tone of voice with which the working man called out the word "whorehouse" caused Robert to jump and move away quickly. He rounded the same corner from which he had come and pondered this new information. He was bumped about by a lumbering pedestrian or two, and he moved out of the walkway between two buildings. Three forms lurched there, encircled in pipe smoke, and the moment the air cleared he recognized the three boys he had seen in the orchard.

He didn't chastise them for their experiments, asking them, rather, whether they would like to do something more useful for the wage of half a dollar.

"What do we have to do?" all three asked at once.

"Do you think you could wear some gloves and put some cheesecloth over your heads and cut the hornet's nest down for me? You will need a corn cob, of course, to plug it with."

All vowed that they had done it many times before, but to what use now?

Robert kindly declined to answer and jingled the money in his hand. As their bare heels disappeared he began to have second thoughts: somewhere he had heard that a bee died after using its stinger.

The longer he waited for the boys, the more the question plagued him. Finally, as they reappeared, walking with great care, the situation had been reduced to the barest of fundamentals: Was the sacrifice of God's creatures permissible for the eradication of an unendurable abomination? Viewed in that light, there never had been a genuine problem in the first place.

He paid for and with extreme care, took his buzzing package from the boys. Going between buildings this time until a back route was searched out, he arrived shortly under the open window of the house whose business transactions would soon suffer.

With all his might he threw his burden inside until, seeing the hornets' nest burst, he reached for the window and pulled it down with such force that the glass rattled. He was rounding the corner before the first shrieks of agony reached his ears.

He was still in listening range when a whole chorus of cries, both male and female, drifted outward into the street.

That night the revival gathering was little better attended than the previous one. For all their preaching and exhortations, they had received but two candidates for the kingdom of heaven.

"Brother Bob, they should be overflowing the aisles and bulging out the sides of the tent. They've got nothing on their minds but the pleasures of the flesh—they fear neither God nor the devil."

For the second night the two of them returned home wearily.

At dawn Robert crept from the house, leaving a note to the effect that he had borrowed the black greatcoat of his host as well as a tool from the barn. "I will see you at meeting time. Save no meals for me, I have taken some of your biscuits also."

Activity around the town started early, but it was eight am before he could enter the dry-goods store to purchase a black silk stovepipe hat. He found one that fitted his head well and marched from the premises.

As the citizens began to stir, and more and more wagons to roll, he paraded alternately up and down both sides of the street to the extent of the town limits. Occasionally he would go out into the center of the slate -impacted street and walk more slowly and deliberately from that location. Before long he was meeting many of the same people coming and going as they went about their business. On occasion, some of the wagons that passed him turned around and doubled back.

By midmorning the perpetual walking tired him until his already drooping shoulders hung even lower and his pace slowed even more. Still he kept going.

It helped some to stop periodically at the store windows and look in for a moment, or pause at the saloons and rest in the doorway. Before long, many he passed and repassed attempted to speak to him, but he forced the evil grin he wore upon his face even harder, refused their overtures, and walked on. Sometimes his arm would tire and he would allow the walking staff he had borrowed from Reverend Bandy's barn to fall horizontal. Just as quickly he would attempt to right it again to walking position, jousting as few people as possible.

His improvised staff might be the only three-pronged hayfork his host possessed, and his care of it must not be one of negligence.

His body in the long coat (it reached to his ankles) sweated terribly, though the June day was overcast. On a vacant lot on the opposite side of the street he spotted a large poplar tree. The tree grew skyward in two forked sections and one of the halves bent sharply eastward a few feet from the ground. Then it straightened again until by force of nature an inverted cane like seating place had been created with a natural back rest. He climbed into the niche with the aid of his fork and settled back to rest.

His heaving lungs slowed after a while but he continued to sit and eat a biscuit. Across the street people gathered to watch him in little groups or individually, casting furtive glances as their steps quickened and they hastened away. Surely he must look like a vulture, he thought, but it was such a peaceful place to rest.

In moments he was glad he hadn't moved, for torrential rains descended from the black skies and he sat warm and dry, protected by his snug alcove and the spreading limbs and leaf cover about him.

As the rain lifted he was aware of the numerous eyes that peered at him from windows on the opposite side of the street. As he came down from his perch his fellow observers likewise fled their positions.

He took up his walk again, facing into a new group of town visitors. He was unaware of friendly forces behind him until mid-afternoon was approaching. From the corners of his eyes he could see an inebriated man following him ever closer until the latter's hand was upon his shoulder.

"Yes? What is it, my brother?" Robert said.

"I've been watching out atcha—we all been watchin' out atcha comin's and goin's—"

"I feel blessed that you have turned from your distractions to see what is going on about you," Robert said.

"Come over here a minute." The other motioned, and led the way behind a livery barn.

Robert drew nearer as requested, but the man backed away a short distance. "Are you who I'm a-thinkin' you are?"

"Who do you think I am?" Robert said.

"I'm thinkin' I know you—now there ain't nothin' you could have agin me—nothin' like that."

"I'm sure we haven't met, but I'd like to see more of you," Robert tried to say at closer range. The back-pedaling steps of the other did not aid the attempt.

"Listen…I want to tell you somethin'…I know I been in church a time or two in the last little while but I was just play actin'…I didn't mean nothin' by it. I want you to know I've been on your side all the time. Honest I been. Now you come on down to th' s'loon with me and my buddies'll tell—"

"I have much walking to do and you must excuse me," Robert said.

But in spite of what he had said, his elderly legs would carry him no further. For what time remained before the end of day, he found a ladder at the rear of a mercantile house and climbed to the roof, walking across the flat surface until a safe perch on a guard-railed parapet afforded a good view of one side of the street. There he sat and looked upon the town. A part of the town looked back, paused briefly, and hurried on.

At supper he gave his colleague the explanation only that he had been doing "some missionary work." He put finality in his voice and ate hungrily.

"Bless your effort, but I've done everything I could do long before you got here, Brother Bob—ran a notice in the paper, announced it from the pulpit several Sundays in a row, and did a lot of personal visitation…Guess I should have done more, but I had hoped the people would understand in view of our loss—"

The congregation was unexpectedly swelled that night—not full by any means, but well over half full.

Reverend Bandy was ecstatic as they labored together to the swell of the foot-pumped organ and the cry of repentant souls.

"At last it looks like a revival!" Bandy said at the close of the meeting. "I don't understand it!"

"Tonight was Saturday, have you forgotten? My experience has taught me that when the week of work is done, public turnouts are oftentimes better."

The following night finalized the services. The crowd had been larger still, but the church and tent enclosure were far from full. Reverend Bandy proclaimed the occasion an unexpected and joyous success. To Robert it was a shameful failure, in spite of the part he had tried to play.

Leaving Richlands, he took the alternate return route he had planned with Aurelius as far as Bland, going by way of Tazewell, Clearfork Valley, Rocky Gap, and Bastian. Zigzagging along the way, churches at Witten's Mill, May's Chapel and Mount Calvary were visited.

The people listened to his camp rebuilding proposal, but their questions caught him off guard. Had the plans been drawn yet? Had the cost been estimated? Had the conference officials been contacted for support, financial and otherwise? How many of the churches in the area to be served were in total support? How many people were represented in all?

He trembled with unpreparedness, and the pressure of new faces seemed unnecessarily demanding. It was never like this before. He had helped build churches and camp grounds too—for almost fifty years he had done it—and there was nothing complex about it. It was as simple as getting a few men together with axes and saws.

But they stared at him doubtfully or unbelieving. Quickly he promised that he would get the information—maybe Brother Frazier or Brother Bailey would have it, or would know how to get it.

"Gideon, I don't know where to find out even half of what they want! I just don't even know where!"

Bland was a blessed sight to see, for he was tired, so dead tired, and his legs and back pained him with a terrible soreness. The truss sandpapered his belly until blood oozed through his trousers.

"I shouldn't have done all that walking I did, Gideon, but we'll stop when we get to Mechanicsburg and see if Dr. Harman can help us."

James Washington Harman was a man after Robert's own heart. He had been a farmer, teacher, merchant, and such a close adherent to the teachings of John Wesley that he lacked little in the way of qualification for preaching. Dr. Harman was also a Confederate war veteran who had served under his brother's command, but the ramrod posture of the soldier had deserted him in the same manner that Robert had lost his own: the good doctor was bent with age and in his seventy-seventh year of life.

The doctor practiced little now, but Robert had no reluctance to stop, preferring medical treatment from old friends if it was possible to patronize them.

He was admitted to the doctor's room—a sort of sun room appendix to the house—facing the village spring. Only one other man waited there.

"I hope you're not in pain, my brother," Robert said.

"No, it's not me. My boy mashed his hand in the tailgate of the wagon. He'll be all right when he gets it wrapped up and salved down."

Robert asked the name of the speaker and was told it was Crockett.

"I know many Crocketts, but most of them come from Crockett's Cove in Wythe County. Do you live here in Bland County?" Robert asked.

"No, as a matter of fact we come from Crockett's Cove. We're just passing through this section returning home."

"There's a special place in my heart for Crockett's Cove. Across the wagon road from the Crockett Cemetery is a grave on the south side of the hill," Robert began.

"Yes, I know where it is, of course. It's a surface grave—almost on top of the ground, I mean. It's walled up with rock and cemented—the grave of a Colonel Robert Sayers, I believe."

"That's right. The grave of the man I was named after. He was an officer in the Revolutionary War and a dear friend of my mother and father. I never knew him, of course. I learned in later life that he died when I was short of six years old. I have been told that my father was one of the executors of his estate."

"The grave never really meant much, but now it takes on a little more personal feeling. It's more of a curiosity to most people than anything else—the place it sits, and all alone too—and the way it faces.... You've given me the Robert Sayers part of your name—what's the rest?"

Robert told him and the other acknowledged his recognition of it. "Brother Sheffey—I guess I can call you Brother Sheffey—everybody else does—I have wanted to ask you something for a long time if and when I ever caught up with you, and I guess I'm about the only one in Crockett's Cove who hasn't seen you."

Robert encouraged the asking.

"It is said that you are fond of honey and that you visited the home of William Tiller in Mercer County on occasion and found no honey there. I believe the story went that you were told by the man of the house that his bees had not swarmed and that he had no fresh honey for you. It is said that you kneeled down on a mat of some kind and prayed for the bees to swarm and that they did. It is important that you tell me whether this information is true or not."

Robert looked his questioner in the eye to determine the sincerity of the question. "There are any number of answers I could give you, but I cannot answer your question until I know or could better feel the image of your life. If I said 'true,' you would brand me a sorcerer and if I said 'false,' I should be denying the majesty of God who is the Creator and Master of all things. You are not yet ready for the answer. I somehow feel that you are not."

A young lad, smiling now, emerged from a doorway. A distinguished older figure hobbled behind him.

"He'll do now," Dr. Harman said gruffly.

The boy's father paid the charge, took his son by the hand, and cast Robert a disappointed glance.

"We'll meet again, Brother Sheffey. I won't forget the question, so be prepared."

"It will be a Lord's blessing if we do. I need no further preparation, but it would pain me if I thought your mind was troubled because of me. Why don't we just say for the meantime that God is good and still Master of our universe."

The other conceded a smile, a nod, and an unhurried farewell.

"Well, Robert, what was that all about?" James Harman said.

"We were just talking of a story your patient's father had heard. I know about it and it's an old tale that the hearers make so complex when it is so childishly simple."

Robert removed his truss and bared his belly. James Harman bathed the raw tissue with ointment and placed a double layer of soft cloth between skin and truss.

"Wear your truss a little tighter from here on home, Robert. You should have gone to Richmond or Bristol and had your malady taken care of long ago. You could still do it, you know."

"At our ages, what does it matter?" Robert countered.

James Harman stiffened his spine at hearing the remark, then let himself relax.

"You can't easily keep that spine as military stiff as you used to do, can you?" Robert said in a fraternal tone of voice.

"You would make an old man admit it? Let me remember my military ancestors with all the glory I can."

The remark needed no interpretation, for Robert was aware of the long line of Harman military men who had distinguished themselves in four wars.

Dr. Harman fingered his neatly trimmed salt-and-pepper beard and suggested that they sit on the outside porch. Robert agreed, saying it would be a good vantage point if other patients came.

"I don't have many patients, Robert. In a way I haven't been able, I've been up and down so much. I'm too old and the people get impatient with me sometimes. There are doctors scattered all around now—it's good that there are."

But James Harman's life belied his words, for James Harman had lifted the practice of medicine above price, and service to humanity above duty. This mutual love and concern for the poor was the thing that had really welded the two men together across the years.

"Brother James, what would you have been if all the patients had been paying customers?"

"A drunken sheep shearer whose trembling hands could do naught else, most probably," the doctor said with a chuckle. "What would you have been if all your pew warmers had dropped even a penny in the plate?"

"That's not much of a question. Most of them didn't have one." Then Robert realized the answer was applicable to the question he himself had posed. "Of course, I've had my share of support from the landed gentry. Many have helped me much and given me clothes and money when I had nowhere to turn."

"But they sure don't come up with the poor—in numbers, I mean."

"I didn't coin the expression, but whoever said that our sweet Lord must have 'loved the poor, for He made so many of them,' surely had the wisdom of the sages placed in his head."

"Well, Robert, I don't possess the gift of the Magi, but you know how much I like to read and study. Everything that you believe in began among the illiterates of the world. Somehow that gentle Man of Galilee was able to instill in those of whom we speak the idea that when their lives seemed lost and hopeless, it was then their souls' full worth became apparent."

Robert stood before his chair, knowing that the sun sank lower and Aurelius Vest's house still lay miles away. He almost forgot to ask the amount of his bill, and when he did so, Dr. Harman refused payment.

"Then I can't ask you my final question," Robert said.

Nevertheless, it was pried gradually from him.

"I want to rebuild the Wabash camp-ground buildings. Would it be upon your heart to give five or ten dollars?"

"I would joyously give you a hundred, Brother Robert, but I have heard this issue discussed throughout the region, and, more specifically, in our own local churches, some of which you have visited. If we were lucky enough to get the basketsful of money it would take, we would find that only old men and old women would show up for the labor. And when it was done, not many years would pass until nobody showed up for worship except those in black bonnets and white beards like our own. The younger generation does not want, and say they do not need, the camp meeting that brought the hearts of our mothers and fathers, and those of our own, to the Lord."

"But the time was when we just all got together and cut some trees down and everybody labored with love…and the people came and were so happy…"

"No matter how much it pains you, Robert, that day will never come again. Go home, Robert! Go home! Sit on the porch and turn your horse out to clover. Our threescore and ten have passed. We have done our due...we have the right to look for a greener land!"

From Mechanicsburg, he pointed Gideon east along the creek and promised the animal that by dark he would be turned into Aurelius Vest's clover.

The feather tick of his bed felt good that night, but when morning came he could not leave it. His knees refused to bend and his back rebelled at obeying the directives of his mind. He tried mightily to rise from the bed which held him prisoner, but his body cried to him of a need for further rest.

Although his recuperation was slow it was soon complete. There was sheer joy in the sunshine of summer and the smell of new-mown hay. On top of it all was the necessity of celebrating his seventy-eighth birthday. Eddie had sent him a special letter and a fruit basket for the occasion. His visitors included a son and daughter of his first marriage, plus a host of neighbors and friends. The number was sufficient for a real revival; had not the good Dr. Blackburn chased them all away before the night had hardly begun.

As complete as his recovery from severe fatigue had been, Aurelius insisted with utmost gentleness that his riding range be limited to a radius of thirty-five miles from home. Lord forgive him, for he pouted a little at the confinement but accepted it obediently. Aurelius was so good to him, and he felt himself now completely in the younger man's care.

For two years he lived with the traveling prohibitions, scanning almost every house and hamlet his diminished territory now encompassed. At every opportunity he would crisscross the unscattered ashes of the Wabash camp ground and keep in touch with those who still helped on behalf of the rebuilding plans. But these loyal few had also lessened as they were transferred to other charges, or fell victim to death or infirmity. He alone seemed to believe that one day victorious voices would rise again under the great oaks and poplars, and that candle-light would flicker in the breeze of eventide as the low hum of song or prayer drifted out into the delicious aroma of night.

The summer of 1901 Robert needed no protective prohibitions other than those self-imposed. For years he had mounted his horse from a fence or stile or some other aid that prevented a strain upon his weak abdomen. Now he could not, with ease, mount his animal in any way except by being lifted into the saddle by friends or family. When he rode off in this condition they all seemed to stand and watch in terror. He had decided they should not be subjected to apprehension on his account; he loved them too much.

Now, instead of riding, he would take his sheepskin out to the meadow knoll and sit under a shade tree, watching Aurelius work. Sometimes Aurelius's little children would sneak up to him and playfully pull his long white beard (a trick he himself had taught them), giggling at their own ingenuity. He would call, "Boo!" to them and they would feign the greatest of fright and come back for more. But there was not enough of any activity to fill the great space of the day. When dusk came he sat upon the porch with Aurelius and talked for a time, time that seemed all too short, until moonlight descended and the crickets and katydids called out the lullaby for sleep.

Even in the softness of his bed his mind would come alive with great flashes of light, and if he thought Aurelius was not asleep, he would call to him for an audience. "Aurelius," he would say to the yawning, night shirted man, "a great thought has come to me! Do you know that Jesus Himself was completely dependent upon prayer for his source of strength? Well, He was, but what I'm leading up to is this: we need to pray over and over again about the same things, to test our sincerity. The necessity of our request is of times tested by repeated prayers. Haven't you ever prayed and prayed for something, Aurelius, and the more you prayed, the more fully you learned that that for which you prayed was not the thing you needed at all?"

Aurelius would give a patient answer, and sometimes he sat by the bed a little longer, occasionally until Robert didn't remember seeing him leave.

Wintertime was bad. It seemed that no matter how close Robert sat to the fire, his outer skin would get hot, but the coldness, which was bone-deep, could not be reached by warmth of any kind. His joints grew cold and stiff, and the medicine for rheumatism that Aurelius applied didn't help at all.

"It won't hurt so bad when springtime comes, Brother Sheffey," Julia Vest would say, and try to massage the hurt away.

Aurelius would relieve his wife of the task when his time would allow, and sometimes Robert whispered the things he felt in his innermost soul: "Save back some good walnut boards for me, Aurelius, the day is drawing near."

But he accepted the kindness of time and felt the smile of another spring upon his up tilted face. Neighbors and friends had plotted during the winter, he discovered, and before the dogwood blossomed forth they came and got him a day at a time to entertain him and make his moments brighter. He would chuckle if he had the strength; it now required more effort to climb into the seat of a buggy than he had once used to scale the highest ridge on his old itinerary.

Two who were both friend and neighbor made the suggestion that thrilled him with a new delight. Since Aurelius did not live by the main road, why not spend an occasional day of the warm spring sitting in a rocker by the side of the traveled thoroughfare?

Calvin Vest, a neighbor and relative of Aurelius, offered to take him first. "Brother Sheffey, it'll give you a new lease on life. You can watch the people go by and talk all day to anybody that'll stop," he said.

The second neighbor, Tom Whittaker, took turns with the transportation. On days that neither of the others could help him, Aurelius himself would carry him to a favorite sitting place in the community by the main roadway.

Both friend and stranger, man and child, paid him friendly homage, but one day in mid-May a lanky young man with thick sandy hair approached him with a furtive countenance and evasive hazel eyes. For a stranger, Robert thought him a poor conversationalist, and, if a friend, completely devoid of brotherly warmth.

Robert asked his name twice before being told, realizing then that something was wrong.

"What is upon your heart, my young brother? I have lived too long not to see the shadow of shame upon the most deceptive face."

"I want you to forgive me for something," the man asked with great effort.

"I hold nothing against any man, for my sweet Lord has told me to be forgiving. My eyes have long ago faded and I do not recognize you. For what can I extend to you forgiveness?"

"You will hate me."

"Hate you?"

"Yes! Hate me! Despise me! Curse me even, and I would deserve it. God forgive me and save my wretched soul!"

"What, my young brother—tell me what?"

"I am one of the guilty who burned down the camp-ground buildings."

"Oh mercy, oh mercy!" Robert cried, and convulsive retching's shook his body. He could not help his tears, yet there was relief in them that he could not explain.

The young man moved to him and steadied his shaking shoulders. "Will you give me your blessing and your forgiveness?"

"You had it from the moment I came upon the smoldering ruins. Only then, I didn't know who was to receive it."

"The camp ground will never be rebuilt, will it?"

"No, son, the camp ground will never be rebuilt. I am told that a new age has eaten freely from the tree of knowledge and that no more spirits live which need enrichment. I am told the classroom will banish hate and hypocrisy; that loneliness and need will wither in a coming intellect which promises to rise to greater heights than anything ever dreamed of at the Tower of Babel."

"Even with your forgiveness I will never be free of it...."

"No, but you can pray that your agony be used to some purpose. I understood you all were toughs? You talk like an educated man."

"I wasn't then."

"How many of you were there?"

"Three—and I set the shed by myself."

"I have already forgiven you, but I want to give you a cross to take up and carry. I want you to be instrumental in saving the souls of your two companions no matter how long it takes. Do not promise me lightly."

There was no hesitation at all. "I promise."

"You realize, of course, that I will never know? My sweet Lord calls to me in the faintest voice. I should ask you again to ponder what you have said."

"With all my heart I promise."

Robert blessed him and asked permission to pray. His rheumatic knees would not allow him to leave the chair, but he bowed his head and felt another head resting against his knees.

The young man got to his feet and started to leave. He turned a few steps away, "Brother Sheffey…I know you understand. For the sake of my mother and father…will you not reveal…"

"A peace that is made with God does not need the censure of man."

Again on his birthday, this time the eighty-second one, Eddie's fruit basket arrived. He could not eat from it, because for weeks his stomach would intermittently take and reject whatever was offered. Nothing Dr. Blackburn gave him changed the rebellious organ that had, once in the wilderness, lived on wild berries and nuts for days at a time.

"Brother Blackburn, can't you recognize an old body with every part worn out when you see it?" Robert whispered.

"Now, if you're going to diagnose yourself, how can I bill you the full fee?"

"You never took a dollar from me in your life—but you ought to have."

As his condition worsened, the almost daily entourage of visitors was turned away. Only his doctor and the closest of friends sat with him, but there were times when he would need to ask even those to leave him when the pain became more than he could bear.

Throughout the remainder of July and until the middle of August his bed was not left except for his bodily functions, and he needed Aurelius even for that. It was agonizing just to sit on the side of the bed, and he sometimes cried out until he could see tears in the eyes of his beloved friend.

"The suffering—the suffering, Aurelius, is my final cleansing. Praise God for it. Praise God."

Rarely a good day would come, and then he would call upon someone to read to him—verses from the Psalms, or religious poems, or a little of the correspondence that continued to arrive.

"You got another letter from that widow woman in Carroll County who's been chasing you for five years," Aurelius would tease him and read into the written lines things Robert suspected were not there. "I expect you've listened to enough letters for today, but here's one more I think you will want to hear," Aurelius said once.

Robert closed his eyes but assured Aurelius that he would not go to sleep until the letter had been read.

Aurelius went on:

> "Dear Reverend Sheffey: I finally got your address from the Holston conference, where I learned you are still listed as a local preacher and a conference deacon. I am told that many years ago you sat at the foot of my unmarried mother's bed in a remote hollow in Wythe County and prayed for me and my family. Tradition handed down further states that you took my little foot in your hand as you prayed and asked God to use me in spite of the circumstances of my birth. You asked, I believe, that God would make a preacher of me and 'stand [me] in many pulpits across the land until [I had brought] a thousand souls into the kingdom.' It is my joy to inform you that I have served churches from Tennessee to Texas (where I now am, as you can see from the postmark) and that the sixth day of August marked the day I baptized my one thousandth convert. I am still a young man and I must tell you I plan to

> work another forty years. Dear friend, you badly underestimated God's power!"

"I think I will sleep now, Aurelius."

The sleep was of five-day duration, he learned, when the coma ended. Eddie stood by his side as cloudy vision returned. He held his son's hand and squeezed it tight when the waves of pain made him conscious again that he was indeed alive.

"Did you hold back the good walnut boards for me, Aurelius?" he asked in the faintest whisper, "Did you?"

"Yes."

"Miter the corners well and polish the wood with oil until the grain shines with the testimony of God's good years."

To life he clung, and sent his son back home to Lynchburg. He remained conscious, but he lost track of the days and hours and needed to ask Aurelius for an accounting. The last he remembered, it was August twenty-fifth, but when he woke up again, it was August twenty-ninth and the day had just broken, for the morning sun shone through his window with such brilliance that the motes seemed as large as raindrops and danced all about the room. He was then aware of other shapes around him, but he did not try to move and see them for himself. He wondered if they could even see *him*, for his own hands looked as white as the satin with which Aurelius lined his caskets, and the starched white counterpane of his bed seemed to blend with the skin of his arms.

"Aurelius...Aurelius...who is present?"

"Brother Calvin Vest and Tom Whittaker. Julia is here with me, and the children are sitting at her feet. Dr. Blackburn will be back after dinner."

Welcomed silence followed. Thoughts would hardly form in his head now. A thought would start to form and then end like a snapping icicle. After a while his brain did clear and he seized the strength to push up a little on one elbow.

"Aurelius! Aurelius! The prettiest things I have ever seen! How beautiful and bright my star is! I have got in a good way...the sweet angels. Praise the Lord. Praise the Lord. So happy. So happy. Tell Eddie to praise the Lord."

His burst of revelation caused a descending blackness, and when he woke again it was night.

"How long will the night be, Aurelius?"

"It isn't night, Brother Sheffey—it is morning again."

"Do my friends bear with me?"

"The same ones are here."

Aurelius had said it was morning, but no sunbeams fell across his bed...Aurelius was surely wrong...it must be night, and it was getting chill. Both his feet were growing numb, and his eyelids could only be opened with his fingers.

"Dear Aurelius...I have not done all...I should have...done for the...sweet L-Lord."

"If you *haven't*, Brother Sheffey, no man ever has," Aurelius whispered.

"You must promise me...all of you...that you will continue... continue the work. Somebody...somebody must carry the...load. Make the people like...crawling babes that know not a stranger... and grab hold of each other...tell all who love me to...do that..."

"We will all do it," Aurelius said.

"Do you...answer me, Aurelius...I can't hear...you...well..."

For a moment he thought he heard his friend and felt his hand, but the voice faded and faded and the touch must have been drawn away, for now there was nothing but a creeping coldness that had reached his neck...

EPILOGUE

Edward Fleming Sheffey finally arrived at his father's bedside two hours after he had died. His summons, when the end was clearly inevitable, was made more difficult by the methods of communication and transportation of the day, but his sorrow at not having seen his father alive once more was borne with dignified grief.

Robert Sayers Sheffey had died at two pm, and Eddie had arrived at four pm, and by six pm funeral arrangements had been agreed upon.

In a matter of minutes horses already saddled and riders mounted and awaiting the word were dispatched in every direction. Some went to newspaper offices, telegraph stations, and telephone switchboards to speed the news of the death and the day and place of the burial; others took the remote roads and mountain trails, calling out at every hamlet and village, "Brother Sheffey is dead. Spread the word." At the isolated houses in the ridges and hollows, the riders would hardly slow their galloping animals except to say, "Brother Sheffey is gone!" and give the details of the funeral.

These Paul Reveres of the wilderness kept up their rides and vigil throughout the night and all the next day. Many of them, who had enlisted dozens of other riders along the way, rode so far and wide that they had hardly enough time to retrace their steps and get back to Giles County in time for the rites.

The effect of the cooperative message carrying became apparent before daylight on the morning of September first. Seemingly endless trains of pedestrians, wagons, buggies, hacks, surreys, and horseback riders came from tributaries out of southern West Virginia to the north, and Roanoke and Lynchburg to the east; Tazewell,

Washington, and sister counties to the west, and Carroll, Floyd, and territories of North Carolina to the south. Trains emptied passengers at the nearest point of disembarkation, and waiting hacks sped off in a cloud of dust to deliver passengers for the eleven am services. Discharged passengers, late in arriving, found themselves unable to get within a mile of the Wesley's Chapel church and walked through powdery dust for the privilege of standing at the outer fringe of a virtual sea of humanity. Shortly after daylight all available pews had been filled and young and old alike took a second nap as they waited for the hour to arrive. Nursing mothers gave their infants a second feeding, which somehow seemed more filling than a previous one, given the confines of a dusty and jolting wagon.

Presently, the hour arrived and Reverend R. F. Jackson, pastor of the Staffordsville Circuit, conducted the services. He was assisted by Reverend Dr. G. A. Maiden, presiding elder of the Radford District, and Reverend Eugene Blake, pastor of the Pearisburg Circuit.

Reverend W. C. Crockett, pastor of the Bland Circuit, preached the funeral sermon from the Book of St. Matthew, drawing from the twenty-seventh verse of the nineteenth chapter.

Robert Sayers Sheffey was lowered into a grave beside his beloved Eliza. The immense concourse of mourners who looked down upon the hillside cemetery were not yet ready to leave the rigid body of this man who, having touched their lives even in a remote way, had somehow enriched them all. This "Saint of the Wilderness," as they had come to call him, was not dead—they would not assent to a fact that gave them such great pain.

As the shovels dug into stockpiled clay and dumped the contents with a dull thud upon "good walnut boards well mitered and rubbed shiny with oil so that God's good years showed well," a petite and well-dressed woman stepped out of the crowd toward the gaping hole in the earth. Her black patent-leather shoes, already dusty, dug more deeply into the clay about the grave, but she walked onward, unconcerned, until her eyes beheld the casket disappearing beneath the clay. From her purse a white flower was drawn, pressed to her lips, and relinquished to the yawning grave.

Uncovered heads stayed bowed long after the grave had again swallowed the dirt taken from it. The terrible quietness which had prevailed after the service continued to hang hauntingly in the atmosphere long after sundown had come, and people yet remained to run their fingers through the loose dirt of the grave one more time.

They vowed to return often and pay homage, and they did. And their number did not diminish each year, but rather increased. Winter, summer, spring, and fall they came, rich and poor alike, until the infant child who had been there on the burial day came back an old man, telling his own grandchildren the story of the Saint of the Wilderness. There he would point to the gravestone before which pilgrimages of two and two hundred would yearly stand, and read the final tribute carved in granite, which said in part:

Robert S. Sheffey
Born July 4, 1820
Died August 30, 1902

"The poor were sorry when he died."
Servant of God, well done; rest in peace.

About the Author

Jess Carr was a prize-winning novelist and nonfiction author from Virginia. Except for a period of schooling in Chicago, a stint in the Marine Corps during the Korean War, and extensive foreign travel, he spent the majority of his life in the South.

As a writer, national recognition came with his third published work, *The Second Oldest Profession: An Informal History of Moonshining in America*, named by Library Journal as one of the one hundred outstanding books published in 1972 for library acquisition. The book went on to gain international acclaim. His fourth book, *The Saint of the Wilderness*, was adapted to the screen in 1978, and his novel, *The Moonshiners*, was also given screenplay treatment. Another one of his books, *A Star Rising*, was granted the Porgie Award as an outstanding historical novel. *Murder on the Appalachian Trail*, perhaps his most recognized book, represented his longstanding desire to write a true life novel.

After a long battle with cancer, Mr. Carr passed away in 1990, leaving behind his wife and three daughters.

CPSIA information can be obtained
at www.ICGtesting.com
Printed in the USA
LVHW030803090221
678800LV00001B/11

9 781641 404006